Cambridge Imperial and Post-Colonial Studies

The Cambridge Imperial and Post-Colonial Studies series is a well-established collection of over 100 volumes focussing on empires in world history and on the societies and cultures that emerged from, and challenged, colonial rule. The collection includes transnational, comparative and connective studies, as well as works addressing the ways in which particular regions or nations interact with global forces. In its formative years, the series focused on the British Empire and Commonwealth, but there is now no imperial system, period of human history or part of the world that lies outside of its compass. While we particularly welcome the first monographs of young researchers, we also seek major studies by more senior scholars, and welcome collections of essays with a strong thematic focus that help to set new research agendas. As well as history, the series includes work on politics, economics, culture, archaeology, literature, science, art, medicine, and war. Our aim is to collect the most exciting new scholarship on world history and to make this available to a broad scholarly readership in a timely manner.

Alexander van Wickeren · Jean Stubbs ·
William Gervase Clarence-Smith
Editors

Tobacco in Global Perspective, 1780–1960

Trade, Knowledge, and Labour

palgrave
macmillan

Editors
Alexander van Wickeren
Faculty of Cultural Studies
TH Köln—University of Applied Science
Cologne, Germany

Jean Stubbs
Centre for Latin American and Caribbean Studies
University of London
London, UK

William Gervase Clarence-Smith
SOAS University of London
London, UK

ISSN 2635-1633 ISSN 2635-1641 (electronic)
Cambridge Imperial and Post-Colonial Studies
ISBN 978-3-031-64410-8 ISBN 978-3-031-64411-5 (eBook)
https://doi.org/10.1007/978-3-031-64411-5

Cover illustration: @ mikroman6/gettyimages

This Palgrave Macmillan imprint is published by the registered company Springer Nature Switzerland AG
The registered company address is: Gewerbestrasse 11, 6330 Cham, Switzerland

Contents

List of Contributors

Nikos Alexis University of Crete, Rethymno, Greece

Guido Cioni Scuola Normale Superiore, Pisa, Italy

William Gervase Clarence-Smith SOAS University of London, London, UK

Santiago de Luxán Meléndez University of Las Palmas de Gran Canaria, Las Palmas de Gran Canaria, Spain

María Dolores Elizalde CSIC (Spanish National Research Council), Madrid, Spain

Nan Enstad University of Wisconsin, Madison, WI, USA

Basma Fahoum Ben Gurion University of the Negev, Beersheba, Israel

Alexandra Ghiţ Department of History, Department of Gender Studies, Central European University, Vienna, Austria

María de los Reyes Hernández Socorro University of Las Palmas de Gran Canaria, Las Palmas de Gran Canaria, Spain

Xavier Huetz de Lemps Université Côte d'Azur, Nice, France

Laird Jones History Department, Lock Haven University, Lock Haven, PA, USA

Martin Kalb Bridgewater College, Bridgewater, VA, USA

Christos Karampatsos National and Kapodistrian University of Athens, University of West Attica, Athens, Greece

Sibanengi Ncube University of the Free State, Bloemfontein, South Africa

Ratna Saptari University of Leiden, Leiden, The Netherlands

Relli Shechter Department of Middle East Studies, Ben-Gurion University of the Negev, Beersheba, Israel

Kathinka Sinha-Kerkhoff International Institute of Social History (IISH), Amsterdam, The Netherlands

Jean Stubbs Centre for Latin American and Caribbean Studies, University of London, London, UK

Alexander van Wickeren Faculty of Cultural Sciences, University of Applied Science, Cologne, Germany

List of Figures

List of Tables

CHAPTER 1

Introduction: Tobacco's Second Globalisation

Alexander van Wickeren, Jean Stubbs, and William Gervase Clarence-Smith

Research into the major changes affecting global tobacco culture from the late eighteenth to the mid-twentieth centuries is currently fragmented and uncoordinated, lacking a clear overall meta-narrative. Here we introduce the concept of a 'second globalisation' to frame a new period in the global history of tobacco that begins around the 1780s. Jordan Goodman's 1993 *Tobacco in History: The Cultures of Dependence*

A. van Wickeren (✉)
Faculty of Cultural Sciences, University of Applied Science, Cologne, Germany
e-mail: alexander.van_wickeren@th-koeln.de

J. Stubbs
Centre for Latin American and Caribbean Studies, University of London, London, UK
e-mail: jean.stubbs@sas.ac.uk

W. G. Clarence-Smith
SOAS University of London, London, UK

A. van Wickeren et al. (eds.), *Tobacco in Global Perspective, 1780–1960*, Cambridge Imperial and Post-Colonial Studies,
https://doi.org/10.1007/978-3-031-64411-5_1

remains what is arguably the most all-encompassing global history. Work published around much the same time, such as by Wolfgang Schivelbusch (in the context of spices, stimulants, and intoxicants), Victor Kiernan, and Ian Gately, broached tobacco over the ages, materially and socio-culturally, in a more popular form for a wider readership.[1] Sander Gilman and Zhou Xun highlighted the breadth and variety of smoking practices across different periods throughout the world, while others explored smoking within popular culture, nation-building, and wartime conflict[2]—all themes reflected in chapters here. The anthropologist Andrew Russell posits a singular global history of tobacco by focusing on the plant's addictive, stimulating effects on people's physical and psychological systems.[3] The particular merit of these studies is that they have examined the globalisation of tobacco in its geographical breadth, analysed different aspects of the tobacco commodity chain in relation to each other, and introduced different methodological approaches to the history of the plant. None of these studies, however, explain why tobacco took such a hold in diverse areas of the world precisely when it did.

As Western imperial dominance expanded more thoroughly beyond the Atlantic and capitalism mutated in multiple ways, major changes took place all along the tobacco commodity chain, in cultivation techniques, labour recruitment, primary processing, trade, manufacturing, and consumption. Increasing commercialisation of cultivation, primary processing, trade, and manufacturing spread across the world. In geographical terms, the centrality of the Atlantic to long-distance commercial flows of tobacco was transcended. This had been the key aspect of tobacco's 'first globalisation' from the sixteenth century, with European conquest and trading in the Americas, where tobacco has its botanical origins.[4] Although both *Nicotiana tabacum* and *Nicotiana rustica* diffused relatively rapidly to virtually all corners of the globe, they were mostly grown on a fairly local basis, or for regional trade. Long-distance trade was concentrated on the sea routes from the Americas to

[1] Goodman (1993). Kiernan (1991). Schivelbusch (1992). Gately (2001). Gately (2002).

[2] Gilman and Xun (2004). See also Hilton (2000). Neuberger (2013). Reeve (2021).

[3] Russell (2019).

[4] Acioli Lopes (2023).

Asia, Europe, and western Africa. Early modern monopolist and mercantilist regulations largely suppressed the cultivation of tobacco in Europe itself. During this era, tobacco produced in South and North America, notably in North American Chesapeake Bay, Cuba, and Brazilian Bahia, remained the key competitor for regionally grown, processed, and traded tobacco in various world regions. The formative power of the Atlantic tobacco regions became even more profound with the increase of colonial trade during the eighteenth century.

We argue that the imperial circumstances of tobacco's transformation since the 1780s provide a central framework to bring together in this collection case studies that invite comparisons across the borders of many empires and provide evidence for the coherence of tobacco's second globalisation. Their focus is on less-known tobacco histories of regions across Africa, the Middle East, Asia, and Europe, testifying to the dimensions of the importance of tobacco, not least in new places and among new players. They demonstrate the rising dominance of new and powerful forces, including transnational corporations, which ranged widely beyond the frontiers of single political units. As the period coincided with the expansion of Western, especially European, imperial rule in the world, we are not only interested in formal land grabbing in non-Western areas, such as Africa and Asia, but focus also on colonial processes within Europe.

The volume shows that colonialism was also informal, characterised by diplomatic, political, cultural, and military power, which did not necessarily deprive political regimes of their territory. Imperialism, as the contributions highlight furthermore, needs to be understood as practices and discourses that state and non-state actors use to mark difference from other groups beyond their regions of origin, in colony and metropolis of formal empires. In the Global South and the peripheries of Europe, Western bureaucrats, entrepreneurs, missionaries, scientists, settlers, migrants, and other groups were responsible for an everyday life structured by imperial inequality and hierarchy. Racism, violence, economic exploitation, and symbolic devaluation were important elements of imperial rule that were reproduced in different situations. This hardly changed the fact that the formal state empires were often rather weak and could hardly establish rule on a large scale.

The authors in this collection highlight that there were many actors in conflict and negotiation within and beyond imperial and territorial confines. The dominance of Europeans and other Western actors was challenged by acts of resistance, denial, rebellion, conflict, or armed intervention. The same applies to forms of collaboration, to the activities of intermediaries and middlemen who benefited from colonial expansion in non-Western areas and European peripheries. Tobacco acts as a lens with which to view imperial and colonial, as well as regional, national, and local interactions, struggles, and conflicts, underlining the agency of subaltern peoples, ordinary people, of farmers and workers, men and women in various global settings. Encompassing global political, economic, and socio-cultural themes, the emphasis of this collection is on trade, knowledge, and labour, juxtaposing micro-histories with macro-historical perspectives.

Mapping the Second Globalisation

The geographical regions under study here are in the Mediterranean and South-Eastern Europe (Greece; Egypt; Transylvania, today in Romania; the Dalmatian/Adriatic region; and Palestine), the Spanish Atlantic and Pacific (the Canary Islands, Cuba, and the Philippines), sub-Saharan Africa (British Southern Rhodesia, today Zimbabwe; German South West Africa, today Namibia; and British East Africa, today Kenya), and East and Southeast Asia (China and Indonesia). In most of these territories, a new generation of experts, scientists, and technocrats, inspired by the spirit of the Enlightenment, set out to develop agriculture and industry. This was an important reason why tobacco took such a hold.[5] Public positions were created for specialist research and training. Trials were conducted with growers to improve cultivation. The École d'application des tabacs, for example, was created in 1824 to train qualified personnel for the French state tobacco monopoly organisation. From the 1840s, French agronomists carried out trials in Algeria, a practice that was also found elsewhere.[6] Experts and scientists not only ensured the spread of tobacco cultivation and the improvement of industrial processing through successful application of their knowledge; through their work and practices, they also helped to consolidate tobacco culture on a symbolic and discursive level as a new normality within people's everyday lives.

[5] Jonsson (2016). van Wickeren (2019, 2020). Davis (1964). Dauser (2015).

[6] Osborne (1985).

Furthermore, the concentration of capital in companies—multinational corporations since the twentieth century[7]—the willingness of governments to cooperate in building transport infrastructures, and most of all the advent of the machine age, creating new technological conditions and spawning manipulators of money and markets, provided further impact.[8] Running alongside the rise of tobacco technical experts was that of marketing specialists, who devised a multitude of ways to promote consumption, most notably through advertising and branding. This was not entirely novel, but new capacities in printing and other forms of communication, as well as literacy and transport, greatly increased the impact of marketing.

During the period, mass consumption emerged, with snuff and chewing tobacco gradually losing market share to the pipe, the cigar, and the cigarette. Regional forms of consumption remained in many places, even as new forms spread. For example, smoking the hookah (water-pipe) persisted in the Middle East and South Asia.[9] In such contexts, local tobacco culture, the tobacco leaf, and the production and consumption of newly spread tobacco products all became highly politicised. In the nineteenth century, the hand-rolled cigar, whose epitome was the Havana made of strong, dark Cuban tobacco, became an elite symbol of Western 'civilisation'.[10] Counterfeits proliferated, for example in Germany, raising the ire of Cuban producers. At the same time, the 'five-cent' cigar, made in the US[11] and all over the world, and increasingly by mechanical means, served a wider market. The twentieth century, especially after World War I, was defined by the global spread of the machine-made cigarette, employing milder and lighter Virginia-type tobacco, competing with and often ousting stronger and darker tobaccos. In the shadow of this, other forms of consumption, such as the Indian bidi or the Middle Eastern hookah, were increasingly stigmatised among upwardly socially mobile groups. And yet indigenous forms of consumption held their ground, both because of their cheapness and as symbols of local identity. Indeed, Western companies capitalised on copying indigenous or local names for

[7] Iwashita (2022).

[8] Lastas and Rentetzi (2016).

[9] Chatterjee (2022).

[10] Stubbs (2018, 2023).

[11] Cooper (1988).

their tobacco products on Western[12] and non-Western markets,[13] playing on ethnic and racial stereotypes.

Accompanying attacks on slavery changed patterns of labour use and enhanced the participation of smallholders in growing tobacco. In the US South, Brazil, and Cuba as part of early and mid-nineteenth-century industrialisation and world-economic expansion, enslaved labourers continued to take a prominent role in growing and processing tobacco, if not to quite the same extent as for sugarcane.[14] Particularly significant in this era, however, was the mass incorporation of women into the tobacco world. Female labour in the tobacco industry was justified by gendered ideas.[15] Mass incorporation also encompassed women consumers. Women had long consumed tobacco products, for example the Manila workers smoking outsized cigars in the Philippines.[16] However, higher-class women became the targets for a novel consumption of mild machine-made cigarettes, with an accompanying discourse on 'feminine' traits.

The early context for tobacco's second globalisation was the radically changing political economy from the late eighteenth to the late nineteenth centuries with a growing wave of free trade, as encapsulated in Adam Smith's famous monograph on the wealth of nations. Increasing commercialisation of cultivation, primary processing, trade, and manufacturing spread across the world, steadily eroding mercantilism and monopolies.

This in no small part arose from conflict and war in the Americas, beginning with the independence of most of Britain's colonies in North America in 1783. The French Caribbean colony of Saint Domingue became the free state of Haiti in 1804, and the mainland colonies of Portugal and Spain in Latin America gained their independence over the years 1806–1826. The resulting interruption of established imperial tobacco supply routes led to new ventures to develop the tobacco commodity chain elsewhere in the world, on a scale hitherto unseen. The Dutch, who had long ago ceded many of their territories in the Americas, and who left Africa altogether in the nineteenth century,

[12] Enstad (2019).

[13] Sinha-Kerkhoff (2020).

[14] Kaye (2009). Barickman (1998). Zeuske (2016). Morgan (2023).

[15] Wernitznig (2022).

[16] Camagay (1986).

developed tobacco in their Asian colony of Indonesia. The Portuguese allowed tobacco cultivation in their Atlantic islands of the Azores and Madeira, and explored the opportunities of their African colonies, especially Angola. The Spanish felt obliged to abolish their tobacco monopoly in Cuba and Puerto Rico, for fear of the secession of these remaining American colonies. Spain also allowed some cultivation in the Canary Islands, while doubling down on the tobacco monopoly in the Philippines.[17] The British took the most radical line, breaching imperial borders in line with their new free trading enthusiasm.

In Europe and outlying regions of the Americas, few governments or state monopolies continued to prohibit tobacco cultivation, leading to a great expansion in the geographical range of the crop. Within Latin America, this led to new tobacco frontiers in emerging countries such as Paraguay. Even more striking was the boom in cultivation across much of Europe, notably in France and Hungary, in the context of persistent state monopolies, and the German, Italian, and Greek lands, as well as Russia. Exceptionally, however, Portugal and Spain continued to ban domestic cultivation, mainly to favour colonial planters. Britain also maintained its ban on tobacco in the home islands, although this was to profit fiscally from import taxes.

A decentralisation of tobacco agriculture away from the Atlantic occurred, especially in Asia. Cultivation grew exponentially in China, Japan, and India, although their markets remained overwhelmingly domestic in nature. Elsewhere, free trade allowed non-Western actors to participate more in the opportunities of exporting tobacco. The Philippines and Indonesia were major examples, as were the Ottoman Empire and other Middle Eastern producers of highly valued 'Oriental tobacco', although their internal markets also expanded fast in every case. Growth in sub-Saharan Africa was slower and more muted, reflecting much lower population densities, as well as quality problems in breaking into Western markets. A particular conundrum is West Africa's continuing reliance on imports of tobacco leaf and manufactures, whereas the rest of the continent became largely self-sufficient, and even a minor exporter. As manufacturing boomed, it turned out to be a particularly precocious form of import-substituting industrialisation across the Global South. The costs of producing cigars, pipe tobacco, snuff, and chewing tobacco were small,

[17] Luxán Meléndez et al. (2024).

the technology was simple, and consumers addicted to nicotine provided a large and growing market.

Although capitalist globalisation had become too firmly entrenched for any complete return to early modern mercantilism, an era of 'neo-mercantilism' began to appear hesitantly in the late nineteenth century. This trend was greatly reinforced by the impact of World War I, the Great Depression of the 1930s, and World War II. The retreat from free trade correlated with renewed imperial expansion by both Western and Asian nations, and concomitant colonial protectionism. Large estates were again favoured over smallholders, and a blind eye was turned to coercive labour regimes. There was further the reinstatement or reinforcement of tobacco monopolies, whether public, parastatal, or corporate.

In this neo-mercantilist phase, even Britain began to backtrack a little from its ideologically driven commitment to free trade. The ban on domestic cultivation remained, but it was now more often justified by the need for 'imperial preference'. London promoted colonial tobacco initially in India and Canada, and later in Southern Africa. However, Britain remained far from providing a completely protected market to its colonies, continuing to import large amounts from the USA and other non-imperial sources. Hesitations could also be seen in France, despite a greater emphasis on imperial autarky from the 1880s. By this stage, domestic producers in metropolitan France had become securely established and politically powerful, and were able to resist colonial imports of leaf and manufactures. Moreover, the nature and quality of colonial tobacco were often unsuited to the French market, necessitating continued imports from non-imperial sources.

A related phenomenon was the rise of the transnational tobacco corporation. Consumption was again revolutionised, with the emergence of the mechanised production of cigarettes from the late nineteenth century. This raised barriers to entry into manufacturing for producers in the Global South and created opportunities for cartels and monopolies in the West. At the same time, Western companies played a special role in marketing on a symbolic level. Newly introduced forms of machine-made cigarettes were equated with Western 'civilisation', while old-fashioned 'uncivilised' ways of enjoying tobacco were frowned upon. Post-1945 liberalisation began under American hegemony, but it remained slow and hesitant in the 1950s. It took a long time to dismantle the barriers that had reached a peak in the command economies of World War II. Furthermore, liberalisation excluded the new 'socialist world', which was fairly firmly closed in economic terms.

Voices critical of tobacco, of which there had been many ever since the 1600s, had gained in strength during the second globalisation.[18] Religious groups had spiritually motivated objections to the consumption of the plant. Physicians warned of the harmfulness of tobacco dust for workers released by processing in factories.[19] The reform movements that emerged in the late nineteenth century carried scepticism about tobacco to a wider public to prevent damage to the 'nation's body'.[20] After World War II, growing health concerns, backed by science and the World Health Organisation, linked tobacco consumption, especially cigarette smoking, to lung cancer, and led to the emergence of a strong anti-smoking lobby. Towards the middle of the twentieth century movements critical of tobacco gained further strength, questioning the spread of tobacco culture.[21] And yet new conditions were generated for tobacco's further global expansion, such that by the 1960s, a 'third globalisation' can be seen to have been under way. This merits further study beyond the well-researched health perspectives, but lies beyond our scope here.

The Structure of the Volume

The volume is structured thematically into three parts, on trade, knowledge, and labour, each comprising four chapters that cover different, though clearly intersecting, facets of tobacco history in regions that have by and large been overlooked. They are authored by a range of senior, mid-career, and postdoctoral scholars, as well as doctoral candidates.

Examining tobacco's second globalisation from the perspective of the history of trade, including approaches to marketing and retail, is the focus of Part I of the volume. While much has been written about the world market in this period, there has been relatively little specific to tobacco, and together the chapters explore competing attempts and means to supply consumers with tobacco products; political expectations

[18] Courtwright (2019).

[19] Jorland (2005).

[20] Elliot (2014).

[21] Dickenson and Crawford (2022).

and strategies that colonised peoples and settlers attached to imperial trade zones; and changes in state influence in global trade with liberalisation, opening up new possibilities for marginalised actors. Tobacco presupposed an infrastructure of supply chains, storage facilities, sales rooms, and marketing campaigns, which was by no means organised and controlled by Western traders alone, but was also shaped by non-Western, region-specific preferences and consumer behaviour.

The part opens with a chapter on the liberalisation of trade in the context of tobacco manufacturing in the Philippines in the last century of Spanish colonial rule. It is co-authored by Xavier Huetz de Lemps and María Dolores Elizalde. The Spanish imperial tobacco monopoly established in the Philippines in 1781 was finally dismantled a century later, after the creation of large companies with Spanish and foreign capital as well as little-known micro-enterprises. The authors show how the growing crisis of the imperial state monopoly model opened up a space in both the export and domestic tobacco markets that benefited not only large but also small companies, the latter in Chinese and Filipino hands, which had previously been marginalised and which in turn brought racial stereotypes and tensions to the fore.

In the following chapter, by Laird Jones, the focus is on early colonial East Africa during the years 1880–1914 and the resilience of locally hand-rolled cigarettes in rivalry with the imperial marketing of machine cigarettes. Despite the increasing influence of British American Tobacco (BAT), with its superior financing, imperial connections, cutting-edge technology, and 'cigarette safaris' of agents travelling the countryside in caravans, attracting crowds with their colourful packaged samples of new machine-made brands, long-established import–export houses such as the Hamburg-Zanzibar firm of William O'Swald & Co. put little effort into advertising. Instead, they quietly continued to work within regional wholesale networks, distributing a variety of shag tobacco and cigarette papers to shop and kiosk vendors. For decades, this 'archaic' approach continued to appeal to smokers, included young migrant workers, for whom it became a badge of identity.

Relli Shecter then investigates Egypt over a similar period of 1890–1939. His chapter documents a glocalised process of 'prosumption' as BAT tried to engage with local consumers through its local subsidiary Eastern Tobacco Company (ETC). It examines corporate considerations and competitivity on the part of local manufacturers and BAT/ETC in a market where, as economic conditions declined, consumers compromised on type and quality, rather than on the quantity of their smoke. ETC only came to monopolise mass production after 1927 by catering to such consumer desires and needs. This is demonstrated by drawing on tobacco import statistics, business and economic reports, smoking patterns, and Egyptian press advertisements.

The case of Anglo-Rhodesian tobacco trade in the aftermath of World War II, by Sibanengi Ncube, is the focus of the final chapter in the part. Before the war, Southern Rhodesia's tobacco industry was constrained by the lack of a steady market, and Britain, the world's biggest leaf importer, obtained most of its tobacco from the United States. With the outbreak of war in 1939, however, the Southern Rhodesian tobacco trade to Britain steadily increased and was consolidated after the war with the 1947 London Agreement, a marketing arrangement between British tobacco manufacturers and Southern Rhodesian farmers to acquire 'Empire' tobacco. It was the London Agreement and Southern Rhodesian state policy to increase white land occupancy in a settler colony that provided the impetus for postwar expansion. Drawing on archival material from the National Archives of Zimbabwe, Adam Matthews Digital Archives, and newspaper reports, this chapter locates the expansion in an era of heightened global trade and fragmented imperial markets and underscores the competing political expectations and strategies of the colonised peoples and the new settlers.

Part II of the volume is on circuits of tobacco knowledge. We are particularly interested in how the political and economic crises of the late eighteenth and early/mid nineteenth centuries accelerated communication about the spread and improvement of tobacco cultivation and industry, within and beyond the Atlantic. The first chapter, by Guido Cioni, looks at imperial rivalries and agronomic reform in the Venetian Ionian islands and Dalmatia, in the late eighteenth century, when the increasing Russian presence in the area culminated in the outbreak of a Russo-Ottoman War, adding to tensions along the triple frontier of the Venetian, Habsburg, and Ottoman empires. The war caused supply chain disruption and Venice searched for alternatives in the overseas domains of the Ionian Islands and Dalmatia of the Stato da Mar, where agronomy was a tool deployed for introducing and consolidating tobacco plantations. In the context of fiscal concerns, scientific knowledge circulation, and commodity frontier pressure, the chapter draws on the Nona plantation in Venetian Dalmatia to explore a tobacco culture that, while developed through links with northern European tobacco experts, transcended centres of the Enlightenment and Atlantic trade.

The following chapter on Spain's Canary Islands, by Santiago de Luxán Meléndez and María de los Reyes Hernández Socorro, also shows how tobacco knowledge was embedded in geopolitical conflict, regional economic crises, and economic restructuring measures, contributing to the globalisation of agricultural and industrial knowledge. With the 1860s cochineal crisis in the Canaries, the established tobacco region of Cuba became a model that influenced the Islands, as it did other colonies and metropoles. Through their focus on the León y Castillo brothers, they call for a revision of Spanish historiography, arguing that while the Canaries tobacco initiative has been seen as a nineteenth-century failure, it nonetheless laid the foundations for the tobacco sector that became one of the Islands' early twentieth-century economic mainstays.

A closer focus on the production of knowledge and technology promises further insights into the significance of violence for the circulation of knowledge and technology—a relationship that perhaps did not carry the same weight everywhere, but which was present, if not prevalent, in certain periods and localities. Previous histories of tobacco have tended to downplay these aspects,[22] whereas more recent histories of colonialism stress the violence, escalating from the late nineteenth century with the new biological racism, especially in times of war. Simultaneously, although this was not always the case, as the example of cigars that continued to be produced primarily by hand in Cuba vividly shows, the new processes of mechanisation massively restructured sectors that had been characterised by craftwork.

In their chapter in this part, Christos Karampatsos and Nikolaos Alexis examine how mechanisation and the repression of manual labour overlapped with imperial conquest. In the expansion of Greece to the Ottoman Balkans in the late nineteenth and early twentieth centuries, they chart how tobacco workers found their craft knowledge undercut in the confrontation with new technologies and territorial claims in mechanised production sites. One of the Greek territory's most overlooked aspects is its constant expansion during this period, annexing parts of the crumbling

[22] Hahn (2008).

Ottoman Empire, and the Greek tobacco industry expanded correspondingly by incorporating the major former Ottoman tobacco centres of Volos, Thessaloniki, and Kavala. The industry that emerged comprised multinational craft workers who crossed borders between former and current Ottoman domains, and their craft economy was under attack at a time when, with the support of the Greek state, mechanisation took off. Mechanisation is thus seen as not only an anti-craft labour process, but also a tool to consolidate the new nation state's political control over sites of craft knowledge with a long imperial past.

Around this same time frame, German South West Africa, while perhaps an extreme example, affords an exploration of how Western experts' creation of a tobacco knowledge economy overlapped with race asymmetries and colonial warfare, as Martin Kalb in the next chapter shows. German efforts to cultivate tobacco in its colonial possession underscore the conflict between imperial fantasies and environmental/logistical realities, in the attempted knowledge transfer, racialised construction of African consumption, and colonial violence. Against a backdrop of existing indigenous knowledge and demands, German attempts to turn an arid landscape into a tobacco-producing paradise were disrupted by colonial war and genocide destroying African lives and livelihoods. Colonial desires to rebuild after, aided by emptied landscapes, discriminatory labour practices, and continued violence, saw German experts struggle in the face of sourcing seeds, curing, locusts, and the lack of water.

The third and final part of the volume takes a closer look at labour in its various forms. A first chapter by Ratna Saptari examines the systematic exploitation of land rights and ensuing political struggles that were increasingly shaped by racial difference. While much has been written on the tobacco plantations in East Coast Sumatra and Central Java, her chapter evidences the diverse nature of Dutch imperial labour regimes by examining the politics of land and labour in tobacco cultivation in the Besoeki Residency of East Java during the mid-nineteenth to early twentieth centuries. The existence of a hierarchical local aristocracy was not characteristic of this region, and plantation owners and colonial authorities had to deal with more diverse power structures. The different types of tobacco, for either the global or domestic markets, also shaped the nature of production, the relationship of the producer to the land, and the different phases of tobacco generating diverse labour needs. Archival research and oral histories evidence disputes over 'native' and 'non-native' rights and obligations regarding access to land and the fluidity of boundaries in vying for control, compliance, and resistance.

Over this same period, Alexandra Ghit directs our attention to the ways in which gender shaped labour control and resistance in the Eastern European Cluj Tobacco Manufactory in the city of Klausenburg/Kolozsvár/Cluj-Napocacity in Transylvania. She explores gendered practices in the tobacco industry persisting across various political regimes, shaped by an imperial past often overlooked in Eastern European tobacco labour history. The legacy of the Habsburg Empire for regulations and state-appointed administrators to control the majority-women's workforce was significant, as workers contested new rules, drew on Austro-Hungarian modes of labour organisation, and supported Austro-Marxist social democrats. Management, social reformers, the male-dominated labour movement, and the particular modes of action on the part of women workers in the state factory are seen in the context of this past legacy.

Labour and management migration and the production of difference are themes explored in the next chapter by Nan Enstadt. She explores how, in the context of late nineteenth- and early twentieth-century global capitalism, BAT-China generated new labour flows and managed large and diverse workforces, in which gender and race played a central role. Critiquing scholarship that sees racial, ethnic, or native place difference in management as an 'add-on' to class, she draws from recent scholarship on the emergence of capitalism within racialised systems of plantation slavery, the 'coolie trade', and other labour migrations to frame her analysis of race, native place, and gender difference among BAT workers, supervisors, and managers.

Finally, there is the case of twentieth-century Palestine, authored by Basma Fahoum. In response to state-sanctioned forms of tobacco trade, 'smuggling' entered the arsenal of protest to actively take control of livelihoods. *Fellahin* smallholder farming households, in the face of what they saw as unfair treatment by local and international companies and colonial governments, throughout Ottoman, British, and Israeli rule, refused to acknowledge the legitimacy of the law, which prohibited independent sale and even personal consumption of their own tobacco crop. Contesting being characterised as 'smugglers', they negotiated their right to sell by lobbying, organising locally and nationally, enlisting nationalist tropes to boost their sales, creating niche markets for their crop, and building a nation-wide reputation. Their defiance revealed the contradictions inherent in liberal state policies and monopolistic, highly regulated practices that operated to their distinct disadvantage.

With the exception of the chapters by Enstad and Ghit, all other chapters build on papers debated at the conference Rethinking Tobacco History: Commodities, Empire, and Agency in Global Perspective, 1780–1960, organised by the editors in December 2021, hosted virtually by the University of Cologne, Germany, and co-sponsored by the Commodities of Empire British Academy Research Project. Kathinka Sinha-Kerkhoff, honorary research fellow at the International Institute of Social History, based in Ranchi, India, gave the closing remarks at the conference and has expanded on them here in her Afterword. Reflecting back on her own work and that of others, she highlights the important glocal approach of the volume, combining diverse local studies in a global perspective. She also underscores the importance of a volume such as this to explain the history behind the continuing resilience of a widespread tobacco culture. As editors, we cannot but endorse her comments, and thank her and all our contributors for their work, confident that this collective volume makes a significant contribution to the field. We also thank the editorial team at Palgrave Macmillan and its Cambridge Imperial and Postcolonial Series, with whom it is our privilege to publish.

Alexander van Wickeren, Jean Stubbs, and William Gervase Clarence-Smith

Cologne and London, January 2024

References

Barickman, B.J. 1998. *A Bahian Counterpoint. Sugar, Tobacco, Cassava, and Slavery in the Recôncavo, 1780–1860*. Stanford: Stanford University Press.

Camagay, M.-L. 1986. A Look into the Working Filipina during the 19th Century. The Cigarreras of Manila. *Archipel* 31: 177–184.

Chatterjee, A.K. 2022. Oriental Dressings, Imperial Inhalations: The Indian Hookah in British Colonial Culture. *Journal of the Economic and Social History of the Orient* 65: 279–324.

Cooper, P.A. 1988. What This Country Needs Is a Good Five-Cent Cigar. *Technology and Culture* 29: 779–807.

Courtwright, D.T. 2019. *The Age of Addiction. How Bad Habits Became Big Business*. Cambridge, MA: Belknap Press of Harvard University Press.

Dauser, R. 2015. Das Wissen der Herrschaft. Wissensgenerierung und Reformen der praktischen Aufklärung in der zweiten Hälfte des 18. Jahrhunderts. In

Geschichte(n) des Wissens. Festschrift für Wolfgang E.J. Weber zum 65. Geburtstag, eds. M. Häberlein, S. Paulus, and G. Weber, 619–633. Augsburg: Wißner-Verlag.

Davis, C. 1964. 'A National Property korregieren'. Richard Claiborne's Tobacco Treatise for Poland. *The William and Mary Quarterly* 21: 93–117.

Dickenson, J., and R. Crawford. 2022. The Global Campaign Against Tobacco. A Brief History. In *The Routledge Companion to Marketing and Society*, eds. K. Kubacki, L. Parker, C. Domegan, and L. Brennan, 287–305. London: Routledge.

Elliot, R. 2014. From Tobacco in the War to the War on Tobacco: Smoking in Britain and Germany from c. 1900 to 1945. In *Health and Citizenship: Political Cultures of Health in Modern Europe*, eds. F. Huisman and H. Oosterhuis, 141–154. London: Pickering & Chato.

Enstad, N. 2019. *Cigarettes Inc: An Intimate History of Corporate Imperialism.* Chicago: The University of Chicago Press.

Gately, I. 2001. *La Diva Nicotiana: The Story of How Tobacco Seduced the World.* London: Simon & Shuster.

Gately, I. 2002. *Tobacco: A Cultural History of How an Exotic Plant Seduced Civilization.* New York: Grove Press.

Gilman, S., and Zhou Xun, eds. 2004. *Smoke: A Global History of Smoking.* London: Reaktion Books.

Goodman, J. 1993. *Tobacco in History. The Cultures of Dependence.* London: Routledge.

Hahn, B. 2008. Paradox of Precision: Bright Tobacco as Technology Transfer, 1880–1937. *Agricultural History* 82: 220–235.

Hilton, M. 2000. *Smoking in British Popular Culture, 1800–2000.* Manchester: Manchester University Press.

Iwashita, H. 2022. Globalisation of a State-Owned Enterprise: A History of Japan Tobacco (1985–2014). *Business History.* https://doi.org/10.1080/00076791.2022.2072487. Accessed by 11 January 2024.

Jonsson, F.A. 2016. Scottish Tobacco and Rhubarb. The Natural Order of Civil Cameralism in the Scottish Enlightenment. *Eighteenth-Century Studies* 49: 129–147.

Jorland, G. 2005. L'hygiène professionnelle en France au XIXe siècle. *Le Mouvement Social* 213: 71–90.

Kaye, A.E. 2009. The Second Slavery: Modernity in the Nineteenth-Century South and the Atlantic World. *The Journal of Southern History* 75: 627–650.

Kiernan, V.G. 1991. *Tobacco: A History.* London: Hutchinson Radius.

Lastas, M., and M. Rentetzi, eds. 2016. Tobacco Roads History: Science, Society and Technology. Special Issue. *Advances in Historical Studies* 5.

Lopes, G. Acioli. 2023. Infiltrando impérios: o tabaco e o mercado Atlântico global (séculos XVI–XVIII). In *História das mercadorias trabalho, meio ambiente e capitalismo mundial (séculos XVI–XIX)*, eds. L. Marques and A. Gebara, 79–123. São Leopoldo: Casa Leiria.

Luxán Meléndez, S.d., J. Figueiroa-Rego, V. Sanz Rozalén, and J. Stubbs, eds. 2024. Tobacco in the Iberian Empires. In *The Oxford Handbook of Commodity History*, ed. J. Curry-Machado, J. Stubbs, W. G. Clarence-Smith, and J. Vos, 145–166. New York: Oxford University Press.

Morgan, W.A. 2023. Tobacco in the Age of Cuba's Second Slavery. In *Social Struggle and Civil Society in Nineteenth Century Cuba*, ed. R.E. Morris, 33–56. New York: Routledge.

Neuberger, M. 2013. *Balkan Smoke: Tobacco and the Making of Modern Bulgaria*. Ithaca: Cornell University Press.

Osborne, M.A. 1985. The System of Colonial Gardens and the Exploitation of French Algeria, 1830–1852. *Proceedings of the Meeting of the French Colonial Historical Society* 8: 160–168.

Reeve, M. 2021. 'Something-to-Smoke, at the Right Time, Is a Godsend': Voluntary Action and the Provision of Cigarettes to Soldiers During the First World War. In *Redcoats to Tommies: The Experience of the British Soldier from the Eighteenth Century*, eds. K. Linch and M. Lord, 120–148. Woodbridge: Boydell & Brewer.

Russell, A. 2019. *Anthropology of Tobacco: Ethnographic Adventures in Non-human Worlds*. New York: Routledge.

Schivelbusch, W. 1992. *Tastes of Paradise: A Social History of Spices and Intoxicants*. New York: Random House.

Stubbs, J. 2018. Beyond Iberian Atlantic Spaces: Trans-imperial and Trans-Territorial Entanglements in Havana Cigar History (1756–1924). In *El tabaco y la esclavitud en la rearticulación imperial ibérica/O trabalho e a esclavagem na rearticulaçåo imperial ibérica (s.XVI–XX)*, eds. S. d. Luxán Meléndez and J. Figueiroa-Rego, 389–426. Evora: CIDEHUS Universidade de Evora. https://books.openedition.org/cidehus/5987.

Stubbs, J. 2023. *Tobacco on the Periphery: A Case Study in Cuban Labour History*. London: Amaurea Press.

Sinha-Kerkhoff, K. 2020. Wooing Indians with New Smokes. Cigarette and Bidi Advertising in British India. In *Globalising Everyday Consumption in India. History and Ethnography*, eds. B. Bhattacharya and H. Donner, 98–120. London: Routledge.

van Wickeren, A. 2019. Territorializing Atlantic Knowledge: The French State Tobacco Monopoly and the Globalization of the Havana Cigar around Mid-19th Century. In *Transnational Cultures of Expertise. Knowledge and the Rise of the Modern State*, eds. L. Schilling and J. Vogel, 181–191. Berlin: De Gruyter.

van Wickeren, A. 2020. The Transformation of an Ecological Policy. Acclimatization of Cuban Tobacco Varieties and Public Scandalization in the French

Empire, c. 1860–1880. In *Environments of Empire. Networks and Agents of Ecological Change*, eds. B. Bennett and U. Kirchberger, 19–38. Chapel Hill: University of North Carolina Press.
Wernitznig, D. 2022. Rauchzeichen: Tabakproduktion und Gender im globalen und historiographischen Kontext. *Österreichische Zeitschrift Für Geschichtswissen schaften* 33: 58–78.
Zeuske, M. 2016. Sklaven und Tabak in der atlantischen Weltgeschichte. *Historische Zeitschrift* 303: 315–348.

PART I

Trade

CHAPTER 2

Liberalising Tobacco in the Philippines During the Nineteenth-Century Late Spanish Colonial Period

Xavier Huetz de Lemps and María Dolores Elizalde

Research to date on the history of tobacco in the Philippines falls short in that it fails to reflect the full gamut of tobacco growing, processing, and consumption in the transformation of the social, political, and cultural life of the archipelago from the late sixteenth century to the end of the nineteenth century. What is best known is the history of the Spanish imperial tobacco monopoly in the period between its creation in 1781 and the final moves to abolition over the years 1881–1883, and the subsequent injection of European capital and technical resources into the liberalised

X. Huetz de Lemps (✉)
Université Côte d'Azur, Nice, France
e-mail: xavier.huetzdelemps@univ-cotedazur.fr

M. D. Elizalde
Spanish National Research Council (CSIC), Madrid, Spain
e-mail: lola.elizalde@cchs.csic.es

A. van Wickeren et al. (eds.), *Tobacco in Global Perspective, 1780–1960*, Cambridge Imperial and Post-Colonial Studies,
https://doi.org/10.1007/978-3-031-64411-5_2

tobacco sector, especially the large international companies that were established.[1]

This is in part due to the nature of the sources. The colonial tobacco administration and its sprawling bureaucracy—inasmuch as Spain's limited administrative resources in the Philippines allowed—deposited at the feet of historians a thick sediment of papers. These are of uneven interest, but easily accessible in the public archives of the Philippines, in the capital city of Manila, and of Spain, in Seville and Madrid. The excellent monograph on the tobacco monopoly by Edilberto de Jesus, published in 1980, remains a key reference, supplemented by more recent research.[2] The suppression of the tobacco monopoly in the Philippines was without a doubt the most important economic reform of the last two decades of Spanish colonial rule in the archipelago. Yet, it has hardly been explored in terms of its social and economic consequences and opportunities beyond the large international tobacco companies, the crisis of the state monopoly, and the subsequent liberalisation 'from below.'

In this chapter, we chart that history, homing in on the small business and outwork sector of what is often termed the Manila tobacco trade, given the city's prominence in the trade. The sector served primarily local markets with tobacco worked in homes and small shops, employing little capital and technology.

To document this history, we draw on secondary and primary sources, the latter in the form of fragmentary information gleaned from contemporary print and archival sources held in the National Archives of the Philippines in Manila, Spain's National History Archives in Madrid, and the Diplomatic Archives of the French Ministry for Foreign Affairs at La Courneuve, France.[3] The archives of many private companies have disappeared—if in the case of smaller companies they ever existed—but documents held in public collections go a long way to fill the gaps, in particular those in the impressive Protocolos section in the Philippine

[1] De Jesus (1971). Delgado (1996). Giralt (1981). Izard (1974). Rodrigo y Alharilla (1996, 2000, 2009). Salazar (2001).

[2] De Jesus (1980). Fradera (1999, 2005). Delgado (1996). Rodrigo y Alharilla (2009). Salazar (2001). Sanz (2019).

[3] National Archives of the Philippines, Spanish Documents Section (Manila), hereafter NAP, SDS. Archivo Histórico Nacional, Sección Ultramar (Madrid), hereafter AHN, Ultramar. Archives du ministère français des Affaires étrangères, Correspondance Consulaire et Commerciale (La Courneuve), hereafter AMAE CCC.

National Archives. Notary offices at the time of the abolition yielded valuable information, for example on La Hensiana, one of the larger tobacco companies that set up operations in Manila, to which we refer later. The industry tax (*contribución industrial*) registers for the years leading up to the start of the Philippine revolution in 1896 and the end of Spanish colonial rule in 1898 contain detailed information on the location of companies, proprietors, number of workers employed, and type of production. We were thus able to build up a snapshot of Filipino and Chinese small ventures.

We document especially Chinese small business and the networks of the Chinese in the tobacco-growing regions. While in the 1750s and 1760s there had been expulsions of the Chinese, from the 1820s onwards the monopoly encouraged immigration from China, albeit with the restriction that the Chinese could not settle freely in the interior of the islands until this was lifted in 1839. Their presence increased during the 1850s, when again migration was encouraged. By the mid-1870s, they officially numbered around 30,000, and almost 100,000 by the early 1890s, though taking into account illegal immigration and a dysfunctional Spanish administration there would have been many more in reality.

Here we first provide an overview of the crisis of the state tobacco monopoly system leading to the establishment of large international tobacco companies. We then trace the emergence of the small tobacco sector, and how the Chinese were able to turn economic crisis and trade liberalisation to their advantage and so improve their economic position. Also, through the reports of Western observers and in particular three consecutive French consuls, we document how their presence was perceived as a threat, fuelling racialised discourse. We conclude with brief reference to salient features emerging in the early twentieth-century tobacco sector when, after Spain's defeat in the Spanish-American War, the Philippines became a territory of the US.

State Monopoly in Crisis

The reasons for the crisis and subsequent abolition of the state tobacco monopoly in the Philippines were manifold. The long-term costs of the monopoly's quest to colonise new tobacco lands on the islands had a detrimental effect on revenue. From the early nineteenth century, the tobacco administration had been opening up new cultivation areas—*colecciones*—in sparsely populated regions, developing them with new settlers, and sending in agricultural experts to improve cultivation, all at considerable cost. The settlers came mainly from Ilocos, the Batanes Islands, and Bohol Island, but there were also captives from military expeditions against Sulu and Mindanao. Cagayan, in northeastern Luzon, was one of the regions deemed particularly suitable for tobacco cultivation from an environmental point of view and for its geographical location, well connected as it was to river traffic for shipping tobacco.

By the 1830s, the tobacco-growing population in the Cagayan Valley alone numbered some 20,000 and continued to grow throughout the century. The military presence to protect the *colecciones* and consolidate the frontier, beyond which the original inhabitants lived, was particularly costly. As early as 1783, a year after the monopoly was established, 30 corporals and 156 guards had already been stationed to repress the illegal cultivation and commercialisation of tobacco, and by the 1840s had increased in number to over 1,500.[4]

As of the 1850s, customs duties from exports of tobacco, along with sugar, abaca, and other products, had become an important source of state revenue.[5] This gave the Philippine treasury a respite, providing it with a broader financial base and encouraging debate on liberalising the tobacco monopoly.[6] Subsequent global transformations, such as the completion of the Suez Canal in 1869, opened up opportunities for international trade and investment across Southern Asia and the Chinese South Sea.

In 1863, however, an earthquake devastated the Philippine archipelago. Despite using public resources to rebuild infrastructure and placing other expenditures on hold, the state tobacco monopoly system fell into debt. The debt continued to grow throughout the decade, generating serious financial problems for the monopoly. In 1872, Governor-General Rafael Izquierdo (1871–1873) estimated that tobacco growers in the *colecciones* were owed 2,000,000 pesos, and, in 1877, after years of delayed and deferred payments for the crops of 1874–1876, the figure had risen to 3,339,909 pesos.[7] In this fiscal crisis, the chits used in lieu of advance payment to the tobacco growers depreciated

[4] Fradera (2005, pp. 471–472).

[5] Legarda (1999).

[6] De Jesus (1980, pp. 178–196).

[7] Fradera (2005, pp. 531–532).

in value, and, compounded by environmental and other factors, meant many growers found themselves facing ruin.

As tobacco monopoly revenue diminished and debts to growers increased, causing great social unrest, numerous studies were carried out to find a solution for the sector, calling for further investment and immediate payment of debts owed to growers. Agronomists and industrial engineers were to be brought in; cultivation was to be improved with tobacco varieties from seeds imported from Cuba; and more solid tobacco barn structures were to be built since most were made of bamboo, wood and nipa, and highly flammable. Recommendations also included better conditions and pay for workers, many of them women, including the creation of a mutual aid society and a school for workers' children, and it was proposed to increase and improve the workforce by bringing highly skilled personnel from Spain. A particular recommendation was to address the rapid turnover in administrative personnel that hindered any meaningful change: in 1868 alone, Carlos Recur noted in his 1880 account, the Dirección de Colecciones had gone through nine directors.[8]

There was also the problem of why Philippine tobacco prices were low. Under the monopoly, leaf and some cigars were not sent to Spain at market prices, but as a form of tribute. Some tobacco was also handed over in the Philippines to creditors of the Spanish state at depressed prices. Some cigars and leaf were auctioned to foreign buyers in the Philippines, at higher prices but not necessarily equivalent to world market rates. Alongside the financial problems caused for the monopoly came increasing political tension in both the Philippines and Spain. The Spanish administration tried unsuccessfully to get a grip on the problem. Rules and regulations were introduced for tobacco cultivation in Visayas, different from those in Luzon, but solutions such as the introduction of cheaper but inferior-quality leaf, combined with setbacks such as poor crops and fires in tobacco facilities, only worsened the situation. Controlling the process of cultivating, harvesting, processing, and selling the tobacco proved costly and unprofitable, and an increase in the price of cigars, aimed at compensating for this, only greatly reduced demand.

In September 1870, the Philippine Governor entrusted an ad hoc board, the Junta de Reformas Económicas, to study reforms in the tobacco economy to increase government revenue. As documented by

[8] Recur (1880, p. 47).

José Jimeno Agius, Intendente General de Hacienda (Director of the Treasury) in the Philippines at the time, the Junta recommended the abolition of the monopoly, arguing that the monopoly generated more problems than it solved.[9] The Junta report ratified that the operational costs of the monopoly outweighed its benefits, and the debt this generated could not be sustained. Declaring the urgency of liberalising the tobacco sector, the Junta advised swift political action,[10] accompanied by a broader fiscal reform that would favour levies on profits, property, industry, and commerce,[11] and there were more subsequently introduced in 1878–1880 and again in 1883–1884.[12]

The Junta's recommendations met with ample support. The Manila press was clearly in favour of abolition, as articles in *El Porvenir Filipino* and *El Diario de Manila*, the main conservative newspaper, convincingly demonstrated.[13] Jimeno Agius himself reaffirmed:

> Public opinion is explicit and unanimous regarding the ending of the tobacco monopoly... Producers as well as consumers, public officers and taxpayers, Europeans as well as natives, all agreed that abolishing the tobacco monopoly is a general aspiration against which no reasons can be upheld, an urgent necessity both for the public interest and private convenience, and a compelling solution to which the archipelago's tax system must be subordinate.[14]

He did, however, warn that ending the monopoly would initially cost the Philippine treasury around 1,750,000 pesos, which would have to be raised elsewhere. The Spanish treasury would also lose the annual remittance of tobacco revenue. Although he did not see these as a principal obstacle, he cautioned such problems should not be lost from sight. Nonetheless, he argued, there could no longer be any going back on liberalisation.

Despite the consensus of the early 1870s, rapid regime change and political events in Spain (from revolution to a new foreign monarchy

[9] Agius (1878, pp. 5–6).

[10] Agius (1878, p. 65).

[11] Ibid. pp. 40–42.

[12] Fradera (2005, p. 532).

[13] Agius (1878, pp. 8, 65–70).

[14] Ibid. p. 10.

and a republic—all of which failed) led to abolition being postponed. The tobacco monopoly recovered from its financial woes thanks to the decrease in the amount of revenue remitted to Spain and an increase in market sales, which finally enabled repayment of the debt accumulated over the two previous decades.[15] Some even lauded the recovery of the sector.[16]

The political situation in Spain stabilised with the restoration of the Bourbon monarchy, and a pact among the main political parties to start a new era. With the Restoration seemingly established, the Spanish Government again turned its attention to the Philippine tobacco sector. Various schemes failed to materialise, one of which was not to abolish the monopoly but to lease it to Spanish interests in partnership with foreigners, including King Leopold of the Belgians, in return for loans to the Spanish state and payment of part of the continuing revenue.

A coincidence of interests, however, among politicians and those in the trade in Spain as well as in the archipelago, along with the conviction that benefits would be forthcoming, finally spurred the government to approve abolition and place the sector in the hands of private enterprise. As soon as the abolition was announced in June 1881, the tobacco market was closely monitored to avoid shortages that could have serious economic and social consequences. The Spanish administration gradually put its stock on the market and tried to increase production, even after the setbacks of the typhoons of late October and early November 1882. It took care to supply quality tobacco adapted to the tastes of smokers in the different provinces. To stave off speculation, the storage and resale of leaf by individuals were prohibited from 30 November 1882 until 1 January 1883. To encourage the creation of business, the collection of taxes on the manufacture and sale of tobacco were suspended until 1 July 1883,[17] and the then Governor-General Primo de Rivera even called on

[15] Fradera (2005, pp. 532–533).

[16] Recur (1880, p. 28).

[17] Dispatch from consul E. Crampon, 8 January 1883, AMAE CCC, Manille, Vol 4, f. 249. AHN, Ultramar, leg. 1447, exp. 23. Memoria reservada que al entregar el mando superior de Filipinas el Exmo. Sr. Marqués de Estella deja a su sucesor, 1 March 1883, AHN Ultramar, leg. 5351, f. 159v–162v.

the clergy to spread the word about the new openings afforded by the monopoly's abolition.[18]

Enter the Large Companies

The Compañía General de Tabacos de Filipinas (or Tabacalera as it came to be known) was a trailblazer for other companies. It was created in Barcelona in November 1881 by a group of industrialists and French financiers with colonial interests,[19] and benefited from late nineteenth-century government patronage designed to attract large-scale foreign capital into the Spanish economy.

As the Spanish newspaper *ABC* noted in a 1964 article celebrating the company's 83 years in existence,[20] Tabacalera leased the factories in Meisic, Malabon, Cavite, Fortín, and Arroceros that the Spanish government still owned. It kept the state networks of providers, buying leaf from Philippine growers and renewing alliances with the groups and intermediaries that controlled growing and buying. It also purchased the government facilities where the harvested tobacco was stored, classified, and processed.[21] The company embarked on a process of agricultural expansion by purchasing 9,230 hectares of tobacco land in the Cagayan Valley, San Antonio, Santa Isabel, San Luis, San Rafael, and La Concepción, bringing under its remit thousands of small tenant tobacco farmers. It brought specialists from Cuba to improve both the leaf and processed tobacco and built new tobacco sheds and a new factory at Arroceros, on the left bank of the Pasig River, which was soon renowned for its cigars, cigarettes, and chewing tobacco under its flagship brand La Flor de la Isabela. Cultivation in Visayas also appears to have benefited from the new opportunities offered by liberalisation.[22] It should be noted the Spanish government had pursued similar expansion plans prior to

[18] Dispatch from consul E. Crampon, 8 January 1883, AMAE CCC, Manille, Vol 4, f. 249.

[19] Giralt (1981), Rodrigo y Alharilla (1996, 2000, 2009), and Izard (1974).

[20] Anonymous (1964).

[21] Recur (1880, p. 9).

[22] Dispatch from consul C. Nodot, 8 February 1885, AMAE CCC, Manille, Vol 5, f. 53–53v.

abolition,[23] which is another indication of how Tabacalera was in many respects following a course already mapped out.

In effect, Tabacalera became the model for other joint-stock companies entering the Philippine market with considerable capital. According to the 1892 *Guía Oficial de Filipinas*,[24] these included the German Baer & Co.[25] and the Spanish La Insular, La Nacional, La Competidora Gaditana, La Constancia, La Exportadora, La Favorita, La Flor de Filipinas, María Cristina, La Honradez, La Hensiana, La Minerva, El Oriente, and Para Usted, among others.[26] Just under a decade later, the *Guía comercial de Manila* for 1901 listed 28 major tobacco-manufacturing concerns in the city alone. Some were founded by European entrepreneurs supported by the capital of foreign trading houses established in Manila. The capital was thus both 'foreign' by virtue of the nationality of the owners and 'local' because it came from Manila-based trading companies. La Hensiana, for example, was set up for five years with a capital of 70,000 pesos in equal parts from six large overseas trading companies—Martin Dyce y Cía, C. Lutz y Cía, Baer Senior y Cía, Tillson Hermann y Cía, Ker y Cía, Smith Bell y Cía—and from Juan Felipe Hens, a Belgian industrialist.[27]

While the monopoly had only introduced one tobacco-shredding machine at its Arroceros factory,[28] Tabacalera fast mechanised. Cigar production was still mainly by hand, but by 1890 three cigarette machines, two French and one American, were in operation, in addition to one shredding machine.[29] By 1895, according to the industry tax registers, Tabacalera had 19 cigarette machines, 10 American and 9 French, as well as 3 shredding machines. A factory owned by Teodorico Cobarrubias was reported as having 5 shredding machines and 18 cigarette machines, and El Oriente had 5 shredding machines and 20 cigarette machines.

[23] De Jesus (1980, pp. 29–56).

[24] Anonymous (1892b, p. 131, and advertisements pp. 14–15, 20–21, 34–35, 42–43, 50–51).

[25] Salazar (2001).

[26] Anonymous (1901).

[27] Protócolos, notary Miguel Torres, 1883, NAP, SDS, Vol 689, deed n°410.

[28] De Jesus (1971, p. 102) and Clarence-Smith (2022, p. 89).

[29] De Bérard (1891, p. 570) and Sawyer (1900, p. 158).

Like all large companies, Tabacalera had the capacity for buying large quantities of leaf each year. The company could choose the best leaf for its most select Isabela products without having to blend them with inferior-quality leaf. It could also store large amounts of leaf from previous years for use only when well cured. It could sell its cigars, cigarettes, and cut tobacco according to quality, whereby the very best were sold under the Flor de Isabela brand and those with some imperfections as La Montañesa, while those made with inferior-quality leaf were sold unbranded.[30] The new companies catered to both local elites and European markets, especially Spain.[31] Tabacalera supplied the Spanish Royal House, having obtained a Diploma of Honor in the 1882 Exhibition of Manila, and in Amsterdam 1883 and Antwerp 1885; a Grand Diploma of Honor in the 1887 Philippines Exhibition in Madrid; and gold medals in the 1888 exhibitions in Melbourne and Barcelona and the 1889 exhibition in Paris.

Again, it is important to note that the groundwork for the international reputation of Philippine tobacco had been laid by changes in trade policy during the monopoly period. As far back as 1785, the metropolitan authorities had begun to liberalise Philippine overseas trade within the framework of the state monopoly, and in the 1820s the first bales of Philippine tobacco were sent to Spanish ports and sold on other international markets. The process of liberalising the trade was complete in Manila by 1834, and in Visayas by 1855, with a greater presence of overseas trading houses. By 1837, tobacco, in the form of leaf and cigars, was one of the Philippines' main export items, along with sugar, cotton, indigo, and coffee, and later also abaca and copra.[32] Cagayan tobacco was especially in demand in Spain and on international markets, and both demand and the price increased when it won the gold medal in the first Great Exhibition of the Works of Industry of All Nations in London in 1851. Spanish demand for Philippine tobacco continued to increase, such that in 1862 the Philippines sent 130,000 *quintales* (13,000,000 kg) of tobacco, which was over half that year's crop of 226,247 *quintales*.[33]

[30] Anonymous (1892b, pp. 6–7).

[31] Nodot (1889, pp. 284–285) and Dispatch of 19 October 1888, AMAE, CCC, Manille, Vol 5, f. 166.

[32] Fradera (2005, p. 479) and De Jesus (1980, pp. 161–166).

[33] Fradera (2005, p. 527).

Spanish producers and consumers soon viewed the quality of Cagayan tobacco as superior to that of Virginia and Kentucky while at the same time much cheaper—in Cadiz, a *quintal* (100 kilos) of Philippine tobacco was sold for 10 pesos, whereas the price of North American tobacco was between 18 and 20 pesos.[34] It was also claimed to be comparable in quality to the Cuban tobacco of Vuelta Abajo, by then the global gold standard in cigars and cigar tobacco leaf. In 1891, less than a decade after the monopoly had been abolished, Gaston de Bérard, the French Consul in the Philippines, who had before been posted to Havana, and who was of the conviction that none could rival Havana cigars, wrote in his report:

> One of the particularities of the Manila factories consists in making cigars that have the shape and colour (but not the finesse) of Havana cigars, and in arranging them well in boxes of cedar that come from Cuba. The labels are as Havana cigars, and they are shipped by their thousands to the United States, where American connoisseurs buy this product from the Philippines and inhale the aroma with the gentle conviction that it has come in a direct line from the Cuban capital. The operation is not insignificant, since 60,000 or 70,000 cigars leave Manila for the ports of the Union.[35]

In establishing this growing international reputation and increase in sales, the political networks of Manila companies and trading houses were of major importance. According to contemporary observers, it was within these networks that sales and price were negotiated for clients in England, Belgium, Germany, and Asia. In effect, this was targeted networking for the Manila companies to open up their overseas markets.

Some smaller companies also appear to have benefitted from the new export possibilities. Thus, shortly after the abolition of the monopoly, a French consular report refers to 'family concerns' selling their products on European markets.[36] For the most part, however, their radius of trade remained extremely limited. It was the large companies that had the trade networks to place their production and keep abreast of market developments and overseas consumer tastes. The domestic market, not least

[34] Fradera (2005, pp. 526–533).

[35] De Bérard (1891, p. 503).

[36] Dispatch from the chancellor Bréjard, 17 July 1884, AMAE CCC, Manille, Vol 5, f. 17v–18.

for cigarettes, was nonetheless by no means inconsiderable. As Bérard reported in 1892, "millions of cigarettes manufactured by the General Tobacco Company of the Philippines and by the other companies are highly appreciated by the natives as well as by the Europeans since they are seen in everyone's mouth from morning to night."[37]

Reports of this nature signalled a wider domestic market for cigarettes. While the large companies targeted especially the financially strong sector of consumers seeking quality tobacco and cigars, they were also focusing on the market for inferior-quality, low-priced tobacco and cigarettes. Competition in the latter segment of the Philippine tobacco market was what would give rise to conflict and hostility towards small local ventures, especially those of the Chinese.

Local Micro-Enterprise

There can be little doubt that micro-entrepreneurship expanded in the shadows of the new large-scale companies, with what appears to have been a spectacular efflorescence in Manila in the mid-1880s of companies of a more modest size. While the constraints and inadequacies of the monopoly had given rise to clandestine production, this could now operate in the open, and local Filipino and Chinese communities began to shape a new outwork and small-shop culture.

A caveat is in order here, which is to clarify how we sought to distinguish Chinese from Filipino in the 1895 industry tax register.[38] Since the ethnicity of the owner-declarants was not specified, we inevitably looked to the surname of the owner. Given the difference between Chinese and Hispanic names, this was a good partial indicator. It was also problematic, however, since a Chinese surname may have corresponded to a Chinese mestizo, a Chinese settler converted to Catholicism, or a freshly arrived Chinese immigrant. Moreover, the Chinese names in the registers are approximate transcriptions. There is similar uncertainty about the ethnic categorisation of the Filipino group. An owner classified as Filipino may have been Spanish, and there is the added complexity of distinguishing between Spaniards from Spain and Spanish creoles and mestizos.

[37] De Bérard (1993, pp. 14–15).

[38] Contribución industrial, 1895, NAP SDS.

Despite these reservations, a statistical analysis of the 1895 industry tax register for Manila provides some very interesting information. There were 201 companies registered in the Manila tobacco sector that year. Of the 188 considered to be either Filipino or Chinese, a little more than half (100) were registered to owners with Hispanic surnames, and a little under half (88) to owners with Chinese surnames. This suggests a significant Chinese presence, albeit not, at least in strictly numerical terms, the alleged Chinese invasion of the sector, to which we shall return later.

Of the 100 enterprises considered to be Filipino, the vast majority were small family affairs. Three-quarters (76%) had fewer than 10 workers and a third (34%) only 1–2. Only 3% of the companies had more than 40 workers, and seemingly only one had more than 100 workers, a company in Binondo, a district on the right bank of Manila, with 205 workers. Most operated on a very small scale, and most likely would have sold directly from the home, on the street, or at local markets. That many were ephemeral was in all likelihood less a reflection on the emergence of an entrepreneurial spirit than the difficult economic situation in the wake of the monopoly. Also, it would be naïve to believe that so many shops flourishing in Manila were all newly founded, but we can nevertheless assume significant growth for the period immediately following abolition. It was clear from the register that only a few companies had machines and a numerically large workforce. In this, Tabacalera with 2,158 workers and El Oriente with 1,800 workers, 1,300 in its cigar factory Binondo and 500 in its cigarette factory in Quiapo, were exceptions. Others such as Scheerer y Cía in Binondo and Baer Senior y Cía in Tambobong had only 20 and 30 workers, respectively.[39]

By contrast, production in the small sector, especially in cigars and to a lesser extent cigarettes, remained fundamentally artisanal, whereby a worktable, that might seat up to 12 workers, was at the centre of production and packaging.[40] Little equipment or infrastructure was required, and even that was beyond the reach of many. A basic requirement was to be under a roof that was sufficiently watertight to protect the leaf and finished product from humidity, but the otherwise low initial capital investment, the limited risk-taking, and the possibility of using the family

[39] Contribución industrial, 1895, NAP SDS.

[40] De Jesus (1971, p. 102) and Camagay (1995).

home as a workplace and family members as workers were all incentives for a successful start to a new small operation.

Almost half of those employed (48%) in these small ventures were women, seeking a means for survival by making use of their know-how and possibly hoping to succeed in setting up a more ambitious venture of their own in the future. Many of the women, like the men, had gained experience in the state-owned factories of the tobacco monopoly before the 1880s. By the end of the monopoly, those factories were employing a total of some 50,000 workers, 18,000 of them women. As reported in several sources, after the monopoly was abolished, a large number of women found themselves out of work and sought work in some small shop, or considered setting up their own.[41]

In effect, considerable practical knowledge and experience of working the tobacco that was acquired during the monopoly period was, from the 1880s on, transferred to the newly emerging small-scale sector. This favoured a geographical continuity of production. The vast majority of the small sector was located in Manila, and in Malabon, the relatively large Philippine municipality to the north of Manila also known as Tambobong, where there were 10 companies and where, prior to 1883, a state-owned factory had been located. In comparison with other cities, Manila had the best connections to the hinterland, including long-established networks to the tobacco-growing regions, and, "as the chief port and capital, Manila also had the best access to current information on overseas style and taste preferences and to superior maritime connections."[42]

According to Isabelo de los Reyes, an observer of the indigenous working classes, the principal trade of the women of Malabon, from the time when the large state tobacco factory was there, was making cigars.[43] After 1883, many were obliged to seek their livelihood in the factories of Manila, but in Malabon there were about 100 small shops rolling cigars and cigarettes, in each of which there were some 5, 10, 15, or 20 workers. The number of shops recorded in the industry tax register was far fewer, which may well be an indication that there were many operating on the margins. In the factories of the monopoly, women were reportedly poorly

[41] Dispatch from consul E. Crampon, 21 August 1881, AMAE CCC, Manille, Vol 4, f. 222v.

[42] Doeppers (1984, p. 20).

[43] De los Reyes y Florentino (1994 [1889], p. 530).

paid, barely able to get by on their meagre wages, although better off than many other workers. In the new shops, the older gender division of the labour market became more blurred, and women and men were to be found in all stages of production in the making of cigars, cigarettes, and cut tobacco.

Regarding the 88 concerns that can be fairly confidently attributed to the Chinese community in the Philippines, in terms of size and number of employees 10% had fewer than 5 workers, 28% between 6 and 10, and 28% between 11 and 20. There were 12 with more than 50 workers, and two were of considerable size, those of Siong Fanten in Trozo with 220 workers and Ricardo Go Chyco in Binondo, with 710 workers split between two establishments of 300 and 410 workers, respectively. Also, 68% of the companies run by Chinese employed between 2 and 20 workers, whereas the proportion was 89% in the case of those run by Filipinos. Some owned by Chinese had relatively modern equipment in comparison with other small ones using older or no technology. In Binondo, one company, that of Sec Quisam, declared only 15 workers and yet was running four hand-operated cigarette machines and five grinders, three of which were manual and two steam operated.

Whereas Filipino companies were to be found more in Manila's poor outlying districts of Tondo (28%) and Santa Cruz (27%), almost three quarters of the Chinese companies were located in Binondo, often referred to as 'Chinatown.' Thus, while the micro-enterprises that emerged from the 1880s onwards had a number of features in common, they also differed, not only in size, number of workers, capital, and use of technology, but also in their geographical location, reflecting Manila's social and ethnic settlement.

The Chinese Presence

The Chinese entrepreneurs stood out for their connections in the tobacco-growing regions. With the abolition of the monopoly, the new small shops all competed for the developing markets of Manila and its hinterland. The advantage of the Chinese was that they were able to buy reliably and cheaply directly at source in the tobacco areas, which gave them a positive edge in terms of the quality and price of the products they sold.

The disappearance of the monopoly also seems to have led to an overall increase in tobacco consumption in the Philippines, as products became more accessible. Poor organisation of the monopoly meant that tobacco was often out of stock or only poor-quality products were available, the best having been diverted upstream.[44] Price reductions for quality cigars after 1882[45] and an end to the obstacles, suspicion, and chicanery of the anti-smuggling guards (*Resguardo*) towards smokers[46]—in particular the most humble who were easy targets for its agents—might have been factors helping explain the increase in consumption. Consumption did not, however, encompass pipe smoking and chewing, which remained virtually absent in the Philippines.

Western observers were nonetheless very struck by how commonplace tobacco was in the archipelago, with women of all ages and conditions smoking in public. Edmond Plauchut, a French traveller to the Philippines, in 1877 described a particular 'Filipino passion' for tobacco[47] and echoed a common colonial belief in particular forms of 'indigenous consumption' for therapeutic and spiritual purposes. Many, of course, consumed inferior-quality tobacco—at least compared to the tobacco Western observers considered superior.

For the years 1884–1885, Charles Nodot, the French Consul who anteceded Bérard, reported a sharp increase in the production of tobacco products "which find in the population of the archipelago an assured clientele because of their low prices."[48] In the Visayas Islands, especially in Iloilo on the island of Panay, in Luzon, in the provinces of La Union, Abra, and Lepanto, different varieties of tobacco could be found, among which the Barili, the tobacco produced on the east coast of the island of Cebu, enjoyed the best reputation.[49]

The dominant tastes in the archipelago thus varied by region, as did the characteristics of the tobacco produced there. Recur referred in 1880 to the failure to take into account the regional differences of the tobacco as yet another of the many complaints levied against the monopoly.[50]

[44] De Jesus (1971, p. 106).

[45] Foreman (1906, p. 297).

[46] Lachica (1977, p. 13).

[47] Plauchut (1877, p. 886).

[48] Nodot (1887, p. 88).

[49] De Bérard (1891, p. 503).

[50] Recur (1880, pp. 38–39).

Officials began to survey the regional diversity,[51] as was reflected in the later 1901 Report of the Philippine Commission, drawn up in the early years of US control over the islands:

> Tobacco coming from the province of Isabela de Cagayan is considered the best in the Philippines. That from the Visayan Islands is coarser, more unequal in color, and of greater strength. The tobacco from Nueva Ecija is fine, but somewhat bitter in taste and yellow in color. That from Union, Ilocos and the Igorrotes is of heavy body, broken, and frequently has but little combustibility.[52]

Companies built on this knowledge, with their own careful packaging and new advertising strategies to attract customers and compete on the market. As a few rare examples discovered in the archives show, even the smallest shops might elaborately decorate their cigar and cigarette packaging, inspired by or openly copying the aesthetics, colours, names, and advertising slogans of the major brands renowned on international markets.

The success of the Chinese as suppliers due to the commercial networks that they had established in the tobacco-growing regions was captured by Edgar Wickberg in the case of Aparri and the Cagayan Valley:

> Basing their operations at Aparri, the Chinese moved up the Cagayan valley, establishing *sari-sari* local stores [where] they retailed imported textiles and household goods and bought tobacco wholesale. As in the hemp regions, Chinese success could be attributed to the cheapness of their operations and their willingness to barter goods from their stores for the tobacco. While other wholesalers stayed in Aparri, paying a transportation fee for having the tobacco shipped to them, the Chinese bought at the point of production, handled the shipping to Aparri themselves and sold it there to other Chinese who sent it on by sea to Manila, where it was sold to foreign buyers or to Chinese cigar and cigarette factories.[53]

[51] Memoria reservada que al entregar el mando superior de Filipinas el Exmo. Sr. Marqués de Estella deja a su sucesor, 1 March 1883, AHN Ultramar, leg. 5351, f. 159v–162v.

[52] Anonymous (1900–1901, Vol 3, p. 267).

[53] Wickberg (1962, p. 282).

The Chinese gained privileged access for tobacco[54] because they were in direct contact with the heads of the networks, and invested directly in them.[55] Furthermore, as the tax records for 1897 show, Chinese merchants opened warehouses in Binondo specialising in wholesale leaf and processed tobacco.[56] The pyramid of intermediaries and the modes of functioning of these networks allowed some Chinese manufacturers to have privileged access to leaf and dominate the transport and storage of leaf en route to the processing centres in Manila.[57]

The Chinese also secured privileged access to leaf tobacco through micro-credits granted to farmers. Dating back to the 1860s in the late phase of the Spanish tobacco monopoly, due to a lack of ready cash, the tobacco administration had started paying some of the growers in chits, not honouring them until months or years later, if at all, and often even confiscating the crop. The purchasing power of the growers was limited by such abuses, and, in order to pay the taxes to which they were subject and underwrite their daily outgoings, growers frequently turned to lenders. They would give them their chits in return for cash or kind, and lenders often took a generous commission of from 20% up to 50% of their stated value. Not all of the lenders were Chinese, but from the 1870s onwards, more and more were. According to the account given in the later 1901 Report of the Philippine Commission,[58] the Chinese thus kindled their networks in the tobacco sector—in which, it should be noted, Chinese merchants had been very present prior to the waves of Chinese expulsions in the 1750s and 1760s, before the creation of the Spanish monopoly.

Lastly, the Chinese may well have dominated the low end of the Philippine tobacco market by making use of retail structures carried over from the monopoly period. We know little, or nothing for certain, about the sale of tobacco for smoking after the disappearance of the outlets over which the state theoretically had a monopoly up to 1882. Yet we do know that tobacco was sold by the countless *sari-sari*, and it is likely that the

[54] De Jesus (1980, p. 191).

[55] Yoshihara (1985, pp. 98–100).

[56] Contribución Industrial, Manila, 1897, NAP SDS.

[57] De Jesus (1980, p. 191).

[58] Anonymous (1900–1901, Vol 1, p. 157) and De Jesus (1978, pp. 101–102, 105–106).

tobacco products of the Chinese shops and factories—and possibly those of others—were sold through the same networks for buying the leaf.

The Chinese Peril

After the end of the monopoly, discourses on people, culture, and identity, which were at the time changing globally, came very much to the fore in the case of the Chinese in the Philippines. They were more and more the target of a barrage of racialized imaginings of a supposed 'yellow peril' that had been growing during the late nineteenth century, in tandem with complaints as to a possible Chinese threat to the international reputation of the Philippine tobacco industry.

It is important to note that the discourse about the Chinese danger emerged around the same time as the liberalisation of the tobacco. After 1881 and before the official abolition of the monopoly, tobacco farmers had been able to count on state administration of cash advances and benefit from a deferral of the payment of personal tax payments. These advantages disappeared with the monopoly and growers needed to sell their crop quickly.[59] Large companies from Manila sent their buyers to the Cagayan Valley and set up drying facilities there, and did not view lightly the Chinese presence.

French consular reports of the time testify to the racialised slant that was given to this. As early as January 1883, the then French Consul, Ernest Crampon, warned:

> The day they [the Chinese] enter the line for the purchase of tobacco, the manufacture and sale of cigars, with their understanding of business, their dexterity of hand, their sobriety, their thrift, their assiduity at work, the admirable spirit of solidarity which unites them, and their numbers, which can be instantly increased by immigration, if it is not restrained by law or police regulations, that day the Compagnie Générale des Tabacs [Tabacalera] will find itself contending with the presence of another and very serious rival... The Chinese, for the moment, are observing and preparing themselves, knowing that they are suspected and feared."[60]

[59] De Jesus (1980, p. 190).

[60] Dispatch from consul E. Crampon, 8 January 1883, AMAE CCC, Manille, Vol 4, f. 253.

Chinese producers were accused of untoward conduct, from unfair competition and tacit agreements to eliminate non-Chinese rivals (in particular by artificially raising or lowering prices) to their collective desire to establish their own monopoly over the entire tobacco sector and alleged inability to defend the 'public' interest. A full range of complaints can be found in the 1901 Report of the Philippines Commission,[61] and French Consul Charles Nodot wrote in his earlier report of 1888:

> [Chinese] speculators care little to encourage the native planter to improve his products and to preserve the superior types of the old classification. Without waiting for the leaf to undergo the fermentation that gives it the desired quality, they endeavour to seize it as soon as possible, pack it immediately and ship it to Manila, in order to make new purchases with the proceeds of the sale of their first jobs. These practices are, moreover, singularly favoured by the inborn defects of the native cultivator who, with no concern about tomorrow, is too often short of money and, consequently, barely in a condition to resist the tempting proposals of the Chinese speculator, who, if he has an ungenerous hand, at least always pays cash.[62]

The typed manuscript of Nodot's report, moreover, omitted a phrase included in his handwritten missive, which referred to "the sordid and mean spirit that characterises their race."[63] Combining two stereotypes—the greed of the Chinese and the indolence of Filipinos—Nodot attributed the existence of poorly processed tobaccos on the markets to the interplay of apparent ethnic characteristics. Chinese entrepreneurs were described as a united block, driven by the sole desire to enrich themselves unfairly, always at the expense of their European competitors or their Filipino workers.

Nodot's successor, Bérard, was hardly more optimistic on the eve of the 1896 revolution, highlighting how tobacco's "inferiority" was due to "insufficient preparation and early harvesting of the tobacco leaf" caused

[61] Report of the Philippine Commission to the President (1900–1901, Vol 1, p. 157).

[62] Nodot (1889, pp. 283–284).

[63] AMAE CCC, Manille, Vol 5, dispatch from consul C. Nodot, 19 October 1888, f. 164v–165.

by "Chinese [who] seek to buy first, in order to resell more expensively."[64] Chinese products were called *beri-beri* cigars, inferring that their poor quality made the consumer dangerously ill.[65] The competition between Chinese entrepreneurs was never mentioned, nor were the socio-economic factors that might have pushed them to focus on the trade and production of inferior-quality tobacco, in which the lack of financial reserves of both Chinese buyers and Filipino farmers played a central role.

Sexual stereotyping was also associated with work in the small tobacco sector. An article titled "Antros industriales," published in 1892 in *La Ilustración filipina,* claimed to give an insight into the "vertiginous work... which would be worthy of praise if it did not also conceal elements that could be called pornographic."[66] The small shops, the article claimed, were places where there were "hundreds of women of all types and ages, half naked, working chaotically amidst hundreds of men, sitting huddled together on the benches in front of the work tables." Such suggestive descriptions with a delight in detail amounted to a clear stereotyping of alleged sexual debauchery among the workers, a trait also observed elsewhere in the world. According to the author Boni (a pen name), the Chinese tobacco shop owner operated like the 'sultan of Turkey' reigning over his harem, employing a logic suggestive of them taking malicious pleasure in compromising the morality of the young as they did in adulterating their tobacco products. Such attributions might be seen as an extension of the stereotypes of the seduction of opium consumption among the Chinese, and also other groups, that were circulating during the later years of the monopoly. On this, Plauchut had commented in 1877: "I've often thought it's mistaken to say the cigars contain opium. Opium is not grown in the Philippines and costs around 3,000 francs a *picul* or 62.5 kg. At that price, it would be difficult to sell a thousand cigars for 40 or 50 francs."[67]

[64] G. de Bérard, Situation des Philippines au 31 décembre 1894, AMAE CCC, Manille, Vol 6, f. 433–433. See also Dispatch from consul E. Crampon, 8 January 1883, AMAE CCC, Manille, Vol 4, f. 253v.

[65] Wickberg (1962, p. 282).

[66] Anonymous (1892a, p. 312).

[67] Plauchut (1877, p. 886.).

There was also the fear that foreign 'inexperienced buyers' would buy tobacco produced by the Chinese.[68] Nodot reported that 'family shops' as well as the large European-owned companies managed to export cigars to European markets, and that these were inferior and detrimental to the good reputation of the colony's products.[69] Bérard wrote that the Chinese, as many observers were convinced, acted as "destroyers of everything based on good faith and commercial honesty." Overlooking the fact that the Chinese did not systematically produce for the world market, but rather produced cheap tobacco products for the local markets, it was, he claimed, the bad faith and imitation skills of the Chinese that had to be seen as the cause of the decline in the reputation of Philippine tobacco around the world and so damaging to the interests of European companies.[70]

Conclusion

As this chapter has shown, the serious dysfunctionality of the Spanish tobacco monopoly and the new liberal atmosphere justified its abolition in the Philippines in the early 1880s. This crucial reform was, however, a leap into the unknown that the French consul in Manila even called a "revolution."[71] With hindsight the abolition of the monopoly can be seen as a success. Not only did it not result in an economic and social crisis, but the number of tobacco workers in Manila and the surrounding area increased to 30,000 by the mid-1890s.[72] There were also related industries, such as rice paper for cigarettes, packaging paper and label printing, and cigar boxes. In terms of capital invested, workers employed, and value of output, the tobacco sector remained of crucial importance for the colonial economy and in particular for Manila until the end of the Spanish period. Only sugar was more important.[73]

[68] Martín Martínez (1896).

[69] Dispatch from consul C. Nodot, 17 July 1884, AMAE CCC, Manille, Vol 5, f. 17v–18.

[70] Dispatch from consul G. de Bérard, AMAE CCC, Manille, Vol 7, 20 June 1896, f. 346–346v.

[71] Dispatch from consul E. Crampon, 21 August 1883, AMAE CCC, Manille, Vol 4, f. 223.

[72] Sawyer (1900, p. 158).

[73] Clarence de Smith (2022, p. 89).

The successful transition from monopoly to free market was due to the combined dynamism of two sets of economic actors: on the one hand, the large Western companies, with powerful financial and technical means, which took over the supply of quality Filipino tobacco to international markets, and on the other hand, a nebulous group of Asian entrepreneurs, Chinese and Filipino, with limited means, who specialised in the supply of an expanding domestic market. Western observers perceived this through the prism of racialised colonial discourses that mixed strong animosity towards the Chinese community, considering Chinese workshops detrimental to the reputation of Philippine tobacco in the world, with a contempt for Filipino entrepreneurial capacity.

Much remains to be researched on the history of tobacco in the Philippines. For the first centuries of Spanish colonial rule, grey areas remain regarding the diffusion of tobacco production and consumption in the archipelago. The historiography remains to this day overly concentrated on the Cagayan Valley, in Luzon, for the cultivation of tobacco, and on Manila and its hinterland, for the production of cigars. The role that leaf or processed tobacco played in the archipelago's internal trade remains poorly studied, in particular the role it played between the evangelised inhabitants of the lowlands and those rebelling against colonial rule in the highlands. For the century of the monopoly's existence, little is known about the intense smuggling that took place between these two areas and, moreover, the central importance that tobacco played in social life during the colonial period. A mass of documentation concerning these phenomena lies dormant in the archives of the administration as well as the religious orders awaiting further investigation.

We wish to end, however, on a note of what happened after the transition to US rule. The early twentieth century did not see the large, highly capitalised Western companies inexorably "gobble up" small Asian factories, as foreseen by Younghusband in 1899.[74] The impetus to create companies of all sizes was sustained and capital concentration was slow, with niches continuing to exist for small entrepreneurs. In 1910, the American Henry Jacobson cautiously estimated the number of tobacco factories at 300, "most of these being small concerns," still concentrated in Manila.[75] At the time, the tobacco industry employed an estimated

[74] Younghusband (1899, p. 140).

[75] Jacobson (1914, p. 14).

40,000 people in and around Manila, and Manila accounted for 93% of all cigar and cigarette factory workers in the country. What the early US colonial period did confirm was a trend, which had already been noticeable in the 1880s and 1890s, for cigar consumption to be replaced by cigarette consumption, especially among the popular classes, such that by 1913 cigarette consumption was quoted as 4.5 billion as against 96.2 million cigars.[76]

After a spectacular boom during World War I, the Philippine tobacco industry went into crisis in the 1920s, with the shift from hand-rolled to machine-made cigars and—including for a new female clientele—cigarettes. On European and US markets, in the Philippines, and particularly in Manila, cigarettes made with dark Manila tobacco faced growing competition from mild cigarettes skilfully advertised and manufactured in the metropolitan area,[77] such that by the 1960s big American cigarette brands had literally flooded the Philippine market and few local brands had survived. Large Filipino manufacturers saw they had little option but to start producing American cigarette brands under licence. Ironically, as if in revenge for how they had been described in the late nineteenth century as the gravediggers of Philippine tobacco, many of the companies still in existence in the 1960s were owned by Sino-Filipinos,[78] but that is a story beyond our remit here.

References

Primary Sources

Unpublished
Archivo Histórico Nacional, Sección Ultramar (Madrid) (AHN, Ultramar).
- Ultramar leg. 5351
Archives du ministère français des Affaires étrangères, Correspondance Consulaire et Commerciale (La Courneuve) (AMAE CCC)
- Manille
National Archives of the Philippines (Manila) (NAP, SDS)
- Contribución industrial

[76] Jacobson (1914, p. 10).

[77] Doeppers (1984, pp. 20–22, 126; 1991, pp. 521–525).

[78] Yoshihara (1985, pp. 43–44, 96).

Published

Agius Jimeno, José. 1878. *El desestanco de tabaco en las islas Filipinas*. Madrid: Conde y Cía.

Anonymous. 1892a. Antros industrials. *La Ilustración filipina*, 21 August.

Anonymous. 1892b. *Guía Oficial de Filipinas*. Manila: Chofré y Cía.

Anonymous. 1901. *Guía Comercial de Manila*.

Anonymous. 1964. Hace ya 83 años fue fundada en Barcelona la Compañía General de Tabacos de Filipinas. *ABC*, 22 December.

De Bérard, G. 1891. Situation économique des Philippines en 1888, 1889 et 1890. *Bulletin Consulaire Français* 22: 488–579.

De Bérard, G. 1993. *Possessions Espagnoles d'Océanie. Situation des Philippines en 1892 (Deuxième Partie). Annexe au Moniteur Officiel du Commerce du 27 Juillet 1893*. Paris: Librairie Administrative Paul Dupont.

De Jesus, E.C. 1971. Manila's First Factories. *Philippine Historical Review* 4: 97–109.

De los Reyes y Florentino, I. 1994 [1889]. *El folk-lore filipino. With an English translation by Salud D. Dizon and Maria Elinora P. Imson*. Quezon City: University of the Philippines Press.

Foreman, J. 1906. *The Philippine Islands*. New York: Charles Scribner's Sons.

Izard, M. 1974. Dependencia y Colonialismo: La Compañía General de Tabacos de Filipinas. *Moneda y Crédito* 130: 47–89.

Jacobson, Henry. 1914. *Tobacco in the Philippines*. Manila: Bureau of Printing.

Martín Martínez, J. 1896. La vida industrial en Filipinas. *Revista quincenal*, January 25.

Nodot, C. 1887. Commerce et navigation des îles Philippines en 1885. *Bulletin consulaire français* 14: 83–98.

Nodot, C. 1889. Commerce et navigation aux îles Philippines en 1886 et 1887. *Bulletin consulaire français* 17: 277–295.

Plauchut, E. 1877. L'Archipel des Philippines. III L'industrie, le commerce, la situation politique. *Revue des Deux Mondes,* 15 June, 886.

Recur, C. 1880. *El tabaco filipino.* Madrid: Fortanet.

Report of the Philippine Commission to the President. 1900–1901. Washington: Government Printing Office, vol. 3.

Sawyer, F.H. 1900. *The Inhabitants of the Philippines*. New York: Charles Scribner's Sons.

Yoshihara, Kunio. 1985. *Philippine Industrialization: Foreign and Domestic Capital*. Quezon City: Ateneo de Manila University Press 98–100.

Younghusband, C.J. 1899. *The Philippines and Round About*. London: MacMillan.

Secondary Sources

Camagay, M.L.T. 1995. *Working Women of Manila in the 19th Century*. Quezon City: University of the Philippines Press.

Clarence-Smith, W.G. 2022. The Industrial Processing of Raw Material in the Philippines, 1814–1898. In *Transforming the 19th Century Philippines*, ed. María Dolores Elizalde, 75–103. Madrid: Polifemo.

De Jesus, E.C. 1978. The Tobacco Monopoly in the Cagayan Valley, 1786–1881. In *South East Asian Transitions: Approaches Through Social History*, ed. R.T. McVey, 86–111. New Haven: Yale University Press.

De Jesus, E.C. 1980. *The Tobacco Monopoly in the Philippines. Bureaucratic Enterprise and Social Change, 1776–1880*. Quezon City: Ateneo de Manila University Press.

Delgado, J.M. 1996. Bajo dos banderas (1881–1910). Sobre cómo sobrevivió la Compañía General de Filipinas al Desastre del 98. In *La Nación Soñada: Cuba, Puerto Rico y Filipinas ante el 98*, eds. C. Naranjo, M. A. Puig-Samper, and L. M. García Mora, 293–304. Aranjuez: Doce Calles.

Doeppers, D.F. 1984. *Manila 1900–1941. Social Change in a Late Colonial Metropolis*. Quezon City: Ateneo de Manila University Press.

Doeppers, D.F. 1991. Metropolitan Manila in the Great Depression: Crisis for whom. *Journal of Asian Studies* 50: 511–535.

Fradera, J.M. 1999. *Filipinas, la colonia más peculiar. La hacienda pública en la definición de la política colonial, 1762–1868*. Madrid: CSIC.

Fradera, J.M. 2005. *Colonias para después de un imperio*. Barcelona: Bellaterra.

Giralt, E. 1981. *La Compañía General de Tabacos de Filipinas*. Barcelona: CGTF.

Lachica, E. 1977. Trade and Commerce in Old Manila. The Manila Cigar: A Sad-Happy Story. *Archipelago* 33: 8–15.

Legarda, B. 1999. *After the Galleons. Foreign Trade, Economic Change and Entrepreneurship in the Nineteenth-Century Philippines*. Quezon City: Ateneo de Manila University Press.

Rodrigo y Alharilla, M. 1996. *Antonio López y López, primer Marqués de Comillas, 1883–1917. Un empresario y sus empresas*. Madrid: Fundación Empresa Pública.

Rodrigo y Alharilla, M. 2000. *Los Marqueses de Comillas, Antonio y Claudio López, 1817–1925*. Madrid: Editorial Empresarial.

Rodrigo y Alharilla, M. 2009. Del desestanco del tabaco a la puesta en marcha de la Compañía General de Tabacos de Filipinas (1879–1890). *Boletín Americanista* 59: 199–221.

Salazar, W. 2001. Baer & Co. and the Transformation of the Philippine Tobacco Industry, 1860–1918. In *Imperios y naciones en el Pacífico. Vol I: La formación de una colonia, Filipinas*, eds. M.D. Elizalde, J.M. Fradera, and L. Alonso, 563–584. Madrid: CSIC.

Sanz Rozalén, V. 2019. Las fronteras del tabaco. Cuba y Filipinas entre el estanco y el libro comercio en el siglo XIX. In *Grandes vicios, grandes ingresos. El monopolio del tabaco en los imperios ibéricos. Siglos XVII–XX*, ed. S. d. Luxán Meléndez, J. Figueiroa-Rego, and V. Sanz Rozalén. Madrid: Centro de Estudios Políticos y Constitucionales.
Sawyer, F.H. 1900. *The Inhabitants of the Philippines*. New York: Charles Scribner's Sons.
Wickberg, E. 1962. Early Chinese Economic Influence in the Philippines, 1850–1898. *Pacific Affairs* 30: 275–285.

CHAPTER 3

The Resilience of Hand-Rolled Cigarettes: Marketing Imported Tobacco in East Africa, 1880–1939

Laird Jones

Introduction

In his biweekly report of October 24, 1912, Georg Döring, the Mwanza branch manager for William O'Swald & Company, a Hamburg-Zanzibar import/export house, informed the Hamburg head office of a potential threat. "A traveling salesman from the British American Tobacco Company [BAT] visited," he wrote, "and sold extremely large lots of cigarettes at very low prices."[1] Döring included several samples in the mail pouch along with his analysis and rated the packaging very good. BAT's cases held 100 airtight tins, each containing 100 packs of five,

[1] Döring, Mwanza to William O'Swald & Co., Hamburg, 24 October 1912, Hamburg State Archives, hereafter HSA, 621–1/22/8, #32:6.

L. Jones (✉)
History Department, Lock Haven University, Lock Haven, PA, USA
e-mail: ljones@lockhaven.edu

A. van Wickeren et al. (eds.), *Tobacco in Global Perspective, 1780–1960*, Cambridge Imperial and Post-Colonial Studies,
https://doi.org/10.1007/978-3-031-64411-5_3

which meant their product remained fresh all the way down the distribution chain. The packs of five, too, were small enough to draw consumers normally accustomed to buying cigarettes one stick at a time. Even more troubling, the price of BAT's low-end cigarette, Palm Tree, appeared below cost, but worst of all Döring suspected that a rival import/export firm arranged the visit, perhaps testing the waters for a business arrangement. Given all these concerns, he nonetheless concluded on a note of seemingly false bravado. "We do believe," Döring opined, "this import will not be able to dislodge our tobacco here."[2]

Perhaps Döring's reaction simply reflected the conservative outlook within an archaic firm. O'Swald had once been a leader in the East African trade, but following the colonial conquests of the 1890s the firm's ageing family leadership grew more cautious, repeatedly hesitating over vital new opportunities. While competitors quickly reorganised to take advantage of scheduled steamship lines, railway construction and new centers of communication, O'Swald fell behind, reluctant to move on from its tramp steamers, caravan-era clientele, and old Zanzibar base of operations. Thus, it should come as no surprise that other O'Swald branches had relayed similar information about BAT's cigarette imports for several years prior to Döring's report; and, despite sporadic experiments with machine-made cigarettes, each time the firm returned to their old favourites—sharp, blended, Rising Hope brand shag tobacco, along with cigarette paper and matches.

It would certainly appear both Döring and his employer missed the plot. At the turn of the twentieth century, BAT wielded seemingly every competitive advantage to saturate export markets with a new product—the machine-made cigarette. An early multinational, it brought together the Imperial Tobacco Company (ITC), a consortium of leading British manufacturers with the behemoth American Tobacco Company (ATC), creating a cartel that carved up the world, pooling their enormous industrial capacity and extensive brand catalogues.[3] British manufacturers provided political access and tariff privileges across the empire. American Tobacco had already made deep inroads in East Asia and even more importantly contributed its state-of-the-art organisation: rail and steamship line distribution logistics, telegraph communication, print

[2] Ibid.

[3] Cox (2000, p. ix).

advertising, and above all single-product direct marketing. The predatory pricing and agency agreement overtures Mr. Döring reported merely formed the opening act.

Ultimately, BAT aimed for vertical monopoly, from the tobacco field to the neighbourhood cigarette vendor. Sometimes, however, even the best laid plans go awry. BAT entered the East African market with much fanfare. Young salesmen, following the company's global marketing strategy, blanketed ports and railway stops with print advertising and free samples, and, as Döring noted, offered wholesale bargains direct to urban shopkeepers. Later, they even organised cigarette "safaris" across the hinterlands to "teach" rural Africans to smoke.[4] Yet, while BAT's brands gradually gained market share, sales fell far short of expectations. A big upsurge in cigarette consumption during World War I could not be sustained. Not even the cash-crop and rural consumer boom of the 1920s significantly altered the trendline. In part, BAT's direct marketing playbook proved ill-suited to colonial East Africa. Fanfare there failed to translate into brand loyalty. But more importantly, BAT faced a very stubborn problem—Döring got it right, Dutch shag tobacco sales proved remarkably resilient.

Very early in the competition, O'Swald employees perceived the problem well. At that time, East African consumer demand was not so much dictated by metropolitan advertising campaigns as it was mediated through long-standing tastes, expressions of status, and local purchasing patterns. Thus, while machine cigarettes attracted many new, younger, urban consumers, shag tobacco had already become firmly entrenched in rural, as well as peri-urban working-class culture. For many rural smokers, shag served as a bridge from pipe to cigarette smoking—foreign yet familiar. Shag was loose tobacco, cut in long, thin strips, and less moist than pipe tobacco, but coarser and less dry than machine cigarette blends. Also, while manufactured from lower-grade tobaccos, compared to the crumbled, unsifted, sun-dried leaf most East African pipe smokers knew, shag appeared uniform and quite fine. Most importantly, the darker, sharper blends, like Van Nelle's Rising Hope, aligned with long-standing, indigenous taste. Caravan porters and migrant labourers, part of a nascent working class, adopted imports that were both practical and set them apart from their rural elders. They picked up cigarette smoking on the

[4] Jones (1995, p. 288).

coast, or along the rail lines, and the hand-rolling kit—tobacco pouch, paper, and matches—travelled well. Finally, in neighbourhoods on the urban fringe, kiosk vendors and peddlers offered an array of daily needs to labourers, and custom, hand-rolled cigarettes served as an important draw, perhaps even a loss leader. Therefore, while the adoption of cigarette smoking might well fit into a broad pattern of globalisation, the process involved considerable local agency.

Quantitative data provide context—timeline, trends, and parameters. Assembled from customs totals reported in colonial statistical abstracts and annual reports between 1895 and 1939, the numbers reveal several distinct phases in imported manufactured tobacco consumption. Imported Dutch shag tobacco exercised near complete dominance between 1895 and 1906. Machine cigarettes gradually increased market share between 1903 and 1913, though by volume still trailed shag considerably. Demand by troops during World War I fuelled a cigarette boom between 1915 and 1919. Thereafter, however, during the 1920s, machine cigarette imports returned to their prewar trendline, and imported shag tobacco regained the lead. Finally, during the Depression years, imported cigarettes remained popular, while imported shag collapsed under price pressure from higher tariffs and competition from cheap, domestically produced machine cigarettes.

Despite its utility, East African customs data present challenges. First, reports largely concern tobacco imports and, apart from occasional exports, give few clues as to the level of domestic tobacco production. This is a considerable blind spot, since "unmanufactured," or domestic sun-dried leaf might well have been the most popular form prior to World War I. Second, the numbers are difficult to disaggregate. Initially, cigarettes were not a significant import, and hence officials lumped them together with other forms of industrially manufactured tobacco, largely shag. Third, the numbers themselves are difficult to render comparable, given that they were gathered across several colonies, protectorates, and trust territories, employing different weights and measures, currencies, and accounting calendars. Fourth, customs officials always noted cash value, since they primarily focused on collecting duties. They referenced weight, the more important consumption indicator, less often. Finally, colonial trade reports provided only sparse commentary on tobacco import numbers and trends.

Fortunately, information buried in commercial correspondence, accounts, and receipts fills in some of the gaps. In this study, customs numbers are disaggregated and analysed through careful reading of the internal correspondence, orders, and shipping records of O'Swald & Co. from 1880 to 1914. O'Swald collected considerable information on African consumer import preferences and was a leading distributor of imported tobacco during the period. This material is supplemented, in particular for the period 1914–1939, by online documents from the British American Tobacco Archive (https://bat.library.ucsf.edu/), a voluminous hodgepodge of materials collected, scanned, and made public as the result of litigation in the 1990s.

O'Swald & Co., Commodities, and Consumer Goods

The O'Swald family and their employees traded on the East African coast for more than 50 years, providing the firm with deep local experience and extensive regional contacts. Successive generations of O'Swald sons rotated between Europe and Zanzibar, directed by their father from the Hamburg office and assisted on the ground in East Africa by a few senior European employees and later junior ones acting as branch managers on the mainland. O'Swald recruited most of their East African staff locally—immigrant South Asian agents, usually the younger relatives of important wholesale clients; Swahili clerks and countermen; and Arab and Somali hide and skin buyers. This not only provided the firm with extensive language skills and a wealth of perspectives, but most importantly provided entrée into many trading networks and communities. O'Swald employees assiduously collected information: marketplace rumours, shipping manifests, caravan counts, sales trends, and commodity forecasts. They made lists and kept files on their clients and their competition. Thus, by the time the machine cigarette appeared on the streets of Zanzibar town or Mombasa, O'Swald correspondents found themselves well positioned to track and assess its progress.

As an old-line import/export house, O'Swald traded in anything and everything. The Hamburg office negotiated with manufacturers in Europe and the US for a wide range of imports: basic consumer goods like cotton textiles, woollen blankets, and glass beads; luxury goods for coastal elites and European expatriates, everything from toiletries to the furnishings for the sultan's palace; foodstuffs like refined sugar, pasta, and rice; tools like hoes, knives, firearms, and ammunition; and, of course, popular vices like alcohol and later tobacco. Returns on retailed imports were generally quite good, but the object was to extend them on credit to networks of local clients who in turn cleared their accounts with deliveries of commodities: ivory, hides and skins, copra, cloves, and later groundnuts or cotton. O'Swald generated much its profits offering East African commodities on metropolitan exchanges or through industrial supply contracts. By the twentieth century, this strategy might have become dated, at least from a marketing or distribution standpoint, but it nevertheless provided O'Swald managers with a clear view of the big picture, and a keen understanding of the market baskets of goods sought by East African consumers.

While admittedly conservative, O'Swald & Co. navigated many late nineteenth-century transitions—from sail to steam, caravans to railways, dispatches to telegrams, and autonomy to colonialism. And O'Swald sometimes caught the wave. The firm scored an early coup trading East African cowrie shells to West Africa, in return for palm oil shipped to Hamburg. They outfitted caravan adventurers during the heyday of the ivory trade and branched into bulk trade in hides and skins. On the coast, they expanded from cloves to copra and later dabbled in plantation agriculture themselves. O'Swald enjoyed success because they attracted clients with much sought-after imports, in particular industrial facsimiles of Indian Ocean textile fashions. The firm faced a myriad of challenges, however, during the early twentieth-century cash-crop boom. Import consumption skyrocketed, consumer tastes increasingly converged, and fashions changed more rapidly. Reading the market became increasingly difficult. O'Swald also scrambled to expand its wholesale clientele to include new rural shopkeeping networks; but an influx of import/export competitors complicated the effort, as did direct marketing efforts like mail order catalogues and travelling factory salesmen. It is not surprising, therefore, when faced with overwhelming change, O'Swald managers relied on their experience and pushed proven products.

When Shag Tobacco Was King, 1895–1913

Customs records and commercial correspondence indicate that initially, in the 1870s, imported cigars proved most popular, largely with European expatriates. Sales remained small, but steady and quite profitable. Machine cigarettes appeared much later, in 1901, and took nearly a decade to break through from European to urban African consumers. Instead, throughout the early colonial period, imported shag tobacco was king—appearing in small quantities in the 1880s, and in bulk by the early 1890s, along with cigarette paper for hand-rolling. Shag caught on quickly with African consumers, as it appealed on taste, form, and price, and continued to dominate tobacco imports by volume and value right up to eve of World War I (Fig. 3.1).

Sorting out patterns within tobacco imports requires detective work. Most early customs tallies lump all forms of tobacco together. Thus, while the aggregate upward trend is clear, the extent to which it resulted from demand for shag tobacco or machine cigarettes is not. However, after 1904, when British East Africa Protectorate customs records designated countries of origin for tobacco imports, it is possible to infer the extent of both. Great Britain exported the lion's share of machine cigarettes, while Holland exported between 80 and 90% of shag tobacco. Therefore, if these numbers are taken as a proxy for each, the two trends would have resembled the graph in Fig. 3.2., and, once customs officials listed machine cigarettes separately from manufactured, or shag tobacco, the trends become increasingly clear, as shown in Fig. 3.3. Numbers from the inland and more rural Uganda Protectorate, see Fig. 3.4.,

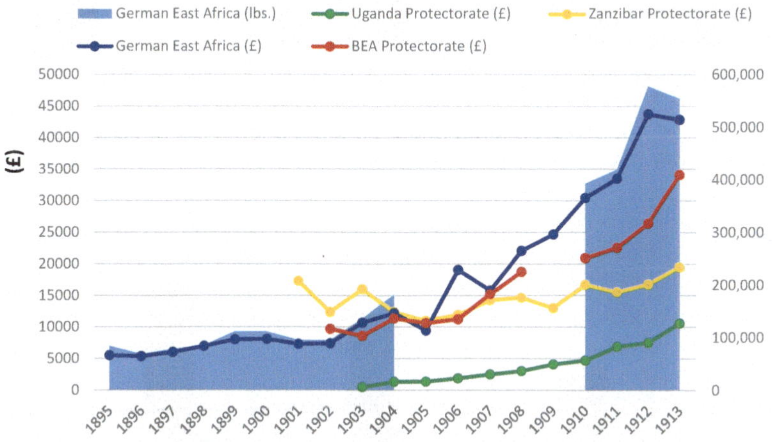

Fig. 3.1 East African tobacco imports (*Source* Compiled from *Statistical Abstract of British Self-Governing Dominions, Colonies, Possessions, and Protectorates from 1901 to 1915*. Government Board of Trade [London, 1918]; and *Statistisches Jahrbuch für das Deutsche Reich*. Vols. 15–36 [Berlin, 1894–1915]. German marks converted to British pounds at prevailing gold exchange rate for that period. For weight, doppelzentner converted to lbs)

provide perhaps the starkest contrast. Machine cigarette imports rose sharply between 1905 and 1913, but shag tobacco imports rose too. Even allowing for some pipe smoking with imported manufactured tobacco, East Africans consumed two to four hand-rolled cigarettes for each machined one, though hand-rolled cigarettes, especially those done by commercial rollers, usually contained slightly less tobacco than machined ones.

According to O'Swald correspondence, the firm began retailing a wide assortment of cigars to Europeans on Zanzibar during the mid-1870s

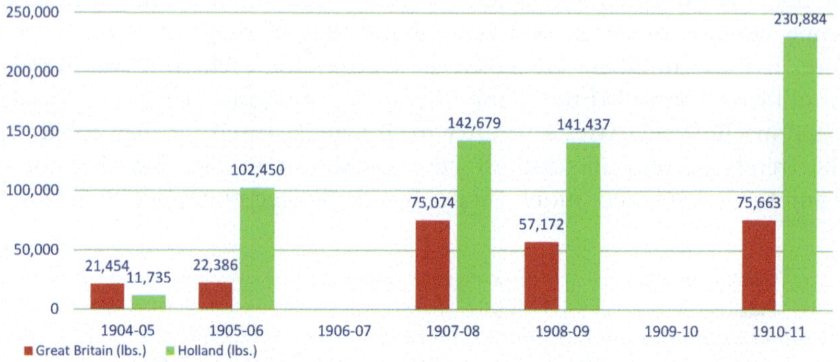

Fig. 3.2 East African protectorate: tobacco imports by point of origin (*Source* Compiled from British East African Protectorate Blue Books, 1903–1911)

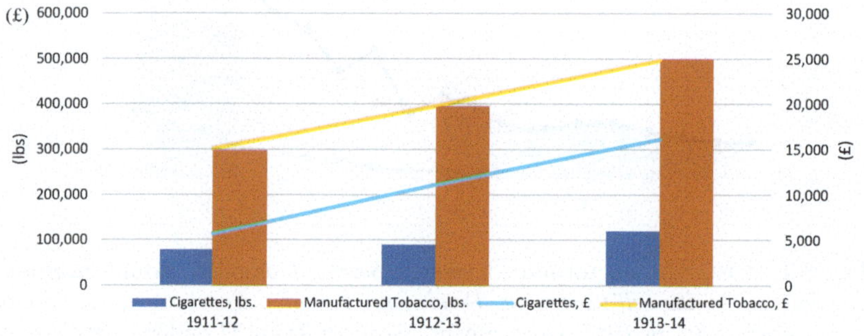

Fig. 3.3 British East African protectorate: Cigarette vs. Manufactured Tobacco Imports (*Source* Compiled from British East African Protectorate Blue Books, 1912–1914)

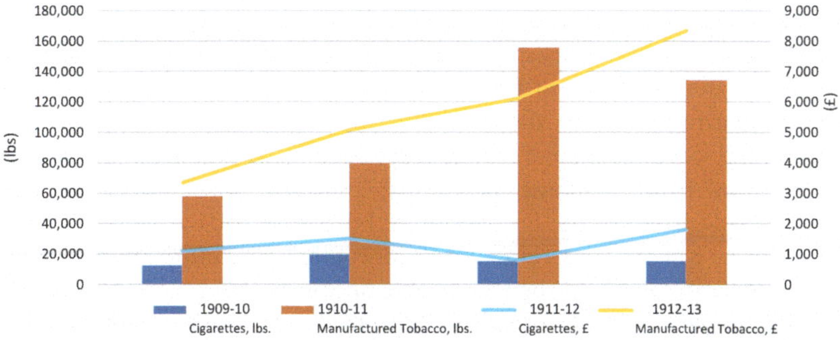

Fig. 3.4 Uganda protectorate: Cigarette vs. Manufactured Tobacco Imports (*Source* Compiled from Uganda Protectorate Blue Books, 1910–1917. For the years 1914–1917, cigarette totals may well have been combined with manufactured tobacco. The country of origin breakdown indicates that at the very least, the ratio between cigarettes and shag did not change as the total number increased)

and then expanded to shag tobacco in the early 1880s. At first, O'Swald experimented with at least fifteen shag brands, but soon narrowed to two: Golden Birds Eye, a bright Virginia blend, produced in Germany, and Rising Hope, a sharp blend, produced by a Rotterdam firm, Van Nelle.[5] Golden Birds Eye appeared most popular early, though largely with European smokers. The Holy Ghost Fathers proved O'Swald's best initial customers, though curiously they never requested cigarette paper. Shag orders picked up, particularly for Rising Hope brand, during the early 1890s, as did orders for matches and paper. Matches, of course, marketed quite widely, beyond smokers. O'Swald offered a higher end, Swedish, Three Stars brand early, and subsequently failed with a South African brand, Lion, before finally settling on a very cheap, nondescript brand 'XXX.' Cigarette paper invoices first appeared in the Hamburg home office's mail packets to Zanzibar in 1890.[6] O'Swald early went with the high-quality Italian brand, Club, but, as African consumption increased, switched to the cheaper, Austrian, Schutz Christ brand. By 1896, O'Swald

[5] William O'Swald, Hamburg to Zanzibar, 19 January 1887, HSA, 621-1/3/30, 66.

[6] William O'Swald, Hamburg to Zanzibar, 11 February 1890, HSA, 621-1/3/33, 72.

had more than half of the shag market on the coast and distributed two-thirds of the cigarette paper.[7] O'Swald first tested machine cigarettes in 1901 and later tried several BAT brands in Mombasa in 1907–1908 and on Zanzibar in 1909, but always returned to shag.[8]

O'Swald correspondents often expressed concern over increased competition from machine cigarettes, especially in coastal towns.[9] However, old hands in the firm countered that shag tobacco still yielded a much better wholesale margin, and the meagre 3–5% return on imported cigarettes hardly justified their financing or logistic efforts.[10] O'Swald & Co. did not go in for loss leaders. Moreover, branch managers considered shag tobacco a key product within their client networks. In coastal towns, O'Swald distributed cases of manufactured tobacco, together with matches, and cigarette paper, through major clients—local laundry operators and wholesalers—who in turn supplied tins and pouches to neighbourhood kiosk and street vendors. O'Swald distributed a whole host of imports through these networks, on account, on three to six months credit, often bundled around deals on imported soap and tobacco.

O'Swald leadership remained firmly convinced shag tobacco better suited African working-class purchasing patterns and tastes. Enslaved and formerly enslaved workers on the coast asserted themselves during the later nineteenth century—politically, socially, and economically. They were at the forefront of popular rebellion[11] and they transformed music and dance and drove fashion as many followed their tastes in imported printed cloth and accessories.[12] The coastal working class also depended on imports, offered in the market or on the street, for much of their basic needs. Tobacco largely retailed on the street as a *taka taka*, or daily need, together with laundry soap, cooking oil, kerosene, matches, and imported rice or pasta. *Taka taka* sales turned on small change. Soap, for

[7] William O'Swald, Hamburg to Zanzibar, 7 January 1897, HSA, 621–1/3/40, ad#1:24–26.

[8] Mombasa sales receipt, 1901, HSA, 621–1/12/1. Meyer, Mombasa to William O'Swald & Co., Hamburg, 2 August 1907, HSA, 621–1/13/13, ad#25:6. Meyer, Zanzibar to William O'Swald & Co., Hamburg, 13 December 1909, HSA, 621–1/3/94.

[9] Meyer, Mombasa to Hamburg, 28 February 1908, HSA, 621–1/13/14, ad#7:1.

[10] Anders, Zanzibar to Hamburg, 30 March 1910, HSA, 621–1/4/99, import report, #14:5.

[11] See Glassman (1995) and Ranger (1975).

[12] See Fair (1998).

example, wholesaled in large bricks but retailed in shavings. Rice wholesaled in 100 lb. sacks but measured out for retail in cut, repurposed kerosene tins. For cooking oil or kerosene, customers brought their own containers. Shag wholesaled in cases but retailed in shops in 50- to 100-gram cloth satchels, a kind of bag, or resealable tins. Some purchases could be wrapped in imported, used newspaper, though it is not clear whether this was later used for smoking. Cigarette papers retailed in booklets of 50 to 80 sheets, and matches were priced by the gross. However, in many shops and on the street, "ready-made," hand-rolled cigarettes sold a few sticks at a time, perhaps with a match or two thrown in. Shop assistants or street peddlers turned them out during down time or on demand.[13] Each vendor competed on style and could, if need be, alter taste or lower cost by blending in lighter, darker, or cheaper tobacco since before machine brands most urban smokers had their own roller. O'Swald banked on smokers' daily routine of buying as a difficult habit to break.

Inland, imported shag found a ready audience. Rural people already consumed a great deal of local loose tobacco. Small farmers around the lakes and on the coast had long produced oriental varieties of dark and sun-dried tobacco for snuff, pipe smoking, and blending with cannabis.[14] Tobacco traded widely from community to community, and in the nineteenth century along caravan routes and coastal sea routes. Production most likely held steady or expanded in the early colonial period. While African tobacco production for local consumption received short shrift in colonial reports, post-World War I Agriculture Department field surveys provide at least a glimpse of the scale.

The earliest survey, conducted in Uganda in 1917, implies a production level of at least 500,000 to as much as 1,000,000 lbs. sun dried, two to four times total manufactured tobacco imports.[15] The survey listed only an estimate of acres planted, not production. Later, from 1927 onward, Agriculture Department reports tracked yields per acre, by African farmers, but only for test plots and fields for commercial production. Yields for local consumption might vary considerably by tobacco type, or intensity of production. Two plantings and harvests per year were

[13] Ibid., 4; and Unger, Mombasa to Hamburg, 18 December 1909, HSA, 621-1/13/17, ad#51:1–2.

[14] Duvall (2017).

[15] Uganda Territory Blue Book. Section 22. 1917ff.

possible, but indigenous farmers might choose to rotate or simply use tobacco as a field break. For the purposes of this estimate, a low yield of 300 lbs. sun dried per acre was used, the range allowing for variations in seasonal rainfall, and single or multiple plantings.

Surveys begun in Tanganyika during the mid-1920s range as high as 2,000,000 lbs. for domestic consumption, four times total manufactured tobacco imports.[16] The acreage surveys fluctuated, sometimes wildly. Tobacco appeared to be a small-plot secondary crop that many farmers moved in and out of frequently. Some returns appear suspect, done on walking tours or flyovers, and some districts repeat the same number for several consecutive years, or abruptly disappear. For the domestic consumption estimate, net exports were deducted from the overall official production estimate. During the early colonial period, coarse, dark, loose tobacco was by far the best known, and most widely smoked, and shag, its closest proximate among imports, was poised to follow in its wake.

Throughout the 1890s, O'Swald supplied regular shipments to caravan organisers in Bagamoyo and Tanga. At that time, during the waning years of the caravan era, shag acquired some cachet as a luxury item. Like fine Arabian or Indian textiles, bottled whiskey, or the occasional cigar, rural elites considered imported, pouched, or tinned European tobacco a status marker, and perhaps many of those around them viewed it as an aspirational good. Caravan porters took it up, along with a range of imports, from firearms to cloth headwraps, and more importantly interacted with people en route, trading their in-kind, cloth and bead wages, and modelling goods and behaviours.[17] After the turn of the century, however, with the gradual extension of steam transport, bulky imports like manufactured tobacco circulated much more widely. Migrant labourers returning from the coast modelled hand-rolling, along with many other imported goods.[18] And networks of shops and peddlers radiated out from the new rail lines. To potential new customers, imported shag appeared familiar in form, even if manufactured, and of course, more expensive. But, its taste appealed, and this proved imported shag's chief selling point. East African smokers termed domestic, dark, loose tobacco *baridi*, literally cool, or smooth. Golden Birds Eye, a light Bright Virginia blend, they

[16] Tanganyika Territory Blue Book. 1929. 193–199.

[17] See Rockel (2006).

[18] Sunseri (2002).

termed *tamu*, literally sweet, owing to its high retention of plant sugars. And Rising Hope, a somewhat darker blend, they termed *kali*, literally strong, or sharp. Shag appears to have appealed most when blended with local tobacco, to alter taster or lower cost for hand rollers, or increased thickness and moisture for pipe smokers.[19]

BAT Goes on Safari, 1907–1929

BAT organised their arrival well. In 1907, the company established a supply depot in Mombasa, the emerging East African commercial hub, since logistics there were ideal.[20] Mombasa served as railhead for the recently completed Kenya Uganda Railway and had become the steam transport gateway to the lake region—Western Kenya, Uganda, Northwest German East Africa, and Eastern Congo. Moreover, international steamship lines made regular, scheduled stops in Mombasa's deep-water port. International telegraphic connections relayed through Mombasa, allowing for rapid communication to BAT's London headquarters, and financial transfers went smoothly through international banks branches there. Thus, older, coastal, caravan-era commodity, and wholesale firms gradually relocated from Bagamoyo and Zanzibar, while new arrivals invariably selected Mombasa as their East African base of operations. BAT, a relative latecomer, got in on the ground floor. Within a few years, BAT set up subdepots at the end of the line in Kisumu, and beyond in Kampala.[21] Then, BAT repeated the strategy, locating a subdepot down the coast in Dar es Salaam, the chief port of German East Africa, to take advantage of construction begun on the rival Central Railway.[22]

BAT had help on the ground. For nearly two decades, the company relied upon a local comprador, Rex Boustead. Boustead came to Mombasa from Zanzibar during the mid-1890s representing his father's

[19] Albers, Mombasa to Hamburg, 26 January 1914, HSA, 621–1/13/21: 1.

[20] Historical Note on BAT Industries, 5 August 1987. Box: gu0504. File: hn0337. BATA. Fol 11. https://www.industrydocuments.ucsf.edu/docs/xhfj0212. Accessed by 11 September 2023.

[21] East Africa: History Prior to 1965 Reorganisation, author and date unknown. Box: us063. File: ac0747. BATA.Fol 1. https://www.industrydocuments.ucsf.edu/docs/tgpy0194. Accessed by 11 September 2023.

[22] Ibid.

partnership, Boustead & Ridley, a long-time coastal caravan outfitter.[23] The original firm dabbled in ivory, but its strengths lay in outfitting European expeditions and supplying Christian missions in the interior. The younger Bousteads subsequently formed a brief partnership, Boustead Bros., in 1901, and a later one, Boustead & Clarke, around 1908.[24] They kept one foot in the caravan business, outfitting professionals, and well-heeled amateurs with camping gear, firearms, and ammunition. But they also moved ahead, realigning old caravan stations around Lake Victoria to the new railways, warehousing commodities, and trade goods; and dealing in stores—imported food, alcohol, clothing, and household items—for European expatriates and settlers. Most importantly, from 1897 onward Rex Boustead acted as proprietor of the Mombasa Club, the favorite European watering hole in East Africa's chief port.[25] Anyone who was anyone in colonial society—business agents, settlers, wealthy tourists, colonial officials—passed through and socialised there. Boustead Brothers acted as sales agent for BAT perhaps as early as 1902 and became sole agents for British and German East Africa by 1907, so presumably they organised BAT's Mombasa supply depot network. Boustead & Clarke continued to manage the Mombasa depot as late as 1923.[26] Yet, while Rex Boustead certainly could provide introductions, information and logistical support, he did have a blind spot: as his biographer noted, "neither (Rex nor his brother Jack) took a serious interest in local languages or culture."[27]

BAT had a plan—the direct sales model, which they implemented successfully in many regions of the world.[28] In the initial phase, company salesmen engaged in promotions, to introduce machine cigarettes and create brand awareness, first in urban ports, and later across the countryside. In East Africa, BAT salesmen had been instructed to push cheaper, mild blends first, like Palm Tree, then attempt to lure customers to

[23] Frankl (2003, p. 432) and Gale (1908–1909, p. 99).

[24] Frankl (2003, pp. 433–434) and Gale (1908–1909, p. 99).

[25] Frankl (2003, p. 432) and Gale (1908–1909, p. 99).

[26] Historical Record of British American Tobacco Company Limited and Associated Companies, Sept. 30, 1924. Box: gu2532,. File: bd0106. BATA, fol 20. https://www.industrydocuments.uscf.edu/docs/mxxn0195. Accessed 11 September 2023.

[27] Frankl (2003, p. 435).

[28] Cochran (1980). Goodman (1993). Cox (2000).

more profitable, strong blends, like Pen Knife.[29] Once demand picked up, in the later phase, salesmen were to distribute cigarettes from supply depots directly to local wholesalers and retailers, cutting free commission agents like Boustead or bypassing import/export houses like O'Swald. BAT intended to deal in machine cigarettes exclusively and dominate that market.

The rollout appeared to go well. In 1908 and again in 1912, O'Swald branches across East Africa reported that BAT salesmen hit the ground running, selling large quantities of discount cigarettes at every rail and lake steamer stop.[30] Seemingly caught by surprise, established importers struggled to respond. They trialled a number of brands, and for a time settled on Van Nelle machine cigarettes, in wholesale tins of 1,000, wrapped 100 to a cloth satchel, intending to compete on price and attract kiosk vendors for single stick sales.[31] But the method failed to consider equatorial heat and humidity and too many cigarettes went bad.[32] Shortly thereafter, O'Swald fell back on imported Dutch shag, offering wholesale discounts and promotions with matches, cigarette paper and even mirrors.[33] BAT, however, soon encountered difficulty as well. While salesmen dispensed tens of thousands of cigarettes per tour, they soon discovered that brand loyalty did not necessarily follow. Many urban smokers simply selected the cheapest, and therefore switched brands readily, or returned to hand-rolling. Customers loved the packaging, especially the thin cardboard 5 and 10 packs. Coastal clothing consisted of cotton cloth wraps, for men sometimes topped with a t-shirt. The outfit lacked pockets. Two single cigarettes could be carried behind the ears, but no more. A pack, on the other hand, could be rolled in a sleeve or placed in a clothing fold.[34] But unfortunately for BAT, a pack could also

[29] Jones (1995, p. 286).

[30] Meyer, Mombasa to Hamburg, 17 January 1908, HSA, 621–1/13/14, ad#2, import report:2–3. Döring, Mwanza to William O'Swald & Co., Hamburg, 24 October 1912, HSA, 621–1/22/8, #32:6.

[31] William O'Swald, Hamburg to Zanzibar, 7 January 1909, HSA, 621–1/3/76, ad#1, import report:2.

[32] Meyer, Zanzibar to Hamburg, 22 December 1909, HSA, 621–1/4/94, ad#45:1.

[33] William O'Swald, Hamburg to Zanzibar, 30 May 1912, HSA, 621–1/3/84, #25, import report:2.

[34] Unger, Mombasa to Hamburg, 18 December 1909, HSA, 621–1/13/17, ad#51:3.

be reused, many times, to carry singles of any brand, or even hand-rolled sticks.

BAT regrouped and increasingly focused on the large, and to their view untapped, rural market. While accounts of BAT's initial urban promotions appear to survive only in competitors' correspondence, in later memoirs BAT salesmen later reminisced most fondly about early East African 'cigarette safaris'—promotional tours in the hinterlands. Their stories became company legend—BAT bringing the cigarette to the heart of darkest Africa—a collection of colourful tropes which followed a predictable plot line.[35] A lone, young white salesman, leading a caravan of 25–50 porters marched 10–15 miles a day for three to four months. The caravan roughed it in the bush, occasionally relaxing at isolated colonial outposts, while the salesman socialised with the district officer. There was plenty of good shooting, with big game hunting in their downtime. When approaching a village or homestead, the salesman staged a gramophone concert to draw out reluctant Africans, who, in the stories at least, often encountered their first white man. Spectators were treated to free matches and cigarettes, even a smoking demonstration if necessary. And if any potential customers lingered with spare change they were offered more at a discounted price. Later, as the safari industry 'modernised,' BAT salesmen took to motorbikes and automobiles, but their stories remained much the same.[36]

BAT engaged in garish promotions worldwide. In China, for example, salesmen paraded in front of brass marching bands, tossing samples to onlookers.[37] The East African 'cigarette safari' scheme appeared to be a variation on that theme, though one stitched together in the very exclusive Mombasa Club bar room. It's 'blind spots' proved considerable. Many rural Africans had previous encounters with travelling 'white men' and approached reluctantly, with good reason. After the turn of the century, Europeans increasingly led small caravans off the beaten track. BAT salesmen borrowed the gramophone concert tactic from Christian missionaries—popular with some but resented by others. Commercial hunters also travelled in small caravans. Heavily armed and

[35] Compiled, from former salesmen's accounts in Jones (1995). See also Steinhart (2006, ch 6).

[36] See ibid., pp. 142–144.

[37] Cox (2000, p. 161) and Cochran (1980, p. 38).

sometimes engaged in poaching, many locals considered them dangerous and approached cautiously.[38] Colonial police records even referenced down-on-their-luck white settlers who engaged in strong-arm livestock buying or roved the countryside impersonating crop inspectors or tax collectors. And finally, labour recruiters visited frequently. They travelled in parade-like caravans, dispensed trinkets, and made dubious promises of well-paid work on railways or coastal plantations. In contemporary folklore, some rural people described them metaphorically as vampires.[39]

Some time before BAT came on the scene, most rural Africans had become aware of new imported consumer goods. They were anything but naïve. Many smoked local tobaccos, and more and more sampled imported shag. Nearly everyone encountered displays in rural shops or wares demonstrated by itinerant peddlers. Older people desired cheap industrial facsimiles of earlier, caravan-era prestige goods like Indian Ocean textiles or glass beads. Most everyone sought basics like unbleached cotton cloth, woollen blankets or drop forged hoes. Young people, moreover, gravitated toward new fashions like printed cloth wraps, t-shirts, playing cards, or hand-rolled cigarettes, introduced from the coast, and modelled by returning caravan porters or migrant labourers. Depictions of these goods appeared in the patterns of popular, printed cloth and were referenced in poetry and popular speech. Thus, rural people had other, more influential sources of information. BAT salesmen simply turned up, played records, spoke 'kitchen Swahili,' and attempted to sell discounted machine cigarettes. They underestimated their audience.

Beyond its poor conception, the 'cigarette safari' faced practical difficulties in its execution, particularly cash sales. Urban smokers usually carried small change. Rural smokers often did not, and sometimes proved unwilling to part with it even if they did. In their accounts, BAT salesmen disparaged rural Africans, contending they either failed to understand money, or preferred it as jewellery.[40] However, at that time, colonial administrations, both British and German, simply could not maintain an adequate money supply in hinterland districts. Trading firms railed cases of coin upcountry for crop-buying seasons. They included it in

[38] See Steinhart (2006, ch. 4).

[39] See White (2000).

[40] Jones (1995, p. 293).

advances to rural shopkeeping networks, along with large quantities of consumer imports. Rural Africans hoarded scarce coin for tax collection, to avoid confiscation of livestock or forced labour if they could not pay. They consumed on credit against their harvest or bartered directly with peddlers or shop keepers, and shopkeepers preferred it that way. Credit bound customers to them, and barter lowered their transaction costs. BAT salesmen could not offer such terms. They could only sell cigarettes to the few willing to part with coin.

Finally, much to their chagrin, during the 1920s BAT salesmen noted their competition adapted and actively competed in roving sales. Groups of professional hand rollers appeared on rural market days across Kenya and Uganda, on foot or bicycle, laden with cardboard suitcases full of imported shag, local sun-dried tobacco and cigarette paper.[41] This approach proved a much more cost-effective promotional model. Itinerant rollers incurred little expense—no porters, no camping gear, no loads of provisions, no boxes of gramophone records. And they wasted little time trekking through the countryside. Nearly everyone went to a scheduled market somewhere. Thus, itinerants had no need to draw a crowd, one always waited for them. Moreover, on market days potential customers were most likely to have cash in hand. Itinerants were always in the right place at the right time. For their part, smokers could observe others, try whatever they wanted, find their blend, and hopefully become repeat customers. In the end, rural smokers could have 'their roller' too.

Breaking into the *Duka* Network

BAT's promotional schemes continued for years with mixed results. To really put their products out there, BAT needed to break into wholesale/retail networks and place cigarettes on shop shelves and into the hands of kiosk vendors and rural peddlers. BAT arrived at an opportune time and had some early distribution success. O'Swald correspondents certainly reported seeing BAT brands in more and more urban shops.[42] Rural shopkeeping networks, however, proved more difficult to penetrate. Just as with its promotions, BAT's over reliance on colonial connections

[41] Jones (1995, p. 292).

[42] Meyer, Mombasa to Hamburg, 28 February 1908, HSA, 621–1/13/14, ad#7, import report:1.

and limited awareness of commercial practice on the ground hindered distribution efforts.

At the turn of the century, a transport revolution transformed East African retailing, and a subsequent cash-crop revolution vastly expanded it. The extension of rail lines to the interior facilitated the export of bulky commodities, and the distribution of a much greater volume and range of imports. The new possibilities of steam transport left coastal caravan organisations scrambling. The more successful redirected porters to feed the rail lines, transformed upcountry depots into warehouses and processing plants, and tapped rural alliances to engage in roving buying operations. Within a few short years, as colonial officials pressed rural people to market crops to generate additional tax revenue, a new influx of coastal and immigrant shopkeepers further enticed them with an array of imported goods. And, after a rather tumultuous decade, former caravan organisations, immigrant shopkeepers, and local traders merged into competing wholesale/retail chains or hierarchies. Historian Martha Honey dubbed these "*duka* networks"[43] of economic and cultural links among the Asian commercial and petty bourgeoisie: shopkeepers and petty traders were tied to wholesalers and shippers through credit, advances of goods and cash, and they were bound together by religious institutions, cultural organisations, and commercial associations.

BAT struggled to find an entry point into rural wholesale/retail. *Duka* networks functioned as ethnic solidarities, often comprising members of immigrant South Asian communities, with relations of trust secured by family ties, language, religion, and culture. Leading merchants acted as patrons, promoting many clients through their organisations, sponsoring them as shopkeepers, and acting as their immediate wholesaler. Older, caravan-era firms, like O'Swald, had long-standing commercial relationships with many *duka* network patrons. Every O'Swald branch employed South Asian agents, some the younger relatives of clients, who communicated well in negotiations and possessed considerable local knowledge. O'Swald branches assiduously collected marketplace rumours, in multiple languages, and tracked the movements of network patrons, all in the hope of gaining the slightest advantage. BAT, on the other hand, employed a collection of junior, sometimes novice British salesmen, new to East Africa, often without language skills or cultural awareness.

[43] Honey (1982).

BAT's early emphasis on wholesale cash transactions also proved limiting. Credit bound most *duka* network clients to their patron and often to larger import/export firms like O'Swald. Out of season, if pressed, shopkeepers met obligations by exchanging *hawala*, third-party promissory notes, endorsed by their patron. Or, they extended their credit by as much as six months and then discharged debt in season by delivering hides, skins, or agricultural produce. For most, retail was not an end but a means to participate in more lucrative commodity buying. They took cash advances, usually from their patron or an import/export firm but expended these on crop buying. At the end of a harvest season, some shopkeepers might have disposable cash on hand, but only those solvent enough to resell or send their collected produce on to an urban auction lot. Thus, out in the field, among rural shopkeepers, credit not cash sales drew wholesale clients.

Yet, despite its difficulties, BAT had opportunity, much further up the supply chain, with urban wholesalers and *duka* network patrons. For years, caravan organisers played rival, metropolitan import/export houses against one another, often dealing with the latest entry to obtain the best terms and avoid becoming entrapped by debt. After the turn of the century, however, innovations like commercial banking services, the telegraph office, manufacturers' catalogues, postcards, and parcel post samples enabled some local wholesalers and *duka* network patrons to go a step further and circumvent import/export firms by ordering some items directly. O'Swald representatives increasingly noted this trend after 1908, reporting local wholesalers receiving shipments of sewing machines, bicycles, drop forged hoes, woollen blankets, and condensed milk. With East African depots, salesmen on the ground, and a stand-alone product, BAT should have broken through, but commercial correspondence and import statistics give little indication they did. Instead, BAT continued to negotiate agency agreements with metropolitan import/export firms. Döring himself received rumour of one in 1912, between BAT regional salesman Emil Winkler and Hansing & Co., operating partner of the German East Africa Company's many affiliates, and O'Swald's chief rival.[44]

East Africa, much like other theatres of World War I, witnessed a dramatic increase in cigarette imports between 1914 and 1919, with BAT capturing the lion's share. At the same time, the volume of manufactured

[44] Cox (2000). Winkler is identified in the caption of a 1912 "safari" photograph, plate 42.

tobacco imports fluctuated widely and fell far below cigarettes in value. BAT salesmen reminisced that the war created a turning point, noting that soldiers modelled smoking for many potential African customers,[45] and throughout the war years Customs Department reports declared a 'remarkable' increase in African demand for cheap cigarettes.[46] Were the story to end here, it certainly would herald the triumph of BAT and the machine cigarette. However, there were several important caveats.

Customs officials repeatedly asserted that increases in machine cigarette imports stemmed from additional demand by expeditionary troops, not local smokers. British, South African, and Indian soldiers posted in East Africa apparently bought a lot of cigarettes. In part this was because their tobacco ration was quite meager, considerably less than troops elsewhere—2 oz of loose tobacco, or in some cases 40 cigarettes weekly.[47] African soldiers and conscripted porters, it should be pointed out, received none. Soldiers with cash were best able to make purchases, and imported cigarette prices rose sharply during the later years of the war, putting them out of the reach of many African smokers.[48]

Customs officials conceded that manufactured tobacco imports, especially popular Dutch shag brands, fluctuated due to wartime supply and delivery difficulties, and not necessarily from a decline in demand. Dutch manufacturers faced periodic restrictions on tobacco export from the continent, as tobacco products were retained for troops on the Western Front.[49] Also, the war disrupted links between Holland and East Africa. The leading prewar commercial shippers and importers of Dutch tobacco had been German, and amid blockades, expired agreements and financial losses that network gradually disintegrated. O'Swald, among several others, shuttered its doors after the war.

After a general, postwar slump, demand for imported machine cigarettes gradually recovered, and sales eventually exceeded war levels by the late 1920s. African smokers accounted for much of that increase.

[45] Jones (1995, p. 288).

[46] East African Protectorate Customs Reports. 1917–1918, 1918–1919. East African Protectorate. Annual Report for the Year 1917–1918. Customs Department (Nairobi 1919, p. 18).

[47] Johnson (2014) and Samson (2018).

[48] East African Protectorate (1920, p. 23).

[49] Customs Department. East Africa Protectorate Annual Report, 1917–1918. p. 18

Rising mid-decade cash-crop prices boosted consumer spending into the early years of the Depression. Also, according to anecdotal accounts, BAT direct sales increasingly succeeded with local wholesalers and rural shopkeepers, but once again there was an important caveat, as imported shag tobacco sales also recovered and by the end of the decade sold in record volumes. Shag, it should be said, never fared as well in Tanganyika Territory owing to competition with local, sun-dried tobacco, and, after 1930, cheaper, domestically manufactured tobacco offered increasingly strong competition. However, in Kenya and Uganda imported shag fared remarkably well.

Despite their success with import brands, BAT still came up against the same two problems competing with imported shag: taste and price. Hand-rolled blends with Dutch shag clearly remained popular.[50] Over the decade Dutch brands, largely Rising Hope, accounted for anywhere from 70 to 96% of manufactured tobacco imports in Kenya and Uganda,[51] and BAT brands comprised from 81 to 99% of cigarette imports.[52] Clearly, many smokers could not find a machine cigarette comparable to their favorite hand-rolled blend, and Rising Hope, a darker, sharp blend, could still block BAT's most profitable cigarette brands. As for price, BAT could not dump forever. Manufactured tobacco, by weight, remained cheaper, and hand-rolled cigarettes often contained far less imported tobacco. Imported machine cigarettes performed well during the 1920s, but, given the resilience of hand-rolling, and with the onset of the Depression, how much better could they do?

By the numbers, it was the Depression years, not World War I that proved the turning point. BAT's cigarette imports simply continued their upward trend, while manufactured tobacco imports declined gradually, then collapsed all at once. BAT had a series of successes which undercut Dutch shag. A new BAT factory in Uganda eventually produced inexpensive machine cigarettes popular with African smokers. And domestic shag tobacco production in Tanganyika also offered a cheaper alternative. But most importantly, BAT's strategies aligned with colonial, Depression-era policies. New official agricultural initiatives, marketing rules, transportation regulations, and tariffs all advantaged BAT's playbook and products,

[50] Kemp (1926, p. 14).

[51] Calculated from Customs data in Kenya and Protectorate Blue Books, 1921–1931.

[52] Ibid.

and disadvantaged rival wholesalers, ***duka*** network solidarity and, above all, Rising Hope.

During the 1930s, BAT finally broke through with a series of dark, strong, inexpensive, domestically produced cigarette brands—Rooster, Crown Bird and finally Crescent & Star.[53] BAT also developed a local shag brand, Red Bird.[54] All obviously were with the intention of competing on taste and price with Rising Hope. Success did not come easily, however. In 1928, BAT opened a factory in Jinja, Uganda, with the intention of producing machine cigarettes from locally grown tobacco. Irregular water supply and electrical service slowed the project, and for several years BAT scrambled to acquire enough fire-cured tobacco. While domestic consumption totals were not reflected in official data, the Uganda Protectorate's export total certainly indicates production eventually picked up, so much so that by 1935 Uganda's cigarette exports exceeded imports, and by 1937 did so by more than fourfold.[55]

The Jinja plant fit an emerging pattern. During the Depression years, well-connected investors moved into agricultural processing and manufacturing across East Africa—dairy, meat-packing, and soap, in addition to tobacco. Most did so in alignment with colonial policy, receiving not only indirect support from officials, but often concessionary terms or monopoly status. A group from Nyasaland, earlier associated with ITC, opened a cigarette factory in Nairobi in 1925–1926, though it promptly failed[56]; a group of German investors opened a cigarette and shag tobacco plant in Dar es Salaam in 1928[57]; and during the Depression, European settlers launched processing operations in the wake of BAT through regional companies such as the Tanganyika Tobacco Company and the East African Tobacco Company. Like BAT, the latter received support from colonial agriculture departments, with experimental and demonstration plantations, extension services, and assistance with crop buying.

[53] Jones (1995, p. 292) and The Kenya Gazette, (1974): 567–568.

[54] Jones (1995, p. 291).

[55] Uganda Protectorate Blue Book, 1935 (1936, p. 154). Uganda Protectorate Blue Book 1937 (1938, p. 145).

[56] Anonymous (1929a, p. 36).

[57] Ibid.

Colonial officials faced a budgetary crisis, with declining revenues across the board as tax, fee, and customs duty receipts all fell at once. At first East African administrations simply sought to stop the bleeding by reducing the level of rural tax default. In the late 1920s, Governor Cameron of Tanganyika Territory identified the decline in African cash-crop production as the chief culprit and sought to reverse it though a 'Plant More Crops' propaganda campaign.[58] District and agricultural officers toured the countryside exhorting local leaders to produce more. In cattle areas, officials voiced fears of an East African "Dust Bowl," and acted more coercively, with 'destocking' auctions.[59] But these efforts proved no match for poor commodity prices, low bids, and scarce buyers. Colonial Agricultural Departments carried on, providing very rudimentary extension services to improve export crop grading, introduced new crop varieties, and above all sought new markets—domestic or export—for African produce.

With its Jinja factory project already underway, BAT found itself in the right place at the right time. In 1927, the Uganda Protectorate Agriculture Department established an experimental tobacco plantation in Bunyoro, with technical assistance from T. R. Hayes, a BAT "leaf man."[60] The Department had long experience interacting with British cotton interests and also had the earlier example of ITC projects in Nyasaland to guide them. However, with the onset of the Depression, officials broke with past practice and took on footing the bill, arranging seed farms, and recruiting local farmers.[61] The Department even organised and carried out initial tobacco buying on BAT's behalf. Apart from providing some advice on leaf disease, Hayes simply dictated BAT's industrial requirements: fire-curing techniques and grading for cigarette quality tobacco.[62] The Uganda administration needed revenue and a policy success. It needed the Jinja plant up and running as badly as BAT did. Thereafter,

58 McCarthy (1982, pp. 62–65).

59 Anderson (1984, pp. 321–343) and Jones (1995, pp. 129–142).

60 Anonymous (1929a, b, c, p. 17).

61 Anonymous (1928, pp. 17–19).

62 Anonymous (1930, p. 13).

BAT went on to extract similar terms in Tanganyika Territory in the early 1930s and Kenya in 1937.[63]

Later, colonial administrators pressed for structural reforms, with new rural market rules and motor transport regulations. Officials blamed rural shopkeepers and roving buyers, the middlemen essentially, for depressing prices, and sought to curb their favoured practices, namely advance sales, store credit, and barter.[64] During the late 1920s, Tanganyika Territory officials restricted most crop buying outside their mapped rural markets. modelled on earlier cotton rules, the Market Ordinance of 1930 required that livestock and crops could only be sold or auctioned at scheduled times, in specific markets, for cash. BAT stood to benefit, having substantial cash for tobacco purchases while smaller buyers did not. The 1930 Control of Carriage of Goods by Motor Ordinance of 1930 limited competition between rail and vehicle transport, restricting truck traffic to routes feeding the rail system. Essentially, the regulations required merchants to ship cargo or receive goods via the nearest railway siding. Done in large part to shore up railway revenue, in which the colonial state had a significant stake, the regulations again benefitted large, market-centered buying operations. The reforms benefitted BAT's imported cigarette marketing strategy, strained *duka* network solidarity, prioritised cash transactions, and favoured rail-centered wholesale distribution for coastal ports.

In a final coup de grâce, Depression-era tariff policy favoured British imports and punished competition. In 1928, Kenya, Uganda Protectorate, and Tanganyika Territory formed a colonial Customs Union, ostensibly to promote inter-colonial trade and encourage domestic production. As the economic depression deepened, however, across the empire officials adjusted tariff rates to also advantage British and imperial exports. After 1933, Dutch manufactured tobacco faced heavy duties.[65] The taste remained popular, and outside the Customs Union, in Zanzibar, Dutch shag sales held steady, but on the mainland the price simply rose too high. Already facing price competition from domestic cigarettes and

[63] Augustus Muir and Mair Davies. Report on the BAT History Project, Folio Two. No date. Box: us119, File: dy0007. BATA. https://www.industrydocuments.ucsf.edu/jyf0197. Accessed by 11 September 2023.

[64] See Jones (1992, pp. 158–185).

[65] Anonymous (1937, p. 10).

shag, Rising Hope sales went into a tailspin and Van Nelle's loss became BAT's gain.

Conclusion

Viewed retrospectively, expecting the triumph of the machine cigarette, BAT's early struggles might be the chief takeaway from this study. Import sales increased gradually from the early 1910s through the late 1930s but failed to sweep away the competition. Moreover, BAT's cutting-edge marketing techniques produced mixed results. Direct marketing to urban shopkeepers made inroads, but colonial-themed 'cigarette safaris' completely missed the rural market, and Western branding failed altogether. Machine cigarettes did not really break through until the Depression years, when BAT's business model effectively aligned with colonial policies; BAT's state-supported domestic tobacco processing and manufacture undercut imports; while high tariffs severely impaired the price competitiveness of their strongest competition, Dutch shag brands like Rising Hope.

Viewed prospectively, the resilience of hand-rolling stands out. Shag tobacco drove the retail market from the colonial conquest until the Depression. It required little marketing effort on the part of importers like O'Swald & Company, which offered desired goods on credit through well-established *duka* network connections, together with an assortment of daily necessities, such that hand-rolled cigarettes became well integrated into urban, street-level retail and rural, outdoor markets and peddling. For consumers, adopting shag tobacco followed easily from precolonial practice, since it could be blended to suit a variety of local tastes. Hand-rolled cigarettes retailed by the stick and were cheap and hand-rolling with shag was widely modelled by urban workers, returning caravan porters and migrant labourers. There was no need to teach Africans to smoke cigarettes, since many were aware, and some already had their roller. In the early colonial era in East Africa, 'modern' marketing campaigns rarely had the impact that salesmen, or contemporary scholars for that matter, assumed. Most people appropriated new goods, like the cigarette, understood them within their own socio-economic or cultural context, and consumed them to fit their needs.

Viewed broadly, the chapter shows that the uptake of the machine-made cigarette was curiously slowed in non-Western regions by the local appropriation of roll-your-own tobacco cigarettes, from the late-1880s through the 1930s. Colonised people helped determine the speed at which machine cigarettes captured trade, retailing, and consumption. In British East Africa, the shag focus of the regional caravan trade, and the *duka* network woven around it, contributed to this in particular. At the same time, the identity-forming importance of shag consumption in rural parts of East Africa and the working classes of coastal cities also led to the resilience of hand-rolled tobacco to the delayed introduction of machine cigarettes. Finally, a general cultural affinity of the East African population to stronger, darker tobaccos long placed tight limits on the machine cigarettes promoted by BAT, which were primarily filled with bright tobacco.

Elsewhere in colonial Africa, too, hand-rolling culture survived the introduction of machine cigarettes well into the first half of the twentieth century by being embedded in regional contexts. In Southern Africa, for example, local tobaccos for pipe smoking competed with BAT cigarette brands, and later locally rolled "penny packs" took market share as well.[66] In Nigeria, Muslims rolled banknotes of the newly introduced imperial currency into cylinders, filled them with tobacco, and then smoked them as a protest against the currency reform.[67] Accordingly, we need further studies that address the importance of regional embeddedness of shag culture in delaying the adoption of machine cigarettes in colonial Africa, as well as in other world regions where shag and hand-rolled cigarettes remained an important alternative to machine cigarettes.

References

Primary Sources

Unpublished
Hamburg State Archives (HSA)
- 621.
British American Tobacco Archive (BATA)
- Box: us119
- Box: us063
- Box: gu0504
- Box: gu2532

[66] Doro and Sandra (2022, pp. 55–74).

[67] Pallaver (2022, p. 12).

Published

Anonymous. 1917. Uganda Territory Blue Book. Entebbe: No Publisher.

Anonymous. 1928. Uganda Protectorate. Annual Report of the Department of Agriculture for the year ended 31st December. Entebbe: No Publisher.

Anonymous. 1929a. Report on the Trade and Commerce of East Africa for the year 1927–1928. London. Entebbe: No Publisher.

Anonymous. 1929b. Tanganyika Territory Blue Book. Entebbe: No Publisher.

Anonymous. 1929c. Uganda Protectorate. Annual Report of the Department of Agriculture for the year ended 31st December 1928. Entebbe: No Publisher.

Anonymous. 1930. Uganda Protectorate. Annual Report of the Department of Agriculture for the year ended 31st December 1929.

Anonymous. 1936. Uganda Protectorate Blue Book, 1935. Entebbe: No Publisher.

Anonymous. 1937. *Report on the Trade and Commerce of East Africa for the years 1934–1936*. Department of Overseas Trade. London. No Publisher.

Anonymous. 1938. Uganda Protectorate Blue Book, 1937. Entebbe.

Anonymous. 1974. The Kenya Gazette, 2 June.

Anonymous. Report on the Trade and Commerce of East Africa for 1924–1925. London. No Publisher.

Customs Department. 1919. East African Protectorate Customs Reports. 1917–1918, 1918–1919. East African Protectorate. Annual Report for the Year 1917–1918. Nairobi: no publisher.

Customs Department. 1920. East African Protectorate. Annual Report for the Year 1918–19. Nairobi: no publisher.

Gale, F.H., ed. 1908–1909. *East Africa: Its History, People, Commerce, Industry and Resources*. London: The Foreign and Colonial Compiling and Publishing Co.

Kemp, C. 1926. *Report on the Trade and Commerce of East Africa for 1924–1925. Department of Overseas Trade*. London: HSMO.

Secondary Sources

Anderson, D. 1984. Depression, Dust Bowl and Drought: The Colonial State and Soil Conversation in East Africa During the 1930s. *African Affairs* 83: 321–343.

Askew, K. 2002. *Performing the Nation: Swahili Music and Cultural Politics in Tanzania*. Chicago: University of Chicago Press.

Chandos, J. 1976. Up in Smoke: An Independent View of Life in the British American Tobacco Company, 1902–1976. Typewritten manuscript, BAT archives.

Cochran, S. 1980. *Big Business in China: Sino-Foreign Rivalry in the Cigarette Industry, 1890–1930*. Cambridge: Harvard University Press.

Cox, H. 2000. *The Global Cigarette: Origins and Evolution of British American Tobacco, 1880–1945*. Oxford: Oxford University Press.

Doro, E., and S. Sandra. 2022. Beyond Agency: The African Peasantry, the State, and Tobacco in Southern Rhodesia (Colonial Zimbabwe), 1900–1980. *Journal of African History* 55: 55–74.

Duvall, C. 2017. Cannabis and Tobacco in Precolonial and Colonial Africa African History. http://africanhistory.oxfordre.com/view/10.1093/acrefore/9780190277734.001.0001/acrefore-9780190277734-e-44. Accessed 23 September 2023.

Fair, L. 1998. Dressing Up: Clothing, Class and Gender in Post-Abolition Zanzibar. *Journal of African History* 39: 63–94.

Frankl, P.J.L. 2003. Who Was Rex Boustead? An Excursus on the Mombasa Club's First Proprietor. *History in Africa* 30: 431–438.

Glassman, J. 1995. *Feasts and Riot: Revelry, Rebellion, and Popular Consciousness on the Swahili Coast, 1856–1888*. Portsmouth: Heinemann Publishing.

Goodman, J. 1993. *Tobacco in History: The Cultures of Dependence*. London: Routledge.

Hilton, M. 2000. *Smoking in British Popular Culture, 1800–2000*. Manchester: Manchester University Press.

Honey, M.S. 1982. *A History of Indian Merchant Capital and Class Formation in Tanganyika, c.1840–1914*. Ph.D. Dissertation. University of Dar es Salaam.

Johnson, N. 2014. World War I, Part 5: Tobacco in the Trenches. Points. https://www.pointshistory.com/post/world-war-i-part-5-tobacco-in-the-trenches. Accessed 14 September 2023.

Jones, L. 1992. *The District Town and the Articulation of Colonial Rule: The Case of Mwanza, Tanzania, 1890–1945*. Ph.D. Dissertation. Michigan State University.

Jones, L. 1995. Commercial Politics and the Overstocking Crisis in Mwanza Province, Tanganyika, 1926–1935. *African Economic History* 23: 129–145.

McCarthy, D.M.P. 1982. *Colonial Bureaucracy and Creating Underdevelopment: Tanganyika 1919–1940*. Ames: Iowa State University Press.

Pallaver, K. 2022. Introduction: Money, Colonialism and African Societies. In *Monetary Transitions. Currencies, Colonialism and African Societies*, ed. Karin Pallaver, 1–30. Cham: Palgrave Macmillan.

Ranger, T.O. 1975. *Dance and Society in Eastern Africa, 1890–1970: The Beni Ngoma*. Berkeley: University of California Press.

Rockel, S. 2006. *Carriers of Culture. Labor on the Road in Nineteenth Century East Africa*. Portsmouth: Heinemann Publishing.

Samson, A. 2018. "It's War, Don't Complain!" Enquiries into African Medical Services during World War I. U.A. Army Center of Military History. https://history.army.mil/curriculum/wwi/docs/AdditionalResources/presentations/WWI_Medical_Pike_report.pdf. Accessed 2 January 2024.

Steinhart, E. 2006. *Black Poachers White Hunters: A Social History of Hunting in Colonial Kenya*. Athens: Ohio University Press.
Sunseri, T. 2002. *Vilimani: Labor Migration and Rural Change in Early Colonial Tanzania*. Oxford: James Currey.
White, L. 2000. *Speaking with Vampires: rumour and History in Colonial Africa*. Berkeley: University of California Press.

CHAPTER 4

Prosumption as Glocal History: Production and Consumption of Cigarettes in Egypt, 1890–1939

Relli Shechter

In 1902, soon after its establishment, British American Tobacco (BAT) was attracted to Egypt for the double reason of taking a share in exporting quality cigarettes from Egypt and supplying the local market. It stayed on after the former business practice crumbled because mechanisation of production allowed it to gain significant control over local production. In 1927, Eastern Tobacco Company, a joint venture that BAT established with the Matossians, cornered the market but, as narrated below, still had to adapt to local demand to make a profit.

This chapter draws on two conceptual terms in narrating the above. First, it employs George Ritzer's study of prosumption—analysing how producers and consumers interact in markets—to study Egypt's tobacco

R. Shechter (✉)
Department of Middle East Studies, Ben-Gurion University of the Negev, Beersheba, Israel
e-mail: rellish@bgu.ac.il

A. van Wickeren et al. (eds.), *Tobacco in Global Perspective, 1780–1960*, Cambridge Imperial and Post-Colonial Studies,
https://doi.org/10.1007/978-3-031-64411-5_4

commodity chain.[1] It uses prosumption to counter familiar narratives of technological trickle down from the centre to the periphery. This chapter further connects prosumption to a process of glocalisation—where the global BAT, through Eastern, closely engaged with local consumers and their particular smoking preferences.

The history of cigarette production in Egypt shows how production and consumption intertwined even during the high age of mass, machine manufacturing, and when only indirect conversation between consumers and producers existed. Manufacturers had to closely consider the contours of market demand for their cigarettes. Eastern, which monopolised mass production in Egypt, had to learn how to accommodate the demand of less-affluent Egyptian consumers. As the Matossian brothers, early players, and the local partners in Eastern showed, big money could be made even in humble markets, if manufacturers paid a close enough attention to local consumer preference. Such an exchange between producers and consumers was crucial for Eastern's economic success.

Second, this chapter consciously inverts and parallels the economist Thorstein Veblen's famous coinage in studying the "inconspicuous consumption" of cigarettes in Egypt.[2] It inverts Veblen's conspicuous consumption because where Veblen discusses the impact of "pecuniary strength" on consumption patterns of a leisure class, this chapter studies the bearing of "survival strategies" on consumption patterns of people living close to subsistence. However, it also parallels Veblen's effort to study money-related living standards and tastes, albeit for consumers of modest means. Inconspicuous consumers have had no lesser impact on production and marketing in developing economies than a more reputed leisure class. Even when producing inexpensive cigarettes, capturing a market and achieving growth in this market depended on manufacturers' attentiveness to consumers' desires and needs. Hence, an intimate understanding of consumers' purchase preferences (their inconspicuous consumer choices) and adapting to such preferences—the prosumption of cigarette manufacturing—was crucial for the success of producers in such markets.

[1] Ritzer (2014).

[2] Veblen (1994, ch. 4).

Inconspicuous Consumption

For the first half of the twentieth century, Egypt experienced what is conventionally described by economists as "development without growth".[3] Such development meant that the material life of the vast majority of Egyptians hardly improved over time. Between 1897 and 1937, a period roughly corresponding to the timeframe of this chapter, Egypt's population increased by about sixty percent, from 9.7 million reported in the 1897 census to 15.9 million accounted for in the 1937 census.[4] Despite this significant demographic growth, we did not observe the creation of a wide and relatively affluent middle-class, a typical aspect of economic development in developed economies. Even later, in mid-century Egypt (1952), about 200,000 persons constituted the higher echelon of society, four million persons could be roughly classified as middle strata, and seventeen million persons formed the lower strata.[5] As influenced by this broad base of the demographic pyramid, purchasing and smoking habits of the lower strata would significantly impact local production.

Under such conditions, the economic gap would not be easily breached. "Trickle down" and convergence in consumer taste were not realisable. Producers would have to come up with solutions to cater to relatively large but income-elastic demands, where, as their economic conditions declined, consumers were ready to compromise type and quality rather than quantity. Quantitative studies of tobacco consumption are few and far between. Their reliability is often dubious, and the data do not allow for a meaningful time-series to account for long-term continuity and change in consumption patterns. Moreover, state-measured per capita consumption, the only data we can use to discuss transitions in tobacco consumption over a sustained period, does not provide city-to-countryside, age-group, or gender breakdowns. To augment incomplete quantitative research, I incorporate qualitative information from various sources into the study of inconspicuous tobacco consumption. Piecing together what little qualitative and quantitative evidence we have in the narrative below should allow some insight into the material culture

[3] Owen and Pamuk (1999, p. 35). Owen and Pamuk borrowed this term from the work of both Bent Hansen and Robert Tignor.

[4] Robinson and El-Zanaty (2006, p. 18, table 2.2).

[5] Amin (1995, p. 132).

of most Egyptians and the ever-present business reality of developing economies.

Like many other commodities consumed in the Egyptian market, tobacco sales were highly income elastic, and demand was often abruptly curtailed by temporary economic constraints. Nevertheless, smoking was a significant, if carefully rationed, consumption practice in the lifestyle of the less-affluent. In the late nineteenth and early twentieth centuries, experts on the Egyptian cigarette industry observed that it benefited from the fact that Egyptians were heavy smokers.[6] One commentator noted that between 1897 and 1907, the population grew by 1.5% per year, suggesting that tobacco consumption probably increased at the same rate.[7] The increase in consumption might have also been explained by the fact that Egypt was at the height of an economic boom accompanied by an influx of economic migrants. Therefore, the above comment reflected an overly optimistic view of the market potential for tobacco based on broader national trends. Indeed, the combination of demographic increase and economic standstill soon brought tobacco consumption levels down: between 1920 and 1936, consumption dropped by about 60%.[8] Even as the world economy gradually recovered from the Great Depression, most Egyptian smokers and consumers faced a future with few smoking opportunities.

Several estimates exist of the relative expenditure on tobacco as a percentage of the income of the "average" urban Egyptian. Around 1911 it was estimated that an Egyptian worker spent one piaster (equal to 100th of a pound sterling) a day on tobacco out of a daily earning of eight to twelve piasters, 8.3% to 12.5% of the worker's salary.[9] In 1920, a government study of the cost of living for low-level employees estimated that they spent 5.8% of their incomes on cigarettes and other minor expenses.[10] For 1938, it was estimated that cigarette expenditures constituted 8.9% of total private spending. Therefore, cigarettes equalled about 14.2% of total food expenditures.[11] By 1945, these proportions had risen

[6] Arminjon (1911, p. 321). Sékaly (1914, p. 350).

[7] Arminjon (1911, p. 321).

[8] Annuaire statistique (1935–1936, p. 463).

[9] Vallet (1911).

[10] Reported in Annuaire statistique (1922–1923, p. 187).

[11] Anis (1950, p. 681, table 6).

to 10.2% and 15.9%, respectively. Although these estimates are suspect for various reasons, taken together they indicate that tobacco, while expensive, remained an essential item for Egyptian consumers and demonstrate that average city dwellers spent a significant proportion of their incomes on smoking.

In 1931, a source unmentioned by name, but characterised as "reliable", calculated expenditure on tobacco consumption in the countryside for the Balfour Mission, studying the economic conditions in Egypt to improve British trade with the country. The calculation was based on a monthly list of living expenses for a family of five (the officially quoted prices applied to Manufia, the most densely populated province in Egypt, in September 1930. It showed that expenditures on tobacco were a meagre 2.4% of the total, a much lower percentage than among city dwellers.[12] The report, compiled during the time that the *fellah*—Arabic for farmer—and his family lived under harsh economic conditions, further suggested that tobacco, meat, and sugar disappeared from household consumption when money was short in the countryside.

Demand for tobacco among inconspicuous consumers showed high elasticity compared to other widely consumed commodities, even though tobacco is addictive. Between 1938 and 1945, the elasticity coefficient of 0.9 for tobacco was higher than for any other essential item, and therefore demand for tobacco corresponded most closely to changes in income.[13] Later, similar calculations were made regarding expenditure elasticities based on the national household survey of 1958–1959.[14] Expenditure-elasticity coefficients for tobacco, cigarettes, and alcoholic drinks, taken together, were 0.86 for urban households and 0.94 for rural families, exposing some disparity between average living conditions in the city and the countryside again.

Consumers responded to changing economic conditions by cutting consumption, but also by switching to cheaper cigarette brands, or changing their smoking habits altogether. In the countryside, smokers gave up machine-made cigarettes and returned to rolling their own. They switched to smoking the water pipe when their economic situation further

[12] Public Record Office, Board of Trade (1952, pp. 65–67).

[13] El-Sherbini and Sherif (1956, tables 13, 23).

[14] Hansen (1979, p. 38).

deteriorated.[15] Consumption rose when economic conditions improved. Cigarette sales in the countryside climbed in November every year after the main cotton sales were completed.[16] They also increased, albeit less sharply, in May, after the sale of cereals. Under such conditions, it was not surprising that consumers were highly price sensitive. Around 1938, the author of a book on the Egyptian peasant commented, "the fellahin love tobacco, but they buy the lowest grade of cigarettes, 20 for 5 piasters".[17] We do not have price lists for the larger manufacturers of the period, Eastern and Coutarelli, the only large-scale Greek producer, which would have constituted the best comparison of cigarette prices. But judging from advertisements in the newspaper *al-Ahram*, where smaller manufacturers promoted their brands, five piasters for twenty was the average price for lower-quality cigarettes. The more expensive brands manufactured by Mahmud Fahmi and Misr li-l-Dukhkhan wa-al-Sajair (The Egyptian [Company] for Tobacco and Cigarettes) cost double that amount.[18]

Such price sensitivity and the readiness to compromise on quality rather than quantity through purchasing cheaper brands correlate well with broader observations on Egyptian purchasing habits found for the early 1930s in the Balfour Mission Report and for the 1950s in a report by economists Abdel Aziz El-Sherbini and Ahmad Fouad Sherif. In addition, consumers adapted their shopping practices to improve their buying power and adjust to cash shortages. For example, some staple commodities were bought in bulk, and food and clothing were mostly processed within the household. Less essential goods (such as cigarettes) were bought ad hoc: "Most consumers [bought] on a hand-to-mouth basis; the purchase of a cigarette, a razor blade, or an egg [was] customary because of [the] inability to finance home inventories, the lack of home-storage space, and the absence of refrigeration".[19] Less-affluent consumers consumed lower-quality goods, and fewer of them, than the affluent, and their shopping habits were also different.

[15] Kamil (1985, p. 8).

[16] Selous (1937, p. 96).

[17] Ayrout (1963 [1938], p. 82).

[18] Anonymous (1936) advertisement for Mahmud Fahm. Anonymous (1939) advertisement for Misr li-l-Dukhkhan.

[19] Boyd et al. (1961, p. 29).

Less-affluent smokers also had different day-to-day practices, which helped them sustain their consumption habits when times were hard. In Naguib Mahfouz's novel *Midaq Alley*, Zaita smokes only half a cigarette at a time.[20] Smokers shared or took a drag from a friend's cigarette, limited the number of cigarettes they smoked daily, or rationed tobacco in other ways. However, little information is available on how fashions were personalised to economise tobacco consumption. We know a little more about social practices related to smoking, which undoubtedly helped to maintain a certain level of smoking and to support the habit, even in hard times. For example, a pack of cigarettes was a welcome gift to a host. Cigarettes (and coffee) were offered to guests at meetings and wedding ceremonies, or to the *fukaha* (reciters of the Koran) in the intervals between recitations.[21] Scarcity increased the social value of cigarettes as tokens of appreciation and expressions of generosity or wealth, attributes that were not necessarily conflated with the meaning of consumption among the more affluent. Last but not least, the proscription against women smoking in public and the absolute ban on smoking by youths in Egypt may, in the context of constrained consumption, be interpreted as an attempt to secure the prerogative to smoke (and the license to spend a considerable portion of the family budget on tobacco) for men in a male-dominated society. Smoking constituted a symbolic boundary that separated men from women and youths and marked entitlement and distinction within and between social groups.

There was thus a quantifiable elasticity in demand coupled with an inelastic desire to smoke, as manifested in the "survival strategies" adopted by smokers under financial constraints. Such strategies reflected the stratification (class-oriented consumption patterns) and real-life choices made by less-affluent consumers. Moreover, they represented a challenge to enterprises that had to adapt to the contours of such demand and its constant fluctuations. The following discusses the emergence of a modern, global tobacco market in Egypt, setting the context for a later discussion of why and how inconspicuous consumption became closely intertwined with changes in this market in the aftermath of World War I.

[20] Mahfouz (1977 [1947], p. 109, 194).

[21] Blackman (1968 [1927], pp. 82–83, 93, 114).

Bifurcation of Production

Following the 1890 reform in the tobacco market (see below), two types of businesses rapidly developed in Egypt.[22] The first type of enterprise catered to upper-class Egyptians, expatriates, tourists, and international connoisseurs by selling high-quality handmade cigarettes. The second type focused on the broader local market and specialised in the mass production of cheap tobaccos and humbler ready-made (but not yet mechanised) cigarettes. Although there was some overlap between the two, the upper-end market was, by-and-large, dominated by Greek manufacturers. At the same time, Armenians came to control the supply for the "average" Egyptian.

The globally renowned Egyptian cigarette significantly impacted the worldwide spread of the cigarette. Its past glory is still discerned from the Camel cigarette iconography. In creating the first brand to be sold in the US nationwide, R.J. Reynolds assigned the captivating images of the Egyptian cigarette (pyramids, Islamic architecture, palm trees, and the camel itself) that were already popularised on Egyptian cigarette packages to its own package design. R.J. Reynolds also mixed American and eastern tobaccos in its product. But the high-end industry crumbled when international production picked up pace and governments, especially in Europe, took protective measures to defend their nascent industries—indigenous demand was not strong enough to keep it going. The less glamorous business flourished by manufacturing cigarettes for the less-affluent consumers—most buyers in Egyptian markets.

From its inception as a modern industry in Egypt, cigarette production was closely linked to events that had largely shaped the region (then under the Ottoman Empire). In 1875, foreign borrowing and state bankruptcy forced the Ottoman government to cede revenues from tobacco tax collection to a group of Istanbul bankers, and later (in 1883) to establish a tobacco administration (Régie) under the auspices of a consortium of several European banks. The Régie drove independent Greek and later Armenian tobacco merchants and producers of ready-to-use tobaccos to migrate to Egypt in search of a less regulated market where they could reinstate their businesses.

In Egypt, which was still nominally under Ottoman suzerainty, a similar process of foreign borrowing and state bankruptcy ended in 1882 in

[22] See Shechter (2003, chs. 2 and 3).

direct British control over the country. This country's tobacco market transformation was a textbook example of the benefits some businesses derived from colonial occupation. After 1882, the opening up of the country and its rapid integration into the world economy enabled the incoming Greek enterprises to launch their export-led cigarette industry. More so, in 1890, under the influence of the Greek merchants, the British-led Egyptian government banned local tobacco cultivation because it was considered inferior in quality, which would potentially harm the reputation of the Egyptian cigarette. The government installed a new tobacco taxation system on imported tobacco, which completely restructured the local tobacco market. The ban turned out to be an important source for the British, who were always searching for new sources of revenues that would pay Egypt's extended public debt.

The ban created a vacuum in supply, since local tobacco was no longer available, and imports of substitutes had only just started. Aggregate tobacco imports increased from 3,248 tons in 1889 to 5,319 tons in 1890.[23] By 1913, tobacco and cigarette manufacturers in Egypt were importing 9,030 tons, almost three times the amount in 1889. At the same time, indigenous producers and sellers of tobacco products were losing their corner of the market to the Greeks, and they were ceding even more of their position to the Armenians, who had begun to specialise in supplying local demand.

Within this period of rapid change, timing was an essential factor in the successful entry into production for the local tobacco market. The biggest Armenian manufacturers and Coutarelli opened or expanded their businesses immediately after 1890, proving that the ban was a crucial wedge facilitating newcomers' entry into the Egyptian tobacco market. No one understood the new opportunities better than the Matossian brothers. Hovhannes Matossian opened a small workshop in Alexandria soon after the family emigrated from the Ottoman Empire in 1882. In 1886, his brother Garabed opened a similar business in Cairo. In 1896, the brothers joined forces.[24] The new company grew rapidly, and in 1899, the Matossians converted their business into a shareholding company with

[23] Statistical and Census Department, Egyptian Ministry of Finance (1914, p. 303).

[24] Topuzyan (1978, p. 101).

a capital of £E100,000. By 1902, they had increased the capital of the factory to £E150,000, which came entirely from the Matossian family.[25]

The Melkonian brothers owned the second largest tobacco enterprise, and the development of their business was similar to the course followed by the Matossians. The family arrived in Egypt in 1875 and started in retail first by opening a tobacco shop in Alexandria and then by expanding to wholesale manufacturing.[26] In 1883 or 1884, the Melkonians established a factory in Zaqaziq, followed in 1888 by a second factory in Fayyum. They later established a factory in Aswan and another in Alexandria. Around the turn of the century, the Melkonian brothers consolidated their business by transferring production to a new factory in Cairo.

Tobacco enterprises shared the conventional practices and business culture of the period. Ownership was restricted to a single family, and the workshops-turned-factories hired Armenians for managerial posts. Armenian factories also took on a large percentage of unskilled Egyptian labourers, but the exact number of workers in the industry is unknown. However, we know that before the transition to machine production, the Gamsaragan factory, the third-largest enterprise, employed 1,200 workers.[27] With minimal mechanisation and an ample supply of cheap labour, the idea behind such large-scale operations was to create economies of scale based on inexpensive work and raw materials. Production for the local market segment was still rudimentary, consisting mainly of cutting, blending, and packaging ready-to-use tobaccos (for water pipes and cigarettes), but it also included preparing handmade economy cigarettes and a few quality brands.

No less important than low production costs was the ability of Armenian manufacturers to develop nationwide distribution networks that promoted their products throughout Egypt, utilising the closures of older retail establishments. By distributing their products directly to consumers, manufacturers cut out the middlemen, rendering the role of the traditional tobacco seller (*dakhakhini*) obsolete. However, producers might have incorporated some tobacco sellers into their distribution networks. A large number of employees in the Armenian enterprises indicate that distribution and, to some extent, retailing were closely integrated with

[25] Statistical and Census Department, Egyptian Ministry of Finance (1910, p. 332).

[26] Al-Imam (1995, p. 92).

[27] Goldberg (1983, p. 313).

production in these companies. For example, by 1918, Melkonian had 80 cigarette-selling outlets in Egypt and the Sudan.[28] Marketing in the cities was probably easier and more profitable because it entailed less travelling and catered to relatively more affluent consumers; still, the countryside, where the majority of the population lived, was not overlooked. Distribution there was facilitated by Egypt's well-developed highway, railroad, and waterway transport systems. These were initially built to facilitate the cotton export trade but also paved the way for introducing novel commodities into rural areas.

Tobacco retailing, however, was not limited to the manufacturers' distribution networks. Smaller retail establishments offered their customers a selection of products from different manufacturers.[29] The growth of nationwide retailing also meant that manufacturers limited the number of their tobacco brands to facilitate distribution and increase brand recognition. For example, Gamsaragan became known for its Abu-Najma brand and Melkonian for its "house special"—the Maden (*Ma'dan* in Arabic) cigarette.[30] Brand recognition was an important stage in retailing nationwide because it enabled manufacturers to employ many salespersons who were not tobacco specialists or sell their cigarettes through general retailing venues (i.e. the Greek stores in the countryside). Packaging, rather than selling in bulk, as had been the custom in the past, also facilitated the retailing process; branding and packaging gave manufacturers an advantage over independent retailers in creating consumer demand for specific brands, which forced such retailers to keep stocks. None of these strategies was unique to tobacco manufacturers in Egypt, but they were all typical of markets for tobacco products and other globally mass-produced goods. In a period of rapid globalisation before World War I, the circulation of standardised commodities worldwide accelerated, as did the marketing and advertising that promoted them.

[28] Advertisement on the back cover of Partevean (1918).

[29] Advertisement by Charisto Demitropolo, in al-Ahram, quoted in Labib Rizk (1997); advertisement by Havhannes Pembedjian, in Partevean (1918, p. 55).

[30] For Gamsaragan, see al-Muqattam (1896, p. 2). For Melkonian, see advertisement in the Egyptian Gazette: Anonymous (1913, p. 5).

BAT in Egypt

The story of BAT's involvement in the local tobacco market, at least until relatively late in the game, was one among several. BAT's chronicle would not play out as a straightforward narrative of imported innovation into a colonial state and the introduction of a novel and modern taste trickling down before achieving wider dissemination. Instead, the details of its entry into Egypt showed subtler interrelations between the business, local production, political economy, and indigenous consumption patterns.

Soon after its establishment in 1902, BAT began to explore various venues in an attempt to enter the Egyptian tobacco market.[31] BAT was motivated to seek inroads into the Egyptian cigarette industry because luxury Egyptian cigarettes sold well in markets worldwide. Moreover, the company hoped to produce cheap cigarettes for the fast-growing local market, as in other places such as China and India.

BAT usually started its operations by importing cigarettes and only later diversified by acquiring local firms and developing its own local ventures. The company had to choose a different strategy for Egypt because the Egyptian market preferred the aroma and taste of Eastern tobaccos to the Virginia tobaccos BAT used in its cigarettes. Indeed, consumers' preference for Eastern tobacco would impact BAT's operations, even after the company came to control most production in Egypt. Instead of imports, BAT purchased existing businesses and produced cigarettes made with eastern tobacco locally. In 1905, Maspero Frères became the first BAT subsidiary and the centre of BAT's activity in the country.[32] The company also acquired the African Cigarette Co. Ltd.[33] In 1908, BAT acquired an interest in the Alma cigarette company through Maspero.[34]

Having only partially succeeded in entering the market by buying local companies and imports, BAT attempted other strategies. In 1907, it seemingly introduced the first cigarette-making machines in Egypt via

[31] Cox (2000, ch. 3).

[32] Cox (1990, p. 385).

[33] Cox (1989, pp. 52–53).

[34] Wright and Cartwright (1909, p. 495).

Maspero Frères, where a reported workers' strike against mechanisation that year may well have taken place.[35]

While this was the standard worldwide for about two decades, the company soon discovered that the production of cheap cigarettes in Egypt did not yield the anticipated advantage over local competitors. Egyptians continued to smoke water pipes (tobacco for water pipes was the cheapest available on the market). When they smoked cigarettes, they preferred to roll their own or, when affordable, to buy handmade cigarettes, which they considered better quality than the machine-made variety.

In 1908, BAT tried again to impose a radical transformation on the existing tobacco market in Egypt.[36] The company approached the Egyptian government and offered financial help and expertise in resuming domestic tobacco cultivation. BAT also offered to compensate the government for the annual sum of its current revenues from import tariffs, which was about £E1,700,000.[37] In exchange, BAT would have the right to control local cultivation, and the government would prohibit tobacco imports to Egypt. This was not a tobacco multinational's first attempt to interfere with the region's market. In 1902, Duke's American Tobacco Company—a forerunner to, and later the American arm of BAT—had attempted to gain control of the Middle Eastern supply market.[38]

In 1913, unidentified Americans, who were probably associated with one of the large cigarette enterprises, made a bid to acquire the Ottoman Régie.[39] BAT's offer, if accepted, would free the company from Egyptian competition in global markets and enable BAT to control the local market by cutting the supply of tobacco to its competitors. It would further help the company to promote its cheap machine-made cigarettes in this captive market.

British exports of manufactured cigarettes to Egypt only started in 1913, and because BAT was responsible for most exports, we may assume that imports from Britain to Egypt were BAT's.[40] Also, and perhaps not

[35] Vallet (1911, p. 103).

[36] Cox (1989, p. 53).

[37] Statistical and Census Department, Egyptian Ministry of Finance (1909, table 3, p. 40).

[38] Goodman III (1987, p. 5).

[39] Cox (1989, fns. 38, 65).

[40] Cox (2000, appendix 3).

entirely by coincidence, BAT's offer came when the Egyptian government was under political pressure to reintroduce tobacco cultivation. Protests against the ban on cultivation were voiced in every opening session of the General Assembly and the Legislative Council.[41] In March 1907, Ali Sha'arawi Pasha, a senior politician, protested against the tobacco ban before the Egyptian General Assembly. He was supported by Shaykh' Ali Yusuf, former editor of the newspaper *al-Mu'ayyad* and leader of the Reform Party. The press backed the suggestion to reintroduce cultivation to protect Egypt from the dangers of total economic dependence on cotton. The journal *al-Muqtataf* devoted two articles to the issue.[42] Although they shared the same interest, there was no open cooperation between BAT and this Egyptian lobby. BAT kept its offer a secret and later even denied the very existence of such a plan.

For the Egyptian government, accepting BAT's offer necessitated making a major overhaul of the existing tobacco revenue system in Egypt, discontinuing a profitable indirect tax, and introducing a new dependence on an external source of revenues. It also required breaking commercial treaties, such as the one it had signed with Greece in 1884 that allowed imports of Greek tobaccos into the country. Government officials were probably more sceptical than the company's directors about the possibility of cultivating quality tobacco in Egypt. They would no doubt have been reluctant to promote tobacco cultivation at the expense of cotton or harm such a thriving local industry. The government preferred to continue with a successful revenue system, rather than risking a completely different one. The entire affair testified to the limits of cooperation between private capital from the metropolis and the local, British-controlled government. When the latter's interests were jeopardised, and with only limited lobbying from the British Foreign Office or other official bodies, the government in Egypt took a decision that best suited its interests.

Although it continued to grow until the end of World War I, BAT operated as one of many players in the Egyptian cigarette industry. The company made two other significant acquisitions: Nicholas Soussa, one of the major early manufacturers of export cigarettes, and Gamsaragan, the third biggest manufacturer for the local market.[43] These acquisitions

[41] Sékaly (1914, p. 362).

[42] Anonymous (1907(a), pp. 318–320); Anonymous (1907(b), p. 849).

[43] Cox (1990, p. 207).

enabled BAT to expand its share in the Egyptian tobacco market. Still, the company did not attempt to mechanise these factories, and even Maspero continued to produce handmade cigarettes until mechanisation swept across the entire industry.

Mechanisation, Integration, and Local Demand

Under the conditions discussed above, and like most other consumer-goods industries and services in Egypt, integration in the tobacco industry was an outcome waiting to happen. Among other factors contributing to this process were infrastructural impediments to manufacturing in a developing country, low levels of investment, and limited entrepreneurial and technical skills. A political economy that encouraged the consolidation of business groups struggling to gain government largesse further encouraged monopolistic conditions in Egypt,[44] with other factors also contributing to integration in the tobacco market, especially the role of local demand in shaping this process. In the case of the tobacco market, the role of demand was even more significant in determining integration because part of the business entailed producing high-quality, handmade cigarettes for the upper end of the local market and, more critically, for export. After the early 1920s, the decline of export-led production enhanced the late mechanisation of cigarette manufacturing and created a duopoly in the business.

Once rapid mechanisation occurred, constraints on local demand and rapid saturation in the new market for machine-made cigarettes led to fierce competition among manufacturers, creating conditions ripe for integration. This process was fast because BAT started buying out companies immediately after mechanisation, and its rival, Matossian, adopted the same strategy. A domino effect ensued because none of the smaller manufacturers could face the mounting competition, nor did they want to be left without any leverage in future selling negotiations.

Although Matossian seems to have suffered from the competition—after World War I, it processed only 10 tons of raw tobacco a day, compared with 15 before the war—it was in little danger of becoming another BAT subsidiary.[45] In the 1920s, it concentrated production in a

[44] El-Gritli (1947, pp. 158–161). Vitalis (1995).

[45] Tigrane Matossian supplied the information on the Matossian factory.

vast factory in Giza, employing 4,000 workers and manufacturing over two billion cigarettes per year. At that time, the factory had 40 cigarette-making machines, each capable of producing 200,000 cigarettes daily. A rough estimate of its capacity compared with actual production shows that the company could increase manufacturing by about a third. Management in the factory also changed. Hovhannes Matossian, the older of the two brothers, who had established the business, died in 1927.[46] His sons, Jacques, Joseph, and Vincent, then took control of the company.

In July 1927, BAT and Matossian merged under the umbrella of Eastern. The strategic alliance between BAT and Matossian significantly took place after the death of the latter's cofounder, making way for a new generation to take control. BAT had made previous overtures and had been rebuffed. The alliance was mutually beneficial because each side brought different assets to Eastern. BAT saw an opportunity to emulate its success in China, where the involvement of a leading domestic firm like Matossian had its parallel in the role played by the Wing Tai Vo Company.[47] In China, BAT mainly managed the production end and used the brands and distribution systems of the Chinese firm to build a nationwide presence, as it would do in Egypt. Before the merger, Matossian tripled its capital from £E250,000 to £E750,000, presumably to increase its financial commitment to the new company.[48] However, BAT, overflowing with resources, increased Eastern's capital to £E5,000,000, the largest investment in any Egyptian joint-stock firm, except the Suez Canal Company.[49] Such an investment also dwarfed capital investments in other factories in the cigarette industry, which were, on average, less than £E100,000—Boustani, £E100,000; Cassimis, £E31,055; Giancalis, £E90,000; Salloam Frères, £E88,000; and Salonica, £E88,320.[50] We have no information on the capital of Coutarelli, but considering the large volume of its business, it must have exceeded that of the smaller enterprises. Nonetheless this did not detract from BAT's optimistic projections for company growth.

[46] Gartashean (1986 p. 146).

[47] I thank Howard Cox for bringing this comparison to my attention.

[48] Mulock (1927, p. 14).

[49] Crouchley (1977, p. 86).

[50] Egyptian Trade Index (1944).

Although BAT invested the lion's share in Eastern, the Matossian family received 50% of the shares.[51] The family retained considerable managerial control over Eastern, and the chairman of the Matossian company also served as Eastern's first chairman of the board.[52] BAT accepted the Matossians' partnership under such generous conditions because they provided their up-to-date factory, which soon became the only production facility of Eastern. Still today, it is colloquially known as "Matossian". The Matossians also supplied well-developed distribution networks, local knowledge of the Egyptian market, and experience in negotiating with the Egyptian authorities. An even greater consideration for BAT was the global rise of nationalism with its possible negative impact on business. The company sought to counter this turn of events by downplaying its direct involvement in such overseas markets and operating via local subsidiaries.[53] While the Matossians were able to secure their position in Eastern, Britons soon filled most of the company's important managerial and administrative positions.[54] BAT also brought to Eastern foreign expertise in production and access to international tobacco markets.

After its subsequent acquisition of Melkonian, the second largest manufacturer, and of the Athena cigarette factory, Eastern controlled nine companies, including some of the largest firms in the industry. Immediately after this merger, Eastern briefly dominated production entirely. According to one source, the company controlled 90 percent of the Egyptian cigarette market, and cigarette sales increased from 2,716.8 million cigarettes in 1927 to 4,789.9 million in 1928.[55]Egypt had become BAT's fourth-largest foreign market after China, India, and Java.[56]

However, two years after the company had been established, the Great Depression undermined Eastern's initial success in increasing sales, emphasising the vulnerability of local demand. The Depression caused the purchasing power of Egyptian smokers to plummet, and per capita

[51] Cox (1990, p. 208).

[52] Mulock (1927, p. 14).

[53] Cox (2000, p. 339).

[54] For a detailed account of Eastern's managerial hierarchies see Shechter (2006, pp. 104–110).

[55] Cox (1990, p. 208, appendix 4).

[56] Cox (1990, p. 386).

consumption fell by about 30% percent, from an estimated 519 grams in 1929 to 363 grams in 1932.[57] Correspondingly, Eastern's sales fell by about 35 percent for the same period, from 4,193.5 to 2,711 million cigarettes, and remained more or less at a constant all-time low until 1939, despite continuous demographic growth.[58] At the same time, the company's exports from Egypt suffered as consumers' purchasing power abroad also diminished.[59] As a result, Eastern had to pare down its operation by closing all its other subsidiaries, moving production to the Matossian facilities in Cairo (Giza), and economising on its distribution chains. According to a BAT internal account, the company had to lay off 12,000 Egyptian workers.[60] In late 1936, after a period in which BAT had to fund Eastern's operations in Egypt, and following a series of shareholding transfers from the Matossians to BAT to compensate for some of the losses, Eastern's shares were written down from £E5,000,000 to £E2,000,000.[61]

Eastern's failure to bounce back when the Depression was phasing out also stemmed from the company's attempt to convert smokers from eastern to British cigarettes, which were made from Virginia tobacco. (I use "eastern" without capitalisation referring to tobacco grown in the East to differentiate it from "Eastern", the company.) Virginia cigarettes were BAT's stock-in-trade in other markets, including China and India, but Egypt was different insofar as local smokers preferred the region's tobacco and would not easily switch to the new taste. Before the Depression, Egyptians were ready to smoke British tobacco when the price was right. Still, an increase in the price of imported Virginia-blend cigarettes quickly drove consumers back to cigarettes filled with eastern tobaccos. The company's failure to cultivate Virginia tobacco locally (and more cheaply) further exacerbated this situation. Although the company began to produce locally Virginia-blend cigarettes, such as Gold Flake, to its dismay, efforts to promote Virginia brands scored only minor

[57] Statistical and Census Department, Egyptian Ministry of Finance (1935–1936, p. 463). Also see Selous (1937, p. 96).

[58] Cox (1990, appendix 4).

[59] Customs Administration (1931, p. 12).

[60] Cox (2000, p. 286, fn. 134).

[61] Levy (1937, p. 362). Cox (2000, p. 287) gives the slightly later date of July 1937.

success.[62] Overall, the company's decision to encourage the consumption of Virginia tobacco in Egypt negatively influenced sales.

Eastern's experimentation with Virginia blends partly enabled its main competitor, Coutarelli, to challenge Eastern's dominant position. Coutarelli was located in Alexandria, where it had opened a new factory in 1920.[63] Unlike other Greek producers of handmade cigarettes, Coutarelli adapted well to machine production. In 1922, the company began machine production when it bought its first three cigarette-making machines. It was the last company to negotiate with Eastern, and it held out for a price slightly higher than what Eastern offered.[64] There is also an indication that rivalry between the Coutarelli and the Matossian families sabotaged the deal.[65]

In 1928, Coutarelli, realising that the competition now was over economies of scale in production, introduced nine new machines into the factory.[66] Moreover, unable to control the wholesale trade, which Eastern dominated, Coutarelli also skilfully developed direct sales to the retail trade, which allowed the company to keep a significant market share while challenging Eastern.[67] To boost its sales and encourage retailers to stock its merchandise, Coutarelli advertised extensively in the press.[68] These schemes were well calculated, and Coutarelli was able to hold up against its rival. In the early 1930s, its factory was estimated to control 30% of the market.[69] In 1948, according to Eastern's unpublished data, the company's share in the total value of tobacco sales in Egypt was 62.5%.[70] Between them, Eastern and Coutarelli dominated tobacco production in Egypt. In 1945, an article in *La Réforme* suggested that Coutarelli employed more than 5,000 persons in production and distribution in

[62] al-Rifa 'i (1935, pp. 450–451). See also Selous (1937, p. 97). Kitroeff (1989, p. 109).

[63] Haritatos and Giakoumakis (1997 p. 140).

[64] Kitroeff (1989, p. 109).

[65] Cox (2000, p. 287).

[66] Kitroeff (1989, p. 109).

[67] Cox (2000, p. 287).

[68] Shechter (2005).

[69] Kitroeff (1989, p. 109).

[70] Abou-el-Fetouh (1976, table 36, p. xlix).

Egypt, slightly less than a third of the total official number of 16,130 working in the industry.[71]

The Egyptian government's decennial censuses of 1927, 1937, and 1947 indicate that several small-sized enterprises were also engaged in production and retailing.[72] With few exceptions, such manufacturers did not produce machine-made cigarettes but concentrated on tobacco products that did not require mechanisation. Unable to enjoy the advantages of large capital, economies of scale, or mechanisation, such businesses survived due to the relative advantage of access to abundant cheap labour. Many continued to produce handmade cigarettes because rollers' wages fell once mechanisation took hold. Thus, the Egyptian tobacco industry had the familiar structure of local manufacturing in contemporary Egypt: a duopoly (or monopoly) controlling most of the production and small-sized manufacturing exploiting the remaining market niches.

Only during World War II did Eastern's fortunes change, when consumption of British cigarettes skyrocketed, owing to the presence of Allied forces in the Middle East. In addition, local consumers faced a new situation as Virginia became the more prevalent tobacco in the market. Eastern stood to gain doubly from the wartime shifts: through close cooperation between BAT and British officials, it secured supplies of raw material from abroad, enhancing BAT's tobacco exports, especially from India and Rhodesia to Egypt; and it greatly increased production as a result of Allied demand. Taking advantage of British (and American) war efforts, Eastern finally overcame the effects of its initial debacle by temporarily evading the constraints of local consumption.[73]

After the war, consumers began to prefer American cigarettes—a mixture of Virginia, Burley, and eastern tobaccos, whose taste was milder than the British brands made only from Virginia tobacco—and American cigarettes made deep inroads into the Egyptian market.[74] This occurred not least due to aggressive promotion and advertising campaigns by American manufacturers. At first, Eastern and other manufacturers felt threatened by this new development and called for an increase in

71 Egyptian Department of Statistics and Census (1944, table 2, p. 15).

72 Statistical and Census Department, Egyptian Ministry of Finance (1927, 1937, 1947).

73 Shechter (2006, pp. 100–104).

74 Guide des industries d'Egypte (1950, p. 39). Public Record Office, Board of Trade (1952, p. 536).

taxation on imported cigarettes. Soon they started making their own cheaper American brands.[75] By 1953, imports of American cigarettes had dropped significantly. Ten years later, most Egyptian smokers in Cairo and Alexandria preferred American cigarettes to British and eastern brands.[76] American brands accounted for 97.3% of Eastern's sales at that time.[77] Unlike in the past, the company was more attentive to consumer demand and knew how to change quickly to bolster its position. However, there was a degree of irony in its success in accommodating local consumption, which made it a greater prize for the Nasserite regime that had begun moving towards nationalisation.

Prosumption as Glocal History

The colonisation of Egypt, coupled with the fast integration of the country into the world economy before World War I, opened a window of opportunity for new businesses in the country, as illustrated by the case of the tobacco market. Since then, however, local and global enterprises have had to involve themselves closely in internal markets and their inconspicuous consumption patterns. Their aptitude in doing so—the indirect conversation between producers and consumers—determined the success of their operations.

Cigarettes sold in Egypt were not simply the standardised, machine-produced commodities we often associate with mass manufacturing by multinationals worldwide. It took mechanisation longer to arrive for reasons specific to the Egyptian market. Even then, Egyptians vastly preferred a different kind of tobacco than the one BAT, through Eastern, was trying to promote. Moreover, this chapter suggests that local consumption, frequently shorthanded as "limited" or "narrow" markets, deserves extensive discussion to realise its impact on the business. The apparent reality was that limited demand restricted supply. However, pecuniary sensitivities of inconspicuous smokers also meant that enterprises had to adapt to the elasticity of demand of such consumers and their employment of distinctive survival strategies in consumption. More

[75] Al-Bank al-Ahli al-Misri (1954, p. 207).

[76] Social Research Center (1964, tables 29–38, pp. 50–56).

[77] Abou-el-Fetouh (1976, table 2.4, p. 34).

so, businesses had to learn to cultivate new tastes for modest but ample markets.

The history of the Egyptian tobacco market, therefore, shows infinitely more complex consumption patterns and consumers' influence on manufacturing than we usually assume for a previous age of Fordism in production. This case study disintegrates the global history of mass tobacco production into a more nuanced narrative of prosumption in a specific market. Furthermore, it demonstrates more local consumers' agency in influencing production than previously suggested. We need more prudence in evaluating consumers' "added value" to contemporary goods and services. In the final analysis, any global history of tobacco is a broad outline of events that should more cautiously or glocally be told worldwide.

References

Primary Sources

Administration, Customs. 1931. *Report on Foreign Trade of Egypt in 1930.* Cairo: Government Press.

Al-Bank al-Ahli al-Misri. 1954. *Al-Nashra al-Iqtisadiyya*, 7, no. 1. Cairo: No Publisher.

Al-Rifa'i, Husayn. 1935. *'Ali Al-sina'a fi Misr*. Cairo: Matba'at Misr.

Anis, Muhammad Amin. 1950. *A Study of the National Income of Egypt*. Cairo: S.O.P. Press.

Anonymous. 1896. Advertisement. *Al-Muqattam*, 21 October.

Anonymous. 1907(a). *All-Muqtataf*, April.

Anonymous. 1907(b). *Al-Muqtataf*, October.

Anonymous. 1913. *Advertisement. Egyptian Gazette*, 8 February.

Anonymous. 1936. Advertisement. *Al-Ahram*, 3 April.

Anonymous. 1939. Advertisement. *Al-Ahram*, 28 June.

Anonymous. Unknown date. *The Egyptian Trade Index of November 1944.*

Egyptian Department of Statistics and Census. 1947. *The Census of Industrial Production, 1944.* Cairo: Government Press.

Guide des industries d'Egypte. 1950. *l'Informateur*, special issue.

Mulock, E. H., Department of Overseas Trade. 1927. *Report on the Economic and Financial Situation of Egypt Dated May 1927*. London: His Majesty's Stationary Office.

Public Record Office, Board of Trade. 1952. Purchasing Power of Egypt's Agricultural Population. 60/29/2.

Registre de l'économie Égyptienne et des industries. 1952. No Place: Near East Publication.
Selous, G.H., Department of Overseas Trade. 1937. *Report on the Economic and Commercial Conditions in Egypt, 1936*. London: His Majesty's Stationary Office.
Social Research Center, American University in Cairo. 1964. *Tobacco Smoking in Cairo and Alexandria*. Cairo: No Publisher.
Statistical and Census Department, Egyptian Ministry of Finance. Years 1909, 1910, 1914, 1922–23, 1935–36. *Annuaire statistique*.
Statistical and Census Department, Egyptian Ministry of Finance. Years: 1927, 1937, 1947. *Industrial and Commercial Census*.

Secondary Sources

Abou-el-Fetouh, M.F. 1976. *A Quantitative Study of the Tobacco Industry in Egypt with Particular Reference to the ETC Firm*. Ph.D. Dissertation, University of Lancaster.
Al-Imam, M.R. 1995. *Al-Arman fi Misr*. Cairo: Matba'at al-Nubar.
Amin, G. 1995. *Egypt's Economic Predicament: A Study in the Interaction of External Pressure, Political Folly, and Social Tension in Egypt, 1960–1990*. Leiden: E.J. Brill.
Arminjon, Pierre. 1911. *La Situation économique et financière de l'Egypte*. Paris: Librairie.
Ayrout, H.H. 1963 [1938]. *The Egyptian Peasant*. Trans. J.A. Williams. Boston: Beacon Press.
Blackman, W.S. 1968 [1927]. *The Fellahin of Upper Egypt*. London: Frank Cass.
Boyd, H.W., Jr., A. Aziz El-Sherbini, and A. Fouad Sherif. 1961. Channels of Distribution for Consumer Goods in Egypt. *Journal of Marketing* 25: 28–33.
Cox, H.T. 1989. Growth and Ownership in the International Tobacco Industry: BAT 1902–1927. *Business History* 31: 44–67.
Cox, H.T. 1990. *The Global Cigarette: BAT and the Spread of International Business before 1939*. Ph.D. Dissertation, University of London.
Cox, H.T. 2000. *The Global Cigarette: Origins and Evolution of British American Tobacco, 1880–1945*. Oxford: Oxford University Press.
Crouchley, A.E. 1977 [1936]. *The Investment of Foreign Capital in Egyptian Companies and Public Debt*. New York: Arno Press.
El-Gritli, A.A.I. 1947. The Structure of Modern Industry in Egypt. *L'Egypte contemporaine* 38.
El-Sherbini, A.A., and A.F. Sherif. 1956. Marketing Problems in an Underdeveloped Country—Egypt. *L'egypte Contemporaine* 47: 5–85.

Gartashean, A.W. 1986. *Nyuter Yegiptosi Hayots' Patmutean Wamar, Patmutyum Yegiptos ahay Barerarneru yev Krtakan Wasta Tutuyunneru*, Vol 2. Venice: No Publisher.
Goldberg, E.J. 1983. *Tinker, Tailor, and Textile Worker: Class and Politics in Egypt 1930–1954*. Ph.D. Dissertation, University of California, Berkeley.
Goodman III, R.C. 1987. *The Role of the Tobacco Trade in Turkish-American Relations, 1923–1929*. MA Thesis, University of Richmond.
Hansen, B. 1979. Income and Consumption in Egypt, 1886/1887 to 1937. *International Journal of Middle Eastern Studies* 10: 27–47.
Haritatos, M., and P. Giakoumakis. 1997. *A History of the Greek Cigarette*. Athens: The Hellenic Literary and Historical Archive.
Kamil, F. 1985. *Ma'a al-haraka al-niqabiyya al-Misriyya fi nisfqarn*. Cairo: Dar al-Ghad al-'Arabi.
Kitroeff, A. 1989. *The Greeks in Egypt, 1919–1937: Ethnicity and Class*. London: Ithaca Press.
Labib Rizk, Y. 1997. Al-Ahram: A Diwan of Contemporary Life. *Al-Ahram Weekly*, 23–29 October.
Levy, C. 1937. *The Stock-Exchange Yearbook, 1937*. Cairo: No Publisher.
Mahfouz, N. 1977 [1947]. *Midaq Alley*. Trans. T. Le Gassick, 2nd ed. Washington, DC: Three Continents Press.
Owen, R., and Ş Pamuk. 1999. *A History of Middle East Economies in the Twentieth Century*. Cambridge, MA: Harvard University Press.
Partevean, S. 1918. *Egyptahay Tarets'uyto'e*. Alexandria: Gasabean Printers.
Ritzer, G. 2014. Prosumption: Evolution, Revolution, Or Eternal Return of the Same? *Journal of Consumer Culture* 14: 3–24.
Robinson, W.C., and F.H. El-Zanaty. 2006. *The Demographic Revolution in Modern Egypt*. Lanham, MD: Lexington Books.
Sékaly, A. 1914. La culture du tabac au point de vue de l'économie égyptienne. *L'Egypte contemporaine* 5.
Shechter, R. 2003. Selling Luxury: The Rise of the Egyptian Cigarette and the Transformation of the Egyptian Tobacco Market, 1850–1914. *International Journal of Middle East Studies* 35: 51–75.
Shechter, R. 2005. Reading Advertisements in a Colonial/Developing Context: Cigarette Advertising and Identity Politics in Egypt, c1919–1939. *Journal of Social History* 39: 483–503.
Shechter, R. 2006. *Smoking, Culture and Economy in the Middle East: The Egyptian Tobacco Market 1850–2000*. London: I.B. Tauris.
Topuzyan, H. Kh. 1978. *Yegiptosi Haykakan Gaghuti Patmutyun (1805–1952)*. Yerevan: Haykakan SSH Ga Hratarakchutyun.

Vallet, J. 1911. *Contribution à l'étude de la condition des ouvriers de la grande industrie au Caire*. Valence: Imprimerie Valentinoise.
Veblen, T. 1994 [1899]. *The Theory of the Leisure Class*. New York: Dover Publications.
Vitalis, R. 1995. *When Capitalists Collide: Business Conflict and the End of Empire in Egypt*. Berkeley: University of California Press.
Wright, A., and H.A. Cartwright, eds. 1909. *Twentieth Century Impressions of Egypt*. London: Lloyd's.

CHAPTER 5

Imperial Markets: The Anglo-Rhodesian Tobacco Trade in the Aftermath of World War II

Sibanengi Ncube

Introduction

This chapter examines the tobacco industry in Southern Rhodesia, a self-governing British colony from 1923 to 1965, in the context of British imperial and Anglo-American economic relations in the aftermath of World War II. It details the growing inroads and ambitions of Southern Rhodesian tobacco growers to dominate the British market in the face of pressure from the US. Despite having a traditional preference for American leaf, the UK was, due to postwar balance-of-payment difficulties, forced to realign its tobacco imports from dollar area sources to within the Empire, and Southern Rhodesia was able to capitalise on this. Unsurprisingly, the US did not take the threat to its global dominance in tobacco leaf exports lightly. This placed the UK at the centre of two

S. Ncube (✉)
University of the Free State, Bloemfontein, South Africa
e-mail: skancube@gmail.com

A. van Wickeren et al. (eds.), *Tobacco in Global Perspective, 1780–1960*, Cambridge Imperial and Post-Colonial Studies,
https://doi.org/10.1007/978-3-031-64411-5_5

competing interests. On the one hand was the US, keen to protect its UK market share, while on the other was Southern Rhodesia, determined to consolidate its position as a permanent tobacco exporter to the UK.

It is this complex Anglo-American-Southern Rhodesian relationship, ultimately characterised by clandestine deals and allegations of double standards, that is explored in this chapter. Drawing mainly on sources in the National Archives of Zimbabwe that offer Southern Rhodesian perspectives on the postwar international tobacco trade, and with a focus on the contested relationship between Southern Rhodesia and the UK, I seek to contribute to key debates on postwar imperial relations. Contrary to conventional wisdom that portrays colonies as hapless victims of an imposing empire, I provide evidence of a complex imperial-colonial relationship as the British attempted to balance competing and conflicting interests. In addition, by analysing the resulting US-Southern Rhodesia tobacco leaf trade rivalry and juxtaposing postwar British imperial relations with the practice of US foreign economic policy, I question the US postwar commitment to its professed notions of freer international trade.

After an initial section outlining the historical background, the period under scrutiny starts in 1947, the year in which the London Agreement, an arrangement between British imperial tobacco manufacturers and the Southern Rhodesian tobacco industry, secured the local tobacco industry a guaranteed market in the UK.[1] It ends in 1960, when the UK abandoned its dollar import restrictions, leaving Southern Rhodesia exposed to the vagaries of the global tobacco market.

Background

Though agriculture was to become a key pillar of the Southern Rhodesian economy, it was not originally at the centre of the territory's occupation in 1890, which was based on speculation by Cecil John Rhodes' British South Africa Company (BASC) that the territory harboured massive gold deposits. Years of prospecting, however, revealed that gold was not there in the anticipated quantities, and to recoup the costs of occupation and appease company shareholders other economic activities were explored, agriculture being one.

[1] Ncube (2019, pp. 28–34).

The exploitation of the colony's agricultural potential began in earnest with the 1908 adoption of its 'white agricultural policy.'[2] After experimentation with different crops, tobacco stood out for two reasons. First, it "had the attraction of offering quick returns on capital invested" which was "a necessity if immigrant settlers were to be attracted."[3] Second, and more importantly for the BSAC, it was "best grown in the previously neglected sandy soils so that the Company could…be able to sell many farms that had hitherto attracted few buyers."[4]

The period coincided with the mass mechanisation of the US and UK cigarette industry and when the UK Imperial Tobacco Company (ITC) was spreading its tentacles to southern Africa, having merged with the American Tobacco Company (ATC) to create British American Tobacco (BAT). ATC had attempted a take-over of the British tobacco industry, and, to counter this move, British manufacturers led by W. D. & H. O. Wills founded ITC. The ensuing rivalry and stiff competition led to the 1902 agreement whereby neither the UK nor the US would attempt to invade each other's markets and the newly formed BAT, owned two thirds by ATC and one-third by ITC, would operate in the rest of the world. BAT went on to set up cigarette-manufacturing operations in countries such as South Africa in 1904 and Nyasaland (today Malawi) in 1908, and actively encouraged the local growing of flue-cured leaf to serve the factories.[5]

For most of the colonial period, the production of nearly all tobacco in Southern Rhodesia was the preserve of white settler farmers. After mining failed to meet expectations and colonial administrators adopted their white agriculture policy, white settlers were regarded as the main agents of agricultural development, and the policy persisted after Southern Rhodesia became a self-governing British colony in 1923. European agriculture remained the cornerstone of settler government policy, based on the view that the attraction of fresh immigrants necessary to develop Southern Rhodesia as a colony of European settlement depended on the success of agriculture. Unlike in neighbouring Nyasaland, where peasant

[2] See Palmer (1970).

[3] Ibid.

[4] Hooper (1988, p. 69). Ncube and Nyamunda (2022).

[5] Ibid. p. 1125.

farmers grew dark tobacco, in Southern Rhodesia the dominant variety was flue-cured Virginia tobacco exclusively grown by white settler farmers.

The white settler government gave two convenient excuses for non-participation of Africans in the industry. First, they argued that allowing Africans to grow tobacco would compromise the quality of the crop and taint the international reputation of Southern Rhodesia as a tobacco leaf producer. This, the settler colonial state added, was because Africans lacked the sophistication to grow quality leaf. Second, the colonial administration patronisingly prevented Africans from embarking on cash-crop farming in general and tobacco growing in particular on the pretext that they lacked the capacity to strike a balance between cash and subsistence farming, which would result in their starvation. They only resorted to African producers when, for one reason or another, white farmers failed or showed no interest in a particular commodity, as was with the case with Nyasaland tobacco after the 1930s depression and Southern Rhodesian Turkish tobacco, after the settler government changed its policy in 1952 and actively encouraged African cultivation of the crop.[6]

The history of Southern Rhodesia's tobacco industry prior to World War II has received significant scholarly attention.[7] Suffice it to say that by the 1920s the colony's crop had outgrown its traditional market, South Africa, prompting the local industry to look for alternative outlets. The UK market became a key target. However, after the UK's long history of trade with the US, which saw British and world smokers accustomed to blends made from American leaf, entering that market was not easy. In addition, UK manufacturers were reluctant to "shatter the Anglo-American marketing understanding" reached in the early 1900s after the "tobacco wars" that led up to the creation of BAT.[8] This did not, however, deter Southern Rhodesia from persistently pursuing the UK tobacco market until the circumstances created by World War II, without which "there might never have been a Rhodesian break-through" and which altered the complexion of the international tobacco trade.[9]

[6] See Ncube (2022).

[7] See Clements and Harben (1962). Haviland (1953). Rubert (1998). Mbanga (1991). and Machingaidze (1980).

[8] Cox (2000).

[9] Tobacco Forum of Rhodesia, November (1961, p. 6).

The war had a considerable impact on Southern Rhodesia's tobacco industry, as it presented local growers with an opportunity to expand their market share in the UK and beyond.[10] Just before war broke out, "the British Government and British buyers were looking towards [Southern] Rhodesia as a reliable source of tobacco supplies in the event of hostilities."[11] Not surprisingly, when the war cut off trade with the US, British manufacturers turned to Southern Rhodesia for supplies. Demand for tobacco increased as the war transformed smoking habits across the world. For instance, under the rigours of the war, consumption of cigarettes increased among soldiers.[12] At the same time, there was an increase in smoking among women as they entered the job market in great numbers during this period. Importantly, demand grew exponentially for Virginia leaf, the variety used primarily in machine-made cigarettes, which was Southern Rhodesia's dominant crop.

Postwar Market Consolidation

The global tobacco trade ushered in by the war continued in a more pronounced manner in its aftermath. The UK emerged from the war bruised and battered.[13] Due to a balance-of-payments disequilibrium, it restricted dollar area imports, which included American tobacco. This set the stage for Anglo-American cleavages and American-Southern Rhodesian trade rivalry. In what has been termed the "second colonial occupation," the UK looked within its Empire for salvation.[14] Among the commodities in high demand in the UK was flue-cured tobacco, which, alongside copper and sugar among other essentials, was accorded first priority status on the UK's Colonial Primary Products Committee (CPPC) commodity priority list.[15]

Southern Rhodesia had already proved itself as one of the non-dollar sources of the crop with the greatest potential. In 1939, the year war broke out; Southern Rhodesia and Nyasaland contributed eleven per

[10] Hooper (1988, p. 78).

[11] Clements and Harben (1962, p. 128).

[12] Tate (1999, p. 119).

[13] Krozewski (2001). Gamble (1985). Gallagher (1982). Hopkins (2018).

[14] See Low and Lonsdale (1976). Hopkins (2018, p. 470).

[15] Matthew (2017).

cent of tobacco leaf used in the UK as compared to seven- and five-per cent contributions from India and Canada, respectively.[16] Given its long-cherished dream of permanently establishing itself on the UK tobacco market, Southern Rhodesia embraced the opportunity presented in the postwar years.

It is important to note that, were Southern Rhodesia to have faced competition within the Empire, it would have been from India and Canada. However, by falling outside the sterling area, Canada posed no threat in the circumstances of the postwar dollar crisis bedevilling Britain. That left India as the only other possible significant competitor. However, Southern Rhodesian tobacco growers had never looked at India as posing any serious threat to their interests in the imperial tobacco market. This is despite recent evidence showing the centrality of Indian tobacco in popularising imperial varieties in Britain, itself a foundation upon which Southern Rhodesian growers later built to expand their UK market share.[17] Whenever Southern Rhodesian tobacco interests complained about Indian tobacco it was for the alleged flooding of the market with poor quality leaf that was bringing down the reputation of Empire tobacco. Interestingly, the same argument was used to prevent Africans in Southern Rhodesia from venturing into tobacco production for export, adding a significant racial dimension to the history of imperial commodities, the details of which lie beyond our remit here.

How did Southern Rhodesia manage to capitalise on the postwar global economic environment? In answering this question, it is imperative to shed light on the colony's constitutional framework. Unlike other colonies, Southern Rhodesia occupied a unique position within the British Empire and Commonwealth. Its Responsible Government status granted in 1923 gave it significant diplomatic and constitutional leverage. The territory passed from the remit of the Colonial Office to the Dominions Office, which after the war became the Commonwealth Relations Office. This explains why Southern Rhodesia was early represented by a High Commissioner in London and was in a unique position to lobby British industrialists.

Significantly, Southern Rhodesia was represented alongside other dominions and the UK at the Ottawa Conference on tariffs in 1932 and

[16] Ibid.

[17] Kuncheria (Unpublished work in progress).

was increasingly treated as a dominion for almost all practical purposes, with its own prime minister and cabinet with internal control of defence. The governor essentially acted only on the advice of his Southern Rhodesian cabinet, with the British government's role being very marginal, and Anglo-Rhodesian relations were channelled through their respective High Commissioners rather than the Governor.[18]

The situation did not drastically change when Southern Rhodesia joined Northern Rhodesia (now Zambia) and Nyasaland (now Malawi) to form the Federation of Rhodesia and Nyasaland in 1953 until its demise in 1963. During its existence, the Federation had autonomy that included the creation of a Dominion-style Department of External Affairs, with the expansion of its diplomatic service not only in Britain but overseas. Sir Edgar Whitehead, for example, served as the Rhodesian representative in Washington, attached to the British Embassy with the rank of Minister, until his return to become Prime Minister. Lobbying by the tobacco industry during this period was not entirely a Southern Rhodesian diplomatic responsibility as the Federal High Commissioner and staff in London also lobbied alongside the Southern Rhodesian High Commissioner and staff also in London at Rhodesia House. Given the dominance of Southern Rhodesia in the Federal set up, and the pre-eminence of tobacco in both the Federal and Southern Rhodesian economies, matters to do with the tobacco trade received serious attention across the board.

Southern Rhodesian tobacco growers' determination to enter the UK tobacco market is well documented.[19] Early efforts to penetrate this market met with little success. When the war and its aftermath loosened the US grip on the UK market to give Southern Rhodesian growers an opportunity to enter, they were conscious of the fact that the favourable environment was temporary. This realisation influenced their approach during deliberations leading up to the 1947 London deal. The major thrust of the local tobacco growers was to stabilise their industry by entrenching local leaf in the UK so that manufacturers or consumers would have no desire to revert to Virginia tobacco from the US.[20] To this end, they were also aware that the advantages afforded by the dollar crisis

[18] Palley (1966). Lowry (2010).

[19] See Phimister (1988). Hooper (1988). Machingaidze (1980). Clements and Harben (1962). and Rubert (1998).

[20] Tobacco General, TMB Meeting Minutes, 22 January 1948, NAZ, 2570/TBC1, Vol. 1.

alone were not a solid basis on which to establish an enduring presence on the UK market.

Southern Rhodesian growers appreciated the need for their product to sell on its own merits. To that end, they fought to make their leaf competitive[21] through coming up with measures to improve the quality of their crop.[22] For instance, they lobbied for the transfer of tobacco research services from the Department of Agriculture to the better-resourced Tobacco Research Board (TRB) and, thereafter, engaged an expert scientist from Canada, Dr F. Stinson, as its head. They proposed three amendments to the Tobacco Marketing Act: first, to prohibit growing unproven and unsatisfactory types of tobacco; second, a provision that would make it compulsory for new entrants into the industry to have at least two years' experience or employ a competent manager; and third, a form of production control whereby, if there were to be market saturation, a method of penalising the consistently lower-grade and lower-yield producer would be introduced.

Among other interventions, they committed to a research programme costing nearly £1m for the five-year period 1955–1960, with the primary purpose of improving the production of quality tobacco suitable for UK manufacturers.[23] Looking beyond the UK market, they sought to penetrate Continental Europe and other markets, a task described by Minister of Agriculture John Graylin as "relentless and unceasing."[24] In 1954, a select committee of the Rhodesia Tobacco Association (RTA) interviewed seven merchant buyers to establish a number of issues. First, they asked whether the merchants were indeed giving worldwide market cover. Second, they elicited suggestions as to how the Rhodesian Tobacco Marketing Board (RTMB) could assist them in their exploitation of new markets. Lastly, they sought their views on the future of the industry from a general marketing perspective. The local industry had to contend in particular with the US, which, in the words of the colony's tobacco

[21] Ncube (2022).

[22] RTA Memorandum, NAZ, RH 27/3/3.

[23] Note of Meeting, Commonwealth Relations Office, 19 April 1955, NAZ, RH 27/3/3.

[24] Anonymous (1961).

representative in London, Captain Ian Morten, was "extremely active in Continental markets."[25]

According to the then RTA President, R.G. Hoskins Davies, Southern Rhodesia and the US were "in direct competition for overseas markets."[26] Across the Zambezi, in neighbouring Northern Rhodesia, J. J. Collins, Chief Tobacco Adviser to the Government, in 1954, also confirmed the strength of US activities, attributing that year's weak demand from the continent of Europe to "the strenuous efforts being made by the US to gain complete dominance in the British tobacco trade."[27] Against this background, Rhodesian tobacco growers mounted a strong campaign for markets, both internally and externally.

There were two external offices directly involved in advancing the interests of Rhodesian agriculture, but mostly tobacco, by then the country's key agricultural commodity. The first was the office of the agricultural representative, mostly referred to as the tobacco representative, who was for the most part Morten, himself a former tobacco grower. The second was the office of the agricultural adviser, occupied during this period by Major Peter Spearing, who was charged among other things with providing periodic reports on the world tobacco outlook as it affected the local industry.[28] The two were supported by the Southern Rhodesian High Commissioner, and after 1953 by the Federal High Commissioner and his assistant. In addition, trade commissioners based at Rhodesia House, due to the sheer importance of the tobacco industry, frequently dabbled in such matters.

As part of his duties, the agricultural representative frequently travelled across Continental Europe to advance the interests of the home industry. Some of his key trips included the 1956 'goodwill mission' to Germany for two weeks at the beginning of May. He contacted "many German government officials and tobacco manufacturers with satisfactory results" during the course of this trip.[29] Towards the end of May, he visited Denmark in the company of the trade commissioner. Again, he took the

[25] Undated Report of the Tobacco Representative, NAZ, RH 27/3/3.

[26] Anonymous (1960 (d)).

[27] Anonymous (1954).

[28] NAZ, RH 27/3/3, Note of Meeting, Commonwealth Relations Office, 19 April 1955.

[29] Annual Report of the Agricultural Adviser, 1956, NAZ, RH 27/3/3.

opportunity to meet with Danish government officials and tobacco manufacturers. In the UK, among the places he visited was Bristol to meet with Directors of ITC and see the Carreras factory, as well as visiting Gallaher's in Belfast.[30]

In 1958, the agricultural representative embarked on a month-long trip to Continental Europe, again on Rhodesian tobacco business. From 15 May to 20 June, he visited Finland, Norway, Denmark, Holland, and France, among other countries. His findings from these visits revealed that the US was penetrating world markets, using both orthodox and unorthodox means. With its own mounting surplus of agricultural stocks due to the government's price-support system, the US passed the Agricultural Trade Development and Assistance Act of 1954, also known as Public Law 480 (PL480). The aim of this piece of legislation was "to reduce agricultural surplus by increasing world consumption of American agricultural products."[31] Under the terms of PL480, the US could make domestic and foreign donations or enter into barter contracts in respect of surplus produce. By an amendment of 1959, the US President was empowered "to make long-term supply contracts to friendly countries" whereby the US could supply surplus commodities to other countries annually over a period of up to ten years and accept payment over a period of up to 20 years.

These arrangements dented Rhodesia's chances of expanding its tobacco markets globally. In Finland, for example, the agricultural adviser discovered that a recent PL480 deal had been arranged between the US and Finland for three million [US] dollars. France was put in a better position to buy American tobacco for their luxury cigarettes than they were to buy high-grade Rhodesian owing to PL480 arrangements whereby they could pay for it in francs.[32]

To promote Rhodesian tobacco, Spearing arranged to send the *Weekly Tobacco Situation*, a newsletter published at Rhodesia House in London, to all his contacts on the Continent. The newsletter was for circulation during the selling season, as well as during the year when there was anything of special tobacco interest to report. The buying and growing

[30] Report of a Mission by the Agricultural Adviser, 11/5/58 to 20/6/58, NAZ, RH 27/3/3.

[31] Fish (1963, p. 114).

[32] NAZ, Box RH 27/2/3-6, File RH 27/3/3.

sides of the Rhodesian tobacco industry complemented their overseas representatives' efforts by forming the Tobacco Export Promotion Council of Rhodesia (TEPCOR) in 1958, and in 1961, the organisation incorporated Nyasaland to become the Tobacco Export Promotion Council of Rhodesia and Nyasaland (TEPCORN).

Changing the organisation into a statutory body enabled its representatives to discuss trade impediments on a government-to-government basis.[33] The organisation's mandate was to foster worldwide interest in local tobacco by "maintaining the most energetic campaign abroad."[34] The incorporation of Nyasaland into TEPCOR was smooth because Nyasaland tobacco did not compete with Southern Rhodesian tobacco. In Nyasaland, unlike in Southern Rhodesia, the collapse of the European flue-cured tobacco industry during the 1930s depression had seen a rise in smallholder fire-cured tobacco production, which became the mainstay of Nyasaland's tobacco industry. Just like in the case of Southern Rhodesia, Britain was the main market for Nyasaland tobacco. However, no rivalry emerged between the two since Southern Rhodesia concentrated on light flue-cured tobacco while Nyasaland grew mainly dark fire-cured varieties. In addition, Nyasaland looked beyond Britain to market its tobacco. It targeted other markets such as Sierra Leone, Belgian Congo, Canary Islands, Netherlands, Belgium, and Sweden.[35]

Some of TEPCORN's objectives included promoting good public relations and friendly personal contacts with all tobacco importers, discussing trends in smoking tastes in their countries, blends, and possible changes required in the leaf, as well as engaging government officials regarding present and future policies on local production or imports. In addition, it collated statistics and commercial intelligence for use in the Council or for dissemination back home. The RTA used such information to make informed periodic production recommendations to growers. TEPCORN representatives also discussed Central African political developments with importers to assure them of continuity of supply, in light of the fears they had about the future prospects of white rule.[36]

[33] Tobacco Export Promotion Council, NAZ, File F226/1217/F29A.

[34] Ibid.

[35] Davies (1964).

[36] Anonymous (1960 (e)).

These activities had the blessings of the government. In 1959, the Minister of Agriculture, accompanied by TEPCORN Chairman Evan Campbell and the trade commissioner at Rhodesia House, led another mission to Europe to establish contacts and promote the sale of Rhodesian tobacco abroad.[37] The mission aimed at developing new markets and expanding existing ones, visiting Finland, Denmark, Norway, Sweden, Holland, France, and London. The next year, another delegation embarked on a tour of Australia, New Zealand, Japan, China, the Middle East, and North Africa. Following the tour, they signed a pact with Japan for middle- and high-grade tobacco, and mounted competition to British and Australian buyers for better-quality tobacco on the Salisbury Auction Floors.

This was before what was described as "the most ambitious international marketing probe ever conducted on behalf of the Federation's tobacco industry," which was "to ensure that when manufacturers think of tobacco they automatically think of Rhodesia and Nyasaland."[38] Individually or together, members of the delegation visited Spain, Portugal, Algeria, France, Morocco, Austria, Czechoslovakia, Germany, Holland, Belgium, Finland, Sweden, Norway, Denmark, Switzerland, and Italy. The tours sought to secure up-to-date information on the production and marketing of tobacco throughout the world and to maintain and widen contacts,[39] and it was the networks and markets established because of these tours that were to prove important in the late 1960s and 1970s, after Rhodesia declared unilateral independence in 1965 and the UK retaliated with sanctions and an embargo on the Rhodesian tobacco export trade.[40]

The rapid expansion of the Rhodesian export trade in tobacco occurred at the expense of the US. According to Frank Clements and Edward Harben in their 1962 study of the Rhodesian tobacco industry, claims were not over-exaggerated when boasting that "after 1947, Rhodesian tobacco…had nothing to fear" and that it was rather the US grower who was on the defensive and saw his share of the international trade

[37] See Federation of Rhodesia and Nyasaland, Parliamentary Debates, Federal Assembly, Vol. 10, April 6 to July 23, 1959, Ministerial Statement.

[38] Tobacco Export Promotion Council, AZ, File F226/1217/F29A.

[39] Anonymous (1960(c)).

[40] See Armstrong (1987).

in leaf steadily declining.[41] Whereas prior to the war the US share of UK unmanufactured tobacco requirements stood at 70%, by 1965 it had fallen to about 40%. India, Canada, Southern Rhodesia, and other minor exporters shared the balance.[42] This was corroborated by Michael Hooper, in his 1988 thesis on the Rhodesian industry 1945–1965, documenting how the US share in the world export trade dropped from 66% in 1954 to 57% in 1961, against Southern Rhodesia's share increasing to almost one-third.[43] Clearly, this became a matter of US concern, seeing Rhodesia—and rightly so—as a fierce competitor in world tobacco markets.

The US Response

To understand the US response to the threat posed by Southern Rhodesia brings us to the complexity of postwar US foreign economic policy, whose intricacies are beyond the scope of this chapter.[44] Suffice it here to provide an overview of the dynamics shaping the agricultural dimension of US economic foreign policy in order to comprehend the source of contradictions inherent in its practice related to Southern Rhodesia.

Michael Mastanduno, in his 1988 study of US trade strategy, provides a perfect starting point in this regard. US foreign economic policy, he observed, was informed by the fact that the US state was relatively weak domestically, yet powerful internationally. According to Mastanduno, domestic weakness enabled private interests to penetrate and influence the state, making it difficult for the state to achieve its policy preference in the face of domestic opposition. International strength referred to the high degree of resources controlled by the US relative to other nation states, as well as the ability to translate those resources into influence over international outcomes.[45]

Therein lay the contradiction that was manifest in US relations with Southern Rhodesia in the postwar era. Whereas for its international stature and geopolitical considerations, the US "adopted the objective

[41] Clements and Harben (1962, p. 153).

[42] Dunlop (1971, p. 45).

[43] Ibid.

[44] See Slichter (1954). Mastanduno (1988). and Hardin (1960).

[45] Mastanduno (1988, p. 121).

of strengthening other economies shortly after the Second World War," in agricultural matters it had to defer to the domestic pressure coming from the powerful 'farm bloc' of Congress in the country's governmental system.[46] Under pressure from its strong domestic agricultural lobby, it was determined to reverse the growing Southern Rhodesian dominance in the UK and global tobacco markets. To this end, it launched a spirited effort not only to reclaim lost markets but also to break into hitherto uncharted territories.

US hyper-activity on the global tobacco market did not escape the attention of Southern Rhodesia's tobacco representative in London, who, in one of his reports, complained about the US "heavy and unremitting" pressure to sell "anywhere" and "everywhere."[47] Reporting on the contradiction between US actual conduct and what it preached, he noted:

> There have been growing signs of impatience with America preaching freer trade to all and sundry and doing nothing to help by her own example … There is hardly a unit of the Commonwealth that has not complained loudly of the unfair competition of America's ruthless disposal of surplus products.[48]

Allegations of US double standards became a source of friction between the two parties and the basis of Southern Rhodesian complaints in various fora.

The increased US presence in world tobacco markets was achieved through a combination of strategies. At policy level, there was greater emphasis on the development of foreign markets and stepped-up international trade. To this end, US Secretary of Agriculture Ezra Taft Benson in 1953 announced the establishment of the Foreign Agricultural Service (FAS) as a new unit in the US Department of Agriculture (USDA). Its task was to devote full time to the development of off-shore markets for US agricultural produce. In addition to other responsibilities, FAS provided information, marketing, and financial assistance to prospective exporters. More significantly, it provided technical assistance and research relating to foreign competition, consumption habits, and transport costs.

[46] Hardin (1960, p. 101).

[47] Tobacco Report No. 45 of 1954, NAZ RH 27/3/3.

[48] Ibid.

This policy statement was immediately followed by a Bill introduced in the House of Representatives to authorise the creation of an Agricultural Foreign Service in the Department of Agriculture.[49] House Bill 8033 provided for the transfer of agricultural attachés from the Department of State to USDA. FAS had first been in the Department of Agriculture, created by an Act of 1930, and this had been reversed in 1939 by a Presidential re-organisation whereby FAS was transferred to the Department of State. In support of the new Bill 8033, Hon. Samuel W. Yorty of California emphasised the US desperation and urgency to set up "the best foreign agricultural service."[50]

In 1954, the Bill was passed into law, after which agricultural attachés were moved from the Department of State to USDA before being posted in foreign markets as the USDA's 'eyes and ears.'[51] In 1956, FAS carried out an assessment of the impact of Southern Rhodesia's tobacco on its own industry.[52] Seven years later, Albert R. Davies was dispatched to carry out yet another 'on-the-spot-survey' of the Federation of Rhodesia and Nyasaland's tobacco, on the basis of which the Director of the American Tobacco Division, Hugh C. Kiger, conceded that the Rhodesian tobacco industry was "of great significance to the US tobacco industry."[53]

The second and more controversial US strategy was what Anthony Hopkins in *American Empire* (2018) described as Washington's use of "financial resources of the US as a crowbar to open protected trading regimes throughout the world, and especially major markets in Europe."[54] In line with this, 'aid' was used to penetrate world tobacco markets. After mounting surplus agricultural stocks because of the government's price-support system—which, according to a 1960 study, the Executive had been forced into by the farm bloc[55]—PL480 was passed "to reduce agricultural surplus by increasing world consumption of American agricultural products."[56] Within a year, the debilitating

[49] Congressional Record, May 26, 1954.

[50] Ibid.

[51] Habenstreit, 'FAS Attachés", 16.

[52] See for instance United States Foreign Agricultural Service (1956).

[53] See Davies (1964).

[54] Hopkins (2018, p. 474).

[55] Hardin (1960, p. 100).

[56] Fish (1963, p. 114).

effect of PL480 deals was clear on countries such as Argentina, Canada, Mexico, and Peru, and the programme was subject to "harsh criticism of interference with production and marketing of other exporting as well as recipient countries."[57] The impact of PL480 on Southern Rhodesia,[58] as we shall see, was particularly hard.

Rivalry in the British Market

Most contentious for Southern Rhodesian tobacco growers was the UK market. In view of their historical desire to permanently establish themselves in this market, they had carved out their industry in its image, and the 1947 London agreement had firmly tied Southern Rhodesian tobacco interests to the UK market. The RTA's huge investment in research was designed first and foremost to fulfil the agreement's quality clause, which obliged them to comply with the expectations of UK tobacco manufacturers and involved sacrificing other markets on the altar of stability. The London deal did not amuse the US tobacco industry, and it did not hide its intention to reclaim lost ground.

The Anglo-American-Southern Rhodesian tension in the global tobacco trade was subdued in the immediate postwar era, as the UK justified its dollar import restrictions in terms of its postwar dollar crisis. However, this lost traction in the mid- to late 1950s when the UK dollar situation improved, and there was a clear movement towards full sterling convertibility,[59] such that "by the mid-1950s the empire had played its assigned, and heroic, part in rebuilding Britain after the war."[60] The UK's new thrust was to "attempt to adjust established imperial relations to the requirements of liberal multilateralism."[61] This entailed "a re-ordering of relationships developed during the war and its aftermath"[62] and marked the beginnings of a clear divergence between the UK and Southern Rhodesian tobacco interests. Leveraging on this, the US intensified its push for the UK to drop its import restrictions and tariff preference, in

57 Hultman (1961).

58 Ncube and Nyamunda (2022).

59 Krozewski (1996).

60 Hopkins (2018, p. 484).

61 Ibid.

62 Krozewski (2001, p. 149).

a move that was sure to set them against Southern Rhodesian tobacco interests.

Nothing demonstrates the divergence of interests within the British Empire better than the sentiments of the British Empire Producers Organisation (BEPO), of which Southern Rhodesia was a member. Whereas under the General Agreement on Tariffs and Trade (GATT) the UK had committed to a reduction in trade restrictions in general, and preferences in particular, BEPO had different views altogether. For BEPO, to create confidence to attract investment within the Empire there was a need "to discriminate in favour of the Commonwealth producer as a matter of deliberate, declared and permanent policy" not "as a make-shift policy imposed ...by balance of payment difficulties."[63] It called for denouncing those sections of GATT that limited their "right to discriminate in favour of... partners in the Commonwealth."[64] This position was not only incompatible with US interests, but, as argued by Gerold Krozewski in his 2001 work on money and the end of the British Empire, was also irreconcilable with the British policy shift from the immediate postwar imperial mentality of a 'second colonial occupation' to liberal multilateralism in the late 1950s; and this was bound to create problems.

BEPO, like the RTA, took exception to US double standards. The US was accused of preaching freer international trade, on the one hand, while, on the other, it was making clandestine and unorthodox moves to gain unfair advantages in world tobacco markets by manipulating its aid policy. According to the Southern Rhodesian tobacco adviser, the US bolstered its export tobacco trade 'by one or other devious means.' Unlike Southern Rhodesia, which exported almost its entire crop, the US could finance the 'devious' means through heavy local consumption and internal excise unlike the Rhodesian industry that was built up on a 96% export market.[65]

The US used PL480 deals not only to penetrate new Continental, Asian, and African markets, but also to effectively limit Southern Rhodesia's chances of entering those markets. The same applied to the British market. Thus, in October 1953 the UK purchased for British sterling US 'surplus' tobacco worth US$20m under another piece of legislation,

[63] 'The Economic Debate,' B.E.P.O Newsletter, 12 August 1952, NAZ, RH27/3/6.

[64] Ibid.

[65] Annual Report of the Agricultural Adviser, 1956, NAZ, RH 27/3/3.

the Mutual Security Act (MSA). This move was condemned as "a blow to the protection afforded by inconvertibility."[66] What most angered the Southern Rhodesian authorities was that neither the Board of Trade nor the Commonwealth Relations Office had consulted them prior to this move, and a delegation from the RTMB, supported by the Acting High Commissioner, directly protested to the President of the Board of Trade in November 1953.

Notwithstanding the 1953 protest, a year later information reached the tobacco representative that there were negotiations between the US and the UK for the supply of a further US$30m worth of American surplus tobacco under MSA terms. Despite the effect of such unfair trading practice on the Rhodesian and Nyasaland tobacco markets, Southern Rhodesia was again not consulted. Then, in the early summer of 1955, the UK took another US$15m worth of tobacco from the US and paid for it in sterling, which was used to build houses for the US Air Force.[67]

The RTA's major worry was that the more readily American tobacco was made available through these non-commercial means, the less incentive there would be to purchase Empire tobacco.[68] While they accepted the inevitability of the results of full convertibility in due course, they considered that purchases of MSA 'surplus' tobacco, 'virtually a free gift' to the UK, distorted the free market forces in the world tobacco export trade. Worse still, around this time the Southern Rhodesian tobacco 'ambassadors' at Rhodesia House received details of the amendments made to the 1954 MSA, according to which it became apparent that pressure by the agricultural bloc had succeeded in removing those clauses in the 1953 Act that related to safeguarding the trade of friendly countries. The Rhodesian industry once again called for a very strong protest to be made against such deals.

Apart from MSA deals, British manufacturers, in connivance with the Board of Trade, were accused of "secret moves ... to get additional American tobacco" by other means.[69] In his monthly report for November 1955, Spearing, in his capacity as the Southern Rhodesian tobacco adviser,

[66] RTA Memorandum on United Kingdom Tobacco Market, Part I, NAZ, RH 27/3/3.

[67] Note of a Meeting, Commonwealth Relations Office, 17 May 1956, NAZ, RH 27/3/3.

[68] RTA Memorandum on United Kingdom Tobacco Market, Part I.

[69] S. S. Murray Memorandum, 17/01/1955, NAZ, RH27/3/6.

reported he had received “a confidential memorandum from the Board of Trade to the British tobacco manufacturers and merchants informing them that they could arrange with Canadian and US tobacco dealers to buy tobacco on their behalf, or borrow dollars from banks there to make their own purchases; no total announced.”[70]

Spearing, and with him the entire tobacco industry back home, found this to be especially galling when it recurred ‘with monotonous regularity’ at a season of the year when local growers were deciding on their acreage to plant for the forthcoming season. Rhodesian local tobacco growers felt that Britain lacked the moral standing to backstab them through clandestine deals given the sacrifices that the local industry had made in the immediate postwar period in prioritising British buyers ahead of others at the Salisbury Auction Floors. Export control permits issued at the instance of Britain, for example, had granted Britain the favoured status of a priority market that needed to be satisfied ahead of competing interests.[71]

Given the ‘somewhat cavalier treatment’ the local industry was receiving over the whole question of these end-of-season advances for additional American leaf, Spearing called upon his government to engage with the UK government to deal with these issues. To counter “the combined pressure of American interests and British manufacturers” which was “being constantly applied to the British Government,” he called on the Rhodesian government to “emphasise the importance of our tobacco industry to the present stability of the Federation, its influence on our food production and its continuing importance in our planned expansion and I would further like to suggest that this should be reiterated not less than annually, for men in government offices change very fast.”[72]

Premising its argument on allegations of double standards on the part of the US, Rhodesia took its protests against PL480 to the 1960/61 GATT negotiations. The Undersecretary for Agriculture, V. M. Wadsworth, delivered the protest to the seventh session of the 1960/1961 GATT conference in strong terms very rarely heard at GATT. Wadsworth admitted that his delegation was “at a loss to find words

[70] Tobacco adviser, 1954 Annual Report, NAZ RH 27/3/3.

[71] See Ncube (2019).

[72] Tobacco adviser, 1954 Annual Report, NAZ RH 27/3/3.

within the language of normal diplomatic use to express its feelings about these transactions."[73] Notwithstanding the 1955 GATT conference resolution on orderly disposal of surplus agricultural products on world markets, compelling a nation carrying out surplus disposals to consult those countries whose trade might be affected by such transactions, the US continued to act with impunity, cutting deal after deal without consulting anyone. Despite repeated protests in GATT, the Food and Agricultural Organisation, and other diplomatic channels, the US continued to roll out its programme of disposing of its surplus tobacco, without any consultations with Rhodesia.[74]

The major cause of discontent among Rhodesian growers was what they felt to be a clear case of US double standards. They considered PL480 deals to be inconsistent with the notion of free trade, viewing them as distorting world trade, the same grounds upon which the US launched its relentless attack on the Commonwealth tariff system. The US, Southern Rhodesia argued, could not have it both ways: using GATT protocols to attack the Commonwealth preferential tariff and at the same time cutting PL480 deals with more deleterious effects on free trade than the Commonwealth preference.

It was against this backdrop that Southern Rhodesian tobacco growers were "of the opinion that a strong line should be taken with the US in any context which might arise."[75] They felt that, contrary to their commitment through GATT to a policy of positively assisting the economies of less-developed countries, US actions did not always square up with words. Through its PL480 deals, it abandoned its "professed desire to promote the well-being of Central Africa," they argued.[76] Graylin himself reinforced this point, arguing that US moves to push for the Commonwealth preference to be scrapped could "only prejudice a major product of an under-developed country which is so essential to the development of its economy."[77]

[73] Agricultural Correspondent (1960).

[74] Tobacco adviser, 1954 Annual Report, NAZ RH 27/3/3.

[75] TEPCOR Secretary Letter to the Minister of Agriculture, 4 August 1960, NAZ, RH27/3/7.

[76] Ibid.

[77] Herald Correspondent (1960).

The 'aid' tobacco deals were just one side of the coin in Anglo-American-Southern Rhodesian relations. Calls for trade liberalisation, which were muted in the early 1950s but later grew louder towards the close of the 1950s, were another matter of great concern to Rhodesian tobacco growers.[78] With liberalisation imminent, and fully aware of its implications for the local industry, the RTA made efforts to ring-fence its only remaining long-held advantage, the Commonwealth preference. However, efforts to have the preference binding and increased were to no avail, since, according to the British, "Any increase in preference would involve a head-on collision [with the US] in the GATT."[79] In the Board of Trade's view, tampering with the preference would set a precedent for a US review of relations, which would harm UK interests on US markets.[80]

Faced with uncertainty, and with liberalisation inevitable, Southern Rhodesia shifted focus to minimise the impact and spelt out the terms and conditions under which they were prepared to accede to liberalisation. First, they urged the UK government to take "the opportunity which liberalisation would present to speak to the US authorities about the more objectionable features of their policy for tobacco disposals in terms of Public Law 480."[81] Second, they required UK assurances that no request for a reduction in the preference would be considered, at least at the 1960/1961 GATT negotiations. Finally, they demanded an undertaking by the Board of Trade to consult at any time should the proposal for a reduction in the preference arose. When the UK acceded to all the conditions, Southern Rhodesia accepted the proposals, after which 1 February was confirmed as the date on which liberalisation took effect.[82]

The abolition of the restrictions that came with liberalisation meant that from then on local tobacco was to compete in the UK on equal terms with American and Canadian tobacco. The only slight advantage it had was the non-binding Commonwealth preference that was under constant US attack. With the 1960/1961 GATT multilateral tariff negotiations approaching, Southern Rhodesia was in a quandary. They had in their possession intelligence to the effect that the US was going to press

[78] Ncube and Nyamunda (2022).

[79] Ibid.

[80] R. Metcalf letter to J. Ward, 14 January 1960, NAZ, File F114/213.

[81] J. M. Caldicott letter to Metcalf, 19 January 1960, NAZ, File F114/213.

[82] Anonymous (1960(a)).

hard for the total removal of the Commonwealth tariff preference. In view of this, the Prime Minister's office mounted a diplomatic offensive in the UK to safeguard the preference, but the response from the UK was not encouraging. According to the British High Commissioner, the UK was increasingly under pressure from the US government "to remove those of our remaining import controls which still affect them; we can no longer plead currency shortage, and the plea that the economy of the Federation benefits by the maintenance of the control on tobacco would not be to the point. We have, therefore, to face the situation that indefinite maintenance of this control cannot be justified."[83]

The Rhodesian situation was compounded by the 'wind of change' behind political challenges from the late 1950s to early 1960s when the Federation was heading towards breakdown.[84] Southern Rhodesia's unsure constitutional future was cause for concern among customers who were worried about continuity of tobacco supply. The then President of the Tobacco Trade Association, the buying side of the industry, was quoted by the main newspaper, the *Rhodesia Herald*, complaining about "the welter of political suspicion and uncertainty" in the country, which he feared would jeopardise business.[85]

Returning from an international trip, Campbell reiterated the same fears. On 5 October 1960, he told the *Rhodesia Herald* that Rhodesian customers in Europe were beginning to believe that Rhodesia would go the same way as the rest of Africa. As Hooper later observed, competitors in the tobacco export trade exploited the uncertainty that this created: "Rhodesia's competitors for tobacco markets, most notably the US were able to use Rhodesia's political problems as a means to win back markets lost to Rhodesia during the period of dollar restrictions."[86] When these fears are added to the hardening of global tobacco markets during this period, it remains unclear as to what would have happened to the local industry even if Rhodesian Premier Ian Smith had not proclaimed the unilateral declaration of independence (UDI) Rhodesia in 1965. Following UDI, the imposition of sanctions by the UK and

[83] Acting UK High Commissioner, Letter to C. H. Thomson, 21 December 1959, National Archives of Zimbabwe, hereafter NAZ, File F114/213.

[84] See Cohen (2017).

[85] Anonymous (1960(b)).

[86] Hooper (1988, p. 9).

the UN triggered a massive reconfiguration of the Rhodesian tobacco industry. Free and unfettered auction sales gave way to sales mediated by the Tobacco Corporation, while the sanctions-inspired suspension of open auctions, introduction of production control through the quota system, and diversification saw a considerable reduction of tobacco growers.[87]

Conclusion

This chapter set out to chart Southern Rhodesian perspectives on the complicated and entangled relationship involving Southern Rhodesia, the UK, and the US in the global tobacco export trade of post-World War II. It also analysed the changes in the trade following changed circumstances brought about by the war, casting light on how, faced with dollar shortages, Britain imposed restrictions on the importation of tobacco from the US. Within the UK, tobacco manufacturers still preferred American leaf and only reluctantly settled for Empire sources due to the dollar import restrictions imposed by the Exchequer. Once the situation permitted, they proved keen to go back to American leaf.

Southern Rhodesian growers, on the other hand, were not content with just being regarded as a stopgap market. They viewed the postwar situation as an opportunity to establish their leaf mainly in the UK and also in Continental Europe and on Asian and other markets. Consequently, they attached much importance to the British imperial and later Commonwealth preferences, which gave them an edge over US tobacco on the UK market. However, this was inconsistent with GATT protocols, to which the three were signatories, and whose major thrust was to eliminate discriminatory commercial practices.

The chapter explored the problems created by this mix, and how each party tried to safeguard its interests. It revealed the contradictions between the US postwar broader foreign policy goals of advancing free international trade and rendering assistance to less-developed countries, and the practicalities of safeguarding its domestic economic interests, which led to the cutting of deals, sometimes clandestinely, exposing double standards. Interestingly, for the US, its foreign economic policy, which was prima facie contradictory to its proclaimed postwar policy towards developing countries, revealed the complexities of balancing

87 Ncube (2022).

domestic interests against foreign policy considerations. The farm bloc in Congress flexed its muscles in a way that defined US agricultural policy even when, as in the case of Public Law 480, it ran contrary to its broader foreign policy direction.

The Anglo-American-Southern Rhodesian relations are also revelatory of how racial and imperial sentiments interacted in shaping the contours of imperial market relations. Rhodesian tobacco growers drew on imperial sentiment to bolster their case against American tobacco's dominance on the UK market: their 'imperial citizenship' was the basis for excluding American tobacco. In this regard, as Cheri Kuncheria has correctly observed in the Indian context, 'Britishness' was an important resource for white producers in the colonies to deploy in marketing their products in the home country.[88] However, when dealing with Indian competition and African producers, the emphasis shifted from imperially constructed identities to racially constructed ones.

Despite the place of Indian tobacco, Empire tobacco was identified most as leaf coming from Southern Rhodesia, a white settler colony. This was in accord with the racialised ideas about fitness for participation in the production of specific imperial goods, which saw Africans excluded from growing certain varieties of tobacco. The same reasoning was deployed in proclaiming the inferiority of both Indian and African leaf. In line with the 'global color line,' whereby whiteness was considered a prerequisite for democracy, in the economic arena whiteness was considered a prerequisite for efficient economic production. While the ethnic and racial dimension to this has only been alluded to here, it certainly played a crucial part not only in Southern Rhodesia as a white settler colony but also in British public opinion supporting sanctions on independent Rhodesia after 1965, and as such merits further study.

References

Primary Sources

Unpublished
National Archives of Zimbabwe (NAZ)
- 2570/TBC1.
- Box RH 27

[88] Kuncheria (Unpublished work in progress).

Published

Agricultural Correspondent. 1960. Federation Protests at Surprise US Tobacco Deal. *Rhodesia Herald*, 12 November.

Anonymous. 1954. *Northern News*, 21 April.

Anonymous. 1960(a). *Rhodesia Herald*, 21 January.

Anonymous. 1960(b). *Rhodesia Herald*, 26 March.

Anonymous. 1960(c). *Rhodesia Herald*, 16 July.

Anonymous. 1960(d). *Rhodesia Herald*, 30 July.

Anonymous. 1960(e). *Rhodesia Herald*, 5 October.

Anonymous. 1961. *Evening Standard*, 14 March.

Davies, A.R. 1964. *Tobacco Production and Marketing in Southern Rhodesia, Northern Rhodesia and Nyasaland*. ed US Department of Agriculture Foreign Agricultural Service. No date: No publisher.

Herald Correspondent. 1960. US Tobacco Preferences Move Was Causing Great Concern. *Rhodesia Herald*, 11 August.

Tobacco Forum of Rhodesia, November 1961.

United States Foreign Agricultural Service. 1956. *Rhodesian Tobacco, What It Means to the American Farmer*. ed US Department of Agriculture Foreign Agricultural Service. No date: No publisher.

Secondary Sources

Armstrong, P. 1987. *Ginger Freeman, Tobacco Spiced with Ginger: The Life of Ginger Freeman*. Welston: Harare.

Clements, F., and E. Harben. 1962. *Leaf of Gold: The Story of Rhodesian Tobacco*. London: Methuen.

Cohen, A. 2017. *The Politics and Economics of Decolonization in Africa: The Failed Experiment of the Central African Federation*. London: I.B. Taurus.

Cox, H. 2000. *The Global Cigarette: Origins and Evolution of British America Tobacco, 1880–1945*. New York: Oxford University Press.

Dunlop, H. 1971. *The Development of European Agriculture in Rhodesia, 1945–1965*. Ph.D. Dissertation, University of Rhodesia, Salisbury.

Fish, M. 1963. *Public Law 480: The Use of Agricultural Surpluses as Aid to Underdeveloped Countries* (with Special Reference to India). Ph.D. Dissertation. University of Oklahoma.

Gallagher, J., and A. Seal. 1982. *The Decline, Revival and Fall of the British Empire*. Cambridge: Cambridge University Press.

Gamble, A. 1985. *Britain in Decline, Economic Policy, Political Strategy and the British State*. London: Macmillan.

Hardin, C.M. 1960. Congressional Farm Politics and Economic Foreign Policy. *The Annals of the American Academy of Political and Social Science* 331: 98–102.

Haviland, W.E. 1953. Tobacco Farm Organisation, Costs and Land-Use in Southern Rhodesia. *South African Journal of Economics* 21: 367–380.

Hooper, M.D. 1988. *The Political Economy of the Rhodesian Tobacco Industry, 1945–1965*, Master's Thesis. University of Aberdeen.

Hopkins, A.G. 2018. *American Empire. A Global History*. Princeton: Princeton University Press.

Hultman, C.W. 1961. Agricultural Disposals as Foreign Aid: An Appraisal. *Journal of Inter-American Studies* 3: 527–537.

Krozewski, G. 1996. Finance and Empire: The Dilemma Facing Great Britain in the 1950s. *International History Review* 18: 48–69.

Krozewski, G. 2001. *Money and the End of Empire: British International Economic Policy and the Colonies, 1947–58*. New York: Springer.

Kuncheria, C.J. *An Empire of Smoke: Indian Tobacco and the Making of an Imperial Commodity in Interwar Britain* (Unpublished Work in Progress).

Low, D.A., and J. Lonsdale. 1976. Introduction. In *The Oxford History of East Africa*, eds. D.A. Low and A. Smith, 1–64. Oxford: Oxford University Press.

Lowry, D. 2010. Rhodesia 1890–1980: The Lost Dominion. In *Settlers and Expatriates: Britons over the Seas*, ed. R. Bickers, 112–149. Oxford: Oxford University Press.

Machingaidze, V.E.M. 1980. *The Development of Settler Capitalist Agriculture in Southern Rhodesia with Particular Reference to the Role of the State, 1908–1939*. Ph.D. Dissertation, University of London.

Mastanduno, M. 1988. Trade as a Strategic Weapon: American and Alliance Export Control in the Early Postwar Period. *International Organisation* 42: 121–150.

Matthew, A. 2017. *Colonial Tobacco. 1944–1949*. Marlborough. Global Commodities. https://www.globalcommodities.amdigital.co.uk. Accessed on 11 July 2017.

Mbanga, T. 1991. *Tobacco: A Century of Gold*. Harare: ZIL Publications.

Ncube, S. 2019. *Colonial Zimbabwe's Tobacco Industry: Global, Regional and Local Relations, 1947–79*. Ph.D. Dissertation, University of the Free State.

Ncube, S. 2022. *Politics, Profits and Protection: Zimbabwe's Tobacco Industry Since 1947*. Makhanda: NISC.

Ncube, S., and T. Nyamunda. 2022. Southern Rhodesia and Britain's Discriminatory Sterling Area: The Dollar Crisis and Post-War Colonial Tobacco Trade, 1947–1960. *The Journal of Imperial and Commonwealth History* 50: 1123–1144.

Palley, C. 1966. *Constitutional History and Law of Southern Rhodesia, 1888–1965: With Special Reference to Imperial Control*. Oxford: Clarendon Press.

Palmer, R. 1970. *Land and Racial Domination in Rhodesia*. Los Angeles: University of California Press.

Phimister, I. 1988. *An Economic and Social History of Zimbabwe, 1890–1948*. London: Longman.

Rubert, S.C. 1998. *A Most Promising Weed: A History of Tobacco Farming and Labour in Colonial Zimbabwe, 1890–1945*. OH: Ohio University Centre for International Studies.

Slichter, S.H. 1954. US Economic Foreign Policy. *Naval War College Review* 7: 13–29.

Tate, C. 1999. *Cigarette Wars: The Triumph of the "Little White Slaver."* New York: Oxford University Press.

PART II

Knowledge

CHAPTER 6

Imperial Rivalries and Agronomic Reform: Tobacco Plantations in the Venetian Ionian Islands and Dalmatia, 1760s–1790s

Guido Cioni

Introduction

In the late eighteenth century, the eastern Mediterranean was a region of commercial and imperial rivalries, as the increasing Russian presence in the area culminated in the outbreak of the Russo-Ottoman War (1768–1774), adding to tensions along the 'triple frontier' of the Venetian, Habsburg, and Ottoman Empires.[1] The war caused supply chain disruption and Venice searched for alternatives in the overseas domains of the Ionian Islands and Dalmatia of the Stato da Mar for the supply of raw materials for local manufactures and exotic goods for its dynamic consumer market. In this context, tobacco was a topic very much on the radar of Venetian officials, entrepreneurs, and experts.

[1] Paladini (2002) and Davies (2016).

G. Cioni (✉)
Scuola Normale Superiore, Pisa, Italy
e-mail: guido.cioni@sns.it

A. van Wickeren et al. (eds.), *Tobacco in Global Perspective, 1780–1960*, Cambridge Imperial and Post-Colonial Studies,
https://doi.org/10.1007/978-3-031-64411-5_6

Agronomy became an important tool deployed for introducing tobacco plantations and consolidating general tobacco farms. Combining examples from other parts of Europe, the German states and France in particular, Venice organized the cultivation, trade, processing, and sale of tobacco within the framework of princely sanctioned privileges to companies that enjoyed fiscal monopolies and privileged trade. In the context of fiscal concerns, scientific knowledge circulation, and pressure on the commodity frontier[2] for the incorporation of new resources in the Venetian economy, a sui generis tobacco culture was promoted. Learning from northern European tobacco experts, the improvement of Venetian imperial tobacco operated in connection with the centers of Enlightenment and Atlantic trade. This highlights the significance of war-related trade interruptions to produce knowledge about tobacco cultivation.

We have a considerable body of research about how the uncertainties over the supply channels of American tobacco caused by the Atlantic imperial wars and revolutions around 1800 forced countries such as France and Great Britain to introduce and promote tobacco plantations in new regions of their empires, from West Africa to India. The Seven Years' War (1756–1763), the revolutionary period including the American War of Independence (1776–1783), and the Napoleonic era have been particularly well researched in this regard.[3] During the period, academies and learned societies began to sponsor the adoption of tobacco as a crop for agricultural development and commerce. They were part of the 'Agricultural Enlightenment', which envisioned harnessing the environment for economic gain through practical knowledge and scientific theories from fields such as botany and, as of the 1770s, agricultural chemistry.[4] Reform circles specialised in the need for specific crops or commodities such as tobacco, its trade requirements, and consumer tastes.[5] The commercialisation of older subsistence-farming regions and the planting of previously non-tobacco regions in this era of tobacco's second globalization were marked by a massive spread of tobacco knowledge.

Far less is known about how the imperial conflicts and wars of the era contributed to the spread of a tobacco-specific, knowledge-based

[2] Beckert et al. (2021).

[3] Sinha-Kerkhoff (2014) and Røge (2019).

[4] Jones (2016).

[5] Van Wickeren (2020).

culture of improvement in the Mediterranean area, and more specifically the Venetian Empire. After the tobacco trade with the Levant faltered with the Russian advance in the region, the expansion of tobacco within its imperial borders became of great interest to the Venetian state. By furthering our understanding of the different contextual conditions of a tobacco-specific Agricultural Enlightenment and its impact on European regions beyond the political struggle of the Atlantic World, this chapter challenges the strong dichotomy between 'centers' and 'peripheries' in the Agricultural Enlightenment debate, as well as a certain disregard for the eighteenth-century Eastern Mediterranean in imperial studies.

Historians today call for conceptualising Venice not as a 'city state' or 'territorial state' but rather as an 'empire' in its own right,[6] and a focus on agronomic projects and tobacco reforms in the Italian states reveals much about the use and creative adaptation of the political theory of physiocracy that underpinned reforms in the empire.[7] The case of Girolamo Manfrin, the financier and entrepreneur from Zara who was the Venetian general tobacco farmer from 1779 to 1797,[8] is under the spotlight in this chapter. Focusing on Manfrin's projects during Venice's struggle for political existence in the Mediterranean space, the chapter shows how imperial concerns, knowledge production, and war contributed decisively to tobacco's rise as a Mediterranean commodity, and how the Mediterranean became an important center of imperial confrontation, land seizures, and territorial development during the late eighteenth century.[9] Moreover, the chapter delves into what tobacco history can tell us about the dynamism of the Mediterranean faced with the rise of a well-established Atlantic economy, with particular reference to the circulation of global commodities.

[6] Fusaro (2015, pp. 1–15).

[7] Ulvioni (1985) and Del Negro (1998).

[8] Fontana (1977, p. 56).

[9] Røge (2019, pp. 51, 54, 170, 191–196, 201).

Mediterranean Tobacco Trade and the Italian General Tobacco Farm

The expansion of tobacco in the Venetian Empire came later than in Western Europe, the Ottoman Levant, or even Eastern Asia, where it had reached full maturity by the end of the seventeenth century.[10] It was only in the eighteenth century that tobacco consumption in the Serenissima saw a spectacular rise, and by the late century many had taken to pipes and snuff enriching coffee-shop sociability and fashionable habits.[11] Levantine snuff was much preferred to that made with leaf from the Americas, and price differences mattered crucially in this regard. The luxury snuff processed in Seville with leaf from Cuba was almost nine-fold the cost of 'Genisè' from Salonika. In 1797, for example, the wholesale price for one lb of 'Spain', as the snuff from Seville was called in Venice, was 42 *lire* as against the price per lb of 4 *lire* and 16 *soldi* for Genisè.[12]

In the mid-seventeenth century, the English and the Flemish, in collaboration with local merchants, were the main agents for importing tobacco to Venice: from Amsterdam, English ports, and also directly from the West Indies in the Americas as some English ships ensured a direct connection with the island of Barbados carrying abundant supplies of Brazilian and Caribbean tobacco.[13] The initial prominence of Atlantic tobaccos was, however, undercut by the success of tobacco being transplanted to several regions of the Eastern Mediterranean, especially in the Ottoman Balkans, such that the bulk of tobacco consumption in Venice and its dominions came from a fragrant Ottoman leaf that had undergone fermentation and seasoning.

Between the second half of the seventeenth century and the first quarter of the eighteenth century, Adriatic ports like Durazzo, Split, and Ragusa had played a crucial role in securing Venetian trade with the Ottoman Balkans, often displacing French, Dutch, and English competition. In 1691, the French consul in Salonika, M. Quenet, complained there are no commodities to be exchanged because "the country is very

[10] Shammas (1993) and Goodman (1994).

[11] Paladini (2003).

[12] Venice 05 January 1797, State Archive of Florence, in the following SAVe, Inquisitori di Stato, f. 942.

[13] Venice 15 December 1654, SAVe, Senato, Terra, f. 609. 08 December 1655. SAVe, Cinque Savi alla Mercanzia, I Series, f. 155, pp. 67r-69v.

deserted by the war. [A]ll the commodities which are collected there pass to Venice by the way of Durazzo and are removed by people of the country [...] who go in the villages to buy them at a good price leaving nothing from the city".[14]

An alliance between the Venetian commercial navy and local Ottoman merchants allowed Venice to emerge as the main Western player in the Ottoman tobacco-growing regions of Albania, Macedonia, and Epirus, even during the periods of open war against the Sublime Porte of Crete (1645–1669) and Morea (1684–1699 and 1714–1718).[15] The alliance was necessary to supply internal markets, as Western European wars made it difficult for Venice to purchase leaf from the Americas. On several occasions, especially during the War of the Spanish Succession (1701–1715), general tobacco farmers were allowed to import leaf from the Americas overland via Genoa and Livorno for consumption on the Venetian mainland, given that "due to the frequent hazards produced by wars between the Western nations tobaccos from those regions were not shipped in this city".[16]

Tobacco revenue significantly increased for the state treasury from the mid-seventeenth century. The Venetian Senate established a tobacco monopoly as early as 1655[17] and relied on it as a pillar of the imperial fiscal system. The monopoly was soon extended to the overseas colonies of the Stato da Mar, in particular to the Ionian Islands of Corfu, Cephalonia, and Zante (1665), and to Venetian Dalmatia and Albania (1667).[18]

From the early days of the monopoly, Venice looked to the general tobacco farm model of the early modern Italian states,[19] which had established their own tobacco monopolies. These were headed by a general tobacco farmer or consortium composed of several financiers concerned

[14] Letter from M. Quenet of 09 July 1691, Archives Nationales de France, in the following ANF, Affaires étrangers, B1 990.

[15] "Consoli – Durazzo", SAVe, Cinque Savi alla Mercanzia, I Series, ff. 661–666.

[16] "Risposte", Venice 22 November 1713, SAVe, Cinque Savi alla Mercanzia, I Series, f. 172, p. 162.

[17] "Tabacco", Decree of the Senate Pregadi, 13 February 1655, SAVe, Cinque Savi alla Mercanzia, II Series, f. 169.

[18] "Tabacco", Decrees of the Senate, Pregadi 12 July 1766 and 25 June 1667, SAVe, Cinque Savi alla Mercanzia, II Series, f. 169.

[19] Levati (2017).

with importing leaf and the finished products through the management of privileged companies, and with the exclusive right to sell tobacco within their territory in return for an annual fee.

The decision to establish the state monopoly was supported by information from Venetian diplomats in Milan, Genoa, and Florence about their tobacco monopolies.[20] The Venetians, however, increasingly looked to the model of the French general tobacco farm. The Serenissima entered into contracts with large privileged companies, which in turn had clout in political debate around the financial structure of the state.[21] The general tobacco farmers and their privileged companies were successful in acquiring knowledge of tobacco, from the selection of the best leaf to the organisation of manufacture. Thanks to their connections with Venetian and Greek merchants,[22] they contributed greatly to consolidating a system whereby leaf harvested in the Ottoman Balkan was imported to Venice for distribution to privileged manufacturers on the Venetian mainland, where skilled workers made ‘Padovano’, ‘Bergamasco’, and ‘Nostrano’ snuff for consumption.[23] While the tobacco monopolies adopted by Spain and Portugal, which were well-observed in Venice,[24] relied on their American colonies and France fostered the trade with British colonies in North America, the Eastern Mediterranean became the central supply space for Venice’s general tobacco farm.

The annual fee paid by the Venetian general tobacco farmers saw an impressive rise: from 46,000 ducats under Francesco Rinaldi (1658–1663) to 400,303 ducats under Paolo Grassi (1708–1713) and 1,371,300 ducats under the privileged company of Salvi and Perulli.[25] While this fiscal success is well documented,[26] the interplay of commercial ambition, scientific knowledge, and agricultural projects has been mostly overlooked. The historiography is undoubtedly richer on how the ‘Gulf’,

[20] Venice 15 September 1654, SAVe, Senato, Terra, f. 609.

[21] Pezzolo (2006, pp. 26–31).

[22] See the contracts signed in 1757 by the general tobacco farmers Salvi and Perulli with Greek and Dalmatian merchants for the supply of Ottoman tobacco in “Diversorum”, SAVe, Cinque Savi alla Mercanzia, f. 371.

[23] Venice 24 August 1742, SAVe, Compilazioni di Leggi, I Series, f. 360, pp. 173–199.

[24] Hanson (1982) and Rodríguez Gordillo (2002).

[25] Miscellanea Soranzo, SAVe, f. 14.

[26] Tolomeo (2013).

as the late eighteenth century Venetian ruling class zealously called the Adriatic Sea, represented an area of greatest importance within the old commercial system. Far less is known about how the imperial conflicts and wars of the late eighteenth-century Eastern Mediterranean eventually undermined the traditional tobacco supply chains that had ensured Venice's preeminent role in the region for a century and pushed the old system toward necessary reform.

War and Rivalry

The Mediterranean tobacco trade suffered in the late 1760s and early 1770s due to the outbreak of the wars in the Levant, compounded by the Russo-Ottoman War. While the Venetian-Ottoman Wars in the previous decades had not compromised trade between Venetian and Balkan merchants, the new intrusion of the Russian military fleet in the Eastern Mediterranean diverted Ottoman tobacco to other Italian markets, in particular the Tuscan port of Livorno.[27] Therefore, traditional tobacco re-exports from Venice to northern Italy and central Europe dropped sharply in the 1770s: from 1,977,138 lbs in the years 1758–1762, a figure that already represented a loss from the tightening of Ottoman export duties, to a mere 514,967 lbs in the years 1771–1778.[28]

During the war Venetian authorities began to demonise the dependence on the Ottoman Empire, not only in terms of the negative consequences this had for fiscal revenue, but also for the great annual monetary outflow. This was estimated as some 160,000 ducats in a report signed by Manfrin and more than 200,000 ducats in a letter written by General Superintendent for Venetian Dalmatia and Albania, Piero Michiel.[29] Government and high officials discussed with alarm the implications for the Venetian economy. In June 1771, the Venetian consul in Salonika informed the Savi alla Mercanzia—the Venetian board of magistrates responsible for external trade—of the difficulties Venetian ships faced in loading tobacco, cotton, and wool due to the military conflict,

[27] See also "Portate dei Tabacchi esistenti nei Maeini pubblici e particolari di Livorno", 1769–1781, SAVe, Azienda del Tabacco, f. 350.

[28] "Tabacco", SAVe, Cinque Savi alla Mercanzia, I Series, f. 889.

[29] "Tabacchi di Dalmazia e Terraferma", Zara, 04 April 1763, Querini Stampalia Library of Venice, in the following QSLVe, Mss. Cl. IV, cod. CCCCLXX (=532), p. 214r. "Tabacco", SAVe, Cinque Savi alla Mercanzia, I, f. 888.

underscoring this would result in a lack of essential goods for trade with Venice.[30]

The Russo-Ottoman War in effect represented a new dimension of trade disruption caused by imperial rivalries in the Mediterranean, and the Venetian Empire was not the only power to suffer. As stressed by the state administrators of the Grand Duchy of Tuscany's general tobacco farm, "in all the European states prices for the tobacco leaf... are considerably higher after the war waged by the Russians in the Levant and after the beginning of the turmoil in the Anglo-American colonies".[31]

While the Western blockade of the Seven Years' War did not affect the tobacco sector in Venice as significantly as in other places, the War of American Independence seriously exacerbated the disruption of tobacco supply from the Atlantic. The Venetian consul in London, Giovanni Valle, had collaborated since 1768 with the general tobacco farmers in Venice for Virginia leaf, praising the periods in which "we can feel the benefit of the quiet in the American colonies", but in 1776 he reported that "given the American turmoil, traffic with the colonies being disrupted, ships sailing from here to Venice have no opportunity to load tobacco from the Americas".[32]

The Russo-Ottoman War closed a period in which Venice had managed to control a large share of the re-export of Levantine tobacco to northern Italy and central Europe. Since the second half of the seventeenth century, Jewish and Greek merchants had increasingly imported tobacco from the Levant to the Venetian territories, where the general tobacco farmers processed them to obtain snuff to be exported to Habsburg territories and other Italian states.[33] This dynamic continued well into the eighteenth century. Having signed an agreement with the state of Milan in 1752 for the supply of the local general tobacco farm with Ottoman leaf and Venetian snuff, the Savi alla Mercanzia reported a promising increase in Levantine tobacco re-exports toward Italian states, Habsburg domains, and other German territories in central Europe, from 645,259 lbs during

[30] "Consoli – Salonicco", Salonika, 18 June 1771, SAVe, Cinque Savi alla Mercanzia, I Series, f. 743.

[31] Florence 02 April 1777, SAVe, Segreteria di Finanze, f. 570.

[32] "Consoli – Londra", London, 20 November 1770 and 16 January 1776, SAVe, Cinque Savi alla Mercanzia, I Series, f. 710bis.

[33] "Tabacco", Decree of the Senate, Pregadi, 26 March 1662, SAVe, Cinque Savi alla Mercanzia, II Series, f. 169.

the previous contract to 2,976,427 lbs under the contract signed by Salvi and Perulli.[34]

Nonetheless, under closer scrutiny, the hegemonic position of Venice in the Levantine tobacco trade had already begun to show signs of weakening. The rise of new Free Ports, notably Ancona and Trieste, granted commercial privileges and fiscal exemptions by the Pope and the Habsburg crown, effectively challenged Venice as the main entrepôt of the region. Along with Filippo Paladini's 'double province' of Venetian Dalmatia and Albania came a 'triple frontier' along porous borders dividing the Venetian domains in the Balkans from the Western provinces of the Ottoman Empire and the Austrian imperial territories in Istria and inland Croatia.[35]

For these empires, the Adriatic Sea was an area of strategic interest, investment, and territorial expansion.[36] The Habsburgs and the Ottomans had already systematically promoted tobacco cultivation in some of their subjected territories, which had impacted the Adriatic trade. Tobacco's successful acclimatisation in the Ottoman Balkans from the early seventeenth century[37] and later in Habsburg Hungary, especially after the Treaty of Passarowitz (1718),[38] provided not only a formidable source of revenue for the Ottoman and Habsburg imperial coffers,[39] but also a competitive export advantage on foreign markets to the detriment of Venetian commercial interests.[40]

To take corrective action and monitor the moves of their imperial rivals, the Venetian Senate and the Savi alla Mercanzia turned to the 'Capi di Piazza' (Venetian representatives appointed from among the most important merchant families in Venice) for their knowledge and expertise. Already in 1754, two 'Capi di Piazza', Demetrio Perulli and Bonhomo Algarotti, were reporting the worrying scenario of the rise of the port of Goro in the territories subjected to the Papal city of Ferrara as

[34] "Diversorum", SAVe, Cinque Savi alla Mercanzia, I Series, f. 357, n. 74.

[35] Paladini (2002, pp. 1–18).

[36] Fodor and Geza (2000).

[37] Balta (2003).

[38] Fotić (2011).

[39] İnalcık and Quataert (1994) and Godsey (2018).

[40] "Risposte", Venice, 25 September 1761, SAVe, Cinque Savi alla Mercanzia, I Series, f. 189.

a threatening alternative to the Venetian route for the rich markets of the Po valley, notably the cities of Milan and Turin.[41] Listing commodities whose trade was about to move away from Venice, the two merchants underscored that "by now much of tobacco supplying the monopolies of northern Italy, and of Tyrol as well"[42] called at the port of Goro, challenging the role of Venice in the trade of Levantine leaf for the numerous general tobacco farms of the region.

A further threat came from Trieste, which handled the growing production of tobacco leaf from Habsburg Hungary. As noted by the Venetian consul, Hungarian leaf was so valued that, when the American War of Independence compromised supplies, merchants in Trieste sought it to replace Virginia tobacco for the supply of Western markets.[43] The fiscal and economic policies of the Ottoman Empire also reduced Venetian access to Levantine tobacco. A serious crisis occurred in 1761, when the Sublime Porte increased export duties from 6 to 24 akce (120 = 1 kurus in the Ottoman monetary system) for each okka (about 1.3 kg) of prime quality tobacco, while taxing second quality ('Caradà') at 15 akce and third quality at 12 akce.[44] Supplies of tobacco from Durazzo and Salonika were hit by an unprecedented price hike,[45] of which the Savi alla Mercanzia were painfully aware, causing concern about the lack of supply for the Venetian tobacco farm. When the Ottoman Empire established another increase in the export duty on tobacco to finance war expenses in 1792, the Venetian consul in Durazzo, Giovanni Antonio Maria Morana, immediately took action with the Bailo in Constantinople to avert a tax tightening that would be "burdensome to the general tobacco farm and all the Venetian merchants, the most important purchasers of tobacco in this market [Durazzo]".[46]

[41] "Diversorum", Demetrio Perulli and Bonhomo Algarotti to Savi alla Mercanzia, Venice, 23 March 1754, SAVe, *Cinque Savi alla Mercanzia*, I Series, f. 359, n. 1.

[42] Ibid.

[43] "Consoli – Trieste", Trieste, 25 April 1778, SAVe, Cinque Savi alla Mercanzia, I Series, f. 756.

[44] Paradise, Bergoin and Haveson to Perulli and Salvi, Salonika, 01 June 1759, SAVe, Archivio Perulli, f. 46.

[45] "Consoli – Durazzo", Durazzo, 02 May 1762, SAVe, Cinque Savi alla Mercanzia, I Series, f. 665.

[46] "Consoli – Durazzo", Durazzo, 08 June 1792, SAVe, Cinque Savi alla Mercanzia, I Series, f. 666.

Behind the decision to increase duties lay the financial difficulties of the Ottoman Empire around 1760,[47] and the spread of the Western habit of snuff led to the Sublime Porte promoting a protectionist policy. For the Ottomans, locally grown tobacco appeared increasingly attractive for meeting the growing domestic market, thereby also becoming a valued source of public revenues.[48] As a consequence, the protectionist policies of the Ottoman Empire and the new importance of other commercial and imperial powers in the eastern Mediterranean posed new challenges for the Venetian Empire regarding tobacco supply, which in turn were further exacerbated by the Russo-Ottoman War.

Nevertheless, we should not view the exacerbation of imperial rivalry and commercial competition in the Adriatic Sea or Russian intervention in the Eastern Mediterranean as an abrupt end for Venetian tobacco purchases from the Levant. Registers based on the solar years between June 1772 and May 1782 documenting the movement of commodities taxed by consumption duties, as was the case with tobacco, suggest there was only a slow decline in the importance of Ottoman tobacco in Venice.[49] The figures quoted by the Savi alla Mercanzia were for the city of Venice, not the entire empire. The data thus undoubtedly underestimated tobacco harvested in the privileged territories of the Venetian mainland, because a part of that was distributed by the general tobacco farm in the inland provinces without passing through Venice. Also, tobacco that arrived overland from the Western Mediterranean ports like Genoa and Livorno was not accounted for. We can, however, roughly approximate these values to an all-encompassing balance for tobacco trade in the Venetian Empire, as leaf that entered the state was required to be negotiated and stored only in Venice, where the general tobacco farm also had its main warehouses.[50]

During these ten years, the city of Venice imported 20.9 million lbs of tobacco, almost exclusively from abroad. Tobacco from the Ottoman Empire amounted for 15,526,955 lbs, of which 3,896,330 lbs came from

[47] İnalcık and Quataert (1994, pp. 947–970) and Darling (1996, pp. 119–190).

[48] Report of the Deputies for the supply of money to the Senate, Venice, 28 November 1761, SAVe, AP, f. 46.

[49] "Registri", SAVe, Cinque Savi alla Mercanzia, ff. 12, 16, 18, 22, 23, 28, 29, 33, 35, 40, 41, 46, 47, 52, 56, 57, 61, 63.

[50] See Sambo (2012).

the 'foreign Levant' (Ottoman Greece) and 11,630,625 lbs from the 'foreign Gulf' (Ottoman Albania). The impact of the Russo-Ottoman War was massive on the import of leaf from the Ottoman Western Balkans: the 2,078,381 lbs imported in 1772 collapsed to 1,064,328 lbs in 1773 and 600,101 in 1774, only rising back to over one million lbs in 1778.

By contrast, the figures show a significant flow of leaf from Habsburg Hungary, which grew significantly in the 1780s. Over the period, 4,533,480 lbs came from Hungary, but almost half—1,829,494 lbs—in only three years between 1780 and 1782. Including the capital outlay for tobacco from the Atlantic and Western Mediterranean ports—which was minimal in comparison with 237,141 lbs throughout the decade—a total of 2,580,727 ducats was spent abroad during the period, so over 258,000 ducats annually. The expenditure for foreign tobacco was thus greater than what was declared in some of the accounting of the general tobacco farmers and Venetian officials, and the exports of snuff processed in Venice, primarily to Milan, were not of sufficient magnitude to compensate for such an expenditure: 65,054 ducats a year during the period. Of a total of 650,545 ducats for tobacco exported, 638,605 derived from exports to other states of northern Italy. Milan was by far the most important market, taking 2,054,844 lbs of tobacco exported during the period.

The New Commodity Frontier

With the exacerbation of commercial competition in the Adriatic Sea and the outbreak of the Russo-Ottoman War, the Venetians began to perceive their own imperial territory more as an area for tobacco cultivation and an alternative to overseas trade. The experimental projects and agricultural reform practices in the newly conquered Venetian territories in Dalmatia and Albania were closely linked to the discussions on tobacco improvement in northern Europe but were adapted to Venetian conditions. Only the new imperial rivalry and the wars of the second half of the eighteenth century made tobacco cultivation an object of increased agro-scientific concern and entrepreneurial investment.

The expansion of tobacco cultivation was part of Venice's eighteenth-century struggle for consolidating what remained of its overseas colonies and integrating them into a coherent economic system. Some Greek Ionian Islands beyond the Adriatic Sea—in particular Corfu, Cephalonia,

Zante, Santa Maura, and Cerigo—were also important in the imperial economy dominated by the capital city of Venice, providing key commodities such as salt[51]; olive oil, which was both a source of energy for many manufactures, such as glass and '*contarie*' from Murano, and a raw material, as for soap makers in Venice[52]; and *uva passa* (raisins, or dried grapes)[53] for the Serenissima. They also appeared to guarantee goods in high demand for competing in regional redistribution and boosting long-distance exchange, especially for Atlantic and European markets. This in turn produced both conflicts and convergence between the imperial dimension of Venice in the Greek Ionian Islands and the Greek and English mercantile networks for the re-export of Ionian goods.[54]

The agricultural development of the overseas colonies was undoubtedly designed to subordinate them to the commercial intermediation of Venice. This was the case in a 1769 proposal from Dalmatia for agricultural improvement in the Stato da Mar, and also one from Cephalonia, from Count Marin Carburi, to introduce in his own landholdings the cultivation of some exotic crops.[55] With the Ottoman fiscal retaliation of the early 1760s, tobacco came to be seen as a commodity worthy of being transplanted to the Venetian overseas colonies, and the first attempt to do so was in 1762. After an initial fiasco over leasing the general tobacco farm, due to the absence of offers, the Senate added to the traditional terms of the contract the possibility of planting tobacco in the overseas territories and signed a contract with Count Iseppo Mangilli granting him permission to cultivate tobacco in Venetian Dalmatia and on the Levantine islands belonging to Venice.[56]

[51] Hocquet (2012).

[52] Ciriacono (1975, pp. 1–18).

[53] Fusaro (1997).

[54] Fusaro (2012).

[55] "Diversorum", Venice, 14 August 1769, SAVe, Cinque Savi alla Mercanzia, I Series, f. 374, n. 32. Venice, 05 January 1778, SAVe, Cinque Savi alla Mercanzia, I Series, f. 338, n. 64.

[56] "Tabacchi di Dalmazia e Terraferma", QSLVe, Mss. Cl. IV, cod. CCCCLXX (=532), pp. 214v–215r.

The yield from Mangilli's first experiment fell short of expectations, and investors in the general tobacco farm looked to the Venetian mainland. They negotiated annual provisions of local tobacco with the privileged territories in the Brenta River valley and the seven municipalities of the Asiago plateau, north of Vicenza, which had turned, sometimes illegally, to tobacco cultivation.[57] Even this did not prove satisfactory, producing only 595,355 lbs of poor-quality tobacco between 1772 and 1782, according to the Savi alla Mercanzia. There was no hope "to get from those lands, though fruitful and rich, a quality of tobaccos similar to those from Ottoman Albania, the favorite flavor for the custom and the mind of the nation".[58] They had to contend with the taste for Ottoman tobacco in Venice and cities of the Venetian mainland, and their preference for tobacco from Salonika.[59]

Contemporary references to the inferior natural features for tobacco cultivation of the mainland compared to the overseas colonies, however, should not distract from the fact that they reflected above all the passivity that characterised Venice's policy toward mainland agriculture in the eighteenth century. Initiatives to develop agriculture were largely left to local elites. Venice focused on more general improvements in a few important areas, especially drainage and soil improvement in the lower plains of the Veronese countryside. The creation of only one magistracy dedicated to reform—the Deputazione all'agricoltura founded in 1768—and the limited success of agricultural academies supported by the state bear witness to the lack of a master plan to make the mainland a central production area for agriculture.[60] It was no wonder that the general tobacco farmers privileged the colonies over the mainland to secure trade autarky.

After the Russo-Ottoman War, this desire for autarky charted a new path and gained in intensity in the 1780s. The Senate sought those willing to take on the general tobacco farm and cultivate tobacco in the overseas

57 See contracts between Iseppo Mangilli and later general tobacco farmers Giammaria Volpi and Girolamo Manfrin and the 'Seven Municipalities' in "Tabacco", SAVe, Cinque Savi alla Mercanzia, I Series, f. 888.

58 "Tabacchi di Dalmazia e Terraferma", QSLVe, Mss. Cl. IV, cod. CCCCLXX (=532), p. 215v.

59 See "Diversorum", SAVe, Cinque Savi alla Mercanzia, I Series, f. 397, n. 119.

60 Knapton (2013, p. 114).

colonies. In 1784, the Avvanzetti Company publicly described its import-substitution project as an opportunity to "mitigate the damage of a passive trade [i.e., the import and redistribution of commodities produced by rival powers] with the tobacco harvest from Ottoman Albania, which nowadays is the source of huge domestic consumption and the reason for a too high passive trade".[61]

In the end, the collection of agricultural projects led to the establishment of the large-scale tobacco plantation in the territory of Nona, near Zara in Venetian Dalmatia, run by the privileged company of Girolamo Manfrin. The activities of Manfrin have been widely researched.[62] Under him the Nona plantation expanded to encompass 1,240 Padoan fields with leaf storage and processing facilities, employing around 2,000 workers after the extension of the contract to 12 years in 1784. It was not by chance that the Senate praised the results of the Nona plantation, because it helped bolster the redistribution of tobacco via Venice toward the traditional markets for re-export.[63]

Most of the workers at Nona were local Morlacchis, which adds another complexity. 'Morlacchi' translates literally as 'Black Vlachs' and is to be interpreted as 'Vlachs of the North'. The terms Vlachs and Aromanians refer to populations speaking Romance dialects related to Romanian and living scattered in the Balkans as muleteer-traders.[64] The Vlachs undoubtedly experienced a process of 'Slavisation' due to migrations from southern regions pushed north by the Ottoman thrust during the early modern age.[65] Sources also refer to the Venetian patriciate employing the term Morlacchis in the eighteenth century more loosely, referring to communities of shepherds in the inland mountain regions of Dalmatia.[66]

[61] "Tabacco", "Prima carta del Progetto Avvanzetti", Venice, 09 January 1784, SAVe, Cinque Savi alla Mercanzia, I Series, f. 889.

[62] See Fontana (1977) and Tolomeo (2013, pp. 67–91).

[63] "Tabacco", "Trapunti della quantità dell'introito, transito e consumo per lo stato de' Tabacchi", Venice, 06 February 1792, SAVe, Cinque Savi alla Mercanzia, I Series, f. 889.

[64] Stoianovich (1960).

[65] "Relazioni finali di ambasciatori, rettori e altri pubblici rappresentanti", "Provveditore generale in Dalmazia e Albania – Progetti e ricordi rassegnati dal sig. Antonio Giusti ai sig.ri Sindici ed Inquisitori in Dalmazia", SAVe, Collegio, f. 70.

[66] "Relazione della Conferenza circa il sopralluogo effettuato sullo stabilimento di Nona dal Conte Rados Michieli Vitturi", Venice, 08 June 1792, SAVe, Miscellanea Soranzo, f. 14.

These areas had become Venetian property through earlier disputes with the imperial rivals of the region. Wars against the Ottoman Empire had strengthened the Venetian presence in the Balkans, with the two enlargements in Dalmatia and Albania after the peace treaties of Carlowitz (1699) and Passarowitz (1718).[67] Territorial extension brought new potential in terms of land resources but also new problems of how to deal with little-known environments and the linguistic, ethnic, and religious diversity of the local populations, whereby since the mid-eighteenth century "General Superintendents reevaluated Dalmatia's agricultural and industrial importance to take into account its land and especially its new inland inhabitants".[68]

The experimental spaces with tobacco cultivation in Venice's imperial peripheries were closely linked to the scientific discussions on agriculture at the time. Manfrin claimed to have chosen the territory of Nona on the basis of "solid and informed agronomic principles". For different reasons related to soil and climate, he discarded other territories of the Venetian Empire: the Venetian mainland, Istria, Venetian Albania, and the Greek Ionian islands of Zakynthos, Cephalonia, and Corfu. By contrast, Dalmatian soil and in particular "the territory of Nona could guarantee all the required land, near to the sea and with excellent soil suited for the production of a tobacco equal to the most perfect leaf of Albania".[69]

Manfrin's scientific endeavor also shows that the Russo-Ottoman War intensified agronomic approaches from an earlier period. He made a first offer for the tobacco monopoly in 1769, which, due to his refusal to declare his financial backers, led to his imprisonment. He later succeeded with the contract for 1779–1787, and, as early as December 1783, proposed to the Senate planting tobacco in 640 Padoan fields in Dalmatia at his own expense during the eight years of the contract (80 new fields each year) and to increase the fee paid into the state coffers by 25,000 ducats each year.[70] Manfrin used the report on Nona by General Superintendent for agriculture in Dalmatia, Rados Antonio Michieli Vitturi, to claim the concession of a larger number of fields for planting. According

[67] Scarabello (1992, pp. 553–567).

[68] Wolff (2003, p. 6).

[69] "Tabacchi di Dalmazia e Teraferma", "Memoria Manfrin", no place and date, probably from 1793, QSLVe, Mss. Cl. IV, cod CCCCLXX (=532), p. 215r–216v.

[70] "Tabacco", Venice, 20 December 1783, SAVe, Cinque Savi alla Mercanzia, I Series, f. 889.

to Vitturi, "a field might yield every year 1,100 lbs of dried leaf",[71] which is why he presented to the Senate his request of 1,150 fields more than the number that had been agreed to produce an annual 2,400,000 lbs of tobacco. The Venetian government agreed.

Venetian agronomic attempts were also inspired by similar initiatives elsewhere in Europe. The privileged path was identified along the lines of the model provided by the Habsburg competitor, which developed flourishing domestic tobacco cultivation within the monopolistic regime of the general tobacco farm.[72] In similar ways, Venetian officials showed growing attention to the port of Trieste as a commercial hub for international tobacco trade and the redistribution of leaf grown in Habsburg Hungary.[73]

In 1790, Nona's success was applauded in a report by Ottavio Cristofoli, one of the agronomists who inspected the plantation that year,[74] and Venetian interest in tobacco extended to other Italian states. Between 1790 and 1795, Manfrin directly promoted several surveys by professors of agronomy and members of agricultural academies.[75] He became fully involved in the networks of agricultural academies and, thanks to the results of the Nona plantation, a correspondent member of the Florentine academy of Georgofili in 1791.[76] His team included experienced and renowned agronomists from various parts of the Venetian Empire and other Italian states: Canon Andrea Zucchini, member of the academy of Georgofili and director of the botanical garden in Florence; Francesco Velluti from Cortona in Tuscany and Count Ottavio Cristofoli from Conegliano in the Venetian mainland, two other members of agricultural academies; Captain Zavoreo, official engineer of the Serenissima; landowners Angleo Muzio from Nona, Lorenzo Lacin from Traù, Andrea Bossi from Milan, and Filippo Cecchi from Florence; and Giovanni

[71] "Tabacchi di Dalmazia e Terraferma", QSLVe, Mss. Cl. IV, cod. CCCCLXX (=532), p. 140r.

[72] Hitz and Huber (1975).

[73] See the inquiry on the Habsburg exports of Hungarian tobacco from the port of Trieste in "Dogane", SAVe, Cinque Savi alla Mercanzia, I Series, f. 838, no place or date, probably from 1767.

[74] See Anonymous (1781) and Cristofoli (1790).

[75] See also in Tolomeo (2013, pp. 71–92).

[76] See Museum Correr Library of Venice, in the MCLVe, Codice Cicogna, f. 2380, n. 71.

Belloni, a farmer from the Polesine.[77] All those competing with Manfrin for appointments as privileged company also had to comply with cultivation practices and techniques highlighted by "the renowned agronomists sent on site by public order",[78] which became a basic prerequisite for entering the sector.

The involvement of agricultural experts was the key to enable a production of tobacco guided by "good rules".[79] The specialist treatises on tobacco cultivation and processing that Venice and other Italian states produced in the period evidence how Enlightenment discussions were adapted to the imperial environments of the Mediterranean in a complex and creative process of appropriation. The Venetian publishing industry was interested in foreign books and treatises on tobacco cultivation written by individual experts and agronomic groups looking for alternatives to the traditional provision of American leaf and translated into Italian as crucial sources for local debate and field trials.

The institutional efforts were accompanied by several publishing initiatives aimed at disseminating know-how on tobacco cultivation. In 1781, the government promoted Abbot Marco Fossadoni's translation of a French manual on the cultivation and manufacture of tobacco—a rarity in pre-revolutionary France, where, since the 1720s, tobacco cultivation had been officially banned in favor of purchases from North America, but it was still allowed in some privileged provinces such as Alsace and Flanders. That same year the *Nuovo Giornale d'Italia* informed readers about the publication in Darmstadt by Johann Gottlieb Backhauss of a book on tobacco cultivation, explicitly aimed at promoting the substitution of American leaf with varieties grown in Europe.[80] And among Manfrin's paper are notes referring to the entry on tobacco written by Louis de Jaucourt in the *Encyclopédie*.[81]

[77] "Tabacco", "Relazione dei tre agrari forestieri canonico Andrea Zucchini, Ottavio Cristofoli e Francesco Velluti", Zara, 22 August 1790, SAVe, Cinque Savi alla Mercanzia, I Series, f. 889.

[78] "Affare Tabacchi – Progetto Manfrin", no place and date, from 1795, MCLVe, Codice Cicogna, f. 3650.

[79] "Affare Tabacchi – Progetto Rigamonti", no place and date, from 1795, MCLVe, Codice Cicogna.

[80] See Nuovo giornale d'Italia (1781, p. 407).

[81] Venice, 05 November 1796, MCLVe, Codice Cicogna, f. 3650.

As the Nona example shows, entrepreneurs such as Manfrin not only immersed themselves in agronomy, but also drew on technical expertise from different regions, encompassing both agricultural and animal husbandry, given the importance of integrating tobacco cultivation and cattle farming for the fertility of the soil.[82] Expertise was acquired through the mobility of individuals with know-how. For Nona, 119 growers were recruited from among farmers of inland Italian states, whose expertise came from tobacco cultivation in the privileged territories and in the interstices where the monopoly was not implemented.[83] Manfrin also employed growers from the Ottoman Empire and the seven municipalities of Asiago to supervise workers at Nona contracted from surrounding villages.[84] The knowledge of farmers was considered of importance for regionalising agronomic research on tobacco cultivation, and a skilled workforce was particularly crucial for the domestic production of quality leaf on a par with that of Ottoman Albania.

Not all were treated with respect. In the early 1760s, Michiel attributed the failure of the introduction of tobacco cultivation in the overseas territories to the Morlacchis' lassitude and recommended more "active farmers, as those in Ottoman Albania are, from families skilled in the cultivation of the plant".[85] Similar arguments were evinced by the financiers, as evidenced in the importance the Avvanzetti company attached to introducing tobacco cultivation in Venetian Dalmatia, which, according to them, needed aid due to the agricultural ineptitude of its inhabitants.[86]

Manfrin himself was paternalistic, blaming and distrusting the local population in Nona for being unreliable and employing 'national soldiers' to control Morlacchis working on the plantation.[87] This attitude certainly

[82] "Tabacchi di Dalmazia e Terraferma", Venice, 08 June 1792, QSLVe, Mss. Cl. IV, cod. CCCCLXX (=532), pp. 137–142.

[83] "Tabacco", "Foglio dimostrante uomini, animali e strumenti trasportati ad Venezia a Nona, 1790–1791", SAVe, Cinque Savi alla Mercanzia, I Series, f. 889.

[84] "Relazione della Conferenza circa il sopralluogo effettuato sullo stabilimento di Nona dal Conte Rados Michieli Vitturi", Venice, 08 June 1792, SAVe, Miscellanea Soranzo, f. 14.

[85] "Tabacco", Zara, 04 April 1763, SAVe, Cinque Savi alla Mercanzia, I Series, f. 888.

[86] "Tabacco", "Seconda carta del Progetto Avvanzetti, Venice, 29 March 1784, SAVe, Cinque Savi alla Mercanzia, I Series, f. 889.

[87] "Tabacchi di Dalmazia e Terraferma", QSLVe, Mss. Cl. IV, cod. CCCCLXX (=532), pp. 61v–63v.

reflects the fact that the Morlacchis had little experience in agriculture but worked mainly as shepherds. Yet, it nonetheless shows how colonial stereotypes all too often determined which rural groups were considered useful and which less so for improving tobacco cultivation.

We should remain skeptical about the agronomic projects, especially with regard to quality,[88] since the Venetian general tobacco farm still needed to purchase tobacco from abroad in the 1790s. Over the years, however, the harvest in the new colonial plantations did become more substantial and an increasing supply of leaf was guaranteed for manufacture on the Venetian mainland. The first experimental harvest in Nona was in 1786, and between 1787 and 1794 the annual average yield was 606,376 lbs, concentrated largely in the latter years it has to be said, due to various initial physiological obstacles.[89] The project protected by the government and financed by Manfrin had moreover enabled Nona to achieve a much more significant output than tobacco cultivation across the Venetian mainland over a century of local privileges.

State Authority and Liberalisation

Venetian authorities spoke of tobacco cultivation in the imperial peripheries benefiting 'Treasury, Nation, and State', helping to avert the great outflow of money toward other empires. The period after the Russo-Ottoman War was accompanied by attempts on the part of the general tobacco farmers and privileged companies to prove their authority as benefactors of the state and demonstrate their agronomic modernity. The privilege of being a state-certified general tobacco farmer and privileged companies and promoting tobacco cultivation in the empire became very attractive to Venetian merchants. Manfrin, himself, was part of an entrepreneurial milieu competing for fiscal monopolies and privileged trade.

[88] For the scarce effectiveness of the Venetian agrarian policy in Dalmatia, see Paladini (2002, pp. 95–100).

[89] "Foglio che dimostra la quantità di cadauna specie tabacchi provvisti per consume anno per anno", no place, 1795, MCLVe, Codice Cicogna, f. 3650. For the organization of tobacco shipping from Nona to Venice, see "Tabacco", Venice, 11 May 1795, SAVe, Cinque Savi alla Mercanzia, I Series, f. 889.

The Senate's appointment of privileged entrepreneurs trained in agronomy was also a strategy to counter the growing mood for liberalisation of tobacco in the Italian states. In Rome, Pope Benedetto XIV, a propagandist of liberal economic reform,[90] abolished the tobacco monopoly in the Papal States as early as in 1757, well before similar measures were adopted by revolutionary France in 1791,[91] granting free economic initiative in the tobacco sector.[92] This came in direct response to the 1756 rule implemented by the British royal navy during the Seven Years' War, which put Civitavecchia, the papal port of call for maritime trade, in serious difficulty for the supply of Western tobacco. The rule stipulated that neutral vessels could not navigate in wartime along the route that French mercantilist policy had not permitted in peacetime and claimed the right to seize ships and goods. Moreover, similar measures were taken by the French navy, further damaging the trade of neutral powers.[93]

The possibility of abolishing the monopoly was discussed also in the Venetian Empire. The liberalisation of tobacco cultivation in the neighboring Papal states led the Venetian authorities to take immediate precautions against the looming prospect of new smuggling channels along the border between the Venetian Polesine and the territory of Ferrara.[94] In the early 1760s, Gabriele Marcello, the member of the Savi alla Mercanzia with the strongest liberalizing convictions, proposed that in the wake of the Ottoman Empire's tax retaliation on tobacco exports there should be "absolute freedom of tobacco cultivation" in the overseas domains. There, the leaf could be sold to the new tobacco general tobacco farmer to "promote the benefit of the subjects without detriment to the monopoly".[95] The liberalisation debate intensified in the 1790s, with the

[90] Dal Pane (1959).

[91] Kwass (2014, pp. 318–353).

[92] Capalbo (1999, pp. 149–152).

[93] See Nys (2013, pp. 50–72).

[94] "Diversorum", Venice, 10 May 1760, SAVe, Cinque Savi alla Mercanzia, I Series, f. 362.

[95] "Risposte", Venice, 12 February 1762, SAVe, Cinque Savi alla Mercanzia, I Series, f. 189, pp. 88v–89r.

interruption of the Levantine tobacco trade, as denounced by a Savi alla Mercanzia report to the Senate in 1791.[96]

This was only partially implemented after the failure of Mangilli and, in 1763, all subjects of Venetian Dalmatia and Albania and the islands in the Levant were permitted to cultivate tobacco under strict regulations to be sold exclusively to the general tobacco farm. The proclamation issued by the Savi alla Mercanzia established a maximum of 800 Padoan fields (500 fields for Venetian Dalmatia and Albania and 300 fields for the Ionian islands, 20 for each territory, city, or island of the *Stato da Mar*) for cultivating varieties of tobacco seeds from Salonika and Ottoman Albania. Everyone could apply to the general tobacco farmer and local subcontractors for planting tobacco on leased or property land. Local growers were encouraged to come forward not only by translating the proclamation in Illyrian for Dalmatia and Greek for the Ionian Islands, but also the offer of generous exemptions on their land and their person.[97]

The shift to the model of the large privileged plantation represented by Nona meant the most liberal ideas of political economy of the time were sacrificed to secure a path that valued advances in scientific agronomy and knowledge-based projects under greater control. In 1784, the Senate received a project from Giovan Battista Martinelli to introduce tobacco plantations in Dalmatia, but this was immediately discarded for being "too generic"[98]; and when the Avvanzetti company raised their bid to an additional 40,000 ducats a year,[99] Manfrin in turn raised his to 45,000 ducats.[100]

The desire for scientifically governed tobacco plantations managed and controlled by enlightened general tobacco farmers and privileged entrepreneurs, also stemmed from the desire to curb the smuggling associated with the 'free' cultivation of tobacco. In the Brenta River valley and the seven municipalities of Asiago, the tobacco plant provided a safe

[96] "Diversorum", no place, 1791, SAVe, Cinque Savi alla Mercanzia, I Series, f. 401, n. 100.

[97] "Tabacco", Venice, 28 February 1763, SAVe, Cinque Savi alla Mercanzia, I Series, f. 888.

[98] Pregadi, 07 August 1784, MCLVe, Codice Cicogna, f. 3650.

[99] "Tabacco", Venice, 09 January 1784 and 29 March 1784, SAVe, Cinque Savi alla Mercanzia, I Series, f. 889.

[100] "Tabacchi di Dalmazia e Terraferma", Venice, 05 April 1784, QSLVe, Ms. Cl. IV, cod. CCCCLXX (=532), p. 25.

and important cash crop for the poor local population of communities in need of cash for paying taxes and purchasing basic necessities when the fodder crop failed.[101] The provinces of the Venetian mainland had created frequent problems for the centralised model of the monopoly granted to the general tobacco farmers in the form of contraband. Throughout the eighteenth century, Venetian authorities issued repeated proclamations forbidding illegal cultivation and reminding local officials of their duty to implement the law.[102] They had such little effect that in 1789 more than 200,000 illegal tobacco plants had to be uprooted in Vicenza.[103]

Privileged companies were not entirely autonomous in their scientific projects to improve tobacco cultivation for the benefit of the state, but rather observed by other institutions. The entire production of knowledge and the disposal of information was under the tight political supervision of the imperial structures of the Serenissima. All the surveys and inspections were reported to the Senate and to the Venetian ruling class, which saw the Nona plantation as of public concern, under the strict jurisdiction of various 'conferences' of imperial officials and General Superintendent in Dalmatia and Albania.

In this context, an enterprising figure such as General Superintendent Michiel personally promoted research and trials to develop tobacco in the overseas provinces. From his correspondence with the Savi alla Mercanzia, we learn that his surveys in the Stato da Mar during the 1760s had already demonstrated the critical obstacles for introducing tobacco cultivation in Venetian Albania, not so much due to the properties of the soil, but rather the current "scarcity of lands".[104] He had also singled out the same territory around Nona as the most suitable for tobacco cultivation and there promoted a small trial, replete with detail on cultivation techniques, leaf properties, and economic sustainability. The leaf produced proved to be of the same quality as the desired Albanian leaf, but the prices set out by the Senate meant a net loss of 4 *soldi* per lb of tobacco harvested.[105] In the decades that followed, General Superintendent Angelo Diedo reported

[101] See Venice, 04 August 1785, SAVe, Inquisitori di Stato, f. 943.

[102] "Diversorum", SAVe, Cinque Savi alla Mercanzia, I Series, f. 348.

[103] Vicenza, 07 November 1789, SAVe, Inquisitori di Stato, f. 126.

[104] "Tabacco", Zara, 17 September 1763, SAVe, Cinque Savi alla Mercanzia, I Series, f. 889.

[105] Zara, 19 November 1763, SAVe, Cinque Savi alla Mercanzia, I Series, f. 889.

to the Venetian Senate on all his efforts for the supervision of the general tobacco farm and the establishment of the Nona plantation.[106]

In 1795, a special "conference of officials" was commissioned to garner knowledge-based "plans and projects to complete and give new impetus to the tobacco plantation already introduced in the province of Dalmatia".[107] Studies commissioned from agronomists and professors of botany on Nona had given new insights into the quality of the product, but estimated at least 12 years as the time needed to produce the amount of tobacco needed for domestic consumption.[108] Officials were looking for proposals of agronomic innovation or reorganisation of production that would speed up the process.

They were, however, forced to consider a broader rethinking of the system, as evidenced by Geminiano Cozzi, former owner of an important porcelain manufactory in Venice, who aimed at introducing "the freedom for everyone to cultivate tobaccos in the overseas territories",[109] for further improving the output from the imperial tobacco frontier. Challenging Manfrin's hegemony over the tobacco sector, Cozzi criticised the Nona plantation by outlining the combined harmful effects of the paternalism toward local populations and the priority accorded to fiscal revenues. Despite the ambitions, a single plantation, though huge in its dimension, he asserted, would not have been able to provide all the tobacco required for the good functioning of the monopoly and for fostering the export trade.

The project elaborated by Cozzi did not challenge the tobacco monopoly, nor did conservative politicians such as the nobleman Angelo Capello, who was an eyewitness of the French revolution in Paris between 1789 and 1792. Capello reported on the 1791 abolition of the tobacco monopoly in France with a sharp negative comment on the "loss of 20 millions of livres tournois on tobacco, the cultivation and sale of which

[106] "Lettere da Zara – Provveditori generali", Zara, 16 November 1789, SAVe, Cinque Savi alla Mercanzia, I Series, f. 572.

[107] "Risposte", Venice, 05 June 1795, SAVe, Cinque Savi alla Mercanzia, I Series, f. 207, p. 158.

[108] Venice, 16 February 1795, MCLVe, Codice Cicogna, f. 3650.

[109] "Progetto Cozzi", Venice, 05 October 1795, MCLVe, Codice Cicogna, f. 3650.

was made free".[110] Capello advocated the Prussian model[111] where local growers could freely adopt the tobacco crop, but only for supplying the general tobacco farm sanctioned by the privileges granted by the sovereign.[112] The outcome was again in favor of Manfrin, bolstered by the "flattering opinion of the renowned agronomist professors dispatched to the site for public inspection".[113] Venetian officials preferred to continue the relationship with Manfrin rather than opening up to new interlocutors due to his financial backing and land for cultivation.[114] Agricultural reform and knowledge-based projects of the Venetian Empire to introduce tobacco cultivation in the overseas domains thus remained highly dependent on the capital, land, and material resources of the privileged entrepreneurs of the general tobacco farm.

Conclusion

Support for the general tobacco farm system among the Venetian population was limited. In 1797, just a couple of weeks after the fall of the Serenissima under the thrust of democratic upheavals and the French revolutionary army, and during the brief interlude of the Municipality (from May 1797 to January 1798), the tobacco monopoly was abolished in Venice[115] and the flourishing book industry of the city put forward biting criticism of symbols and institutions of the old oligarchic power. A satirical booklet was published poking fun at the general tobacco farmers and privileged companies. The main target was Manfrin himself. While swelling the public coffers, he was resented by consumers for the full-fledged war on fraud and contraband he unleashed with the swordsmen and armed guards he enlisted to that end. His pursuit of financial yield

110 Antonio Capello to the Venetian Senate, Parigi, 02 December 1790, MCLVe, Codice Cicogna, f. 3650.

111 See also Rogozinski (1990, pp. 70–71).

112 "Risposte", "Relazione di minoranza della Conferenza sui Tre Progetti per il completamento della piantagione a tabacchi", Venice, 26 March 1796, SAVe, Cinque Savi alla Mercanzia, I Series, reg. 208, pp. 43v–47v.

113 "Progetto Manfrin", no place, 1795, MCLVe, Codice Cicogna, f. 3650.

114 "Risposte", Venice, 26 March 1796, SAVe, Cinque Savi alla Mercanzia, I Series, f. 208, pp. 47v–57v.

115 Decree of the Municipality, Venice, 09 June 1797, SAVe, Municipalità provvisoria, Comitato finanze e zecca, f. 2.

had pushed up the prices of tobacco sold by the official farm, hitting a widely consumed product that many considered almost a necessity. Manfrin's assets were temporarily seized, and Nona was dismantled by the Habsburg government after the occupation of Dalmatia.[116]

Despite the final outcome, tobacco cultivation represented a topic of major concern for economists, officials, experts, and government in the late eighteenth-century Venetian Empire. Due to the significant growth in the consumption of snuff manufactured in Venice with Levantine-style tobacco, the general tobacco farm became a fundamental item of the imperial budget, but also a profitable opportunity for entrepreneurs with financial strength and consolidated connections with merchant networks that had access to the market of the tobacco-growing regions in the Ottoman Balkans.

The system entered a crisis starting in the 1760s as tobacco trade assumed increasing importance in the commercial competition in the Adriatic Sea and in the imperial rivalry between Venice, Vienna, and Constantinople in the Eastern Mediterranean. The traditional supply chain for Ottoman tobacco exploited in Venice for the privileged manufactures of the general tobacco farm and for the re-export trade witnessed further disruption with the outbreak of the Russo-Ottoman war (1768–1774). These multiple tensions initiated a political process. At the urging of officials and entrepreneurs inspired by principles of a new political economy and by the attention to agronomy aroused by the spread of physiocratic ideas in the Italian peninsula, the Senate turned to the overseas domains of the Stato da Mar to promote experiments and agricultural projects for the introduction and development of tobacco cultivation.

The case of Girolamo Manfrin is revealing. As general tobacco farmer for the Venetian Empire, he responded to the political needs to consolidate state finance and the balance of trade with the establishment of a large tobacco plantation in Venetian Dalmatia. The project was carried out by drawing on the agronomic knowledge disseminated by specialistic treatises, journals, and agricultural academies. He benefitted from the collaboration of experts, but also from the recruitment of specialized workers from the Venetian mainland and the Ottoman Empire who were skilled in tobacco cultivation. Also, the state controlled the process

116 Tolomeo (2013, pp. 87–92).

with a particular attention to agronomic principles, entrusting the supervision of the agricultural project to special "conferences of officials" and by commissioning site inspections of experts in the field.

In the final analysis, the Nona experiment registered some success, ensuring an increasing supply of good quality tobacco leaf to the general tobacco farm's privileged manufactures. However, there was no shortage of contradictions holding it back. Distrust and ethnic prejudice against local people, especially the Morlacchis, may have limited the possibilities for growth in the region. The conservatism of the Venetian ruling class held back more radical proposals to liberalise tobacco cultivation. Not only was the monopoly never seriously challenged, but a model prevailed that concentrated the supply of leaf in large modern plantations administered by the general tobacco farm itself. In Venice, tobacco's Agricultural Enlightenment remained deeply intertwined with the pressure from state finance and the system of patronage that linked the Venetian patriciate to privileged companies and entrepreneurs through the awarding of contracts and fiscal monopolies.

References

Primary Sources

Unpublished

Archives Nationales de France, Archives diplomatiques (ANF)
- B1 990.

Museum Correr Library of Venice (MCLVe)
- Codice Cicogna.

Querini Stampalia Library of Venice (QSLVe)
- Mss. Cl. IV, cod CCCCLXX (=532).

State Archive of Venice (SAVe)
- AP.
- Archivio Perulli.
- Cinque Savi alla Mercanzia.
- Collegio.
- Compilazioni di Leggi
- Inquisitori di Stato.
- Miscellanea Soranzo.
- Municipalità provvisoria, Comitato finanze e zecca.
- Senato, Terra.
- Azienda del Tabacco.

- Segreteria di Finanze.

Published

Anonymous. 1781. *Della coltivazione e Manifattura del Tabacco. Memoria tradotta dal Francese dal signor Abate Marco Fossadoni*. Venezia: presso Benedetto Milocco.

Cristofoli, O. 1790. *Memoria agraria scritta in Zara dal sig. Ottavio Cristofoli di Conegliano*. Venezia: Unknown Publisher.

Nuovo giornale d'Italia, 1781, Vol v.

Secondary Sources

Beckert, S., U. Bosma, M. Schneider, and E. Vanhaute. 2021. Commodity Frontiers and the Transformation of the Global Countryside: A Research Agenda. *Journal of Global History* 16: 1–16.

Capalbo, C. 1999. *L'economia del vizio: il tabacco nello Stato pontificio in età moderna fra produzione e consumo*. Napoli: Edizioni scientifiche italiane.

Ciriacono, S. 1975. *Olio ed ebrei nella Repubblica veneta del Settecento*. Venezia: Deputazione di Storia Patria.

Dal Negro, P. 1998. Introduzione. In *L'ultima fase della Serenissima*, eds. P. Del Negro and P. Preto, 1–80, Roma: Istituto dell'Enciclopedia italiana.

Dal Pane, L. 1959. *Lo Stato pontificio e il movimento riformatore del Settecento*. Milano: Giuffrè.

Darling, L.T. 1996. *Revenue-Raising and Legitimacy: Tax Collection and Finance Administration in the Ottoman Empire 1560–1660*. Leiden and New York: Brill.

Davies, B.L. 2016. *The Russo-Turkish War, 1768–1774: Catherine II and the Ottoman Empire*. London: Bloomsbury.

Fodor, P., and D. Geza, eds. 2000. *Ottomans, Hungarians, and Habsburgs in Central Europe: The Military Confines in the Era of Ottoman Conquest*. Leiden and Boston: Brill.

Fontana, V. 1977. Girolamo Manfrin e la Manifattura Tabacchi a Venezia di Bernardino Maccaruzzi. *Bollettino Dei Musei Civici Veneziani* 22: 51–63.

Fotić, A. 2011. The introduction of coffee and tobacco to the Mid-West Balkans. *Acta Orientalia* 64: 89–100.

Fusaro, M. 1997. *Uva passa: una guerra commerciale tra Venezia e l'Inghilterra (1540–1640)*. Venezia: Il Cardo.

Fusaro, M. 2012. Cooperating mercantile networks in the early modern Mediterranean. *The Economic History Review* 65: 701–718.

Fusaro, M. 2015. *Political Economies of Empire in the Early Modern Mediterranean: The Decline of Venice and the Rise of England (1450–1700).* Cambridge: Cambridge University Press.

Godsey, W.D. 2018. *The Sinews of Habsburg Power: Lower Austria in a Fiscal-Military State 1650–1820.* Oxford: Oxford University Press.

Goodman, J. 1994. *Tobacco in History: The Cultures of Dependence.* London: Routledge.

Hanson, C.A. 1982. Monopoly and Contraband in the Portuguese Tobacco Trade, 1624–1702. *Luso-Brazilian Review* 19: 149–168.

Hitz, H., and H. Huber. eds, 1975. *Geschichte der österreichischen Tabakregie 1784–1835.* Vienna: Verlag der Österreichischen Akademie der Wissenschaften.

Hocquet, J.C. 2012. *Venise et le monopole du sel: production, commerce et finance d'une république marchande.* Venezia: Istituto veneto di scienze lettere ed arti.

İnalcık, H., and D. Quataert. 1994. *An economic and social history of the Ottoman Empire, 1300–1914.* Cambridge: Cambridge University Press.

Jones, P.M. 2016. *Agricultural Enlightenment: Knowledge, Technology, and Nature, 1750–1840.* Oxford: Oxford University Press.

Knapton, M. 2013. The Terraferma State. In *A Companion to Venetian History, 1400–1797*, ed. Eric R. Dursteler, 85–124. Leiden: Brill.

Kwass, M. 2014. *Contraband: Louis Mandrin and the Making of a Global Underground.* Cambridge, MA: Harvard University Press.

Levati, S. 2017. *Storia del tabacco nell'Italia moderna: secoli 17.-19.* Rome: Viella.

Nys, E. 2013. *La Guerre Maritime Étude de Droit International.* Farmington Hills, MI: Gale.

Paladini, F.M. 2002. *Un caos che spaventa: poteri, territori e religioni di frontiera nella Dalmazia della tarda età veneta.* Saggi Marsilio. Presente storico. Venice: Marsilio.

Paladini, F. 2003. Sociabilità ed economia del loisir. Fonti sui caffè veneziani del XVIII secolo. *Storia di Venezia-* Rivista, 1: 153–281.

Pezzolo, L. 2006. *Una finanza d'ancien régime: la Repubblica veneta tra 15. e 18. secolo.* Naples: Edizioni scientifiche italiane.

Rodríguez G. J. M. 2022. *La creación del estanco del tabaco en España.* Madrid: Fundación Altadis.

Røge, P. 2019. *Economistes and the Reinvention of Empire: France in the Americas and Africa, c.1750–1802.* Cambridge: Cambridge University Press.

Rogozinski, J. 1990. *Smokeless Tobacco In The Western World: 1550–1950.* New York: Praeger.

Sambo, A. 2012. La balance de commerce de la République de Venise: sources et méthodes. *Cahiers de la Méditerranée*: 381–410.

Scarabello, G. 1992. Il Settecento, In *La Repubblica di Venezia nell'età moderna: dal 1517 alla fine della Repubblica*, eds. G. Cozzi, M. Knapton and G. Scarabello, 553–696, Torino: Utet.

Shammas, C. 1993. Changes in English and Anglo-American consumption from 1550 to 1800, In *Consumption and the World of Goods*, eds. J. Brewer and R. Porter, 199–227, London: Routledge.

Sinha-Kerkhoff, K. 2014. *Colonising Plants in Bihar (1760–1950): Tobacco Betwixt Indigo and Sugarcane*. Gurgaon: Patridge Publishing.

Stoianovich, T. 1960. The conquering Balkan Orthodox merchant. *Journal of Economic History* 20: 234–313.

Tolomeo, R. 2013. *Imprenditoria e società in Dalmazia: il partito del tabacco e lo Stabilimento Manfrin nel Settecento*. Venice: La Musa Talìa editrice.

Ulvioni, P. 1985. Politica e riforme a Venezia nel secondo Settecento. Il "piano daziale", In *Profili di storia veneta*, eds. Umberto Corsini, 65–94. Venice: Università degli Studi Ca' Foscari.

van Wickeren, A. 2020. *Wissensräume im Wandel. Eine Geschichte der deutsch-französischen Tabakforschung (1780–1870)*. Cologne, Weimar, and Vienna: Böhlau Verlag.

Wolff, L. 2003. *Venice and the Slavs: The Discovery of Dalmatia in the Age of Enlightenment*. Stanford, CA: Stanford University Press.

CHAPTER 7

Knowledge and Politics: The León y Castillo Brothers and the 'Cuban Model' of Tobacco in the Canary Islands, 1852–1914

Santiago de Luxán Meléndez and María de los Reyes Hernández Socorro

Introduction

In the liberalisation following the Spanish Royal Decree of 1852 granting Free Ports status to the Canary Islands, landowners, entrepreneurs, merchants and politicians turned their gaze to applying the 'Cuban model' for promoting tobacco and sugar. They looked to the agricultural and industrial knowledge and expertise deriving from the perceived success of what had been achieved in Cuba in both tobacco and sugar,

The authors would like to thank Helena Luezas Hernández for her work and contribution to this study.

S. de Luxán Meléndez (✉) · M. de R. Hernández Socorro
University of Las Palmas de Gran Canaria, Las Palmas de Gran Canaria, Spain
e-mail: santiago.deluxan@ulpgc.es

A. van Wickeren et al. (eds.), *Tobacco in Global Perspective, 1780–1960*, Cambridge Imperial and Post-Colonial Studies,
https://doi.org/10.1007/978-3-031-64411-5_7

but in particular, for our purposes here, from how renowned Cuba had become for its tobacco and its cigars.

The Canaries, conquered by Spain in the fifteenth century and located off the coast of Morocco in northwest Africa on the route to the Americas (*Carrera de Indias*), had long constituted an important link between mainland Spain and her American territories (*las Indias*). The Spanish crown, having lost its mainland American territories by the start of the nineteenth century, saw Cuba as its 'pearl of the Antilles', and the economy, society and people of the Canary Islands and Cuba became ever more intertwined.

Against this backdrop, Juan de León y Castillo (1834–1912) and his brother Fernando de León y Castillo (1842–1918)—whose individual and collective trajectories have been well documented[1]—were two major actors who supported the 'Cuban model' for the Canary Islands. They helped set in motion a process to create a new economic, social and political framework for the islands, with steam-powered infrastructure and good local and overseas connectivity, to address the vulnerability of the Canaries economy and society. In the case of tobacco, this meant acquiring and adapting a diverse set of bodies of knowledge ranging from the liberalisation of the tobacco sector to the careful research of tobacco cultivation and the skills involved in the cigar industry.

The main thrust of the historiography to date has been to highlight the failure of late nineteenth-century Canaries tobacco. It is our contention here, however, that the period starting with the Free Ports Declaration of 1852 was a defining period in which the transfer of knowledge and experience from the 'Cuban model' and the acumen of actors such as the León y Castillo brothers played a central role in shaping the longue-durée. While it is true that in the short term neither tobacco nor sugar proved a panacea for the islands, in the long term they laid the foundations for developments in the twentieth century, when the Canary Islands achieved regional specialism in tobacco and became a significant tobacco exporter, and the alcohol industry (rum and spirits) replaced the production of sugar.[2]

[1] Del Castillo (1995). Hernández Gutiérrez (1995). Hernández Gutiérrez (1991). Hernández Gutiérrez (2006). Calvo Cruz and Castro Pérez (2010).

[2] Luxán Meléndez (2006). Luxán Meléndez (2007). Luxán Meléndez and Bergasa Perdomo (2010).

The León y Castillo brothers were involved in this in different ways. Juan, the elder of the two, directly engaged in the production of both tobacco and sugar and had a central role in the design and construction of major infrastructure projects, notably Puerto de La Luz (which literally translates as Port of Light), in the city of Las Palmas de Gran Canaria. He also became interested in politics, but it was Fernando, the younger brother, who became most active in political life. Following the constitutional changes of the early nineteenth century, Fernando, having joined the Liberal Union Party in the 1860s, was elected deputy in 1871 and then became senator. He later joined the Constitutional Union and in 1873 was fiercely against a Federal Constitution and supported the coup d'état that dissolved the Spanish Parliament. In 1874, he was made Overseas Undersecretary, and in 1876, he was a prominent member of the Liberal Party (dubbed 'Leonista' in the Canary Islands).[3] Immersed as he was in what has been described as a 'cacique-based system', he also played an active role in national and international politics and argued for extending the 1876 Spanish Constitution to Cuba.

In the case of both Juan and Fernando, and especially Fernando, iconography played a significant part.[4] Their images were bolstered through photographs, often with personal dedications, and many personal and institutional portraits, including some commissioned by Canary Islanders abroad.[5] Several were paraded around the streets to a show of public support,[6] and commemorative monuments were erected in public places, such as that of Fernando in Doramas Park in Las Palmas de Gran Canaria, commissioned after his death.

Here we home in on the role of each of the brothers in drawing on the Cuban model for tobacco during the latter part of the nineteenth century and attempting to break free from the controls of the Spanish tobacco monopoly, while also later arguing for a modicum of protection within it. The chapter first looks at how the 1817 abolition of the Spanish imperial tobacco monopoly in Cuba played a key role in the new transfer of agricultural and industrial knowledge to the Canaries, which

[3] Archivo Histórico Provincial de Las Palmas, in the following AHPLP, Fondo Juan de León y Castillo, nº 269.

[4] Hernández Socorro and Luxán Meléndez (2020, 2009).

[5] Letter dated 1 October 1904 by the Centro Archipiélago Canario, AHPLP, Fondo Juan de León y Castillo, nº 266.

[6] Luxán Meléndez (2008).

in turn played a role in the later 1881–1883 abolition of the monopoly in the Philippines, evidencing the respective roles of the brothers León y Castillo in this. It then documents their respective involvement in tobacco in the search for an economic alternative to cochineal—the carmine dye widely used in the global textile industry, produced by the insect living on the prickly pear plant, in which the archipelago had been a world leader and which was in crisis. Finally, it highlights the drive for a level of protection for Canary Island tobacco, in which Fernando in particular became a strong political advocate, especially in the face of the block put on Canaries tobacco on the Spanish national market as of 1887 by the newly established Compañía Arrendataria de Tabaco, the successor company to the Spanish national state monopoly under a private leasing arrangement.

Promoting Tobacco and the 'Cuban Model'

Our point of departure is that the agricultural and industrial developments in tobacco in the Canary Islands cannot be understood without reference to the 'Cuban model' of liberalisation in the wake of the 1817 abolition of the Spanish tobacco monopoly in Cuba. Juan de León y Castillo, greatly inspired by his uncle Francisco María de León y Falcón, was one among others who saw the importance of the transfer of seeds, growing and drying techniques, and leaf blends from Cuba for the prospects of developing Canary Island tobacco. Alongside other manuals and reports on tobacco cultivation published in Tenerife and Gran Canaria,[7] in 1870 he published his own *Guía del cultivo del tabaco* (Guide for Tobacco Cultivation), in which he declared, "I read the memoires [such as Mr Demoor, *Du Tabac* and *El manual del veguero de José María Dau* (José María Dau's Tobacco Grower's Manual) [published in Havana in 1847] and all the facts that came into my hands, keen as I was to know if this new specialty of agriculture could be really profitable or not in our islands".[8]

Dau, a Cuban-based agronomist, whose book featured numerous facets of tobacco cultivation, from sowing to fertilising to harvesting,

[7] Anonymous (1859). Nepomuceno Deniz (1863). Anonymous (1861). Mitjans (1872).

[8] León y Castillo (1870).

drew international attention to his writing, with French experts likewise interested in his work in the 1860s. In Cuba, agricultural research on tobacco cultivation dated back to the Bourbon reforms of the eighteenth century, and Cuban leaf and cigars had by the 1830s become established beyond Cuban shores as a model to be imitated. It was also clear to contemporaries that knowledge from Cuba, not least agricultural knowledge, had to be tested and adapted to respective environments.

The first small-scale trials in cultivating tobacco in the Canary Islands began in 1827, when, during the last decade of Fernando VII, authorisations were granted to conduct trials using Cuban seed in the Canary Islands. Spain was looking to foster its own production of leaf to curb the large-scale smuggling of tobacco and the cheaper tobacco being brought in from the USA and Brazil as an alternative to the more costly leaf from Cuba. Against this backdrop, it was by virtue of Spanish Royal Decree 14/XII/1827, together with additional rules and regulations, that trialling tobacco was envisaged.

The Junta de Fomento de las Islas (Islands Development Board) was created by Spanish Royal Decree 23/IX/1830, and it saw tobacco as a possible alternative to the then decline of wine, which had been the island's main export since the mid-sixteenth century; *barilla*, which was cultivated for its sodium carbonate, a basic ingredient for soap production; and orchilla lichen (*Roccella canariensis)*, the source of a purple dye. There was at the time little confidence in what appeared to be an uncertain future for cochineal, given declining prices and the large amounts of capital required in order to establish the prickly pear farms, and it was mooted that under the Provincial Councils tobacco might be a potential 'quick' switch. We know from Royal Commissioner Manuel Rafael Vargas, however, that the Spanish government only reluctantly authorised the tobacco trials, and each evidently failed.[9]

It was not until the late 1860s and early 1870s that Juan de León y Castillo turned to tobacco, growing the leaf on his farm *Jaraquemada* in Telde, on Gran Canaria. He wrote in his *Guía* that the soil conditions, height above sea level, winds and insects were such as to be favourable for tobacco and other crops, especially types of corn, and the farming method to be followed should vary the planting, fertilising and watering seasons. Over two harvests, his farm averaged a successful yield of 70

[9] Luxán Meléndez (2006).

quintales (approximately 3,220 kg, since at the time a *quintal* was the equivalent of 46 kg, not the standardised 100 kg after 1892) per *fanega* (bushel). This led him to extrapolate from his experience to the rest of the archipelago and become instrumental in developing procedures for selling initially leaf and subsequently cigars within the Spanish state monopoly, though he sold only cigars.

The will to change the agricultural landscape through knowledge from Cuba corresponded to the technocratic spirit of the age that would have shaped Juan de León y Castillo's education and training. As he observed retrospectively, he could have followed in his parents' footsteps on the land or "migrated like so many others to the Americas".[10] However, having been a boarding student (1845–1850) at the influential San Agustín School—the first private high school established in the city of Las Palmas, at a time when there were no public schools—he went on to study civil engineering in Madrid (1850–1858). There he acquired his 'industrialising ideology'[11] and after graduating became a road engineer, travelling France and Belgium, as well as the Spanish mainland.

While less directly involved in politics than his brother, he became an influential figure in economic and cultural circles through two major institutions in Las Palmas de Gran Canaria: the Real Sociedad Económica de Amigos del País de Gran Canaria (Royal Economic Society of Friends of the Country of Gran Canaria) and the Gabinete Literario (Literary Forum). Then, after his years dedicated to tobacco (and sugar), he resumed his work as engineer and in 1883 embarked on his grand project of Puerto de La Luz. The port became one of several causes of friction with his brother and the source of a bitter controversy later in life, when he confronted Prudencio Morales, the author of a 1907 book titled *Política de mi tierra*, for attributing the port to Fernando.[12]

The brothers were descended from Canary aristocracy. Their parents José de León y Falcón and María de la Concepción del Castillo Olivares were the second son and daughter of nobility. This meant they were excluded from the main part of their respective parents' inheritance under the right of primogeniture (the *mayorazgo* or *majorat*), and they went into business, first in wine and then cochineal. Their mother, Concepción

[10] AHPLP, Fondo Juan de León y Castillo, n° 90, 93, 94, 97,99, 100 and 280.

[11] Luxán Meléndez and Bergasa Perdomo (2019).

[12] AHPLP, Fondo Juan de León y Castillo, Numbers 252, 253, 255 and 257.

del Castillo, in 1857 started up a company with Mariano González y Cía to manage their cochineal business. In several letters to his mother,[13] Juan enquired about cochineal production. My mother, he wrote, "started businesses like a man" (clearly considering business to be a male enterprise). He also congratulated himself for having achieved a good cochineal harvest and having sold a plot in El Monte Lentiscal, on Gran Canaria, to tobacco and sugar financier and businessman Alfonso Gourié, and it was this that financed his civil engineering studies and stay in Madrid.

His interest in the introduction and improvement of tobacco in the Canary Islands, along with sugar, was part of his broader aim to promote a modern development of the Canaries with a great infrastructure. He saw the potential in tropical plant species, and among them tobacco specially stood out. In agriculture, he wrote in his *Guía*, there is an axiom: a country that grows tobacco becomes rich. On the basis of this, his aim was to see the creation of an industry, drawing on the Cuban experience; as a tobacco expert and entrepreneur, he acquired symbolic capital; and, in addition to publishing his *Guía,* he founded the newspaper *El Omnibus*.[14] In 1875, when Canaries tobacco began to be marketed on the Spanish mainland, his name did not figure among the tobacco leaf sales of the agrarian and industrial company El Porvenir Agrícola de Canarias, owned by Alfonso Gourié. However, he had by then become a member of the cigar manufacturers' guild and established his own factory producing Jaraquemada cigars. This we know from a cigar band that has been handed down to us today, bearing the name of his son Germán.

Improved processing of the tobacco was as important to Canary Island experts as managing the cultivation of the tobacco plant in the fields. For tobacco's future on the Islands, Juan de León y Castillo noted in his *Guía*, one had to learn from processing in the world-famous rolling shops in Havana and also other places, such as Germany, where manufacturing factories were the greatest sources of income and reached a level of perfection worthy of study. The fact that he referred to the cigar factories in the German states—which have barely been considered from a global history perspective, and until the 1860s were concentrated mainly in the Hanseatic cities of Hamburg and Bremen (two benchmark ports in

[13] Letters dated 27 March, 12 May, and 12 June 1857, AHPLP, Fondo Juan de León y Castillo, nº 99, in numbers 191–192, 195 and 197.

[14] Juan Rodríguez Suárez, Biografía ms., AHPLP, Fondo Juan de León y Castillo, nº 97.

Europe and for the Atlantic trade)—demonstrates the breadth of knowledge experts were acquiring at the time in the newly emerging tobacco regions such as the Canary Islands.

Knowledge about tobacco from Cuba also encompassed design expertise. Julián Cirilo Moreno, Juan de León y Castillo's civil engineering assistant, included in his memoirs a fascinating description of the great interest in the '*habilitaciones*' (labels), stating that he was "honoured with drawing in colour the illustrations on the cigar boxes and the brands of the cigarette packets".[15] Gran Canaria was depicted lying on top of tobacco bundles surrounded by palm trees in the front. Behind this was an idealised view of the imagined tobacco field of Jaraquemada with its drying barns and in the background a calm sea, cloudless sky and rising sun. Cuban cigars were already famous in the 1830s and 1840s for their decorative presentation on cigar bands and cigar box labels. These were soon being imitated across the world, and the visual regionalisation of Jaraquemada is suggestive of knowledge appropriation from the cigar culture of Cuba.

The significance of the new conditions created by the 1852 Spanish Free Ports Decree to promote the improvement of tobacco cultivation, processing and retail cannot be overestimated. Before the 1850s the Canary Islands were consumers not producers of tobacco. They had been subject to the restrictions on cultivation and production of the Spanish state tobacco monopoly and its general licensing regulations.[16] Their geographical location on the route to the Americas had, however, facilitated a direct relationship with Cuba, which was exempt from the Spanish state monopoly control after 1817. Granting Free Ports status to the Canary Islands meant easing the controls of the Spanish state monopoly, enabling Canary Islanders first to grow their own leaf and later manufacture their own tobacco on a commercial scale, and Canary Island politicians and the tobacco sector used this to good advantage.

The liberalisation in Cuba had come largely in response to the pressure of the local sugar lobby headed by Francisco Arango y Parreño, who also argued that tobacco, given its importance for Cuba, should be freed from monopoly constraint.[17] A central part of the Preamble to the 1817

[15] Cirilo Moreno (1947).

[16] Luxán Meléndez et al. (2012). Luxán Meléndez (2018).

[17] Sanz Rozalén (2009). Sanz Rozalén (2018).

Spanish Royal Decree that approved the abolition was couched in this vein:

> (…) My royal attention has been drawn to the promotion and farming of the precious tobacco plant, this being so important due to the exclusive privilege that Nature has given to the soil in the Island of Cuba, in order to produce the most exquisite quality in the world. Spain, which has in this agrarian and manufacturing industry one of the most precious items to be delivered in European markets, has been deprived of immense capital due to a state monopoly, as well as a lack of freedom in its planting, manufacturing and trading, and the inhabitants of the Peninsula have also been deprived of enjoying a product that they deeply appreciate and have ended up consuming the unhealthy Brazilian tobacco and the most despicable leaf of English America.[18]

The Spanish government was undecided for many years as to whether or not monopoly control over the Canary Islands should also cease. A Spanish Act of 1837 ratified the main difference between the Spanish mainland and the rest of overseas territories in terms of distance, the nature of their population, and their different material interests, and an 1841 Spanish Review Committee of the Laws of the Indies concluded that the Canary Islands should also follow special regulations.[19] Among those who promoted the 1852 Spanish Royal Decree of Free Ports status in the Canary Islands and also earlier supported the Cuban precedent, were the two uncles of the León y Castillo brothers: the Member of Parliament Jacinto de León y Falcón and his brother Francisco María, who as Royal Commissioner for Agriculture strongly promoted Canaries tobacco.[20]

Juan de León y Castillo himself decried how many countries had established an 'artificial monopoly' (as had the Spanish state in 1636), but the liberalisation, he also argued, could result in an unfettered increase in production and loss in value. He took from Thomas Robert Malthus and John Stuart Mill their concept of the 'natural monopoly' a territory might have, and he, among others, envisaged this would be the case with

[18] Spanish Royal Decree as of 23 June 1817, signed by Martín de Garay, Archivo General de Indias, in the following AGI, Ultramar, leg. 245.

[19] Martínez Navas (2007). Elizalde (2019). Concerning the Cuban case, the most recent references can be found in Gárate Ojanguren (2019). Sanz Rozalén (2019).

[20] Luxán Meléndez (1993). Luxán Meléndez (2006).

Canary Islands tobacco after abolishing such an artificial restriction as the state monopoly. But the result of liberalising the tobacco economy along the lines of the 'Cuban model' was that the Canary Islands were then competing on both the Spanish and international markets with Cuba, and also the Philippines, where the Philippines' monopoly had been a key source of crown revenue from the end of the eighteenth century.[21] Abolition of the state tobacco monopoly there, between 1881 and 1883, was eventually carried through when Fernando de León y Castillo was appointed Overseas Minister.

The decree by virtue of which the state monopoly in the Philippines was abolished, which was reproduced in full in Fernando's memoirs, published in 1918, argued:

> if from the economic point of view, the state monopoly has the wealth of the Philippines in a stranglehold, from the political [point of view] the means employed in order to sustain that are unacceptable… The tobacco state monopoly, yielding revenues of approximately two and a half million *pesos*, is imposing in return for this material sacrifices which are infinitely greater than their advantages.[22]

The appointment of Fernando helped Antonio López, Marqués de Comillas and his French partners to play a decisive role establishing in Manila, in place of the monopoly, the privately owned Compañía General de Tabacos de Filipinas. Accounting for a large part of Philippine production, the company was one in which Fernando became a shareholder.

In effect, the abolition in Cuba in 1817 became a model that was applied de facto in the Canary Islands in the 1850s, and subsequently in the Philippines in the early 1880s. In the process, a new tobacco transborder dynamic of agricultural and industrial knowledge was created. When in the late 1880s, however, the Spanish national state tobacco monopoly was replaced by the private leasing arrangement of Arrendataria, new problems were created for Canaries tobacco, as we shall see below.

[21] Alharilla (2009). Alharilla (2021). de Jesus (1980). Fradera (1999).

[22] León y Castillo (1978 [1918]).

Tobacco as an Economic Alternative

After the abolition of the monopoly in Cuba, the Cuban tobacco sector expanded greatly and by the mid-1850s was second only to sugar in terms of exports.[23] In the Canaries, by the mid-1870s, tobacco, along with sugar, was being taken seriously as a future alternative to cochineal, which had seen a renewed expansion after 1852. This bottomed out during the depression of 1873, by which time technological innovation of artificial aniline dyes (a by-product of coal tar) meant cochineal ceased to be profitable. For Juan de León y Castillo, the prospect of crisis was already apparent. As he wrote in his *Guía*:

> The history of industry always proffers the same features - each victorious effort brings along a victim and many winners. Rich regions, important industrial centres, are destroyed because of an improvement. Exorbitant yields must be reduced. Natural or artificial monopolies end up disappearing under the weight of the law of production. This is the history of our wine… as it is of our cochineal industry too. Our mild and uniform temperatures – unique in the whole world – created a natural monopoly for cochineal farming. Excessive yields were obtained. Properties everywhere increased their values… but nonetheless we have been producing so much that at last cochineal has fallen…

The earlier cochineal crisis and downturn in wine production, on the heels of the turbulent wars earlier in the century,[24] compounded by prolonged droughts and outbreaks of yellow fever in 1846 and cholera in 1851, had resulted in extreme poverty across the islands. Lanzarote, Fuerteventura and El Hierro experienced particularly high levels of out-migration, and those who did not migrate—as many already had earlier, not least to Cuba—were reported unable to feed themselves. Despite the growth of cochineal after 1840 and through the boom years after 1852, not all the islands were involved in its production, and the 1873 cochineal crisis only worsened the situation. Since the 1852 Free Ports Declaration, the Canaries had lost precious time. Diagnosing an uncertain future for cochineal, Juan de León y Castillo declared it unwise to depend on just one product. In his *Guía,* he saw tobacco as an alternative for cochineal farmers—if every farmer would turn some *celemines*(1 celemín = 537m2)

[23] Stubbs (2003 [1985]). González Fernández (1992).

[24] Luxán Meléndez (2011). Cabrera Armas and Díaz de la Paz (2011).

over to growing tobacco, the knowledge of tobacco cultivation in the Canary Islands would improve rapidly.

Despite the new advocacy for tobacco, cultivation and processing remained limited. As Juan de León y Castillo wrote in his *Guía*, people who had made their living from cochineal still looked to it, ignoring the new. Even in 1880, there still seemed to be hope of a future for cochineal and tobacco was still viewed with a certain anxiety. The records of the Tenerife Real Sociedad Económica de Amigos del País cautioned:

> It is not to tobacco farming that we should turn our gaze. Tobacco, besides having competitors in many countries, is a new crop among us that requires some years for improvement and expansion, and our situation does not allow for any delay; it requires at least a minimum of investment to perform trials, and that capital does not exist; it requires the farmer to harvest immediately, and this is not possible for the time being. Caution recommends not abandoning what we already know for the unknown.[25]

In response to an 1880 enquiry into the main agrarian issues facing the islands, agriculturalists did, however, support a gradual reduction of cochineal,[26] and, aware of the importance of tobacco, insisted on more intensive exploitation of cultivating the plant in the Canary Islands for it to be economically viable. Experts and industrialists recommended the compatibility of tobacco with sugar, whose regional cultivation in the Canary Islands was more familiar, and the solution put forward was the creation of an agro-industrial complex of tobacco and sugar, combined with the introduction of new crops (mainly bananas and tomatoes) and the development of infrastructure (a network of roads and ports). This was reflected in the local fortnightly journal *Las Palmas Quincenal*, put out between 1875 and 1876 by El Porvenir Agrícola, the company owned by Alfonso Gourié, who had interests in both tobacco and sugar, and was particularly close to Fernando de León y Castillo. For his part, Juan de León y Castillo wrote, "Given the terrible perspective that the agrarian future of our Province is presenting, we shall all try, to the extent of our possibilities, to clear its enveloping dark clouds". In addition to tobacco, he also showed a strong interest in sugar as a possibility for diversification in an 1875 article in *Las Palmas Quincenal*. He even considered

[25] Hernández García (1978, p. 56).

[26] Anonymous (1880).

building his own factory in 1881, for which we have the budget quote he requested from a French company located in Cannes.

The more it seemed that cochineal would not recover, the more Canary Island growers and manufacturers, through their associations, saw that the future might lie in the advantages that tobacco could deliver. In an article published in *Las Palmas Quincenal* in September 1875, Alejo Luis Yagüe argued "Although America is the first and main source of this essential item, the one produced in our lands must not be ignored... and a new path to prosperity shall be forged".[27] Some voices were raised in favour of developing the tobacco option exclusively, advising against the sugar option when sugar was undergoing a world crisis in 1884–1885 and its price halved. In the world market, production of beet entailed a latent threat, whereby a letter reproduced in the Las Palmas newspaper *El Liberal* in December 1885 suggested:

> It seems by far more logical to give preference there to tobacco farming over sugar cane, due to the fact that the former does not require such big investments as the latter for its exploitation in good conditions, and also being this a more manageable item, but above all, more able to withstand foreign competition, since its quality is as good as some people I must consider competent have assured.[28]

The letter went on to suggest that the model to follow was that of Sumatra tobacco, which had recently been introduced in the North American market, and that it would be absolutely essential to establish an agency in New York.

Tobacco Seeks an Export Market

Gradually, there was growing consensus in support of tobacco cultivation given that its start-up did not require great sums of money or labour; it could be combined with other crops such as corn and with livestock, leading to an increase of animal manure; it would foster transport and port activities; and it would be a stimulus to industry. However, this had, it became increasingly argued, to take place in a commercial framework that provided a certain level of protectionism. This was seen as essential

[27] Yagüe (1875).

[28] Anonymous (1885).

to develop an emerging industry, aiming to sell its production on the Spanish mainland market, and Fernando de León y Castillo became one of the major political actors aiming to secure the future of the agricultural and industrial tobacco sector through a market partially protected with customs tariffs.

The conditions for expanding exports to the Spanish mainland were quite promising. Between the years 1877/1878 and 1878/1879, a total of 1,000,000 Canary Island cigars were sold on the Spanish mainland,[29] and Table 7.1 details cigar shipments for the previous two years from manufacturers, including Juan de León y Castillo:

Parallel to increasing sales on the Spanish mainland, Canary Island tobacco had been garnering accolades in international trade exhibitions, likening the tobacco to that of Cuba. As the Canaries newspaper *La Defensa* reported in March 1872 on the participation of Canaries tobacco in the Exhibition Fair that our compatriots have promoted in Matanzas (Cuba): "Among thousands of tobacco types sent there, several brands with leaf harvested in the Canary Islands (Guanarteme) and manufactured in the factory of La Afortunada, owned by Sr Marcial Melián, achieved distinguished places, competing with important manufacturers like Gener and Partagás".[30]

For some, Canary Islands tobacco was already being considered among the finest. "This new tobacco that has been assessed according to some samples is very similar to that coming from Havana. Hence, prices must reflect this accordingly".[31] Samples that were sent to the London market, Juan de León y Castillo wrote, were mistaken for tobacco from Havana, whereby, he concluded, in the Canary Islands we know how to produce tobacco. He had requested three *quintales* (138 kg) from the Sotomayor family on the island of La Palma "since they never gave out this crop" and sent samples to the London market through the firm *Casa de Menéndez y Laza*, which sold on commission. He obtained 632 *reáles de vellón* (1 shilling and 4 pennies per lb) per quintal, and the firm notified him that it was mistaken for Havana tobacco:

[29] Anonymous (1875a, p. 16).

[30] Anonymous (1872).

[31] Anonymous (1872, p. 3).

Table 7.1 Canary Island cigar manufacturers and shipments to the Spanish mainland, 1885–1887 (Units)

	José García Torres	*Melián Hnos*	*Luis Román y Lugo*	*Antonio Navarro y Mandillo*	*Miguel Sotomayor y Lugo*	*Tomás Miller e Hijos*	*Juan de Léon y Castillo*	*Juan Cumella*	*Marcial Melián*	*Sin distinguir*
26/V/85		60.000	27.300	28.950						
23/XI/85		40.000	76.000	38.150	10.500					
23/III/86		25.000	100.000							
22/V/86					40.000					
23/VI/86		90.000	250.000		12.500					
8/VII/86	59.200									
23/X/86	125.000		305.000		45.000	80.000	38.000	195.000		
8/I/87	27.000		117.250		40.500	27.250				
22/IV/87	55.000		105.000		63.000		43.000	145.000	15.000	
Total	**628.550**	**215.000**	**990.300**	**67.100**	**175.750**	**107.250**	**81.000**	**340.000**	**15.000**	**277.000**

Source AHT FTM, DGRE, Adm, sig. 723–726

After seeing it, people here believe it comes from Havana, although they are puzzled by its type. We let them go along with this mistake, and they certainly think that it is tobacco known by the name of *Partido*. Concerning its aroma and taste, it has obtained a second place. The Philippine [type] is more expensive due to its leaf being excellent for rolling.

The optimistic assessments were rather misleading as to the wider export situation. Canary Island tobacco, despite its presence at exhibitions and the positive assessments, was not a big seller on the world market. International markets such as Hamburg were focused on other tobacco types, such as those from Havana, Santo Domingo, Puerto Rico or Brazil. Juan de León y Castillo himself wrote in 1872, "up until now, nothing has been exported from these [Canary] islands".[32] For his 1870 *Guía*, he had studied the market conditions and produced a price chart (Table 7.2) in English and Spanish currencies for each tobacco type:

Table 7.2 shows significant price fluctuations and British consuls might have been closer in their assessments than London, when they recommended Canaries manufacturing cater to the need for low-quality products, for which there was a growing market on the coast of Africa.[33]

Table 7.2 Price chart for different tobacco types

Type	*English currency (Shillings)*	*Variation*	*Spanish quintal in* reales de vellón	*Variation*
Maryland	4 ½	10	180	401
Virginia	4	2	160	961,20
German	5	1,9	190,96	841,44
Santo Domingo	6	9	240,56	360,33
Turkish and Greek	3	9 ½	119,77	380,62
Colombian	8	2	320,74	1201,76
Brazil	10	2	400,92	961,20
Java	6	1	240,55	481,71
Manila	6	7,6	2884,63	3606,29
Havana	1	8	681,07	3845,54

Source Juan de León y Castillo, *Guía del cultivo del tabaco* (1870)

[32] Ibid.

[33] Quintana Navarro (1992).

Numerous proposals were put forward as to how a closer trade connection with the Spanish market could be achieved. Both consular representatives and Canary Island growers insisted on the need to locate in the Canaries a state factory that could guarantee the growers the sale of their leaf. In 1878 a specific request was made from Tenerife for a state establishment in the Canary Islands responsible for purchasing and manufacturing Canaries tobacco.[34] In 1882, this request was repeated in *La Correspondencia de Canarias*,[35] which saw a brilliant future for tobacco, if state stores could be established which had direct links with Madrid and measures could be taken for the tobacco from the Canary Islands to be known and compete on all markets.

Faced with the impracticality of this proposal, the alternative consisted in the implementation of tobacco drying facilities. However, these remained vulnerable to unpredictable contingencies, and private interests were eventually left responsible for trading on local and national markets. Arguments in 1875 from El Porvenir Agrícola and the Sociedad Agrícola e Industrial del Fomento del Tabaco de La Laguna (Society for the Agricultural and Industrial Development of Tobacco of La Laguna) in Tenerife were to no avail. The Liga de Agricultores y Fabricantes de tabaco (League of Tobacco Farmers and Manufacturers), which had the political support of Fernando de León y Castillo,[36] that same year also called for an expansion of exports to the Spanish mainland. The League called for higher customs duties on tobacco coming from Cuba and from foreign countries entering the Spanish market, so as to promote Canary Island tobacco.[37]

When Fernando de León y Castillo was appointed Overseas Minister in 1881, the newspaper *El Independiente* requested his intervention for allowing tobacco from the Canary Islands to enter territories of the state monopoly on the following grounds:

> This country, being in a state of prostration, and once disappointment has dissipated all bright hopes founded on formal promises, cannot by any means continue living on dreams, nor on nominal offers. Something more

[34] Hernández García (1980).

[35] Anonymous (1882).

[36] Anonymous (1875(a), p. 16).

[37] Anonymous (Ibid., 1875(b), p. 13).

positive is demanded, in order to cease this uncertainty that is astonishing, this despondency that is killing us. Can our country live and improve on the honour and glory achieved for having climbed the seats of power, due to his exclusive merits and political consequence, of the distinguished son of the Canary Islands, Don Fernando de León y Castillo? No, as honour does not provide for life, and glory does not provide for prosperity. It might represent a mark of honour shining in history, but it will not be a source of welfare solving the eventful situation we are facing (...) In his Ministry, Don Fernando de León y Castillo can certainly do a great deal for the Canary Islands: for us, to do justice (not favour), to fulfil the promise, will suffice. Our main issue is the purchase of tobacco by the [Spanish] Government, the only way of ceasing this atrocious crisis we are experiencing, as it has been evidenced over and over again. The regulation approved in Parliament must be enforced...[38]

In 1885, Fernando formed part of a committee in Madrid with the aim of managing the sale of Canary Island tobacco in Madrid and presenting a statement to this effect before the minister of finance.[39] The creation of Arrendataria in 1887, however, made things worse for Canaries tobacco. No longer able to count on any safety net that had been provided within the state monopoly market, the Canaries soon found that not only were special rights for Canaries tobacco off the agenda, but leaf and manufactured products from elsewhere, notably Cuba and the Philippines, were favoured, and Canaries tobacco was disadvantaged. According to consular reports, in 1893–1894 more than 90% of Canaries tobacco was sold on the local Canaries market.

The situation turned more critical after 1898, when Spain lost its three colonies of Cuba, Puerto Rico and the Philippines, and was compounded with the renewal of Arrendataria's contract in 1900, as well as a Free Ports reform and further regulations in 1901 and 1903. Its treatment on a par with overseas products on the Spanish market was such that in parliament, in 1905, the Marqués de Casa Iglesia addressed the finance minister as follows:

The Arrendataria, which buys in all parts of the world, [knows] that the cheapest tobacco is sold in the Canary Islands... Tobacco has been the sole commercial bond linking the Canary Islands with the Spanish mainland,

[38] Anonymous (1881, p. 1).

[39] Anonymous (1884, p. 48).

> and although the reasons for the monopoly and its purpose are worthy of consideration, I heartily recommend the Minister of Finance to put this condition to an end.[40]

From 1899 to 1914, 80% of tobacco imports were from the UK and Germany, followed by 10% from the USA (including Puerto Rico as of 1905), and in small proportions from several other countries. The interest in the Canaries on the part of Arrendataria, insofar as it existed, was primarily in leaf, and the buying system was shipments of leaf in bulk, not from individual growers, designed to counter smuggling. The important point to make here is that the Canary Islands tobacco option continued to be mainly agrarian. This caused friction not only between the Canaries tobacco sector and Arrendataria but also between Canaries growers and manufacturers, and left the manufacturing sector in a precarious state. In 1905 there were 39 small concerns, 18 in Tenerife, 12 in Gran Canaria and 9 in the island of La Palma. In 1909 there were only 16, and fragmentary and contradictory data for 1914 suggest they might have increased in number but were small scale and often ephemeral.

Conclusion

Our intention, as stated at the outset, was to evidence the importance of the León y Castillo brothers in promoting the 'Cuban model' of tobacco in the Canary Islands over the years 1852–1914. It can be argued that the presence of Juan was initially the more important, as a tobacco grower and manufacturer, and having been the one who penned the *Guía del Cultivo del Tabaco*. It was, however, the intervention of Fernando that was crucial in political negotiations on a national level, arguing for the importance of a level of protection for Canaries tobacco within the Islands' Free Ports status.

In the case of tobacco, the brothers together demonstrate the significant role business and political figures can play at a key moment in time. What was achieved in defending the interests of the Canary Islands cannot be understood without the presence of a political intermediary like Fernando de León y Castillo, and the network of connections he created. He and his brother Juan were complementary to each other in the modernisation of the Canaries economy and society.

[40] Anonymous (1905, p. 1).

This is not to say that either, and especially Fernando, were always portrayed in a positive light, and the two of them parted ways in later life. By way of an epitaph for their, and especially Fernando's, contentious trajectory, in 1910 *La Opinión* of Santa Cruz de Tenerife ran an article critical of the political system created by Fernando, one in which Juan was also implicated, referring to the 'cacique system', which merits quoting at length:

> Spanish Governments have always understood as the unique ideal for governing the State that this should be developed under the wildest cacique system, ignoring other trends of opinion, and surrendering to the great provincial caciques instead, who ruled over those beneath them at their pleasure, thus forming a vast network of caciques that have been the sole support of the Government and institutions up until our day. These did not hesitate, once León y Castillo reached the high spheres of the Overseas Ministry, to give him complete control of politics in the Canary Islands Archipelago.

In the article, Juan was explicitly implicated:

> For forty years, the people of the Canaries have considered León y Castillo as their unique bond between them and the central power, and his own power has reached such a level of omnipotence that those who did not surrender have been quickly annihilated. Not even his own brother was spared from the rage of this great cacique. When Don Fernando de León y Castillo was elected MP for Las Palmas for the first time, his brother Don Juan was a person with a great political influence in the Canary Islands… When some years later and in view of the huge benefits that the building of the port represented, the idea of raising two statues of the León y Castillo brothers was requested and unanimously accepted, Don Fernando, who already had enough power to overshadow his brother, not only did not consent to a statue for his brother, but also gave orders to his newspapers and supporters to engage in his political extermination.

The sad epitaph for Juan was that, in view of the war directed against him, he retired to a private life and:

> He continues like that until our days, cornered and forgotten by everyone, with no more friends than three or four men of independent hearts and souls who are defending the misfortune of this second 'Abel'. The rest of the politicians, fearing the anger of Don Fernando, are doing what they

can to avoid consorting with Don Juan and even harass him whenever the occasion arises.

This sorry indictment on their lives should not detract, however, from what they each achieved in laying the foundations for significant long-term developments. Neither Juan nor Fernando de León y Castillo lived to see the new twentieth-century expansion of the Canaries tobacco sector. This did not come until after World War I, and more precisely until the 1920s, when Arrendataria recognised the full legality of Canary Island producers within the monopoly market, and, alongside cigar rolling, there was an expansion of mechanised cigarette production. There would be continued tension, however, with Arrendataria, which was exacerbated in the late 1930s and 1940s during the Spanish Civil War and World War II and their aftermath.

The second globalisation of tobacco from the late eighteenth century to the mid-twentieth century saw the emergence of many new centres of tobacco production. In the case of Spain and its last colonies (Cuba, Puerto Rico and the Philippines), the Canary Islands became one of these centres in the nineteenth century. The Islands' creative minds, such as Juan and Fernando León y Castillo, sought to learn from the knowledge and experience that the Cuban model offered. The liberalisation of the Cuban tobacco economy after 1817 and Cuba's industrial and agricultural knowledge, hailed globally as a successful model, was one they saw could be adapted to the needs of the Canary Islands. They, along with other agriculturalists, entrepreneurs and politicians, aspired to share in the opportunities afforded by the growing global tobacco trade and ever-widening circles of cigar and cigarette smokers. They crafted an antidote to economic recession and the decline of cochineal, and, in both the build-up to and aftermath of the creation of the Arrendataria, sought to frame a level of protection to secure markets for Canaries tobacco on the Spanish mainland.

While the Canary Islands cannot be seen to have been at the forefront on international tobacco markets, it would, nevertheless, be misleading to dismiss the efforts of those such as the León y Castillo brothers as a 'failure'. They provide us with a significant case study of the Canary Islands, illustrating how the intensified circulation of knowledge and experience about the Cuban model and Cuban tobacco in the earlier and middle parts of the nineteenth century, while frustrated towards the end of the century, would forge a path for the Canary Islands that would eventually reap rewards.

References

Primary Sources

Unpublished

Archivo Histórico Provincial de Las Palmas (AHPLP).
- Fondo Juan de León y Castillo.
Archivo General de Indias (AGI).
- Ultramar.

Published

Anonymous. 1859. *Manual del Cultivo del Tabaco.* Santa Cruz de Tenerife: Imprenta Madrileña de Salvador Vidal.

Anonymous. 1861. *Memoria redactada por las clases de agricultura y comercio de la Sociedad de Amigos del País de Palmas de Gran Canaria sobre el cultivo del tabaco.* Gran Canaria: Imprenta de la Verdad.

Anonymous. 1872. *La Defensa*, 23 March.

Anonymous. 1875(a). *Anales de la Sociedad Económica de Amigos del País de Las Palmas de Gran Canaria*, 31 December.

Anonymous. 1875(b). *La Opinión*: periódico liberal conservador, 16 December.

Anonymous. 1880. *Memoria sobre las causas de la actual decadencia de la provincia de Canarias y medios para evitar su ruina. Interrogatorio referente a las principales cuestiones relacionadas con el porvenir agrícola de estas Islas.* Cf. "La Correspondencia de Canarias" 13 y 27-IX and 2-X-1880.

Anonymous. 1881. *El Independiente*, 13 March.

Anonymous. 1882. *La Correspondencia de Canarias*, 2 February and 2 November.

Anonymous. 1884. *Anales de la Sociedad Económica de Amigos del País de Las Palmas de Gran Canaria*, 21 December.

Anonymous. 1885. Letter from Rob. Hérques (Monaco, 6/XII/1885). *El Liberal*, 25 December.

Anonymous. 1905. *El Tiempo: diario de asuntos generales e información*, defensor de los intereses del país, 22 December.

León y Castillo, F.d. 1978 [1918]. *Mis tiempos.* Las Palmas de Gran Canaria: Cabildo Insular de Gran Canaria.

León y Castillo, J.d. 1870. *Guía del cultivo del tabaco.* Gran Canaria: Imprenta de La Verdad.

Mitjans, B. 1872. *Memoria sobre el tabaco de la isla de Cuba en la que se indican algunas mejoras de que es susceptible su cultivo y preparación.* Santa Cruz de Tenerife Imprenta: Librería y Encuadernación de J. Benítez y Cía.

Nepomuceno, D.J. 1863. *Instrucción para el cultivo del tabaco*. Gran Canaria: Imprenta de la Verdad.
Yagüe, A.L. 1875. *Las Palmas Quincenal*, 15 September.

Secondary Sources

Cabrera Armas, L., and A. Díaz de la Paz. 2011. La quiebra de las bases económicas tradicionales. In *Historia Contemporánea de Canarias*, eds. A. Millares Cantero, S. Millares Cantero, F. Quintana Navarro and M. Suárez Bosa, 17–33. Las Palmas de Gran Canaria: Obra Social de la Caja de Canarias.
Calvo Cruz, M., and C. Castro Pérez. 2010. El fondo documental Ingeniero D. Juan de León y Castillo: Estudio descriptivo de las principales cuentas utilizadas en el registro de las obras de construcción del Puerto de La Luz y Las Palmas, 1891–1901. *Revista Española De Historia De La Contabilidad* 13: 3–40.
Cirilo Moreno, J. 1947. *De los puertos de la Luz y de Las Palmas y otras historias*. Las Palmas de Gran Canaria: Ediciones del Gabinete Literario.
Delaunay, J.-M., and F. Quintana Navarro. 1982. Inventario del fondo documental de los hermanos León y Castillo. *Coloquio De Historia Canario Americana* 5: 546–600.
De Jesus, E.C. 1980. *The tobacco monopoly in the Philippines. Bureaucratic, Enterprise and Social Change 1776–1880*. Manila: Ateneo de Manila University Press.
Elizalde, M.D. 2019. Filipinas en el marco del Imperio español en el siglo XIX. *Estudis. Revista De Historia Moderna* 45: 93–116.
Fradera, J. 1999. *Filipinas, la colonia más peculiar. La hacienda pública en la definición de la política colonial 1762–1868*. Madrid: Consejo Superior de Investigaciones Científicas.
Gárate, O.M. 2019. *Cuba: tabaco y hacienda imperial (1717–1817). Un siglo de gestión del estanco: funcionarios, ilustrados y militares*. San Sebastián: Universidad de Las Palmas de Gran Canaria/Real Sociedad Bascongada de Amigos del País.
González, F.D. 1992. La manufactura tabacalera cubana durante la segunda mitad del siglo XIX. *Revista De Indias* 52: 129–155.
Hernández García, J. 1980. La Económica de Tenerife ante la crisis del XIX canario: Los nuevos cultivos de recambio. *I Jornadas De Estudios Canarias-América* 3: 45–73.
Hernández Gutiérrez, A.S. 1991. *El Puerto de La Luz en la obra de Juan de León y Castillo*. Las Palmas of Gran Canaria: University of Las Palmas of Gran Canaria.

Hernández Gutiérrez, A.S. 1995. *Juan de León y Castillo. Ingeniero, Científico y Humanista*. Santa Cruz of Tenerife: Consejería de educación, Cultura y deportes.

Hernández Gutiérrez, A.S. 2006. *Juan León y Castillo*. Madrid: Dikinson.

Hernández Socorro, M. de los Reyes and Luxán Meléndez, S. de. 2009. La imagen de los hombres del azúcar en Canarias (Siglos XV-XX). In *La empresa azucarera en Canarias*. Sevilla, ed. Destilerías Arehucas (Gran Canaria)—Ayuntamiento de Los Llanos de Aridane (Isla de La Palma).

Hernández Socorro, M. de los Reyes and S. de Luxán Meléndez. 2020. Retratos de promotores del cultivo del tabaco y representaciones plásticas del hábito placentero en Canarias (Siglos XIX-XX). In *Los monopolios ibéricos del tabaco, Millars, Espai i Història*, eds. S. de Luxán Meléndez, J. Stubbs and J. Figueiroa, 162–185.

Luxán Meléndez, S. de. 1993. La agricultura canaria en vísperas de los Puertos Francos: El informe del comisionado regio Francisco María de León y Falcón en 1849. *Revista De Estudios Regionales* 37: 281–294.

Luxán Meléndez, S. de. 2006. *La opción agrícola e industrial del tabaco en Canarias. Una perspectiva institucional. Los orígenes, 1827–1936*, Las Palmas de Gran Canaria: Universidad de Las Palmas de Gran Canaria and Sociedad Canaria de Fomento Económico S. A. (PROEXCA).

Luxán Meléndez, S. de. 2008. El retrato de Fernando de León y Castillo de Nicolás Massieu Falcón. In *El despertar de la cultura en la época contemporánea. Artistas y manifestaciones culturales de Canarias en el siglo XIX*, eds. S. Hernández, G. Fuentes Pérez, and C. Gaviño de Franchy, 132–133. Santa Cruz de Tenerife: Gobierno de Canarias.

Luxán Meléndez, S. de. 2011. Guerra y economía: Canarias durante el conflicto bélico de 1808-1814. In *Conflictos bélicos y relaciones internacionales 1739–1927. Canarias en la encrucijada de la Guerra de la Independencia*: 305–359. Santa Cruz de Tenerife: Ediciones Idea.

Luxán Meléndez, S. de. 2018. El proceso de construcción del estanco imperial hispánico 1620–1786. Las reformas borbónicas del siglo XVIII. In *Anuario de Estudios Atlánticos*: 961–1011. Las Palmas de Gran Canaria.

Luxán Meléndez, S. de and O. Bergasa Perdomo, 2010. Destilerías Arehucas. *La industria Alcoholera en Canarias 1940–2010*. Las Palmas de Gran Canaria: Destilerías Arehucas.

Luxán Meléndez, S. de and O. Bergasa Perdomo. 2019. Entre los siglos XX y XXI. El discurso de la industrialización en Canarias. In *Reflexiones sobre el desarrollo actual y futuro de la economía canaria*, eds. C. L. González, M. G. Hernández and J. de León Ledesma, 15–43. Madrid: Delta Publicaciones.

Luxán Meléndez, S. de, M. Gárate Ojanguren and J.M. Rodríguez Gordillo. 2012. *Cuba, Canarias-Sevilla. El estanco del tabaco español y las Antillas*

(1717–1817). Las Palmas de Gran Canaria: Ediciones del Cabildo Insular de Gran Canaria.

Martín del Castillo, J.F. 1993. Juan de León y Castillo y las sociedades científicas, literarias, artísticas o de recreo de su tiempo. *Anuario De Estudios Atlánticos* 39: 401–430.

Martín del Castillo, J.F. 1994. *Ciencia y política en el pensamiento de Juan de León y Castillo*. Las Palmas de Gran Canaria: Ediciones del Cabildo Insular.

Martín del Castillo, J.F. 1995. Juan de León y castillo (1834–1912): Ingeniero y político. Apuntes de una biografía. *Anuario De Estudios Atlánticos* 41: 369–382.

Martínez, I.N. 2007. *El gobierno de las Islas de Ultramar. Consejos, Juntas y Comisiones consultivas en el siglo XIX*. Madrid: Universidad de la Rioja-Dykinson.

Millares Torres, A. 1982. Biografías de canarios célebres. *Historia General de las Islas Canarias*, eds. A. Millares Torres et al. Las Palmas of Gran Canaria: Edirca.

Quintana Navarro, F. 1992. *Informes consulares británicos sobre Canarias (1856–1914)*. Las Palmas: CIES.

Rodrigo Alharilla, M. 2009. Del desestanco del tabaco a la puesta en marcha de la Compañía General de Tabacos de Filipinas (1879–1890). *Boletín Americanista* 59: 199–221.

Rodrigo Alharilla, M. 2021. *Un hombre, mil negocios. La controvertida historia de Antonio López, marqués de Comillas*. Barcelona: Ariel.

Sanz Rozalén, V. 2009. Arango y el mundo del tabaco. Estanco, reforma y abolición. In *Francisco Arango y la invención de la Cuba azucarera*, eds. M. Dolores González-Ripoll Navarro and I. Álvarez Cuartero, 277–288. Salamanca: Ediciones de la Universidad de Salamanca.

Sanz Rozalén, V. 2018. Francisco Arango y Parreño. In *Nueva historia de la España contemporánea (1808–2018)*, eds. J. Álvarez Junco and A. Shubert, 620–631. Barcelona: Galaxia Gutenberg, S.L.

Sanz Rozalén, V. 2019. Las fronteras del tabaco. Cuba y Filipinas entre el estanco y el libre comercio. In *Grandes vicios, grandes ingresos. El monopolio del tabaco en los imperios ibéricos (siglos XVII-XX)*, eds. S. de Luxán Meléndez, S. de J. Figueiroa Rego, J and, V. Sanz Rozalén, 179–195. Madrid: Centro de Estudios Políticos y Constitucionales.

Stubbs, J. 2003 [1985]. *Tobacco on the Periphery: Case Study in Cuban Labour History, 1860–1958*. Cambridge: Cambridge University Press.

CHAPTER 8

Tobacco Fantasies in German Southwest Africa, 1884–1915

Martin Kalb

Introduction

Graf von Schweinitz was dreaming big in 1892. A lieutenant in the *Schutztruppe* (German colonial troops), he assessed the soil of German Southwest Africa (1884–1915, modern-day Namibia). After his "thorough examination" in Otjimbingue, Schweinitz concluded that "tobacco can completely cover" the landscape.[1] Major Curt von François, the commander of the German colonial troops, had similar plans. He

[1] Graf von Schweinitz, Eindrücke von Deutsch-Süd-West-Afrika, 29 September 1892, Bundesarchiv Berlin-Lichterfelde, in the following BArch-B, Reichskolonialamt (R) 1001/1135, p. 28, as referenced in Blackler (2017, p. 125). See also Schweinitz-Dieban (1892).

Thank you to Dag Henrichsen (Basel), Rob Gordon (Vermont), and editors, as well as to librarians and archivists; I am also grateful for funding from Bridgewater College.

M. Kalb (✉)
Bridgewater College, Bridgewater, VA, USA
e-mail: mkalb@bridgewater.edu

A. van Wickeren et al. (eds.), *Tobacco in Global Perspective, 1780–1960*, Cambridge Imperial and Post-Colonial Studies,
https://doi.org/10.1007/978-3-031-64411-5_8

authored a comprehensive text discussing the colony's terrain, climate, soil, and colonial life. Sent to Chancellor Leo von Caprivi in Berlin, von François added a facsimile of a prospective German garden showing plots for "tobacco, cabbage, peas, melon, and grapes."[2] "Our Southwest-African colony is certainly not as useless as many think," another colonial enthusiast noted in 1888. Writing in the newspaper *Deutsche Kolonialzeitung*, the mouthpiece of the German Colonial Society, he conceded that German Southwest Africa "is still uncultivated land." However, he continued, "with capital and German diligence and hard work the land will be made arable soon."[3] Missionary gardens had already demonstrated the potential for transforming existing landscapes. Experimental stations focusing on the cultivation of tobacco and wine, and manned with competent experts from the metropole, could achieve even more. The colony's future was promising.

In what was Germany's first and only settler colony, desert landscapes and a lack of water provided few opportunities for farming cash crops. Nonetheless, shortly after the official creation of the German protectorate in 1884, colonists dreamed of transforming arid lands into an agricultural paradise. German farmers, along with the colonial government and all kinds of enthusiasts, began to experiment with a variety of plant and animal resources, including tobacco. After the 1904–1908 war and genocide on the Herero and Nama peoples, colonists saw an opportunity to expand the colony's tobacco cultivation throughout the settlement area known as the police zone, favouring the needs of white settlers and ideally imperial Germany.

Fuelled after 1908 by an increasingly scientific approach to tobacco cultivation, fantasies of economic autarky go a long way to explaining why the Germans set their sights high, but their objectives and optimism are also deeply tied to the violence and racial exclusion embedded in the transformative nature of settler colonialism. Historians have researched

[2] Major Curt von François, Garten der Südwestafrika Schutztruppe, June 1890, BArch-B, R 1001/1134e, 29, as referenced in Blackler (2017, p. 123).

[3] Deutsche Kolonialzeitung (1888). See also Deutsche Kolonialzeitung (1889).

the German empire,[4] tobacco in German and African history,[5] and agricultural and farming developments in Namibia,[6] as well as commodity chains.[7] Yet those studies have not always given sufficient consideration to the fact that improvement programmes constructed around cash crops such as tobacco overlapped with the racist excess violence that occurred not least, but by no means exclusively, in the so-called settler colonies.[8] *Siedlungskolonialismus* (settler colonialism) and *Lebensraum* (living space) remain key concepts in that context as discriminatory and racist policies were ingrained in settler structures. Imperial forces dragged indigenous cultures into the German sphere of influence, with Africans resisting well before 1904. "The first genocide of the twentieth century," to take George Steinmetz's phrase,[9] was that of the 1904–1908 partial extermination of the Herero and Nama people in Southwest Africa by the German colonial forces. Violence continued thereafter. According to Marie Muschalek, "the quotidian, normalized violence that was orchestrated by the police force" after the war "differed from the belligerent, destructive violence that had come before."[10] This chapter thus draws on the violent history of settler colonialism linked to tobacco history to cast new light on the knowledge history of imperial improvement projects, including friction between agro-scientific visions from the metropole and settler mentalities.

Environmental conditions by no means provided a blank canvas or simple backdrop. Nature seemingly set clear limits to any prospects of success. Today's Namibia is testimony to this with its desert landscapes, most famously the Namib and the Kalahari. Temperatures range widely, and rain is hard to come by. Depending on the region and season, precipitation can reach from 600 millimetres in the northern Caprivi Strip to

[4] Naranch and Eley (2014). Fitzpatrick (2022).

[5] Cremer (2004). Roberts (2004). Duvall (2017). Prowse (2020). Gately (2003). Prowse and Niño (2022). On Germany see: Jacob and Dworok (2015). van Wickeren (2020).

[6] Lau and Reiner (1993). Declerq (2016). Zollmann (2020).

[7] Snyders (2011). Press (2021). See also Zimmerman (2010).

[8] On broader debates regarding continuities within German history see Zimmerer and Zeller (2008). Olusoga and Erichsen (2010). Zimmerer (2011). Kreienbaum (2015). Häussler (2018).

[9] Steinmetz (2005).

[10] Muschalek (2019). See also Zollmann (2010).

less than 50 millimetres in the Namib Desert along the coastline, and rainfall shows great inter-annual variability.[11] Torrential rains at times disrupt plans, and the sudden arrival of pests such as locusts repeatedly foils otherwise successful growing seasons. Such threats to large-scale agricultural operations defined agricultural schemes as well as prevalent settlement stories; according to Christo Botha, Namibia's colonial period was "pervaded by European perceptions of toil and battle to tame a hostile landscape."[12]

Questioning colonial perceptions is essential for our understanding of this settler space. Such colonial views are to be found in an array of sources, many of them coming from colonial records. They include government and personal files at the National Archives in Berlin-Lichterfelde, Koblenz, and Windhoek focusing on the cultivation of tobacco. There are also countless reports tracking progress and pitfalls, pamphlets, books, newspaper articles, and photographs. The underlying narratives and visual culture, and colonial photographs in particular, are often staged portrayals or stories of progress.[13] And with few oral histories tied to tobacco cultivation to combat existing silences and racist storylines,[14] disrupting the colonial gaze is challenging. A quest for fragments, slippages, and traces of suppressed and subaltern voices in the tradition of reading against the grain; the questioning of widespread settler premises; and the awareness of inherent violence within settler colonialism are thereby key when trying to think critically about the German cultivation of tobacco in Southwest Africa.

Racist Stereotypes and Delayed Transformation

German officials and early settlers initially focused on local tobacco demand and preference. While framed as an effort to keep products from neighbouring South Africa out, problems with logistics and funding, along with local resistance and a delayed commitment to the colony, allowed for little more than the production of tobacco for African

[11] Goudie and Viles (2015, pp. 37–38).

[12] Botha (2005, p. 170).

[13] Hayes (2002a). Hayes (2002b). Steinmetz and Hell (2006). Otte (2014). Rizzo (2014).

[14] Förster (2008, p. 65). Krüger (2008, p. 4).

consumers. With some colonial voices already advocating agronomic improvement and investment, the initial years of German rule were characterised by a silencing of indigenous knowledge, racial stereotypes of African consumers, and slowly expanding localised ambitions.

Scholars know remarkably little about how American tobacco became part of African agricultural economies.[15] Unknown to many, there is indigenous tobacco (*Nicotiana africana*) in Namibia. It can be found in at least three isolated regions (Brandberg, Erongo, and the Spitzkoppe mountains).[16] The introduction of *Nicotiana tabacum* came from the Americas in the late sixteenth century.[17] The plant "gained rapid, widespread popularity," according to Ian Gately, "and Africans developed distinctive modes of tobacco production and use."[18] In a territorial expanse inhabited by Khoisan-speakers (e.g. Nama, Damara) and Bantu-speakers (e.g. Herero, Ovambo), consumers had long been smoking cannabis (*dagga*).[19] This later facilitated the spread of tobacco, especially snuff, which seemed to be more widespread than chewing tobacco.[20] By the beginning of the nineteenth century, European travel accounts distinguished between the cultivation of "wild tobacco" (*Nicotiana glauca*) and "cultivated tobacco" (*Nicotiana tabacum*).[21] In 1909, German botanist and explorer Kurt Dinter described what he considered Argentinian tobacco (*Nicotiana glauca*) growing along the riverbed of the Swakop, adding that it likely arrived with missionaries from the Cape Colony.[22] Decades later in 1981, one commentator referred to it spreading "today along almost all riviers [dry riverbeds or ephemeral rivers]."[23] The plant's introduction and subsequent expansion speaks to the region's connections to Atlantic trade networks.

Until the advent of industrial capitalism and consumer goods, African tobacco production in garden economies sustained local and regional

[15] Ambler (2022, pp. 194–195).

[16] Marlin et al. (2014). Cremer (2004, pp. 105–112). Giess (1982).

[17] Cremer (2004, pp. 60–66).

[18] Duvall (2017, p. 1). Rubert (2005, p. 23). Gately (2003, p. 59).

[19] Cremer (2004, pp. 28–36).

[20] Gately (2003, pp. 60–61). Ambler (2022, p. 193). Cremer (2004, p. 84 and 99).

[21] Schinz (2021, p. 302). Schwabe (1899, p. 6). Von Bülow (1893, p. 52).

[22] Dinter (1909, p. 2 and 120–121).

[23] Giess (1981, p. 20).

trade networks. Namibia's precolonial tobacco topographies defined trade and consumption throughout the region. According to historians, tobacco became an important commodity for the Herero throughout the nineteenth century, especially for poor Herero groups [Ovatjimba].[24] Nama commando groups grew tobacco and *dagga*. Soon imported tobacco began replacing that which was home grown.[25] The neighbouring Cape Colony produced an annual output of three million lbs by 1875,[26] much of it for export. Early accounts sustain such findings. Scottish traveller James Edwards Alexander in 1838 wrote of having discovered gardens in Namaland that included tobacco and at one point coming across a warm spring serving "to irrigate a tobacco and melon garden below, in which the chief and some of his head men had plots, but which laboured under the disadvantage of having a brack soil." He also mentions the spread of tobacco into Namaland first from the south side of the Great River.[27] In 1857, missionary Carl Hugo Hahn commented on efforts by the people of Kandambo to grow tobacco in the riverbed of the Swakop. In his view, "the soil was rather brackish and sparse."[28] In 1864, explorer Thomas Baines wrote about the introduction of cultivated tobacco several years prior to his travels in the region.[29] And, in 1882, fellow explorer Charles John Andersson described the cultivation of tobacco north in Ovamboland.[30] In 1896, German accounts referred to a gardening place once utilised by Africans to grow tobacco, pumpkins, corn, and melons and how Damara at one point grew tobacco in a riverbed.[31] According to missionary Heinrich Vedder, Damara "provided tobacco for the Herero from gardens specifically laid out for this purpose."[32] By then the Dutch had long begun commercial cultivation, especially once they had "found that Khoesan [Khoisan] people accepted

[24] Henrichsen (2011, p. 101).

[25] Lau (1986, pp. 34–35).

[26] Akehurst (1981, p. 11). See also Goodman (1995, p. 213). Rubert (2005, p. 24).

[27] Alexander (1838, p. 82, 111, 122–123, 131 and 147).

[28] Moritz (1980, p. 7).

[29] Baines (1864, pp. 23–24).

[30] Andersson (1882, p. 209).

[31] Bülow (1896, pp. 178–179). Baines (1864, pp. 61–62). Vedder (1923, p. 152). Von Falkenhausen (1905, p. 134).

[32] Vedder (1966, p. 43).

it in exchange for labor, livestock, and land at rates that Europeans found quite profitable."[33]

German sources repeatedly described the demand for tobacco among the African population in discriminatory and blatantly racist terms. Expeditions had long commented on how Khoisan "vociferously demanded" tobacco.[34] German missionaries later described similar interactions. Jakob Irle, who worked for the *Rheinische Missionsgesellschaft* (Rhenish Missionary Society) and came to the territory in 1870, wrote about Herero calling *"tu pao makaja" or "tuako! Give me tobacco, pack my pipe."*[35] *Later, settler Helene von Falkenhausen described a note reading "arikana, mohana Voigtsa, tubao makaia" (please Mr Voigts, give me tobacco).* She added that local Africans repeatedly begged for tobacco.[36] Other accounts document "irritating beggars" with their pipes seemingly growing out of their mouths.[37] According to one German soldier, smoking tobacco constitutes the "main pleasure" of the Herero,[38] while a female settler spoke of indigenous consumption as a "passion."[39]

References mentioning tobacco and alcohol together speak volumes about broader discourses of morality. Grounded in concepts of *Sittlichkeit* (ethical life) that emerged in the early nineteenth century, debates about *bürgerliche Normen* (civic middle-class norms) had long become distinctive elements in German society. Such traditional values, by no means broadly endorsed, had much in common with British Victorian-era ideals and their emphasis on morality, work ethic, and personal improvement.

Beginning in the 1880s, an expanded sense of urgency, debates about social hygiene, and increased "scientification" also defined the discourse.[40] In the empire's settlement colony, a place meant to become a better Germany, such values clashed with real or imagined indigenous behaviour. It was claimed the Nama only valued two things: the tobacco

[33] Duvall (2017, p. 17). See also Cremer (2004, p. 70). Gordon (1996).

[34] Duvall (2017, p. 17).

[35] Irle (1906, p. 115).

[36] Falkenhausen (1905, p. 18, 45, 149, and 169). Karow (1909, p. 164, 195, 198, and 245).

[37] Belwe (1906, p. 66 and 136). Schwabe (1899, p. 20 and 318).

[38] Auer (1911, p. 47).

[39] Karow (1909, p. 192).

[40] Tschurenev et al. (2014, p. 9, 17, and 19).

and the schnapps.[41] In 1911, one account referenced the supposed "passionate and impulsive nature" of African consumers and the "excessive amounts" of tobacco they allegedly devour.[42] For the author, tobacco and alcohol were the most useful tools for Europeans hoping to control Africans.

That African men, women, and children smoked raised concerns as well.[43] German societal norms marked women smoking as a sign of immorality and promiscuity. That then fed into existing discourses of overly sexual natives presumably seducing upstanding German men and spreading all kinds of venereal diseases.[44] References to smoking children pointed to the moral failures of parents and juvenile delinquency. Addiction, dependency, and laziness, along with discourses of immorality, neglect, and deviancy were characteristics of German views of indigenous tobacco consumption.

German accounts included an array of demeaning descriptions of particular forms of consumption. Sources mostly questioned the use of loose leaf or Cavendish—named after Sir Thomas Cavendish and obtained by adding sugar or dark rum, leaving the leaves generally milder and sweeter (*Plattentabak* in German)—long bartered and sold in sticks each weighing about an ounce.[45] Unlike the presumed sophistication of the cigar, the loose leaf was seen as "uncivilized," a discourse comparable to mid-nineteenth-century British India where hookah smoking of the indigenous people was demarcated from the civilised cigar smoking of the Europeans.

Europeans who tried indigenous tobacco products described them as harsh and biting.[46] Alexander, who favoured products with "the oriental refinements" and saw European habits as "disgusting," was an exception in that context.[47] For most, such a type of tobacco and its consumption were repellent. According to one German missionary's description of the Herero, "their way of 'drinking in tobacco' is disgusting; they

[41] Bayer (1907, p. 7).

[42] Hartwich (1911, p. 74).

[43] Vedder (1923, p. 77). See also Alexander (1838, p. 156).

[44] Walther (2015).

[45] Galton (1853, p. 18).

[46] Von Deimling (1906, p. 21).

[47] Alexander (1838, p. 186).

pull the smoke in and blow it out again through the nose."[48] According to another account, "indulgent" African men and women possessed no refined taste.[49] That African consumers also smoked and valued cannabis (*dagga*), a substance Europeans looked down upon, meant their taste must be unsophisticated.[50]

Ignorance of the medicinal uses associated with tobacco formed part of how the discourse on indigenous populations became increasingly racialised in the late nineteenth and early twentieth century, after a long history of consumer and group distinctions in Southern Africa. As early as the seventeenth century, Johan (Jan) van Riebeeck, a navigator and administrator who led the Dutch settlement of Cape Town in the service of the Vereenigde Oostindische Compagnie (Dutch East India Company), recounted in a conversation with nine Saldanhars (a term the Dutch employed to describe mainland groups of Africans): "They will not accept rotten tobacco but haggle over a finger's length of tobacco twist"[51]; and Dutch physician Willem Ten Rhyne, also employed by the Dutch East India Company, referred to the addiction and dependency on tobacco of unnamed Khoikhoi individuals he met, including children.[52] Fast forward to the nineteenth century and Baines described "tears glistening," "humorous grimaces," and "witty aphorisms" when characterising the demand of Africans for tobacco.[53] Edwards pointed to tobacco "when all else fails to move the natives of South Africa",[54] commenting that in Namaland "men would not hesitate to give up their wives and daughters" for some tobacco, and denial of tobacco resulted in anger and "great passion."[55]

By the nineteenth century, a new hygiene discourse had increasingly begun refining observations. German commentators noted that Africans in Southern Africa enhanced leftover tobacco leaves with cow dung. For

[48] Irle (1906, p. 115).

[49] Kolonie und Heimat in Wort und Bild (1910). See also Blackler (2017, p. 137).

[50] Duvall (2017, p. 1). Ambler (2022, p. 194).

[51] Goodwin (1952, p. 10).

[52] Cremer (2004, p. 66).

[53] Baines (1864, p. 144).

[54] Alexander (1838, p. 18). See also Baines (1864, p. 14).

[55] Alexander (1838, p. 82 and 106).

them, this was not only uncivilised and odd but had clear health implications apparent in numbing and convulsions. That these mixtures point to the critical role of tobacco in local medicine, including dealing with snake bites after they had been sucked or burned out,[56] did not make sense to the Germans. Instead, what they perceived was simply unsanitary. After all, animal excrement had gradually disappeared from the everyday life of many Europeans over the course of the century. A similar hygiene discomfort existed when Europeans described the ceremonial and often communal nature of smoking.[57] Local groups typically shared pipes, passing them around. Baines declared he could not even paint Damaras smoking—it was just "too revolting."[58] Such an act of sharing would also characterise European working-class culture and the supposed deviancy of workers with the rise of the cigarette. At the time, however, German observers were obsessed over it as a possible cause of disease.[59] "Sitting around" smoking and "being lazy" became essential narrative tools in demeaning descriptions of the "inferior" indigenous consumption habits of Southwest Africa,[60]

Meanwhile, most of the German 'improvements' were unsystematic. Missionaries and early settlers frequently grew tobacco in their gardens for local or regional consumers. The sites they preferred were not identified at random. Rather, they established themselves near indigenous settlements—and the latter had carefully selected their locations close to water. Over time, and as German newcomers pushed indigenous populations off their ancestral lands, such gardens emerged on long-standing plots. Later, it would become easy to dismiss previous indigenous efforts as "miniscule in scale" while claiming the Germans initiated the cultivation of tobacco.[61] Missionaries and settlers carefully tended their gardens, work that carried connotations of transformation and progress.[62] A report submitted to the German parliament in 1902 summed up that "both in the South as well as in the North good harvests [of tobacco] have been

[56] Cremer (2004, pp. 100–102). See also Karow (1909, p. 107).

[57] Wanless (1991, pp. 125–143).

[58] Baines (1864, p. 202).

[59] Irle (1906, p. 115).

[60] Brockmann (1912, p. 183). Von Eckenbrecher (1907, p. 84). Wegner (1885, p. 28).

[61] Schwonder (1922, p. 147).

[62] Petermanns Geographische Mitteilungen (1885, p. 135).

achieved. Moreover, the fermentation of tobacco progressed as well, and tobacco produced on the land is becoming more and more widespread among local smokers."[63] The next year's report declared the harvests in Grootfontein, Okahandja, and Gobabis "found a ready market mainly among Boers."[64]

Expansion beyond local markets required investment; plus, African resistance and environmental factors hampered initial efforts. German Chancellor Otto von Bismarck's plan to outsource development to private companies was deemed a failure. Following his departure in 1890, and faced with local resistance led by Nama Captain Hendrik Witbooi and others, a more direct commitment to Germany's first colony eventually materialised. However, logistical nightmares tied to a lack of natural harbours, difficult travel inland across the Namib Desert, and a Rinderpest epidemic complicated and delayed German desires to transform the colony. In 1902, the colony thus imported 14,000 kilograms of cigarettes and cigars and 42,000 kilograms of Cavendish.[65] The Cape Colony was by far the leading supplier for Southwest Africa. By then the focus of attention had turned to the development of the local tobacco industry to decrease overall imports.[66] In 1904, the magazine *Der Tropenpflanzer* called for more investment and government involvement when it came to lowering imports from neighbouring South Africa; that publication equally hoped for the tobacco lobby to get involved.[67] However, with the exception of efforts at Osona and Grootfontein,[68] where production increased mainly due to deliveries to railway construction sites, cultivation remained tied to personal use and domestic consumers.

Over time, state initiatives to support the cultivation of tobacco in Southwest Africa began to emerge. In 1901, the Colonial Government in Windhoek produced a 38-page pamphlet informing and educating those interested in the cultivation of tobacco. Based on lessons from

63 Verhandlungen des Reichstages (1900, /1903(b), p. 2938).

64 Verhandlungen des Reichstages (1900/1903(a), p. 5289).

65 Deutscher Tabakverein, Gemeinsame Sitzung des Hauptvorstandes und Abtheilungsvorstände, 11-12 November 1902, BArch-B, R 1001/8050, Tabak in Deutsch-Südwestafrika, Vol 1 (Febr. 1902-Juni 1910), p. 24.

66 Ibid.

67 Der Tropenpflanzer (1904).

68 Jaeger and Waibel (1920, p. 111).

neighbouring South Africa,[69] the main point of reference for German colonists, Governor Theodor Leutwein pushed for the free distribution of 200 copies.[70] Parliament later praised such efforts.[71] Leutwein had also initiated state-funded awards handed out at the Agricultural Exhibition in 1902. The Kolonial-Wirtschaftliche Komitee (Colonial Economic Committee), a private–public partnership founded to support economic development in the colonies, provided funding to improve tobacco cultivation as well.[72] Leutwein also tried capturing Berlin's attention by reaching out to the lobbying group Deutscher Tabakverein (German Tobacco Association).[73] An initial meeting held in the luxurious Savoy Hotel in Berlin took place on 11 November 1902. It included Leutwein, Angelo Gollineli from the colonial department, and interested parties from the private sector.[74]

Previous setbacks elsewhere overshadowed the discussion. Early efforts in New Guinea had failed; Councillor of Commerce Biermann recalled his own enthusiasm about an opportunity in Cameroon but noted how little had come of it.[75] Moreover, a reference was made to the "fiasco" in German East Africa.[76] There, the Deutsch-Ostafrikanische Plantagengesellschaft (German East African Plantation Society), founded in 1886, had anticipated a more conducive environment and "quick profits."[77]

[69] See, for instance Bülow (1896, p. 360). Der Tropenpflanzer (1906).

[70] Kaiserl. Deutsches Gouvernement für Südwestafrika an Kolonial-Abteilung Auswärtiges Amt, 10 December 1901, BArch-B, R 1001/8050, Tabak in Deutsch-Südwestafrika, Vol 1 (Febr. 1902-Juni 1910). For the pamphlet see Watermeyer (1902).

[71] Verhandlungen des Reichstages (1904, p. 123).

[72] Kolonial-Wirtschaftliches Komitee an Kolonial-Abteilung, Auswärtiges Amt, 8 January 1903, BArch-B, R 1001/8050, Tabak in Deutsch-Südwestafrika, Vol 1 (Febr. 1902–Juni 1910).

[73] Deutscher Tabakverein, Gemeinsame Sitzung des Hauptvorstandes und Abtheilungsvorstände, 11-12 November 1902, BArch-B, R 1001/8050, Tabak in Deutsch-Südwestafrika, Vol 1 (Febr. 1902–Juni 1910), pp. 24–25.

[74] Ibid., p. 24.

[75] Ibid., p. 28.

[76] Deutscher Tabakverein, Gemeinsame Sitzung des Hauptvorstandes und Abtheilungsvorstände, 11-12 November 1902, BArch-B, R 1001/8050, Tabak in Deutsch-Südwestafrika, Vol 1 (Febr. 1902-Juni 1910), p. 30. See Der Tropenpflanzer (1902). Der Tropenpflanzer (1904).

[77] Wagner (1888, p. 110).

However, an uprising at the coast in 1888 smashed this early experiment.[78] Gollineli's clarification that Southwest Africa would not see a plantation system meant for export helped soothe some concerns.[79] In the end, it was in large part thanks to Leutwein's insistence and presumed knowledge of local circumstances that the authorities agreed to the employment of a tobacco expert for Southwest Africa.[80]

By the turn of the century things started to look up for tobacco cultivation in Southwest Africa. The Colonial Economic Committee began providing funding.[81] According to Leutwein, early tobacco trials received good reviews—although these came only from the inhabitants of the colony.[82] Plus, proponents of tobacco cultivation anticipated the arrival of an expert. The authorities picked Ludwig Wunderlich from Heilbronn.[83] There were delays regarding the arrival of Wunderlich. Then the war erupted in January 1904, destroying the lives and livelihoods of Herero and Nama and putting German initiatives regarding the cultivation of tobacco on hold.

To sum up, tobacco cultivation in German Southwest Africa faced an array of issues. Grounded in racist stereotypes and a focus on indigenous demands, logistical problems, a lack of commitment from the metropole, and local resistance all hampered success. Colonists remained positive, however, with some still dreaming big. Arguably, underlying racist stereotypes and a broad disregard for indigenous knowledge hampered initial efforts and ultimately delayed scientific improvements.

[78] Bückendorf (1997, p. 308). See also Tabak in Deutsch-Ostafrika (Vol 1-6), BArch-B, R 1001-8042-8047.

[79] Deutscher Tabakverein, Gemeinsame Sitzung des Hauptvorstandes und Abtheilungsvorstände, 11-12 November 1902, BArch-B, R 1001/8050, Tabak in Deutsch-Südwestafrika, Vol 1 (Febr. 1902-Juni 1910), pp. 28–29.

[80] Ibid., p. 32. See also General-Anzeiger (Mannheim) (1902).

[81] Kolonial-Wirtschaftliches Komitee an Kolonial-Abteilung Auswärtiges Amt, 8 January 1903, BArch-B, R 1001/8050, Tabak in Deutsch-Südwestafrika, Vol 1 (Febr. 1902-Juni 1910).

[82] Kaiserl. Gouvernement für Südwest-Afrika in Windhoek to Kolonial-Abteilung Auswärtiges Amt, 28 September 1903 and Kolonial-Wirtschaftliches Komitee to Kolonial-Abteilung Auswärtiges Amt, 8 January 1903, BArch-B, R 1001/8050, Tabak in Deutsch-Südwestafrika, Vol 1 (Febr. 1902-Juni 1910).

[83] General-Anzeiger (Mannheim) (1902). Joseph Hammerschlag, director of the Kaiserliche Tabakmanufaktur in Strasbourg, in the Alsace, had also been recommended. On the tobacco industry in Strasbourg see Silverman (1971, pp. 34–53). Dehn (1880).

Genocide, Settler Mentalities, and Agricultural Science

War and genocide transformed the German cultivation of tobacco. For one, the extermination of a large part of the Herero and Nama population radically changed the consumer market. At the same time, there was increasing investment to fund the implementation of an agro-scientific infrastructure, with some dreaming about exports to the German metropolis. Colonial stakeholders, however, did not always agree on how to actively pursue the cultivation of tobacco.

Due to war and genocide, which resulted in the murder of about 80% of Herero and 50% of Nama people, African consumers of Cavendish disappeared in large numbers. While some demand remained, imports of Cavendish, mainly from South Africa, decreased. The colonial government's annual report for 1910/11 claimed that tobacco grown by farmers locally had more or less pushed out imported Cavendish in the northern part of the colony.[84] That was a success, according to colonial records.[85] The newspaper *Windhuker Nachrichten* noted, "Tobacco can be grown in the whole country and the protectorate itself provides a receptive internal market for tobacco and tobacco products. With a rational planting of the tobacco plants and the right treatment of the harvested tobacco, many settlers will still recognise a profitable culture."[86] However, such trends had little to do with the colony becoming more self-sufficient. Instead, it was the destruction of an existing consumer base wrought by war and genocide.

With African demand presumably met and the war over, the conversation began to shift. By 1910, publications increasingly speculated about Germans in the metropole soon enjoying tobacco from Southwest Africa.[87] According to economists, scientists, and bureaucrats, there was potential. Estimates regarding the production of tobacco worldwide had

[84] Reichs-Kolonialamt (1911, p. 142). See also Der Farmer (1910). Deutsch-Südwestafrikanische Zeitung (1913(b)).

[85] Zimmermann (1926, p. 30).

[86] Windhuker Nachrichten (1909(a)).

[87] Kolonie und Heimat in Wort und Bild (1910). See also Blackler (2017, p. 137).

gone beyond one billion (1,000 million kilograms).[88] Most of the globally consumed tobacco came from the US (about 240 million kilograms), followed by British India (about 175 million kilograms); other countries produced less than 100 million kilograms, with Germany adding only about 35 million. That tobacco came mainly from Baden, Alsace, and other parts of the Southwest. As a result, Germany had to import more than half of its tobacco by the late 1890s[89]; by 1912/13, the import of manufactured tobacco products alone reached 252 million pounds per year.[90] Plus, cigarette sales went above 10,000 million sticks in the early 1900s for the first time in Germany.[91]

In 1907, toward the end of the war in Southwest Africa, a meeting in Mannheim was convened to discuss future prospects. According to the Governor of Cameroon Theodor Seitz, son of a tobacco businessman, "unsuitable" and "inadequate" methods had been used in Southwest Africa so far. The arrival of Wunderlich was about to change that, he noted.[92] Others later agreed when it came to the piecemeal efforts of settlers. It seemed sensible to establish agricultural scientific centres, institutions that oscillated between laboratories, research stations, and model farms. Such institutions were also meant to disseminate modern agricultural knowledge. In 1902, the Department of the Interior had already proposed the creation of "centres for the cultivation of tobacco."[93] According to one official in Berlin, centralised factories would make it much easier when trying to build a tobacco industry.

The organised cultivation of tobacco officially began with the arrival of Wunderlich in September 1907.[94] Wunderlich submitted numerous hand-written reports to the government in Windhoek[95]; offered advice in

[88] Der Tropenpflanzer (1898). See also Lewinstein (1897, p. 4). Wolf (1912, p. 132 and 164–172).

[89] Der Tropenpflanzer (1898).

[90] Hannah (2006, p. 44).

[91] Ibid., p. 48. See also Südwestbote (1912(d)).

[92] Der Tropenpflanzer (1907).

[93] Staatssekretär des Inneren to Kolonial-Abteilung Auswärtiges Amt, 10 October 1902, BArch-B, R 1001/8050, Tabak in Deutsch-Südwestafrika, Vol 1 (Febr. 1902-Juni 1910).

[94] Eintreffen des Landwirtschaftsinspektor Wunderlich, 29 April 1908, BArch-B, R 1002/1992, Wunderlich, Ludwig, Landwirtschaftsinspektor, 1907-1911.

[95] Wunderlich to Gouvernement Windhuk, 4 November 1909, BArch-B, R 1002/ 1992, Wunderlich, Ludwig, Landwirtschaftsinspektor, 1907-1911.

local publications, especially concerning the transfer of seedlings, curing, and fermentation[96]; gave talks on the cultivation of tobacco; and was involved in the preparation, publication, and distribution of ten basic rules regarding the cultivation of tobacco in German Southwest Africa.[97] Initially, Wunderlich argued against major investments. In his view, it was simply not worthwhile. The tobacco was currently of poor quality, and low humidity made curing and fermentation risky. It required slow drying, which seemed impossible in Southwest Africa. Hail, locusts, and an arid climate also made cultivation difficult. According to Wunderlich, "At the very beginning, we want to produce tobacco suitable for the indigenous population. Even if they will at first not take it with particular pleasure, because they are used to *Plattentabak* (Cavendish), that does not mean much, because over time they will get used to it—granted the *Schneidetabak* [tobacco meant to be smoked] is of good quality."[98] Early on, revenues might become a welcome subsidiary income for farmers but economic independence would come much later. In other words, Wunderlich called for more time and patience.

Local tobacco farmers had some access to funds. For one, there was money for irrigation.[99] And, there were some funds for the cultivation of tobacco. Take the construction of expensive curing barns.[100] To fund them, the Wohlfahrtslotterie (Welfare Lottery), a major funder of infrastructure projects in German Southwest Africa, planned to step in, providing 20,000 Marks for each barn.[101] Since Wunderlich noted that existing facilities were not effectively utilised, the local government began

[96] Der Farmer (1908(b)). Der Farmer (1908(c)). Windhuker Nachrichten (1908(a)). Der Farmer (1908(d)). Der Farmer (1908(f)). Der Farmer (1908(e)).

[97] Windhuker Nachrichten (1908(b)). Windhuker Nachrichten (1908(c)). Windhuker Nachrichten (1908(d)). Der Farmer (1908(g)). Deutsch-Südwestafrikanische Zeitung (1909). Südwestbote (1911(a)). A poster of these rules was also available for purchase at the bookstore in Swakopmund.

[98] Der Farmer (1908(a)). In October 1908, Wunderlich elaborated on his views at a presentation in Windhoek. Windhuker Nachrichten (1908(b)).

[99] Von Lindequist, Denkschrift über die Besiedelung Deutsch-Südwestafrikas, 19 September 1906, BArch, R 1001/1142, Ansiedlung insbesondere deutscher Bauern in Deutsch-Südwestafrika, Vol 9 (Okt. 1906-Febr. 1907). See also Oelhafen (1926, p. 63).

[100] Verhandlungen des Reichstages (1911, p. 843).

[101] Abschrift, Reichs-Kolonialamt, 11 March 1909, BArch-B, R 1001/8050, Tabak in Deutsch-Südwestafrika, Vol 1 (Febr. 1902-Juni 1910). See also Windhuker Nachrichten (1909(b)). Der Tropenpflanze (1909).

dispersing the money among farmers interested in constructing their own barns.[102,103] At that point, discussions about the high costs of importing tobacco from Germany ran on the front page of the local newspaper *Windhuker Nachrichten*. In 1907/08 alone German Southwest Africa imported tobacco worth 940,895 Marks—814,567 from Germany and 126,328 from South Africa. Commentators therefore hoped that the recent increase in prices for such imports would help strengthen the colonial tobacco industry and bring in more investments.[104]

There were also calls for a government monopoly meant to strengthen the emerging tobacco industry. In line with debates surrounding alcohol, officials in Windhoek hoped to support a struggling business. The monopoly "would initially be limited to the establishment of a smaller facility, manned by a manager, a foreman, and four to six natives, in which the production of an affordable native-tobacco for the needs of the protectorate could be tackled." Next would be "experiments regarding the fabrication of a medium-tobacco meant for the consumption of whites." Only over time would there be the production of tobacco, cigars, and cigarettes also meant for export.[105] The sum of 100,000 Marks would cover initial costs, including 10,000–15,000 Marks to reimburse existing investments made by settler businesses such as Wecke and Voigts. According to one report, "Presently fragmented efforts are not useful for the cultivation of a high-quality tobacco, [and] settlers are not the suitable entity for conducting such trials."[106] Wunderlich chimed in as well, pointing out that the quality of the products offered for sale had been terrible. The company Bachstein-Koppel, for instance, which built railways in the colony, had received tobacco samples grown by settlers. Meant

[102] Kaiserl. Gouverneur für Deutsch Südwest-Afrika to Reichs-Kolonialamt, 17 December 1910, BArch-B, R 1001/8051, Tabak in Deutsch-Südwestafrika, Vol 2 (Sept. 1910-Jan. 1914). For concise guidelines see Amtsblatt für das Schutzgebiet Deutsch-Südwestafrika (1910).

[103] See Reichs-Kolonialamt to Gouverneur von Südwest-Afrika, 15 February 1911, BArch-B, R 1001/8051, Tabak in Deutsch-Südwestafrika, Vol 2 (Sept. 1910-Jan. 1914).

[104] Windhuker Nachrichten (1909(c)).

[105] Kaisl. Gouverneur von Deutsch Südwestafrika to Reichskolonialamt, 16 October 1910, BArch-B, R 1001/1819, Einführung von Handelsmonopolen (Febr. 1909-Febr. 1914, 1920).

[106] Kaiserl. Gouverneur von Deutsch-Südwest-Afrika to Reichs-Kolonialamt, 8 March 1911, BArch-B, R 1001/8051, Tabak in Deutsch-Südwestafrika, Vol 2 (Sept. 1910-Jan. 1914).

mostly for contract workers from South Africa, the presumed consumers turned down this awful product. According to Wunderlich, monopoly or not, a centre for tobacco experimentation should be prioritised.[107] The scientific production process, he added, not individual farmers trying to figure things out as they go, would result in high-quality products easily sold domestically—and maybe eventually good enough for export.[108]

During his tenure in Southwest Africa, Wunderlich extensively promoted scientific experiments and experimental stations, and in August 1910 summarised his work and findings in a letter. He described how low humidity made curing tobacco difficult. He had to run his trials at the farm of Richard Voigts adding that he needed a curing barn and long term studies. Such dependencies on Voigts' facilities and workers, plus the need for tobacco samples from a farm in Osona and his required presence on sight to oversee operations, bothered him as well. After the 1909/10 growing season, he concluded, the cultivation of high-quality tobacco in German Southwest Africa was possible, requiring funds for a curing barn and steady scientific trials—not private investments into cigarette factories.[109]

When back in Germany, Wunderlich actively promoted the creation of a government experimental station and an assistant on site to guarantee a quality product. But he would never return to Southwest Africa: he contracted malaria[110] and also later suffered from chest pains.[111] Although the local farming society hoped he could be retained for three more years, he had left the colony in 1910 for good.[112] Finding a replacement turned out to be difficult. Correspondences between Wunderlich

[107] Kaisl. Gouverneur von Deutsch Südwestafrika to Reichskolonialamt, 16 October 1910, BArch-B, R 1001/1819, Einführung von Handelsmonopolen.

[108] Ibid.

[109] Wunderlich, letter to Reichskolonialamt (Lindequist), 21 August 1910, BArch-B, R 1001/1819, Handelsmonopole.

[110] Kaisl. Bezirksamtmann (Swakopmund) to Kaisl. Gouvernement, 2 April 1909, BArch-B, 1002/1992, Wunderlich, Ludwig, Landwirtschaftsinspektor (1907-1911).

[111] Abschrift, Seemannskrankenhaus und Institut für Schiffs- und Tropenkrankheiten, 31 October 1910, BArch-B, R 1002/1992, Wunderlich, Ludwig, Landwirtschaftsinspektor (1907-1911).

[112] Deutsch-Südwestafrikanischer Farmerbund to Kaiserl. Gouvernement Windhuk, 7 December 1910, BArch-B, R 1002/1992, Wunderlich, Ludwig, Landwirtschaftsinspektor (1907-1911).

and officials accessible in the colonial records describe all kinds of problems, especially since he had never trained a potential successor. There was also some confusion. Heinrich Sohnrey, a farmer employed to assist with tobacco cultivation in Okahandja, was seemingly under the impression that he would replace Wunderlich.[113] Sohnrey, who had prepared by researching the cultivation of tobacco,[114] arrived in the colony in November 1911.[115] The actual replacement for Wunderlich, however, was Kurt Schwonder, a former expert at Silesia's agricultural commission in Breslau. The latter had gained practical experience in farming in Eastern Prussia before attending university to study agriculture in Königsberg and Berlin.[116] Schwonder later noted that Sohnrey repeatedly complained about the work and drank extensively. Sohnrey eventually ended up working for another farming institution at Fürstenwalde.[117] Once Schwonder was recruited, the new governor and tobacco advocate Seitz recommended that he visit experimental stations at Hochburg (near Emmendingen) and in Kaiserslautern, and also stop by at the cigarette factory in Berlin-Pankow.[118] Schwonder finally arrived in the colony in February 1912,[119] almost two years after Wunderlich had departed.

Settlers in Southwest Africa voiced concerns about the actual expertise of such experts. According to an editorial published in the paper *Südwest*, Wunderlich had not been a specialist in tobacco at all. At best, he was an

[113] Sohnrey, Heinrich, Tabaksachverständiger, Schwonder to Kaisl. Gouvernment in Windhuk, 22 July 1913, BArch-B, R 1002/1665.

[114] Staatssekretär des Reichs-Kolonialamts to Kolonial-Hauptkasse, 11 October 1911, BArch-B, R 1002/1665.

[115] Kaisl. Gov. Windhoek to Kaisl. Distriktamt (Okahandja), 9 November 1911, BArch-B, R 1002/1665.

[116] Lebenslauf, BArch-B, R 1002/1614, Schwonder, Kurt, Dr., Tabakbausachverständiger, Vol 1 (1912–15).

[117] Schwonder to Kaisl. Gouvernment in Windhuk, 22 July 1913, BArch-B, R 1002/1614, Schwonder, Kurt, Dr., Tabakbausachverständiger, Vol 1 (1912-15). Schwonder to Kaisl. Gouvernment in Windhuk, 3 October 1913, BArch-B, R 1002/1614, Schwonder, Kurt, Dr., Tabakbausachverständiger, Vol 1 (1912-15).

[118] Staatssekretär Kolonialamt to Dr. Schwonder, 2 January 1912, BArch-B, R 1002/1615, Schwonder, Kurt, Dr., Tabakbausachverständiger, Vol 2 (1912-15).

[119] Staatssekretär des Reichs-Kolonialamts to Governeur, 22 January 1912, BArch-B, R 1002/1614, Schwonder, Kurt, Dr., Tabakbausachverständiger, Vol 1 (1912-15). Kaiserl. Bezirksamt, Verzeichnis, 19 February 1912, BArch-B, R 1002/1614, Schwonder, Kurt, Dr., Tabakbausachverständiger, Vol 1 (1912-15).

agricultural expert. His replacement Schwonder raised chickens prior to coming to Southwest Africa, the paper alleged. His assistant Sohnrey was merely a farmer. Should the money not be spent elsewhere? Could these so-called experts not at least be employed for several years to gain the required experience? The paper's anonymous informant suggested that settler Aimé Weiß would be a better choice.[120] Weiß had long tried to cultivate Turkish tobacco in Southwest Africa;[121] the *Südwestbote* also prominently featured a story about his efforts to sell his tobacco to the French state tobacco monopoly.[122] Such complaints emphasised the inexperience of the alleged experts and their short-lived tenure in Southwest Africa, while touting settler experience and independence. Settlers did not always agree with officials in Windhoek or Berlin and criticised government efforts to centralise cultivation. The colonial government certainly tried steering farmers toward cooperating, with a competition for a minimum of 5,000 bags of "tobacco for the indigenous populace," officially advertised in 1912. The newspaper *Südwestbote* was concerned, however, that this would leave behind small farmers.[123] The government reconsidered, ultimately allowing individual contributions without a required minimum.[124]

The institutionalisation of agricultural improvement ultimately came with the opening of an experimental station in Okahandja.[125] In line with Wunderlich's recommendations, discussions about a monopoly had been put aside for now.[126] Funds from the Wohlfahrtslotterie, combined with a private donation of 15,000 Marks specifically earmarked for the

[120] Südwest (1912(c)).

[121] Südwestbote (1912(a)).

[122] Südwestbote (1912(b)).

[123] Südwestbote (1912(c)). For a private competition see Südwestbote (1912(d)). Deutsch-Südwestafrikanische Zeitung (1910). For another criticism see also Südwestbote (1913(a)).

[124] Südwestbote (1912(c)).

[125] Amtsblatt für das Schutzgebiet Deutsch-Südwestafrika (1912).

[126] By November 1911, governor Seitz noted that the creation of a monopoly is not on the agenda anymore. Kaisl. Governeur to Reichskolonialamt, 1 November 1911, BArch-B, R 1001/1819, Einführung von Handelsmonopolen.

cultivation of tobacco in Southwest Africa, helped pay for the facility.[127] Meant to centralise cultivation and curing, the station employed local African workers. It had an irrigation system and by October 1912 a curing barn.[128] The aim was to support German farmers, who could make use of a blowing device (*Windfege*) and a sieve-rack (*Schüttelsieb*) to clean tobacco seeds free of charge.[129] Schwonder spent 121 days during the 1912/13 growing season visiting farmers to offer advice.[130] And the private company Tabakfabrik American Gebr. Risser, owned by the brothers Philipp and Heinrich Risser in Osona, received assistance from the experimental station.[131]

The station also embarked on a comprehensive study regarding the cultivation of tobacco and the most suitable plant species. Experiments were undertaken with seeds from Turkey and elsewhere.[132] Schwonder built on the work of Voigts and Wunderlich, both of whom had tried 26 different types of tobacco, resulting in "good" quality.[133] By October 1912, he felt the product was "gaining in quality" though exporting the leaf would be out of the question "for the foreseeable future."[134] Schwonder hoped for the involvement of a German factory on site.

[127] Kaiserl. Gouverneur von Deutsch Südwest-Afrika to Reichs-Kolonialamt, 23 July 1911, BArch-B, R 1001/8051, Tabak in Deutsch-Südwestafrika, Vol 2 (Sept. 1910-Jan. 1914).

[128] Kaiserl. Gouverneur von Deutsch Südwest-Afrika to Reichs-Kolonialamt, Bericht Schwonder, 7 June 1912, BArch-B, R 1001/8051, Tabak in Deutsch-Südwestafrika, Vol 2 (Sept. 1910-Jan. 1914).

[129] Amtsblatt für das Schutzgebiet Deutsch-Südwestafrika (1913). See also Deutsch-Südwestafrikanische Zeitung (1913(b)).

[130] Fühlings Landwirtschaftliche Zeitung (1914).

[131] Amtsblatt für das Schutzgebiet Deutsch-Südwestafrika (1914(a).

[132] Abschrift, Reichs-Kolonialamt to Gouverneur in Windhoek, 12 July 1910, BArch-B, R 1001/8050, Tabak in Deutsch-Südwestafrika, Vol 1 (Febr. 1902-Juni 1910). For efforts to get seeds namely from Turkey see Metropole to Reichs-Kolonialamt, 2 July 1910, BArch-B R 1001/8043, Tabak in Deutsch-Ostafrika, Vol 2 (Jul. 1899-Juni 1911). On seed samples from the United States see Gov. Windhoek (Blumenhagen) to Kaisl. Distriktamt Okahandja, 10 October 1912, National Archives Namibia (NAN), DOK, 121, T.1.C., Tabakanbau.

[133] Abschrift, Bericht, Wunderlich, 14 January 1911, BArch-B, R 1001/8051, Tabak in Deutsch-Südwestafrika, Vol 2 (Sept. 1910-Jan. 1914).

[134] Kaiserl. Governeur von Deutsch Südwest-Afrika to Reichs-Kolonialamt, 25 October 1912, BArch-B, R 1001/8051, Tabak in Deutsch-Südwestafrika, Vol 2 (Sept. 1910-Jan. 1914).

In his view, that would save costs for consumers, producers, and the government.[135]

During 1912/13, the experimental station utilised 62 hectares to run trials with 31 different species of tobacco.[136] Hoping he could find suitable plants for Southwest Africa, Schwonder also planned further investments that were required for irrigation, the cultivation of alfalfa for working animals, and additional experiments regarding curing and fermenting.[137] Okahandja, along with farms in Omaruru, Osona, and Grootfontein, promised an expansion of scientific initiatives for tobacco cultivation on land freed for cultivation for the German settlers through discrimination and genocide. Kawab (literally a flower-rich place), for example, had been a Herero settlement, and after the war Count Bentheim grew tobacco there.[138]

In addition to an array of subsidies and the German takeover of African lands, changes in the post-war work environment also made such developments possible. In August 1907, the colonial government institutionalised the *Eingeborenen-Verordnungen* (Indigenous Ordinances). These laws cemented the subjugation of Africans while creating a permanent pool of black labourers. The government barred black Africans from owning cattle or land and curtailed their freedom of movement by having them carry *Passmarken* (passes).[139] As a result, many black Africans found themselves dependent on working for the Germans. Although labour statistics, or the voices of Africans growing tobacco for the Germans, are hard to come by, there is evidence that Ovambo migrant workers from the north came south to work on tobacco farms. As in other sectors, scientific experts and their assistants were often the only whites on site. Since tobacco was a labour-intensive crop,[140] it is clear that forced and contract labourers sustained German efforts. Harsh work environments, and at

[135] Wolf (1912, p. 164).

[136] Fühlings Landwirtschaftliche Zeitung (1914).

[137] Schwonder (1914).

[138] Karow (1909, p. 121).

[139] Deutsche Kolonialzeitung (1911). See also Steinmetz (2007, p. 171). Zimmerer (2008). Zimmerer (2001, pp. 68–94).

[140] For discussions of labor and tobacco in colonial Zimbabwe see Rubert (1998, p. xi).

times brutal conditions, have long been documented when it comes to African labour in the colony.[141]

Settlers barely acknowledged the importance of land, subsidies, African knowledge, or black labour. Instead, they spoke about their own hard work on the frontier. While there was a settler distrust toward experts from the metropole, stories of improvement define most colonial narratives. Government reports constantly spoke about "substantial progress"[142] and "pleasing growth."[143] Karl and Gustav Holtz from Osona heralded the cultural mission of Europeans. Maria Karow, who spent time on a farm in Southwest Africa, described daily routines and ordinary life in harsh environments: "What one does not understand one learns out of necessity in Africa." Thanks to the supposed addiction of Africans, she could rely on their dilligence. "Yes, for that [tobacco] they had an appreciation," she noted, before explaining how workers at her farm presumably observed her closely as she was tending the crop.[144] Descriptions of alleged African dependencies, not harsh labour conditions regulated and enforced by "violence as usual," to borrow Muschalek's term,[145] thus became narrative tools in colonial stories when discussing work conditions. Settler Margarethe von Eckenbrecher dipped into a similar discourse when emphasising the cultivation of tobacco as a response to local demand. Although noting that the African population became interested and involved during the growing process,[146] von Eckenbrecher did not appreciate the agency, knowledge, and practices of the African population in tobacco cultivation. She, like other Germans, rather envisioned a racially inferior and addicted farm hand who was informed about the new introduction of cultivation practices by the settlers in close collaboration with the scientists of the agricultural experiment station.

Newly formed private initiatives meanwhile had trouble establishing themselves. In 1911, the limited liability company "Otjomikambo"

[141] See, for instance, Deutsche Kolonialzeitung (1911). See also Zimmerer (2001, pp. 68–94). Zollmann (2020, pp. 133–138).

[142] Reichs-Kolonialamt (1912, p. 127).

[143] Reichs-Kolonialamt (1914, p. 148).

[144] Kolonie und Heimat (1908). See also Karow (1909, p. 61).

[145] Muschalek (2019).

[146] Eckenbrecher (1907, p. 157).

Farmgesellschaft für Straussenzucht und Tabakbau G.m.b.H, overseen by farmers Walter Carpzow (in Grootfontein) and Kurt Woite (in Hoffnung), shared its plans to establish a large-scale operation.[147] Graf von Bernstorff-Hinrichshagen, who had been elected to the governing body, seemed unsure about the trustworthiness of Carpzow and Woite;[148] there were also worries about inconsistencies regarding the ownership of certain stretches of land.[149] Bureaucratic delays, along with the sudden disappearance of Carpzow, ultimately ended the endeavour.[150] Two years later, in early 1913, the Bremen-based business F. Undütsch & Co. requested information about the possibility of opening a tobacco factory in the colony. Although in contact with a farmer in the region, and willing to invest, the company was unsure about the prospects and asked for specific production privileges.[151] While some officials in Berlin were willing to support the proposal,[152] stakeholders in Southwest Africa had reservations.[153] At the time, there were also fears about British-American Tobacco (BAT) in Southwest Africa.[154] Instabilities and wars in the Balkans had increasingly upended the lucrative tobacco industry for Turkish cigarettes. Would BAT now become even more dominant? According to the *Deutsch-Südwestafrikanische Zeitung*, "there are some

[147] Woite to Lindequist, 8 March 1911, BArch-B, R 1001/1723, Otjomikambo Farmgesellschaft. Otjomikambo Farmgesellschaft fuer Straussenzucht und Tabakbau G.m.b.h., BArch-B, R 1001/1723, Otjomikambo Farmgesellschaft.

[148] Graf von Bernstorff-Hinrichshagen to Reichskolonialamt, 3 April 1911, BArch-B, R 1001/1723, Otjomikambo Farmgesellschaft.

[149] Carpzow to Reichskolonialamt, 13 September 1911, BArch-B, R 1001/1723, Otjomikambo Farmgesellschaft.

[150] Lawyer Paul Meyer to Reichskolonialamt, 21 October 1912, BArch-B, R 1001/1723, Otjomikambo Farmgesellschaft. Reichsamt für deutsche Einwanderung, Rückwanderung und Auswanderung (Reichswanderungsamt), to Reichskolonialamt, 4 December 1919, BArch-B, R 1001/1723, Otjomikambo Farmgesellschaft.

[151] Letter/ memorandum, Undütsch to Kaisl. Governeur, 21 February 1913, BArch-B, R 1001/1819, Einführung von Handelsmonopolen.

[152] Ibid.

[153] Ibid., Anlage: Abschrift, Vertrag; Verordnung, Begleitschreiben, Seitz, BArch-B, R 1001/1819.

[154] Ibid., Array of newspaper articles included in the file outline German fears, many of which tied to the situation in the Balkans, BArch-B, R 1001/1819. See also Deutsche Tageszeitung (1913(a)).

anxieties among German tobacco producers."[155] For some commentators, this was a "time of reckoning" for the German tobacco industry.[156] An inquiry regarding potential connections of Undütsch with BAT took months and bore no fruit.[157] In early 1914, a year after Undütsch's original proposal, debates in the Reichstag regarding a state monopoly put discussions on hold.[158] General anxieties, bureaucratic delays, and confusions regarding the situation on the ground made private investment seemingly impossible and protected those settlers already cultivating tobacco in German Southwest Africa.

Overall, disruptions tied to war and genocide transformed the German cultivation of tobacco and a changing consumer structure rarely acknowledged at the time paved the way for an increasingly centralised agro-scientific infrastructure starting to emerge in the colony. This was one of many subsidies German settlers enjoyed during colonial rule—even though settler narratives claimed individualism and independence. Private entities, on the other hand, experienced bureaucratic nightmares.

Tobacco Fantasies?

Different stakeholders had their own narratives about the cultivation of tobacco between 1908 and 1914. Although ecological limitations of the colony, the lack of imperial infrastructure, the shortage of labour grounded in genocide, and the entrenched behaviour of settlers in the face of models coming from the metropole were evident for most contemporaries, debates in colonial newspapers and other avenues selling empire nonetheless continually highlighted the Southwest Africa's potential for tobacco cultivation.

Tobacco of a desired quality was presented in euphoric ways in many colonial newspapers and tobacco publications. In 1910, the magazine *Kolonie und Heimat* reprinted an article praising the virtues of tobacco farming in German Southwest Africa, referring to "really good

[155] Deutsch-Südwestafrikanische Zeitung (1913(a)).

[156] Deutsche Tageszeitung (1913(a)). Frankfurter Zeitung (1913).

[157] Auskunftei Schimmelpfeng to Reichskolonialamt, 13 October 1913, BArch-B, R 1001/1819, Handelsmonopole.

[158] Handschriftlich, Undütsch to Reichskolonialamt, 8 March 1914, BArch-B, R 1001/1819, Handelsmonopole.

prospects" not just to meet local demand but also for export.[159] In 1911, The *Deutsch Tabakzeitung* referenced a London-based businessman and expert travelling to Southwest Africa praising the excellent quality of tobacco in Grootfontein and Okahandja.[160] The *Deutsche Kolonialzeitung*, while acknowledging some difficulties, always remained positive about the next season.[161] "Our fine experiences and success in the cultivation of tobacco in a relatively short amount of time," it noted in 1914, "entitle us to speak of tobacco in Southwest [Africa] as an economic opportunity with a great future."[162] The *Süddeutsche Tabakzeitung* agreed with that assessment, highlighting efforts in Osona.[163] An undated photograph capturing a man in a field of tobacco pointing to "his success" encapsulates that as well. Adverse climatic conditions of the colonies for cultivation and fermentation were dismissed as obstacles worth conquering; a lack of water hindering initial efforts was identified as a challenge within this frontier spirit. Farmer Ferdinand Gessert of Inachab, quoted in *Der Tropenpflanzer* in 1899, noted that tobacco could do well "without artificial irrigation on flooded land."[164] In 1911, the *Deutsche Tabakzeitung* featured tobacco industrialist Johann Ludwig Reiner's assessment of probes arriving from Okahandja and Osona. Although unable to give a full evaluation given that fermentation had not been completed, Reiner painted a promising picture when highlighting that the current quality could serve the domestic market in Southwest Africa.[165] By 1914, there was thus an exceptional amount of confidence regarding the future, which became apparent in reporting about Southwest Africa's national exhibit in June.[166]

And yet, the rosy picture was clouded by some scepticism. First and foremost, there were concerns about whether the quality of tobacco could be improved by means of science in view of adverse environmental

[159] Kolonie und Heimat in Wort und Bild (1910). See also Blackler (2017, p. 137). Amtsblatt für das Schutzgebiet Deutsch-Südwestafrika (1911).

[160] Deutsche Tabakzeitung (1911(a)).

[161] Deutsche Kolonialzeitung (1913).

[162] Holtz (1914). See also Lau and Reiner (1993, p. 38).

[163] Süddeutsche Tabakzeitung (Mannheim) (1914).

[164] Der Tropenpflanzer (1899).

[165] Deutsche Tabakzeitung (1911(c)). See also Südwestbote (1911(b)).

[166] Südwest (1914).

conditions. Schwonder, who described agricultural trials in meticulous detail,[167] discussed the impact of drought, sudden downpours, and sand storms. Hail, locusts, and aridity brought additional problems, not even to mention mildew, the groundnut leaf miner (*Aproaerema modicella*), the European mole cricket (*Gryllotalpa gryllotalpa*), and the potato tuber moth (*Phthorimaea operculella*).[168] Then there was the question of curing—air-curing or flue-curing?[169] Given previous issues with flue-curing in Osona, Schwonder promoted the use of closed curing barns. Controlling humidity to around 65% was key but difficult given the climate. Schwonder suggested blowing mist into the barns and hanging up wet rags.[170] Still, the quality of the product lagged behind. In 1911, three cigarettes from Omaruru arrived at the Garbaty Company. Although of decent quality, they did not compare to Turkish or so-called Oriental products widely consumed.[171] Another company noted that "maybe only the better of these tobaccos" could be used in small batches for the cheapest cigarettes sold. Samples arriving from Omaruru at Thorbecke in Mannheim could not be properly assessed because they had not fermented enough.[172] In 1912, some evaluations still referred to a "harsh" and "ordinary" product, wild in character.[173] Some discussed marketing a "Southwest African cigarette" in Germany, which raised fears in Windhoek about promoting a weak product and thus deterring future customers.[174]Secondly, the shortage of labour and insufficient infrastructure worried officials. The lack of African workers,[175] which

[167] Schwonder (1913).

[168] Schwonder (1922(a), pp. 185–187).

[169] Schwonder (1922(b), pp. 222–227).

[170] Kaiserl. Governeur von Deutsch Südwest-Afrika to Reichs-Kolonialamt, 25 October 1912, BArch-B, R 1001/8051, Tabak in Deutsch-Südwestafrika, Vol 2 (Sept. 1910-Jan. 1914). Wolf (1912, p. 164).

[171] Südwest (1911(e)).

[172] Zigarettenfabrik to Reichs-Kolonialamt, 30 March 1911, BArch-B, R 1001/8051. See also Fühlings Landwirtschaftliche Zeitung (1914).

[173] Gutachten, 9 December 1912, BArch-B, R 1001/8051, Tabak in Deutsch-Südwestafrika, Vol 2, (Sept. 1910-Jan. 1914).

[174] Kaiserl. Gouverneur von Deutsch Südwest-Afrika to Reichs-Kolonialamt, 9 February 1913, BArch-B, R 1001/8051, Tabak in Deutsch-Südwestafrika, Vol 2, (Sept. 1910-Jan. 1914).

[175] Reichs-Kolonialamt (1914, p. 148).

speaks to the shallow labour pool following war and genocide, made it difficult to keep farms running. Scholars estimated that about 15,000 workers were needed by 1911, a stunning 75% of the labouring male population.[176] While publications focusing on tobacco mentioned the indigenous population mostly in the context of consumers, newspapers in general repeatedly discussed labour shortages.[177] Delays in the construction of infrastructure meant to reach international markets did not help either. At one point the newspaper *Deutsch Tabakzeitung* most directly outlined the issues at hand when pointing to "inadequate infrastructure and a lack of labour" in one of its articles.[178] Finally, there was resistance by local farmers, many of whom, like the tobacco farmers in Osona, did not see the point of collaboration.[179] In general, settlers wanted little interference from the metropole. In their view, they knew best how to grow tobacco. After all, they had been in the country for years. Hence, efforts by the government in Windhoek to incentivise the production of larger quantities received pushback from a front-page *Südwest* editorial pointing to the value of small-scale efforts by settlers.[180] It is hardly surprising then that there was often uncertainty about the development of tobacco in the colonies. Of course, all colonists could agree that only the loss of the colony due to World War I had disrupted the realisation of German tobacco fantasies.

Conclusion

German tobacco fantasies in Southwest Africa are deeply tied to racial exclusion, inherent violence, and settler stories about transformations of nature. Complex logistics and limited funding, along with local resistance and environmental limitations, initially meant the cultivation of "inferior" tobacco to meet local demands. After the war and genocide,

[176] These are estimates of Farmer Schlettwein in Zimmerer (2001, p. 177).

[177] See, for instance Südwest (1911(a)). Südwest (1911(b)). Südwest (1911(c)). Südwest (1911(d)). Südwest (1912(a) and 1912(b)).

[178] Deutsche Tabakzeitung (1911(b)).

[179] Schubert (1913, p. 24 and 91).

[180] Südwestbote (1912(c)) For governor Seitz's assessment see Bericht über die Tätigkeit in Südwestafrika (ca. 1919), Marchivum (Mannheim), Nachlass Seitz, Theodor, 50/1968_00006, p. 7.

a changing consumer structure that was a direct outcome of the extermination of a large part of the Herero and Nama people created a shift in the market. Various difficulties ultimately undermined imperial fantasies, and the desire to cultivate tobacco for white settlers and the metropole never materialised. While the production of tobacco increased, ecological limitations, a lack of imperial infrastructure, labour shortages grounded in war and genocide, and the entrenched behaviour of settlers hampered anticipated development and progress. Colonial narratives, framed as battle-stories meant to overcome adversities, silenced the indigenous history of precolonial tobacco and settler violence. According to those storylines, progress and success (for whites) was always just around the corner.

References

Primary Sources

Unpublished

Bundesarchiv Berlin-Lichterfelde (BArch-B)
- Reichskolonialamt (R 1001).

Bundesarchiv Koblenz (BArch-K)
- 1138/59–63, Nachlass Kastl, 1911–1928.

Namibian National Archives (NAN), Windhoek
- BSW (Inventar der Akten des Kaiserlichen Bezirksamt Swakopmund), 1892-1914, 95, T.1.D.: Tabaktrockenschuppen, 1910. - DOK (Inventar der Akten Kaiserlichen Distriktsamts Okahandja), 1894-1915, 121, T.1.A., T.1.C., T.1.H.: Tabakbau.

Marchivum Mannheim
- Nachlass Seitz, Theodor.

University Library Frankfurt am Main
- Koloniales Bildarchiv.

Published

Alexander, J. 1838. *An Expedition of Discovery into the Interior of Africa*. London: H. Colburn

Amtsblatt für das Schutzgebiet Deutsch-Südwestafrika. 1910. Bekanntmachung des Gouverneurs vom 9. November 1910 betr. Beihilfen zum Bau von Tabaktrockenschuppen, 15 November.

Amtsblatt für das Schutzgebiet Deutsch-Südwestafrika. 1911. Verschiedenes, 1 May.
Amtsblatt für das Schutzgebiet Deutsch-Südwestafrika. 1912. Personalien, 1 March.
Amtsblatt für das Schutzgebiet Deutsch-Südwestafrika. 1913. Bekanntmachung, 15 February.
Amtsblatt für das Schutzgebiet Deutsch-Südwestafrika. 1914(a). Bekanntmachung, 1 February.
Amtsblatt für das Schutzgebiet Deutsch-Südwestafrika. 1914(b). Bekanntmachung, 1 July.
Andersson, J. 1882. *Notes of Travel in South-Western Africa*, 2nd ed. New York: G.P. Putnam's.
Auer, G. 1911. *In Südwestafrika gegen die Hereros. Kriegstagebücher des Obermatrosen G. Auer*. Berlin: Hofmann.
Baines, T. 1864. *Explorations in South-West Africa*. London: Longman.
Bayer, M. 1907. *Der Krieg in Südwestafrika und seine Bedeutung für die Entwicklung der Kolonie*. Leipzig: Friedrich Engelmann.
Belwe, M. 1906. *Gegen die Herero 1904/1906. Tagebuchaufzeichnungen von Max Belwe*. Berlin: Mittler.
Brockmann, C. 1912. *Briefe eines deutschen Mädchens aus Südwest*. Berlin: Mittler.
Bülow, F.J. von. 1896. *Deutsch-Südwestafrika: Drei Jahre im Lande Hendrik Witboois*. Berlin: Mittler.
Darmstaedter, P. 1896. *Die geographische Verbreitung und die Produktion des Tabakbaus*. Ph. D Dissertation, University Halle-Wittenberg.
Dehn, P. 1880. *Die kaiserliche Tabaksmanufaktur in Strassburg als Vorläuferin eines deutschen Tabaksmonopol*. Berlin: no publisher.
Der Farmer. Mitteilungen über Farm-, Garten-, Forstwirtschaft und Bergbau. Gratis-Beilage der Windhuker Nachrichten. 1908(a). Die nächsten Ziele des deutsch-südwestafrikanischen Tabakbaues, 14 March.
Der Farmer. Mitteilungen über Farm-, Garten-, Forstwirtschaft und Bergbau. Gratis-Beilage der Windhuker Nachrichten. 1908(b). Das Trocknen der grünen Tabakblaetter bei mittlerem und kleinerem Anbau in Deutsch-Suedwestafrika, 25 April.
Der Farmer. Mitteilungen über Farm-, Garten-, Forstwirtschaft und Bergbau. Gratis-Beilage der Windhuker Nachrichten. 1908(c). Das Trocknen der Tabakblaetter am Tabakstengel, 16 May.
Der Farmer. Mitteilungen über Farm-, Garten-, Forstwirtschaft und Bergbau. Gratis-Beilage der Windhuker Nachrichten. 1908(d). Pflanzweite und Boden beim Tabakbau, 22 July.
Der Farmer. Mitteilungen über Farm-, Garten-, Forstwirtschaft und Bergbau. Gratis-Beilage der Windhuker Nachrichten. 1908(e). Das Versetzen der in

Saatbeeten Töpfen und Blechbüchsen gezogenen Tabakpflanzen ins Feld, 19 August.
Der Farmer. Mitteilungen über Farm-, Garten-, Forstwirtschaft und Bergbau. Gratis-Beilage der Windhuker Nachrichten. 1908(f). Die Anzucht von Tabakpflanzen in Tontöpfchen oder Blechbüchsen, 22 August.
Der Farmer. Mitteilungen über Farm-, Garten-, Forstwirtschaft und Bergbau. Gratis-Beilage der Windhuker Nachrichten. 1908(g). Die zehn Grundregeln für den Tabakbauer in Deutsch-Südwestafrika, 4 November.
Der Farmer. Mitteilungen über Farm-, Garten-, Forstwirtschaft und Bergbau. Gratis-Beilage der Windhuker Nachrichten. 1910. Etwas über den Tabakbau im Erntejahr 1908/09, 15 January.
Der Tropenpflanzer. 1898. Statistisches über Tabak, March.
Der Tropenpflanzer. 1899. Etwas über Winterfrucht im Namaland, April.
Der Tropenpflanzer. 1902. Die Tabakproduktion in den deutschen Schutz gebieten, July.
Der Tropenpflanzer. 1904. Über den Tabakbau in den deutschen Kolonien, July.
Der Tropenpflanzer. 1906. Tabakindustrie in Britisch-Südafrika, May.
Der Tropenpflanzer. 1907. Tabakbau in den Kolonien, August.
Der Tropenpflanzer. 1909. Tabakbau in Deutsch-Südwestafrika, November.
Deutsch-Südwestafrikanische Zeitung. 1909. Die zehn Grundregeln für den Tabakbauer in Deutsch-Südwestafrika, 23. January.
Deutsch-Südwestafrikanische Zeitung. 1910. Aus dem Schutzgebiet: Neues Tabak-Preisausschreiben, 5 October.
Deutsch-Südwestafrikanische Zeitung. 1913(a). Tabakhandel und Trust, 25 January.
Deutsch-Südwestafrikanische Zeitung. 1913(b). Aus dem Schutzgebiet: Aus dem Norden, 18 March.
Deutsche Kolonialzeitung. 1888. Zur Wasserfrage in Südwestafrika (Schluß), 11 February.
Deutsche Kolonialzeitung. 1889. Deutsche Pflanzer für die deutschen Kolonien, 12 January.
Deutsche Kolonialzeitung. 1911. Arbeiternot und Eingeborenenpflege in Südwestafrika, 29 April.
Deutsche Kolonialzeitung. 1913. Rundschau: Tabak in Deutsch-Südwestafrika, 1 November.
Deutsche Tabakzeitung. 1911(a). Vermischtes. Zunehmende Bedeutung des Tabakbaues in Südwest-Afrika, 19 January.
Deutsche Tabakzeitung. 1911(b). Tabakkultur und Zigarrenfabrikation in den deutschen Kolonien, 24 August.
Deutsche Tabakzeitung. 1911(c). Beurteilung des Südwest-Tabaks, 30 November.
Deutsche Tageszeitung. 1913(a). Der Tabaktrust im Orient, 28 May.

Deutsche Tageszeitung. 1913(b). Auskunftei Schimmelpfeng to Reichskolonialamt, 13 October
Deutsche Tageszeitung. 1914. Handschriftlich, Undütsch to Reichskolonialamt, 8 March.
Dinter, K. 1909. *Deutsch-Südwest-Afrika. Flora, Forst- und landwirtschaftliche Fragmente*. Leipzig: T. O. Weigel.
Dornan, S. 1925. *Pygmies and Bushmen in the Kalahari*. London: Seeley.
Eckenbrecher, M. von. 1907. *Was Afrika mir gab und nahm*. Berlin: Mittler.
Falkenhausen, H. v. 1905. *Ansiedlerschicksale: Elf Jahre in Deutsch-Südwestafrika 1893–1904*. Berlin: Reimler.
Foreign Office/Board of Trade, eds. 1914. *Germany, Report for the Year 1913 on the Trade of the Consular District of German South-West Africa*. London: H.M. Stationery Office 1914.
Frankfurter Zeitung. 1913. Die Schicksalsstunde der Zigarettenindustrie, 6 September.
Fühlings Landwirtschaftliche Zeitung. 1914. Anbauversuche mit Zigarettentabak auf der kaiserlichen Versuchsstation für Tabakbau Okahandja (Deutsch-Südwestafrika). Vegetationsperiod 1912/13, 1 August.
Galton, F. 1853. *The Narrative of an Explorer in Tropical South Africa*. London: Ward, Lock and Co.
General-Anzeiger (Mannheim). 1902. Der Tabakbau in Deutsch-Südwestafrika, 19 November.
General-Anzeiger (Mannheim). 1907. Die Tabakindustrie und die Kolonial politik, 11 June.
Gentz, P. 1905. *Deutschland und England in Südafrika: Vergleich der Kriegsführung und der Erfolge beider Staaten in ihren südafrikanischen Kolonialkriegen*. Berlin: no publisher.
Giess, W. 1981. Die in der zentralen Namib von Südwestafrika/Namibia festgestellten Pflanzenarten und ihre Biotope. *Dinteria* 15: 20.
Giess, W. 1982. Zur Verbreitung des Tabaks in Südwestafrika: Nicotiana africana Merxmüller. *Dinteria* 16: 11–20.
Hartwich, C. 1911. *Die menschlichen Genussmittel: Ihre Herkunft, Verbreitung, Geschichte, Anwendung, Bestandteile und Wirkung*. Leipzig: Chr. Herm. Tauchnitz.
Henkel, F. 1908. *Der Kampf um Südwestafrika*. Berlin: Paetel.
Hoffmann, M, ed. 1914. *Jahres-Bericht über die Erfahrungen und Fortschritte auf dem Gesamtgebiet der Landwirtschaft*. Braunschweig: Vieweg und Sohn.
Holtz, K. G. 1914. Der Tabakbau in Südwestafrika. Das Ergebnis siebenjähriger Erfahrungen. Landwirtschaftliche Beilage des Amtsblattes für das Schutzgebiet Deutsch-Südwestafrika, 1 March.
Irle, J. 1906. *Die Herero: Ein Beitrag zur Landes-, Volks- & Missionskunde*. Gütersloh: Bertelsmann.

Jaeger, F., and L. Waibel. 1920. *Beiträge zur Landeskunde von Südwestafrika*. Berlin: S.W.A. Wissenschaftliche Gesellschaft.

Karow, M. 1909. *Wo sonst der Fuß des Kriegers trat. Farmerleben in Südwest nach dem Kriege*. Berlin: Mittler.

Kissling, R. 1925. *Handbuch der Tabakkunde, des Tabakbaus und der Tabakfabrikation*, 5th ed. Berlin: Parley.

Kolonie und Heimat. 1908. Vom Tabakbau in Deutsch-Südwest. 6 December.

Kolonie und Heimat in Wort und Bild. 1910. Neues vom Tabakanbau in Südwestafrika, 13 March.

Koning, C.J. 1900. *Der Tabak. Studie über seine Kultur und Biologie*. Amsterdam: Van Heteren.

Lewinstein, G. 1897. *Der Tabakkonsum in den einzelnen Staaten der Erde und die Einnahmen der Staaten aus dem Tabak*. Berlin: Peiser.

Moritz, W. ed. 1980. *Erkundungsreise ins Ovamboland 1857 Tagebuch Carl Hugo Hahn*. Schwäbisch Gmünd: Lempp 1980.

Oelhafen, H. von. 1926. *Die Besiedelung Deutsch-Südwestafrikas bis zum Weltkriege*. Berlin: Dietrich Reimer.

Petermanns Geographische Mitteilungen. 1885. Das Gebiet zwischen Angra Pequena und Bethanien. Vorläufige Mitteilungen aus Lüderitzland von Dr. Adolf Schenck, 31: 132–136.

Reichs-Kolonialamt, ed. 1911. *Die deutschen Schutzgebiete in Afrika und der Südsee 1909/10. Amtliche Jahresberichte*. Berlin: Ernst Siegfried Mittler und Sohn.

Reichs-Kolonialamt, ed. 1912. *Die deutschen Schutzgebiete in Afrika und der Südsee 1910/11. Amtliche Jahresberichte*. Berlin: Ernst Siegfried Mittler und Sohn.

Reichs-Kolonialamt, ed. 1913. *Die deutschen Schutzgebiete in Afrika und der Südsee 1911/12. Amtliche Jahresberichte*. Berlin: Ernst Siegfried Mittler und Sohn.

Reichs-Kolonialamt, ed. 1914. *Die deutschen Schutzgebiete in Afrika und der Südsee 1912/13. Amtliche Jahresberichte*. Berlin: Ernst Siegfried Mittler und Sohn.

Schinz, H. 2021. *Deutsch-Südwest-Afrika. Forschungsreisen durch die deutschen Schutzgebiete Gross-Nama- und Hereroland, nach dem Kunene, dem Ngami-See und der Kalahari*, Oldenburg: Schulze.

Schnee, H., ed. 1920. *Deutsches Kolonial-Lexikon*. Leipzig: Quelle & Meyer.

Schubert, E. 1913. *Landwirtschaft und ihre Nebenbetriebe in Südwestafrika*. Ph. D Dissertation, University of Heidelberg.

Schwabe, K. 1899. *Mit Schwert und Pflug in Deutsch-Südwestafrika. Vier Kriegs- und Wanderjahre*. Berlin: Mittler.

Schweinitz-Dieban, G. von. 1892. Die Wasserfrage in Deutsch-Südwestafrika. Deutsche Kolonialzeitung, 2 April.

Schwonder, K. 1905. *Die landwirtschaftlichen Betriebssysteme: Eine Kritik der verschiedenen Einteilungen und Vorschläge zu einer Neueinteilung, begrüendet durch die Wirtschaftsweise auf dem Gute Wermten und der Herrschaft Friedrichstein.* Ph. D Dissertation, Albertus-University Königsberg.
Schwonder, K. 1913. Tabaksamenbau und -züchtung in Deutsch-Südwestafrika. Landwirtschaftliche Beilage des Amtsblattes für Deutsch-Südwestafrika.
Schwonder, K. 1914. Jahresbericht der Kaiserlichen Versuchsstation für Tabakbau in Okahandja 1913/14. Landwirtschaftliche Beilage des Amtsblatts für das Schutzgebiet Deutsch-Südwestafrika, 1 June.
Schwonder, K. 1922. Anbauversuche mit Zigarettentabak in den deutschen Schutzgebieten. Sonderabdruck aus dem Tropenpflanzer 25. September-December, 147–154, 185–189 and 222–232.
Süddeutsche Tabakzeitung (Mannheim). 1914. Tabakbau in Deutsch-Südwestafrika, 28 May.
Südwest. 1911(a). Ein Vortrag über den Arbeitsmangel, 6 January.
Südwest. 1911(b). Vorschläge zur Abhilfe der Arbeiternot, 19 May.
Südwest. 1911(c). Ein weiterer Vorschlag zur Abhilfe der Arbeiternot, 2 June.
Südwest. 1911(d). Erwiderung auf "Ein weiterer Vorschlag zur Abhilfe der Arbeiternot", 18 July.
Südwest. 1911(e). Aus dem Schutzgebiet. Ein Urteil über Omaruru-Tabak, 25 July.
Südwest. 1912(a). Die Arbeiterfrage, 23 January.
Südwest. 1912(b). Die Arbeiterfrage, 30 January.
Südwest. 1912(c). Mit den Sachverständigen für Tabakbau, 29 March.
Südwest. 1912(d). Anbauversuche mit türkischem Tabak, 4 August.
Südwest. 1913. Aus dem Schutzgebiet. Reinigen von Tabaksaat, 21 February.
Südwest. 1914. Landesausstellung 1914, 23 June.
Südwestbote. 1911(a). Die zehn Grundregeln für den Tabakbauer in Deutsch-Südwestafrika, 23 August.
Südwestbote. 1911(b). Beurteilung des Südwest-Tabaks, 7 October.
Südwestbote. 1912(a). Anbauversuche mit türkischem Tabak, 4 August.
Südwestbote. 1912(b). Südwesttabak in Frankreich, 4 August.
Südwestbote. 1912(c). Die Tabak-Ausschreibung des Gouvernements, 6 September.
Südwestbote. 1912(d). Schutzgebiets-Chronik: Neues Tabak-Preisausschreiben, 2 October.
Südwestbote. 1912(e). Etwas vom Welthandel in Tabak, 20 October.
Südwestbote. 1913(a). Tabakbedarf der Eisenbahn-Verwaltung, 9 March.
Südwestbote. 1913(b). Tabaksamenbau und -Züchtung in Deutsch-Südwestafrika, 23 March.
Vedder, H. 1923. *Die Bergdama.* Hamburg: Friederichsen.

Vedder, H. 1966. The Berg Damara. In *The Native Tribes of South West Africa*, eds. C.H. Hahn, H. Vedder, and L. Fourie, 37–78. London: Routledge.

Verhandlungen des Reichstages. 1900/1903(a). Denkschrift über die Deutschen Schutzgebiete. 196: 5289.

Verhandlungen des Reichstages. 1900/1903(b). Denkschrift über die Entwicklung der Deutschen Schutzgebiete im Jahre 1900/01. 193: 2938.

Verhandlungen des Reichstages. 1904. Denkschrift über die Deutschen Schutzgebiete: Aktenstück Nr. 54. 205: 123.

Verhandlungen des Reichstages. 1909. (Entwicklung d. deutschen Schutzgebiete in Afrika u. d. Südsee), Anlage E.IX, Bericht des Sachverständigen für Tabakbau über den Stand und die Aussichten des Tabakbaues in Deutsch-Südwestafrika. 252: 6980.

Verhandlungen des Reichstages. 1911. Bericht des Sachverständigen für Tabakbau über die Entwicklung des Tabakbaues im deutsch-südwestafrikanischen Schutzgebiet. 271: 843.

von Deimling, B. 1906. *Südwestafrika. Land und Leute, Unsere Kämpfe, Wert der Kolonie*. Berlin: Eisenschmidt.

Wagner, J. 1888. *Deutsch-Ostafrika: Geschichte der Gesellschaft für deutsche Kolonisation der Deutsch-Ostafrikanischen Gesellschaft und der Deutsch-Ostafrikanischen Plantagengesellschaft nach den massgebeneden Quellen*. Berlin: Engelhardt.

Watermeyer, ed. 1902. *Anleitung für Anbau und Behandlung des Tabaks unter Berücksichtigung der klimatischen Verhältnisse Deutsch-Südwest-Afrikas*. Berlin: Reichsdruckerei.

Wegner, E. 1885. *Aus Deutsch-Afrika! Tagebuch-Briefe eines jungen Deutschen aus Angra Pequena (1882–1884)*. Leipzig: Schloemp.

Windhuker Nachrichten. 1908(a). Anzucht der Setzlinge in Saatbeeten, 4 July.

Windhuker Nachrichten. 1908(b). Tabakkultur in Südwestafrika. Vortrag gehalten in Windhuk am 4. Oktober 1908, 10 October.

Windhuker Nachrichten. 1908(c). Deutsch-Südwestafrika: Vortrag über Tabakbau, 14 October.

Windhuker Nachrichten. 1908(d). Deutsch-Südwestafrika: Vortag über Tabakbau, 31 October.

Windhuker Nachrichten. 1909(a). Die Kleinsiedlungen, 20 February 1909.

Windhuker Nachrichten. 1909(b). Deutsch-Südwestafrika: Unsere Tabakpflanzer, 18 September.

Windhuker Nachrichten. 1909(c). Die Verteuerung des Tabaks, 17 November.

Witte, H. 1919. *Tabak und Tabakerzeugnisse. Ein Leitfaden und Ratgeber*. Leipzig: Akademische Verlagsgesellschaft.

Wohltmann, F. 1905. *Unsere Lage und Aussichten in der Kolonie Deutsch-Südwestafrika: Ein offenes Wort*. Bonn: Cohen.

Wolf, J., ed. 1912. *Der Tabak und die Tabakfabrikate*. Leipzig: Voigt.

Wunderlich, L. 1908. Tabakkultur in Deutsch-Südwestafrika. Windhuker Nachrichten, 10 October.

Zimmermann, P. 1926. *Tabakforschung in aller Welt. Ein Rundblick*. Dresden: Die Tabakwelt.

Secondary Sources

Akehurst, B.C. 1981. *Tobacco*. London: Longman.

Ambler, C. 2022. Drugs in Africa from the Slave Trade to Colonialism. *The Archaeological Bulletin* 7: 192–210.

Blackler, A. 2017. *Heathens, 'Hottentots', and Heimat: Colonial Encounters and German Identity in Southwest Africa, 1842–1915*. Ph.D Dissertation, University of Minnesota.

Botha, C. 2005. People and the Environment in Colonial Namibia. *South African Historical Journal* 52: 170–190.

Bückendorf, J. 1997. *'Schwarz-weiss-rot über Ostafrika!' Deutsche Kolonialpläne und afrikanische Realität*, Münster, LIT.

Cremer, W. 2004. *Pfeifen, Hanf und Tabak in Schwarzafrika: Eine historische Darstellung*. Idstein/Ts.: Baum.

Declerq, R. 2016. Building Imperial Frontiers: Business, Science and Karakul Sheep Farming in (German) South-West Africa (1903–1939). *Journal of Modern European History* 14: 54–77.

Duvall, C.S. 2017. Cannabis and Tobacco in Precolonial and Colonial Africa. *Oxford Research Encyclopedia of African History*. Oxford: Oxford University Press [Online]. https://doi.org/10.1093/acrefore/9780190277734.013.44. Accessed by 7 January 2024.

Fitzpatrick, M. 2022. *The Kaiser and the Colonies: Monarchy in the Age of Empire*. Oxford, Oxford University Press.

Förster, L. 2008. The Concept of Oral History. In *What the Elders Used to Say: Namibian Perspectives on the Last Decade of Colonial Rule*, ed C. Erichsen, 63–74. Windhoek: John Meinert Printing.

Gately, I. 2003. *Tobacco: A Cultural History of How an Exotic Plant Seduced Civilization*. New York: Grove/Atlantic Inc.

Goodman, J. ed. 2005. *Tobacco in History and Culture. An Encyclopedia*. 2 Vols. Detroit: Thomson/Gale.

Goodman, J. 1995. *Tobacco in History: The Cultures of Dependence*. London: Routledge.

Goodwin, A.J.H. 1952. Jan van Riebeeck and the Hottentots 1652–1662. *The South African Archaeological Bulletin* 7: 2–6.

Gootenberg, P., ed. 2022. *Oxford Handbook of Global Drug History*. Oxford: Oxford University Press.

Gordon, D. 1996. From Rituals of Rapture to Dependence: The Political Economy of Khoikhoi Narcotic Consumption, c. 1487–1870. *South African Historical Journal* 35: 62–88.

Goudie, A., and H. Viles. 2015. *Landscapes and Landforms of Namibia*. Dordrecht: Springer.

Hannah, L. 2006. The Whig Fable of American Tobacco, 1895–1913. *Journal of Economic History* 66: 42–73.

Häussler, M. 2018. *Der Genozid an den Herero: Krieg, Emotion und extreme Gewalt in Deutsch-Südwestafrika*. Weilerwist: Nomos.

Hayes, P., J. Silvester, and W. Hartmann. 2002a. "Picturing the Past" in Namibia: The Visual Archive and its Energies. In *Refiguring the Archived*, ed. C. Hamilton et al., 103–134: Dordrecht: Springer.

Hayes, P., J. Silvester, and W. Hartmann. 2002b. Photography, History and Memory. In *The Colonising Camera: Photographs in the Making of Namibian History*, eds. W. Hartmann, J. Silvester, and P. Hayes, second edition, 2–9, Cape Town: University of Cape Town Press.

Henrichsen, D. 2011. *Herrschaft und Alltag im vorkolonialen Zentralnamibia*. Basel: Kuiseb Verlag.

Hess, H. 1987. *Rauchen. Geschichte, Geschäfte, Gefahren*. Frankfurt am Main: Campus.

Hewitson, M. 2018. *Germany and the Modern World, 1880–1914*. Cambridge: Cambridge University Press.

Jacob, F. and G. Dworok. 2015. *Tabak und Gesellschaft: Vom braunen Gold zum sozialen Stigma*. Göttingen: Nomos.

Kaulich, U. 2001. *Die Geschichte der ehemaligen Kolonie Deutsch-Südwestafrika 1884–1914*. Frankfurt am Main: Lang.

Kreienbaum, J. 2015. *'Ein trauriges Fiakso': Koloniale Konzentrationslager im südlichen Afrika, 1900–1908*. Hamburg: Hamburger Edition.

Krüger, G. 2008. The Golden Age of the Pastoralist: Namibia in the 19th Century. In *Genocide in German South-West Africa: The Colonial War (1904–1908) in Namibia and its aftermath*, ed. J. Zimmerer and J. Zeller, 3–18. Monmouth: Wales Merlin Press.

Kundrus, B. 2003. *Moderne Imperialisten. Das Kaiserreich im Spiegel seiner Kolonien*. Köln: Böhlau.

Lau, B. 1986. Conflict and Power in Nineteenth-Century Namibia. *The Journal of African History* 27: 29–39.

Lau, B. 1987. *Namibia in Jonker Afrikaners Time*. Windhoek: National Archives of Namibia.

Lau, B., and P. Reiner. 1993. *100 Years of Agricultural Development in Colonial Namibia. A Historical Overview of Visions and Experiments*. Windhoek: National Archives of Namibia.

Marlin, D. et. al. 2014. The Only African Wild Tobacco, Nicotiana africana: Alkaloid Content and the Effect of Herbivory. *PLoS ONE* 9.

Muschalek, M. 2019. *Violence as Usual: Policing and the Colonial State in Southwest Africa*. Ithaca: Cornell University Press.

Naranch, B., and G. Eley, eds. 2014. *German Colonialism in the Global Age*. Durham: Duke University Press.

Olusoga, D., and C. Erichsen. 2010. *The Kaiser's Holocaust: Germany's Forgotten Genocide*. London: Faber and Faber.

Otte, W. 2014. *Weiß und Schwarz–Black and White: Photos aus Deutsch-Südwestafrika/ from Namibia, 1896–1901*. Wendeburg: Krebs.

Philips, J.E. 1983. African Smoking and Pipes. *Journal of African History* 24: 303–319.

Press, S. 2021. *Blood and Diamonds: Germany's Imperial Ambitions in Africa*. Cambridge: Cambridge University Press.

Prowse, M., and H.P. Niño. 2022. Tobacco and Transformation in Southern Africa. *Journal of Southern African Studies* (Special Issue) 48.

Prowse, M., and P. Grassin. 2020. *Tobacco, Transformation and Development Dilemmas from Central Africa*. Cham: Palgrave Macmillan.

Rizzo, L. 2014. Faszination Landschaft–Landschaftsphotographie in Namibia. *Basler Afrikabibliographien Working Papers* 1: 1–15.

Roberts, A.F. 2004. Smoking in Sub-Saharan Africa. In *Smoke: A Global History of Smoking*, eds. S.L. Gilman and X. Zhou. London: Reaction Books.

Rubert, S. 2005. Africa. In *Tobacco in History and Culture. An Encyclopedia*. Vol 1, ed. J. Goodman, 23–31. Farmington Hills, MI, Thomson Gale.

Rubert, S.C.A. 1998. *Most Promising Weed: A History of Tobacco Farming and Labor in Colonial Zimbabwe, 1890–1945*. Athens: Ohio University Press.

Seibert, T., and G. Hechler. 1976. *Tabakbau in Deutschland*. Neustadt/Landau: Pfälzische Verlagsanstalt.

Silverman, D. 1971. The Economic Consequences of Annexation: Alsace-Lorraine and Imperial Germany, 1871–1918. *Central European History* 4: 34–53.

Snyders, H. 2011. "Stinky and Smelly—But Profitable": The Cape Guano Trade, c. 1843–1910'. Ph. D Dissertation, Stellenbosch University.

Steinmetz, G. 2005. The First Genocide of the 20th Century and its Postcolonial Afterlives: Germany and the Namibian Ovaherero. *The Journal of the International Institute* 12 [Online]. http://hdl.handle.net/2027/spo.4750978.0012.201. Accessed by 7. January 2024.

Steinmetz, G. 2007. *The Devil's Handwriting: Precoloniality and the German Colonial State in Qingdao, Samoa, and Southwest Africa*. Chicago: University of Chicago Press.

Steinmetz, G., 2006. The Visual Archive of Colonialism: Germany and Namibia, Public Culture 18: 147–183.

Tschurenev, J., F. Spöring, and J. Große. 2014. Einleitung: Sittlichkeitsreform, Biopolitik und Globalisierung. In *Biopolitik und Sittlichkeitsreform: Kampagne gegen Alkohol, Drogen und Prostitution 1880–1950*, eds. J. Tschurenev, F. Spöring, and J. Große, 7–46. Frankfurt am Main. Campus.

Walther, D. 2015. *Sex and Control: Venereal Disease, Colonial Physicians, and Indigenous Agency in German Colonialism, 1884–1914*. New York: Berghahn Books.

Wanless, A. 1991. Public Pleasures: Smoking and Snuff-Taking in Southern Africa. In *Art and Ambiguity: Perspectives on the Brenthurst Collection of Southern African Art*, ed. Johannesburg Art Gallery, 125–143. Johannesburg: no publisher.

Wickeren, A. van. 2020. *Wissensräume im Wandel*. Eine Geschichte der deutsch-französischen Tabakforschung (1780–1870). Köln: Böhlau.

Zimmerer, J. 2000. *Deutsche Herrschaft über Afrikaner: Staatlicher Machtanspruch und Wirklichkeit im kolonialen Namibia*. Münster: LIT Verlag.

Zimmerer, J. 2008. War, Concentration Camps and Genocide in South-West Africa. In *Genocide in German South-West Africa: The Colonial War of 1904–1908 and Its Aftermath*, trans. E. Neather. Monmouth, Wales: Merlin Press, 30–35.

Zimmerer, J. 2011. *Von Windhuk nach Auschwitz? Beitrag zum Verhältnis von Kolonialismus und Holocaust*. Münster: LIT.

Zimmerer, J., and J. Zeller, eds. 2008. *Genocide in German South-West Africa: The Colonial War of 1904–1908 and Its Aftermath, trans. E. Neather*. Monmouth, Wales: Merlin Press.

Zimmerman, A. 2010. *Alabama in Africa. Booker T. Washington, the German Empire, and the Globalization of the New South*. Princeton: Princeton University Press.

Zollmann, J. 2010. *Koloniale Herrschaft und ihre Grenzen: Die Kolonialpolizei in Deutsch-Südwestafrika 1894–1915*. Göttingen: Vandenhoeck & Ruprecht.

Zollmann, J. 2020. Becoming a Good Farmer — Becoming a Good Farm Worker: On Colonial Educational Policies in Germany and German South-West Africa, Circa 1890 to 1918. In *Education and Development in Colonial and Postcolonial Africa: Policies, Paradigms, and Entanglements, 1890s–1980s*, eds. D. Matasci, M. Jerónimo, and H. Dores, 109–142. Cham: Palgrave Macmillan.

CHAPTER 9

Mechanising the Greek Tobacco Industry: Worker Knowledge, Protest, and Territorial Expansion, 1890–1925

Christos Karampatsos and Nikos Alexis

For Greece, the early-twentieth century witnessed war and territorial expansion on a scale far beyond that which had come before during the nineteenth century. Between 1912 and 1922, there were two Balkan Wars (1912–13), World War I (1917–18) and the Greco-Turkish War (1919–1922), known today as "The Asia Minor Expedition" or "The Asia Minor

This research is co-financed by Greece and the European Union (European Social Fund—ESF) through the Operational Programme "Human Resources Development, Education and Lifelong Learning" in the context of the project "Reinforcement of Postdoctoral Researchers – 2nd Cycle" (MIS-5033021), implemented by the Greek State Scholarships Foundation (IKY). The research work of Nikos Alexis was supported by the Hellenic Foundation for Research and Innovation (HFRI) under the 3rd call for HFRI PhD Fellowships (Fellowship Number: 5915).

A. van Wickeren et al. (eds.), *Tobacco in Global Perspective, 1780–1960*, Cambridge Imperial and Post-Colonial Studies,
https://doi.org/10.1007/978-3-031-64411-5_9

Disaster". During this period, Greece annexed significant new territories from the Ottoman Empire, including Southern Epirus, Southern Macedonia, Crete, and Thrace (Fig. 9.1).

This was also the period in which the Greek cigarette industry was mechanised. After two decades of failed sporadic attempts, the first concerted mechanisation efforts began in 1910, just before the Balkan Wars. The introduction of cigarette machines continued intermittently between 1914 and 1918 and escalated between 1919 and 1921. However, albeit the collapse of the Asia Minor Expedition in 1922 and the ensuing territorial stabilisation witnessed the stagnation of the then mechanised cigarette industry.

The focus of this chapter is on the process of Greek mechanisation in this context. We begin by addressing the technological questions already evident in the time lag between the early invention of cigarette machines and the first serious efforts to introduce them in Greece. We then explore the interplay between the mechanisation process and the historical context of war and the Greek annexation of former Ottoman territories. We call into question the perception of cigarette machines as embodying the perfection of engineering knowledge during the Second Industrial Revolution, detailing the dysfunctional aspects of the machinery. In tandem with the ambivalence of the employers and the opposition of the craft workers, we subsequently argue that cigarette manufacturers decided to mechanise on a large scale only after it became apparent that the machines could be advantageous in terms of anti-labour policies and expectations. Efforts to undercut craft workers and their knowledge of the craft through the introduction of machinery have been studied elsewhere, not least in the US where many of the machines originated.[1] The Eastern Mediterranean region studied here, however, situates this

C. Karampatsos (✉)
National and Kapodistrian University of Athens, University of West Attica, Athens, Greece
e-mail: chriskaraba@phs.uoa.gr

N. Alexis
University of Crete, Rethymno, Greece
e-mail: nik.alexis@yahoo.gr

[1] Montgomery (1979). Cooper (1988). Smith (1991). Braverman (1998).

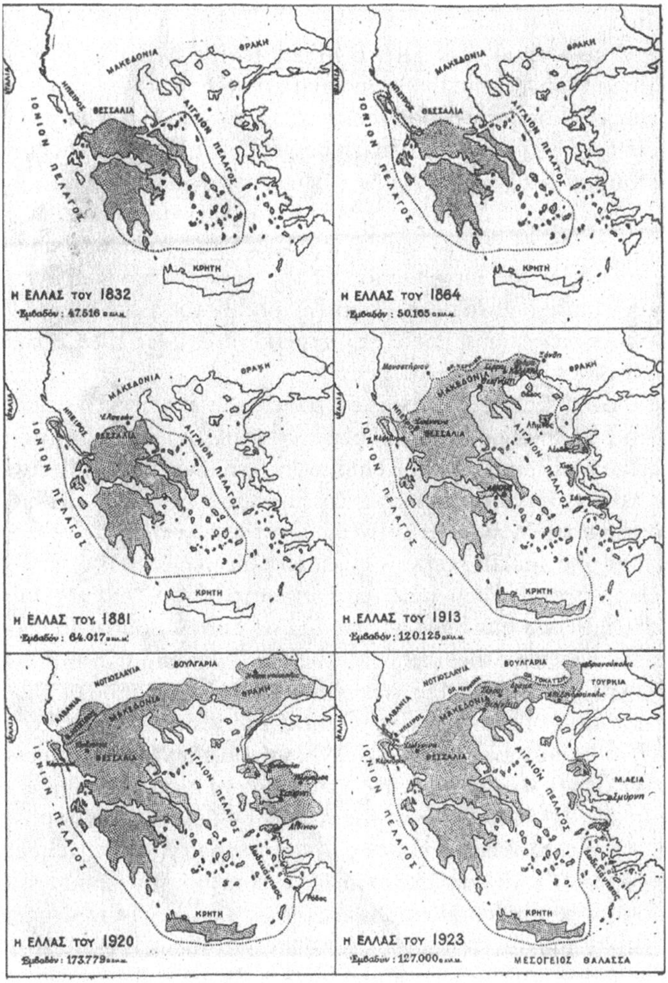

Fig. 9.1 Greek territorial expansion, 1832–1923[2]

within two important broader contexts: that of regional fragmentation, between 1900 and 1923, when the crumbling Ottoman Empire gave way

[2] Μηλιός (2000, p. 389).

to nascent nation-states, and also that of an extensive network of craft culture and know-how that carried over into the new nation-states as a common denominator in labour and economic policy.[3]

The chapter comprises four sections. In the first, we emphasise the problems faced by the cigarette machines, problems that had been present from the outset but which became particularly evident during the introduction of the new technology in Mediterranean countries such as Italy, France, and Greece. These were technical, environmental, and sociocultural, such that the introduction of the new machines under specific conditions required more time, extensive modifications, changes in preexisting production systems, and costly expenditure. Even then, a successful outcome was not a priori guaranteed.

In the second section, we focus on the cigarette rollers. We detail their knowledge and methods of workplace control and their positioning at the epicentre of dispute with the employers. We trace their collective ingenuity to craft organisation and practices and show how this informed their actions during the May 1910 strike against the first imported machine.

The third and fourth sections chart the mechanisation efforts during the 1910s, a period when war, territorial expansion, and the introduction of machinery went hand in hand. The annexation of the so-called New Lands widened the scene of the mechanisation dispute, adding further actors and raising the stakes involved. It brought to the fore a broader tradition of artisanal organisation and resistance characteristic of the newly annexed tobacco regions. Whether in the form of appeasement or suppression of the craft, active state intervention was required, and the state played a central role in the mechanisation process, with various wartime pro-mechanisation policies that culminated in the implementation of a one-off severance payment. We conclude by summarising the findings of our research and emphasise the link between the struggle over mechanisation and the transition from the Ottoman Empire to nation-states. The Greek case, we argue, highlights the need for further scrutiny of the complexities involved in the glocal transfer of technological knowledge, and craft resistance to it, across empires and nation-states during the Second Industrial Revolution.

[3] Khuri-Makdisi (2010).

Revisiting Engineering Knowledge

The cigarette machine that was patented in the early 1880s by James Bonsack, a Virginia woollen mills owner, was arguably the one that subsequently travelled the world most. A wave of similar later inventions then swept through cigarette-producing countries ranging from Germany to Japan,[4] and companies that adopted the machines went on to dominate first the domestic and then the international tobacco industry.[5]

The Bonsack machine was much heralded as having an initial production capacity amounting to 133 cigarettes per minute, equalling the output of forty-eight skilled hand rollers. Widely quoted as they are, these figures for the Bonsack machine's productivity do not stand up to careful scrutiny. A source often cited to substantiate the 133 cigarettes per minute is B. W. E. Alford's seminal history of the Wills company and the UK tobacco industry, Wills having been the first to gain exclusive British rights to the Bonsack machine.[6] Alford's sources report a 15-minute run "producing at the rate of 133 cigarettes per minute". However, the same sources also indicate that this was "the best result obtained", indicating there must also have been an unknown number of less successful runs.[7] Alford himself ventured into a problematic instance of the machine's introduction, when he quoted an 1884 letter written by D. B. Strouse, president of the Bonsack Machine Company, who was at the time trying to sell the machine to Italian interests. The Italians, he reported, remained "very suspicious" of the novel artefact, and Strouse described the source of their suspicion as follows: "Having no other way to put the tobacco in order they sprinkled it, and this caused some particles of the tobacco to be too wet & it slightly stained the wrappers (...). Now (...) these people require another experiment".[8]

The problem Strouse identified can be explained by reference to actual workplace practice. What he casually described as "putting the tobacco in order" was in fact a complicated work process. Tobacco was sorted into different qualities and then mixed by master craftsmen called blenders.

[4] Roberts and Knapp (1992). Hannah (2006).

[5] Chandler (1999, p. 250).

[6] Ibid., p. 250. Roberts and Knapp (1992). Rifkin (1996, pp. 128, 129). Porter (1969, pp. 68–69).

[7] Alford (1973, p. 145).

[8] Ibid., p. 154.

The blends thus produced were cut by hand tools or machines and delivered to the cigarette-rolling rooms where craft rollers made them into cigarettes.[9] Regulating the humidity of the blend was a crucial part of the pre-rolling processes. The oriental tobaccos, the varieties of the plant growing around the Eastern Mediterranean,[10] and used in specific portions in cigarette blends all over the world, were particularly demanding in the humidity department. If "very moist" they were liable to "ferment and spoil by mildew"; if "very dry" they should be "liquored carefully and sparingly by a fog pump and never (...) be moistened by wet cloths as that will develop bitterness".[11]

In sharp contrast to this meticulous handling of tobacco humidity, the Bonsack machine required "sprinkling" in order to reach capacity, even in the context of a controlled experiment. By intervening in the crucial process of humidity regulation, it was incompatible with the preexisting work processes in the cutting and sorting rooms. This incompatibility was evident in Bonsack's own descriptions: upon its first contact with the machine, tobacco was likely to be "pulled in clots or bunches", "string across" the rollers, and "break or stick irregularly" on the surface of the card-teeth.[12]

No wonder the Italians remained "suspicious" of Strouse and his machine. Experienced cigarette manufacturers such as these oversaw complex systems comprising a detailed division of labour and a body of knowledge garnered over decades of practice. An obvious truth about technological systems is that "if a component is removed (...), or if its characteristics change, the other artifacts in the system will alter characteristics accordingly".[13] The Bonsack machine demanded a radical reorganisation of the whole system, beginning with an immediate conversion of the sorting, blending, and cutting processes so as to produce a machine-compatible product. Its introduction resulted in change that in

[9] Nacar (2019, pp. 61–67). Καραμπάτσος (2019, pp. 62–67).

[10] Carmona-Zabala (2022, p. 539).

[11] Constantinides (1912, pp. 68–71). Balsoy (2009, p. 57).

[12] Cigarette-machine, US 238640 A, Patented. 08 March 1881. https://patentimages.storage.googleapis.com/c8/ea/24/463c1e13d10bd7/US238640.pdf. Accessed on 15 July 2024.

[13] Hughes (1993, p. 51).

practice proved to be much more radical than initially promised. Reference to failed expectations can be found in the primary sources in the form of a constant "humidity problem" that results in cigarette "mold", in the constant laments over the lower quality of the machine-made cigarettes, and consumer reluctance to adopt them—a prejudice against the machine-made cigarette that did not go away.[14] This also explains why every introduction of cigarette-rolling machines had to be accompanied by new cutting machinery: it was the cutting processes that had to adapt to machine production rather than the other way round.

In 1893, some ten years after the Italian incident, the Greek industrialist Gerasimos Aspiotis arrived in Paris under orders from the Greek Ministry of the Economy. His mission was to inspect the machines employed in the French cigarette industry and report on the feasibility of employing them in Greece.[15] He did this, providing a detailed description of the Central Tobacco Factory of Paris where craft cigarette production co-existed with the "système Decouflé", a French variant of the Bonsack machine[16].

Aspiotis witnessed more than 100 Decouflé cigarette machines, each producing 20,000 cigarettes per day. However, he reported that the preceding tobacco-cutting process was also mechanised. In the Paris factory, the French-made cutting machines were being replaced by the "admittedly much superior" cutting machines imported from Robert Legg & Co. of London, which confirms our point that the introduction of cigarette machinery imposed a radical reorganisation of the pre-rolling processes.[17] Aspiotis inquired whether the British cutting machines could be used for cutting Greek tobacco, but the response was discouraging. According to his fellow Frenchmen, Greek tobacco was "too thick" relative to the tobacco they usually processed and thus incompatible with their English cutting machines. The humidity problem was also present and approached in a mechanical manner: the factory equipment included a ventilator of 1.5 metres diameter and 6 metres length.

[14] Shechter (2006, p. 87). Constantinides (1912, p. 71).

[15] Gerasimos Aspiotis to the Ministry of Economics, 15 March 1893, Greek Literary and Historical Archive, hereafter E.L.I.A, Aspiotis Archive, File 1, Section 2.

[16] Hannah (2006, p. 64).

[17] Alford (1973, p. 20).

Aspiotis was all the same enthusiastic. From an informed standpoint though, his report is a catalogue of the immediate problems that would face any attempted mechanisation. The Decouflé machines had to be accompanied by more sophisticated machinery, not to mention a new division of labour in the cutting shop. Cigarettes had to be mechanically dried, resulting in a final product that had a very different taste and feel. Moreover, even the British top-notch cutting machinery imported by the French in order to keep up with their rolling machines was reportedly inadequate for cutting Greek tobacco.

In 1895, two years after Aspiotis visited Paris, former Istanbul tobacco manufacturer Christos Angelidis, likely taken in by the alleged productivity of the cigarette-rolling machines, imported the first machine in Greece.[18] The machine can hardly have met expectations, for there is no further reference to it or its owner. Some years later, Fotis Papafotis, president of the Greek tobacco manufacturers' union, bought another machine. It was sold just a few years later for a sixth of its original price and was eventually destroyed by workers during incidents described below.[19]

That the first systematic effort to mechanise was not until 1910 mirrors the case in Egypt, a major cigarette producer of the time, where manufacturers, many of whom were Greek, were also "reluctant to venture into the unknown territory of machine production".[20] This "delay" in a process widely thought to be "inevitable" is explainable: the introduction of the machinery was much more technically and politically demanding than anticipated. Initial high expectations were not met, and the meagre outcomes reinforced the hesitation of other manufacturers who were reluctant to undertake the political and economic costs of mechanisation. An important question to ask then is why, beginning in May 1910, certain Greek cigarette manufacturers eventually decided to mechanise. For an answer, we need first to take a look at the cigarette rollers.

[18] Labrianidis (1982, p. 124) and Anonymous (1895).

[19] Anonymous (1910c), (1910m).

[20] Shechter (2006, pp. 87–88).

The Craft Cigarette Industry

In Russia and the Ottoman Empire, the craft of hand-rolling cigarettes dates back to the second half of the nineteenth century and later spread west with the migration of Greek and Jewish cigarette rollers.[21] Rolling was a process that could be carried out by the same worker, as has been well documented in the case of women working in the US cigarette industry.[22] And yet in the former and current Ottoman territories, as in Greece and Egypt, a detailed division of labour was followed: *macaronistes* rolled and glued cigarette papers, fillers placed the tobacco in the rolled cigarette papers, and *psalidistes* (croppers) cut the rolled cigarettes to make the finished product.[23]

In Greece, hand-made cigarettes were produced at least from the mid-1880s,[24] and the first attempt to organise dates back to 1902 and the establishment of a Cigarette Rollers Society in Athens.[25] In the following years, local organisations emerged all around the country and made their presence felt through a variety of strikes and protests, culminating in a major strike that broke out in October 1909 to demand higher piece rates.[26] The employers quickly capitulated, although not without planning for the future. Their thinking, according to the newspapers of the time, was "to order cigarette-making machines through which they will be freed from any future demands".[27]

The first of the machines arrived at the port of Piraeus on 10 May 1910. It had been ordered by Konstantinos Varkas, a well-known tobacco manufacturer of the time, who employed some 150 workers.[28] Varkas' machine was part of a concerted move, as in the following months

[21] Rogoff (2001).

[22] "Long Record for Steady Work Held by Woman Who Began Her Duties in Duke's First Factory." *Durham Morning Herald*, 17 January 1926. https://www.ncpedia.org/anchor/working-tobacco-factory. Accessed 2 January 2024.

[23] Χαριτάτος and Γιακουμάκη (1998, p. 61). Shechter (2006, p. 40). Beinin and Lockman (1988, p. 50). Καραμπάτσος (2019, pp. 62–66). Nacar (2019, pp. 68–69).

[24] Labrianidis (1982, pp. 123–124).

[25] Anonymous (1902).

[26] Anonymous (1909a), (1909b).

[27] Anonymous (1909a).

[28] Χαριτάτος and Γιακουμάκη (1998, p. 241).

other cigarette manufacturers imported more machines. The manufacturers' motives were explained by Efstathios Lertas, a nephew and business partner of Varkas, in an interview published on the day of the machine's arrival. After a brief reference to "the country's industrial progress", Lertas turned to a different matter:

> The cigarette rollers, through their council, literally have us under their control. And here is why. They have coerced us into employing cigarette rollers that were not of our liking. They have coerced us into retaining in service more croppers than actually needed. They demanded that we replace people who enjoy our trust with their own people.

Summarily, declared Mr. Lertas, "[the rollers] aim to run our cigarette production themselves. All this has obliged us to purchase a machine and follow the obligatory path of progress".[29]

The cigarette rollers immediately went on strike, which lasted more than a month. Throughout the whole time, Lertas' accusations were met with silence. However, a careful scrutiny of the workers' demands and workplace descriptions of the time back up his claim. Based on the technical aspects of their knowledge, cigarette rollers were able to impose their own rules in the workplace threatening the employers' control of the work process.

First, the cigarette rollers' union could hire and fire workers at will. Their demand to replace "people of trust", referred to Vasilios Meksis, a trusted foreman for the preceding 25 years, and was obviously the culmination of a trend.[30] Control over the workforce had severe repercussions on workplace discipline. On 15 May 1910, with the strike going full steam, Varkas sent a written protest to the Prime Minister claiming that the rollers "went about the tobacco shop, armed", clubbing strike breakers' hands. When it came to identifying their leader, however, Varkas could offer nothing more than "Lorentzo, of unknown surname".[31]

Second, the cigarette rollers exerted control over the design of the production process. They had devised and imposed particular workplace positions, such as the *psalidistes*, and defended them through collective

[29] Anonymous (1910d).

[30] Anonymous (1910e).

[31] Anonymous (1910l). Petition of Konstantinos Varkas, 15 May 1910. Gennadius Library, Stephanos Dragoumis Archive, file 71.

action. Such positions were often reserved for children connected to adult rollers by family or acquaintance. In Greece, as elsewhere, children worked alongside their parents and relatives. The work process served as both an apprenticeship and childcare,[32] and the children's employment provided adult male workers with a considerable source of power. The young workers of the Piraeus tobacco shop, for example, had been out on strike at least once in the months preceding the introduction of machinery.[33]

Third, the cigarette rollers worked a "stint". As recorded in the US case, the "stint" was "an output quota set by the workers themselves".[34] It reflected what the workers thought to be a "fair" daily production. It was collectively imposed by the workers and was adhered to "even when doing so meant thinner pay envelopes".[35] Of course, agreements of this sort do not suggest management control over the work process, but rather the opposite.[36] The "stint" also characterised cigarette manufacture in Greece and the former Ottoman territories. As reported some years later, in a 1918 open letter of the Association of Tobacco Manufacturers, "the cigarette rollers, working for 25 days a month, deliver to the manufacturers 50,000 cigarettes, receiving the price [αντίτιμον] of 375 drachmas (…). However, they are perfectly able to deliver 3,000 cigarettes per day (…)".[37] The figure of 50,000, amounting to 2,000 cigarettes per day, was an "informal limit on output" agreed by the workers and tacitly accepted by the employers. Of course, variations in "stint" numbers reflected the balance of power inside the workplace at any given time and place. This helps explain the wild fluctuations of the rollers' productivity found throughout the relevant literature ranging from 1,200 to 3,000 cigarettes per day.[38]

Fourth, the rollers shared particular worldviews concerning the relations between workers, employers, and the product of labour. According

[32] Shechter (2006, p. 40). Nacar (2019, pp. 64–65). Φουντανόπουλος (2005, pp. 138–141).

[33] Anonymous (1910g).

[34] Montgomery (1979, p. 12).

[35] Cooper (1988, p. 789).

[36] Thompson (1967, p. 78).

[37] Anonymous (1918d).

[38] Nacar (2019, pp. 69 and 72). Shechter (2006, p. 40).

to these worldviews, the product of labour (i.e. cigarettes) was not exclusively the employer's property. The rollers also had property rights and these rights were expressed as concrete demands. As stated in a rollers' "ultimatum" addressed to Varkas on 16 May 1910, "the price of internal consumption of cigarettes in relation to the labour of the cigarette rollers should remain at their current level for five years; as for the prices of external consumption, they will be arranged by the cigarette rollers' association".[39] The rollers' remuneration was already connected to the market price of cigarettes, providing them with a constant share of the value produced and a say regarding cigarette prices.[40] Notably, this practice seemed quite natural to the employers. Accordingly, the words "price" and "wage" are often confused in the primary sources.[41]

Last but not least, the rollers' struggle for workplace control was expressed via customs and everyday habits. They had the right to smoke freely cigarettes they made during their work.[42] Another habit noted was to "stop working or even cause grievances upon approach of the foreman", in a "manly" display of defiance.[43] In short, the rollers could use their knowledge of the production process to assert workplace control. This knowledge was not exclusively technical but rather a mixture of custom, ideology, and practice that served as a crucial component of cigarette production. Craft autonomy and its enmeshing "moral code"[44] were in evidence over the years in the Varkas shop, fuelling a daily war of attrition; the introduction of the machine transformed this everyday war into open conflict.

The hand cigarette makers' repertoire of action during the strike of May 1910 went far beyond the strike per se. They blockaded the Varkas shop, hindering the transfer of cigarettes to the market.[45] They used friendly newspapers to publicise their demands and opinions. They employed violence against the strikebreakers and the Varkas family. They enlisted their colleagues from the state-owned tobacco factory in Piraeus

[39] Anonymous (1910e, 1910i).

[40] For the same practice in Salonica, see Φουντανόπουλος (2005, p. 143).

[41] Anonymous (1899, 1918d).

[42] Anonymous (1911b).

[43] Anonymous (1918c).

[44] Montgomery (1979, p. 12).

[45] Anonymous (1910k).

to attack and destroy the only preexisting cigarette machine and implied in the press that they could also destroy any new machine.[46] They declared a boycott against tobacco manufacturers who intended to mechanise, calling on the people of Athens for support. Children roamed the streets carrying placards with the slogan "If you love the workers, do not smoke Varkas cigarettes".[47]

State suppression was crucial for the defeat of this multi-faceted mobilisation. It culminated on 17 May 1910, when a demonstration intended to break Varkas' machine was attacked by a "cavalry charge". An emergency meeting of the ministerial cabinet ensued and the chief of police was given "permission to support the police force with soldiers".[48] Police and army control of the centre of Athens continued until at least the middle of June.[49] The cigarette rollers arrested "for abusing Varkas' associate Mr. Lertas" met with extreme juridical severity and three of them ended up facing felony charges.[50] In November 1910, membership of the cigarette rollers union was reason enough to be laid off.[51] In 1911 things had quietened down, the accused awaited trial, and the new machinery was put to work as efficiently as possible (Fig. 9.2).

For reasons explained in the previous section, however, the rolling machines imported in Greece were accompanied by no fewer than 26 imported cutting machines[52]; the central tobacco factory was now guarded by police on a permanent basis; and in the Varkas shop hand-rolled cigarettes were still being produced, which suggests they were not being easily replaced by the machine-made ones.

The humidity problems recorded in 1884 in Italy and 1893 in France also resurfaced in Greece, despite the intervening years of "technological progress". The tobacco fed into Varkas' new imported cutting machines had to be thrown "in a large tub" where it was "rubbed" by hand in an attempt to regulate moisture.[53] According to expert advisors enlisted

[46] Anonymous (1910j).

[47] Anonymous (1910a).

[48] Anonymous (1910c, 1910j).

[49] Anonymous (1910b).

[50] Anonymous (1910f, 1910l).

[51] Ποταμιάνος (2011, p. 310, fn 90).

[52] Labrianidis (1982, p. 128).

[53] Anonymous (1911b).

Fig. 9.2 One of the two cigarette machines belonging to Varkas, as demonstrated to the newspaper *Εμπρός* in October 1911[54]

by the Greek parliament in March 1911, rolling by hand required "dry tobacco", while "it [was] impossible to produce machine-made cigarettes if the tobacco isn't moist". As a result, the machine-made cigarettes were of vastly inferior quality and could be identified "by their disgusting taste alone".[55] The tobacco-producing region of Agrinio, moreover, was left "with no tobacco demand whatsoever", as "the machine owners, would not buy it",[56] seeking lower-quality tobacco and leaving prime tobacco unsold. Meantime, Greece was entering one of the most crucial periods of its history, to which we now turn.

Tobacco in the "New Lands"

The period beginning in 1912 and ending in 1922 was a veritable war decade. The 1912–1913 Balkan Wars enabled Greece to annex significant parts of Epirus and Macedonia.[57] The new territories came to be known as the "New Lands", as opposed to the original "Old Greece"

[54] Anonymous (1911b).

[55] *Εφημερίς των Συζητήσεων της Βουλής* (1911, pp. 1126–1129).

[56] Ibid., pp. 1127–1128.

[57] Douglas (2012).

territory. They included some of the Ottoman Empire's major tobacco-processing centres, namely Kavala, Siroz (Serres), Salonica, and from 1920 onwards İskeçe (Xanthi). Beginning in 1884, the tobacco economy of these lands, except for leaf exports, had come under the monopoly of the Régie Company, which founded factories around the Empire to produce cigarettes and other tobacco products (Fig. 9.3).[58]

The cigarette rollers of the New Lands are often absent from historical accounts. In a way, this is to be expected as they were fewer in number than other tobacco workers in Macedonia and Thrace and their regular participation in general strikes often went unrecorded. However, cigarette factories of the Régie had operated in Salonica since the 1880s, contributing to the company's expanding presence in the Ottoman domestic market.[60] In the early 1890s, about 75% of the workforce in these factories were women, mainly Jewish, "very skillful and quick in

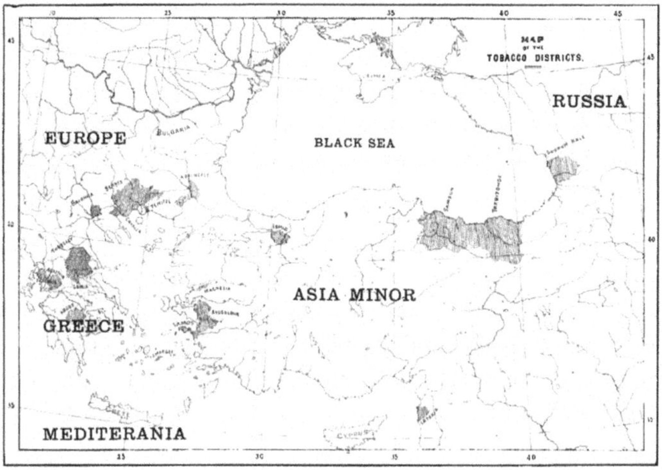

Fig. 9.3 Major tobacco regions of the Balkans and the Anatolian peninsula in 1912, including the New Lands in the northwest annexed by Greece after 1913[59]

[58] Nacar (2014, p. 535).

[59] Constantinides (1912, p. vii).

[60] Nacar (2014, p. 535).

the manufacture of cigarettes".[61] This significant women's presence in cigarette rolling differentiates the Ottoman territories from Greece and even Egypt, where cigarette rolling was mainly carried out by men. One of Salonica's popular Ladino songs was "La cigarrera", testifying to their significance in the public sphere.[62]

In 1910, the union of the Régie workers in Salonica claimed 500 members, and in 1911, the women workers spearheaded a "strike wave", clashing with the union's male leadership.[63] Organisationally and ideologically, the workers in the cigarette factories of Salonica were part of the larger whole working in the former Ottoman tobacco centres and were no strangers to the customs and habits described in the previous sections. They too worked in groups linked together by familial and residential bonds[64]; they aspired to control entry into their craft and were accused by employers of trying to run the shop on their own[65]; and they ascribed to customs, informal rules, and worldviews as they struggled to retain autonomy over their work. When, for example, Ottoman tobacco workers broke the windows of tobacco warehouses in Kavala, they did so with the strategic aim of spoiling the tobacco by drying. This potent blend of custom, knowledge, and agency was witnessed since the 1890s; in fact the Ottoman tobacco industry had become a veritable "hotbed of labor unrest", with strikes one after the other all over Macedonia and Thrace.[66]

It was somewhat to be expected, then, that the "severest tobacco strike ever faced by any Greek Government"[67] began in the spring of 1914, lasted for three weeks, and quickly spread to all tobacco centres of the New Lands. The 30,000 men and women strikers belonged to all the main ethnic groups of Macedonia. Familial and ethnic ties were mustered against the employers, and there were violent confrontations between Muslim women strikebreakers and Jewish women workers under

[61] Nacar (2019, p. 68)

[62] Μόλχο (1988, p. 143).

[63] Nacar (2019, pp. 38, 65, 68, 113 and 154) and Ilicak (2002, pp. 121 and 132).

[64] Hadar (2007, p. 138). Nacar (2019, pp. 33 and 104).

[65] Anonymous (1918c).

[66] Nacar (2019, pp. 35, 62 and 89).

[67] Φουντανόπουλος (2005, p. 183).

male leadership.[68] The main demands of the strike concerned entry into the workforce and the particular division of labour in the warehouses, including a request that the employers officially accept the presence of a union representative inside each and every workplace. Eventually, after consultation with the Greek authorities, the employers complied.[69]

It goes without saying that Greek dominion over the new territories was by no means a given. For example, the first impulse of the Greek authorities after Salonica's conquest, was to ethnically cleanse the city by a wide pogrom that took place in 1912 resulting in 60 dead and 50 reported rapes of Jewish women. However, the consuls of England and France immediately warned that the Greek occupation of Salonica would depend on the "safety of the city's inhabitants", and the Greek authorities had to put an immediate end to the atrocities.[70] Salonica's "inhabitants" had been saved thanks to foreign intervention, but for Greece remained politically suspect, along with all workers of the former Ottoman tobacco-processing centres. In fact the Greek State had inherited a tobacco working class akin to that which had recently caused so much trouble in Old Greece, and one that was much greater in number, more organised, and multicultural. Most disturbingly for Greece, the red-flag-wielding Jewish strikers of 1914 insisted on wearing the fez, a symbol of Ottoman rule that had come to represent both "the pride of the tobacco worker" and "scorn towards the Greeks".[71] In the war decade that followed, the national interest and the "labour question" continued to be in delicate balance as Greece attempted to secure the New Lands and subdue the tobacco workers.

Mechanisation in Times of War

The Greek state favoured covert means to support mechanisation. This was already evident during the Balkan Wars, when "soldiers" of the victorious Greek Army, "the Army officers and public servants" transferred in droves to the New Lands to staff the new Greek administration and were

[68] Avdela (1998, p. 429).

[69] Φουντανόπουλος (2005, p. 183).

[70] Μόλχο (2006, pp. 245–251).

[71] Hadar (2007, pp. 127–152, 137 and 146).

"for the most part followed by the Varkas cigarette packet".[72] The extensive consumption of machine-made cigarettes by the army and public servants favoured the dissemination of the new product and implies an informal promotion of machine-made cigarettes by the Greek State. In any case, not only did it support the recently undertaken mechanisation ventures, it also addicted politically important parts of the population to the new product, thus weeding out the persistent prejudice against the machine-made cigarette mentioned in the previous sections, initiating a standardisation of the smoking habit in the whole country.

Implicit state support accompanied military victory, nurturing grand expectations. In the months following the 1914 strike, the Greek tobacco manufacturers attempted a new wave of mechanisation and demanded to be granted a monopoly of cigarettes in the New Lands, claiming they would employ only Greek workers.[73] When their demand to replace the Régie was rejected by the government, they resorted to opening new mechanised tobacco factories in Salonica.[74]

Their ambitions, however, proved to be premature. They once more were met with fierce worker resistance,[75] and over the next few years, the Greek State became entangled in perpetual military conflict and political instability. Events such as the Entente's naval blockade of November 1916 resulted in extreme shortages of food and other necessities, and one of the raw materials in short supply was cigarette paper. In the autumn of 1916, Varkas informed his clients that he could no longer work his machines,[76] and a few months later his cigarette paper was confiscated, allegedly to be used for hand rolling by underemployed cigarette workers.[77]

Greece entered World War I on the side of the Entente in June 1917. In the autumn, the cigarette rollers of Old Greece went on strike demanding better payment in order to compensate for skyrocketing war inflation; the tobacco workers of Salonica followed suit in May 1918[78];

[72] Ηλιάδης (1919, p. 126).

[73] Αβδελά (1993, p. 176, fn 14).

[74] Anonymous (1914b).

[75] Anonymous (1914a).

[76] Anonymous (1916).

[77] Anonymous (1917a).

[78] Εφημερίς της Κυβερνήσεως του Βασιλείου της Ελλάδος [Φ.Ε.Κ.], Vol A, no. 6, 4 January 1918.

and in January 1918, the Greek government imposed a temporary ban on cigarette-making machines in Old Greece.[79]

At the time, such spectacular moves were implicitly or explicitly presented as state protection against technological unemployment, made all the more morally acceptable by the ongoing participation of many cigarette rollers in the war effort. However, they were perfectly compatible with wartime political and macroeconomic imperatives. The state appeased the tobacco workers, many of whom were serving in the Greek Army. At the same time, the resulting decrease in cigarette consumption[80] was perfectly aligned to the "mandatory restriction of consumption among the popular classes", widely regarded to be one of the principal economic strategies to be followed in wartime.[81] Moreover, when restrictions were lifted after more than a year, people who had stopped smoking for months could easily disregard cigarette quality upon their return to the habit, thus undermining even further any prejudice against the machine-made cigarette.

If the succession of wartime laws and bans was rather chaotic, the outcome was anything but. In 1919, the conflict between Agrinio tobacco producers and cigarette manufacturers noted in 1911 had somehow been overcome. Greek smokers could now be described as "detesting" the taste of the "feminine aromatic blends" of the New Lands, as opposed to the "manly taste of Agrinio tobacco" used in machine-made cigarettes.[82] Meanwhile, in the rest of the world the aromatic tobacco varieties of the New Lands were considered to be of much higher quality and were for the most part exported, thus improving the Greek external trade balance.

The complex interplay of worker appeasement, labour policy, and wartime tactics culminated in the post-war debate concerning the compensation of cigarette makers due to technological unemployment. The idea of a severance pay was an old one. It resurfaced immediately after the end of World War I and was gradually presented as the sole solution to

[79] Νόμος 1133 "Περί αναστολής της λειτουργίας των εν τοις καπνεργοστασίοις του Παλαιού Βασιλείου εγκατεστημένων μηχανημάτων τελείων σιγαρέττων", *Εφημερίς της Κυβερνήσεως του Βασιλείου της Ελλάδος* [Φ.Ε.Κ.], Vol A, no. 6, 4 January 1918.

[80] Ηλιάδης (1919, p. 130).

[81] Ζολώτας (1940, pp. 3, 19–20).

[82] Ηλιάδης (1919).

unemployment.[83] It of course required ample state funding, as thousands of workers would have to be compensated in order to leave their trade. Nonetheless, at the beginning of 1919, the employers presented compensations as their proposal; the state quickly adopted it; and the rollers' leadership grudgingly complied after a few weeks.[84] The state funded the project by imposing special taxes on cigarette and tobacco consumption and rollers began leaving their jobs, first in Old Greece and later in the New Lands.[85] Although the new territories had been part of Greece for more than five years, the state avoided implementing a common legislation for the whole territory, starting the severance pay in Old Greece and expanding it in the New Lands some months later.

The severance pay was, in effect, a state-funded service to mechanisation. Employers could relieve themselves of all "irrational workers' demands", a feat rendered more urgent after in 1917–1918 workers displayed their capacity to mobilise even under various forms of martial law. The impending march of the Greek Army into Asia Minor in effect revived the vision of a Greek "Empire" that would span "two continents and five seas", and the accompanying "tobacco empire" imagined by Greek tobacco industrialists would require huge production capacity only attainable through machines.

In practice, the debate over the severance pay concealed a rapid abandonment of all wartime protective legislation. The use of the machines in Old Greece was once more allowed in the summer of 1918,[86] initiating a rapid wave of mechanisation all over Greece and the New Lands. Between 1919 and 1920, as Greece was preparing to embark on what turned out to be its disastrous Asia Minor Expedition, thousands of workers were compensated to leave their trade, while cigarette-making machines were being imported by the dozen. In 1918 fewer than 20 machines existed in Greece. By 1923 their number had risen to 167, accompanied by 257 tobacco-cutting machines of the Legg system. Salonica was second only to Athens in the number of imported machines, with 32 machines in

[83] Anonymous (1910e) and Αλέξης (2021).

[84] Εφημερίς της Κυβερνήσεως του Βασιλείου της Ελλάδος [Φ.Ε.Κ.], Vol A', no. 42, 27 February 1919; Εφημερίς της Κυβερνήσεως του Βασιλείου της Ελλάδος, Vol A, no. 279, 4 December 1920.

[85] Εφημερίς της Κυβερνήσεως του Βασιλείου της Ελλάδος [Φ.Ε.Κ.], Vol A, no. 6, 4 January 1918.

[86] Anonymous (1918a).

comparison with Athens with 44.[87] The 1919–1923 wave of mechanisation was unprecedentedly rapid and nationwide in scale, accompanied by a new faith in the future of mechanised cigarette production. In some cases, employers were quick to fire their rollers even before the actual arrival of the machines.[88]

As for the rollers, the mobilisation and organising evident during the 1910s were strangely absent in the 1920s, the perpetual state of war, military enrolment, and political manipulation seemingly having taken a heavy toll on their potential for mobilisation. Even so, between 1920 and 1930, a number of rollers kept on producing diminishing volumes of hand-made cigarettes, and the debate concerning their compensation continued until the mid-1930s.[89]

Machine-made cigarette production can hardly be described as an outright success. The exports of Greek-made cigarettes remained marginal during the 1920s, and domestic consumption was no more than stable from 1926 to the early 1930s. The volume of cigarettes produced during this period was much lower than the promising potential of the machines, and in the early 1930s, as the financial crisis unfolded, a significant percentage of the machines in Greece stood idle.[90]

Conclusion

It might be tempting to see mechanisation as straightforward. The machine is presented as the perfect embodiment of advanced engineering knowledge. Its arrival immediately renders workers redundant, and any initial problems are quickly overcome through inexorable technological progress. The Greek case is one that belies this. The introduction of machinery was long delayed, there were further delays when it was eventually attempted, and it subsequently succumbed to diminishing returns.

[87] Μικέλης (1923, p. 350).

[88] Ελληνική εταιρεία βιομηχανίας καπνού, Χρήσις Α: Έκθεσις του Διοικητικού – Συμβουλίου και της Εξελεγκτικής Επιτροπής προς την Γενικήν Συνέλευσιν των μετόχων της 27 Φεβρουαρίου 1920, 4 February 1920, Historical Archive of National Bank of Greece, Series 20, Subseries 67, File 182.

[89] Ioannis Anagnostakis to Artistotelis Dimitratos, 10 December 1937, Hellenic Literary and Historical Archive (E.L.I.A.), Aristeidis Dimitratos Archive, File 3, Section 2.

[90] Βαρβερόπουλος (1935, p. 153).

In our explanation for this, we began by questioning the efficiency of the machines, documenting how the machines introduced into preexistent technological systems demanded a radical change of other components of the system. Cigarette-rolling machines required mechanisation of the cutting process, faced severe problems of humidity regulation, and produced a very different kind of cigarette, thus demanding a change in consumer tastes. Whether it was Italy in 1884, France in 1893, or Greece in 1911, the introduction of machinery in the cigarette industry was much more complicated than often assumed.

Our research highlighted the agency of the cigarette rollers, who, like other craft workers of the Second Industrial Revolution, asserted their workplace control through informal practices based on collective knowledge of the production process. Their knowledge was imbued with a moral code stemming from their everyday class experience and resulted in concrete collective worldviews and practices described by some as "a chronic battle" in the workplace and beyond.[91] Mechanisation was weaponised in this battle.

In our case study, the stakes in the battle soon acquired wider political significance, for the cigarette rollers were located in an imperial setting. Their knowledge, moral codes, and ideas transcended borders and served as a unifying factor for a multinational labour force.[92] During a time of war, rapid renegotiation of borders, and ethnic homogenisation, undoing all such connections became a national Greek imperative.

From 1910 onwards, the Greek state became mechanisation's most faithful proponent. Police repression was paired with an array of more covert policies. Consumer tastes were changed through political manipulation. Even seemingly pro-worker initiatives concealed wartime economic imperatives. The money needed for the concerted purchase of new machines and the rollers' remuneration was found, even in times of preparing for yet another war. From an economic standpoint, the outcome was far less spectacular than expected. The Greek cigarette empire failed to materialise. From a political standpoint, however, the Greek state had wiped out the power exerted by a multinational and,

[91] Montgomery (1979, p. 559).

[92] Khuri-Makdisi (2010, p. 54). Betas (2020, p. 162). Παλούκης (2021).

from the state's perspective, politically suspect workforce. State power in this sense "rested more and more on successful industrialization".[93]

Our inroads into the Greek mechanisation story brought to the fore connections and commonalities with other former Ottoman territories. In Egypt, for example, the introduction of machinery was also delayed until after World War I and the hand-rolled cigarette persisted for a long time. The Egyptian rollers were in all likelihood aware of the compensation policy of the Greek state when they petitioned for their own severance payment.[94] Workers and their customs constitute another significant commonality. Reference to the "stint" is to be found in most of the cigarette hand-rolling processes described in the secondary sources. The same holds true for a worker owning the tools of his or her craft, and for the free consumption of tobacco and cigarettes.[95] Machine-breaking is also repeatedly encountered. It was present in the Egyptian strikes against mechanisation in the 1910s,[96] encountered in 1910 in Greece, and feared by the employers in 1911 in Istanbul.[97] And aspects such as these were found to be commonplace across the former Ottoman territories for a good part of the twentieth century.

Approaching the Eastern Mediterranean as a region of rich connections and interactivity, including those of an Ottoman past, rather than as one of diverse nation-states,[98] as we did, highlighted the complexities of cross-border processes of technology transfer, circuits of knowledge transfer, and forms of struggle in a crucial early-twentieth-century period of war and nation-state building. As such, we hope our case study can serve as a historiographical tool for exploring other such processes in specific glocal settings.

[93] Beckert (2014, p. 249).

[94] Shechter (2006, pp. 84, 86–95).

[95] Nacar (2019, pp. 50 and 92) and Radcliff (1993, p. 93).

[96] Shechter (2006, p. 89).

[97] Nacar (2019, p. 146).

[98] Papastefanaki and Erdem Kabadayi (2020, p. 1).

References

Primary Sources

Unpublished

Hellenic Literary and Historical Archive (E.L.I.A.)
- Aristeidis Dimitratos Archive
- Aspiotis Archive
- Historical Archive of the National Bank of Greece

Gennadios Library
- Stefanos Dragoumis Archive

Published

Anonymous. 1895. Ελληνική σιγαροποιία – Χρήστος Αγγελίδης. Ακρόπολις, 23 January.

Anonymous. 1899. Ευχαριστήριον. Εμπρός, 29 January.

Anonymous. 1902. Οι σιγαροποιοί. Εμπρός, 11 February.

Anonymous. 1909a. Η απεργία των σιγαροποιών του Πειραιώς. Εμπρός, 7 October.

Anonymous. 1909b. Η απεργία των σιγαροποιών – Απειλείται γενική. Εμπρός, 5 October.

Anonymous. 1910a. Η πολυθρύλητος μηχανή του κ. Βάρκα - μετεφέρθη με κοστωδία. Ακρόπολις, 19 May.

Anonymous. 1910b. Αι σκηναί του καπνοκοπτηρίου. Εμπρός, 14 June.

Anonymous. 1910c. Αι χθεσιναί ταραχαί των σιγαροποιών – Καταστροφή μαχανήματος. Σκριπ, 18 May.

Anonymous. 1910d. Η Απεργία των σιγαροποιών – Πώς έχουν τα πράγματα – Τι λέγει ο κ. Λέρτας. Καιροί, 10 May.

Anonymous. 1910e. Η Απεργία των Σιγαροποιών – Τελεσίγραφον προς τον Βάρκαν. *Σκριπ*, 17 May.

Anonymous. 1910f. Η Απεργία των σιγαροποιών. Εμπρός. 19 May.

Anonymous. 1910g. Η Εξακολούθησις της απεργίας του Πειραιώς - Απεργία και εις το καπνοκοπτήριον. *Σκριπ*, 23 March.

Anonymous. 1910h. Η Απεργία των σιγαροποιών. Εμπρος, 17 May.

Anonymous. 1910i. Καταστροφή μηχανής εις το καπνεργοστάσιον Πειραιώς - Επάλασις (sic) του ιππικού κατά των απεργών. Αστραπή, 17 May.

Anonymous. 1910j. Τα πακέτα. Χρόνος, 23 May.

Anonymous. 1910k. Το βούλευμα δια τους σιγαροποιούς. Εμπρός, 30 August.

Anonymous. 1910l. Τραυματισμοί και δυστυχήματα. Εμπρός, 2 July.

Anonymous. 1910m. Η απεργία των σιγαροποιών - Καταστροφή Μηχανής, Αθήναι, 18 May

Anonymous. 1911a. Egyptian Cigarettes and Tobacco. Journal of the Royal Society of Arts, 13 January.

Anonymous. 1911b. Το πσιγάρο που καπνίζετε: Πού και πώς κατασκευάζεται. Εμπρός, 9 October.

Anonymous. 1914a. Η απεργία των σιγαροποιών – Δήλωσις Γιαννουκάκη Πρωτόπαπα. Αθήναι, 17 December.

Anonymous. 1914b. Νέα καπνεργοστάσια εις την Θεσσαλονίκην – Το νομοσχέδιον περί καπνού. Έθνος, 16 December.

Anonymous. 1916. Ο καπνεμπορικός οίκος Κ. Βάρκα και Σίας. Σκριπ, 15 October.

Anonymous. 1917a. Επίταξις σιγαρόχαρτου. Εμπρός, 26 January.

Anonymous. 1917b. Η απεργία των καπνεργατών και σιγαροποιών – Πώς έχει η υπόθεσις. Ριζοσπάστης, 14 October.

Anonymous. 1918a. Το χθεσινόν υπουργ. συμβούλιον. Εμπρός, 8 June.

Anonymous. 1918b. Η απεργία των καπνεργατών – Εργατική αλληλεγγύη. Μακεδονία, 5 July.

Anonymous. 1918c. Η απεργία των σιγαροποιών - Υπεβλήθη η απάντησις των εργοστασιαρχών. Μακεδονία, 11 July.

Anonymous. 1918d. Οι σιγαροποιοί. Τελευταία Ώρα, 19 May.

Anonymous. 1919a. Εργατικά - Σιγαροποιοί. Ριζοσπάστης, 8 February.

Anonymous. 1919b. Ανακοινωθέν σωματείου σιγαροποιών καπνεργατών. Εμπρός, 23 February.

Anonymous. 1926. Long Record for Steady Work Held by Woman Who Began Her Duties in Duke's First Factory. *Durham Morning Herald*, 17 January. https://www.ncpedia.org/anchor/working-tobacco-factory. Accessed on 28 July 2022.

Βαρβερόπουλος, Β. 1935. Ο μονοπωλιακός χαρακτήρ της του καπνού οργανώσεως (part 1). *Αρχείον Οικονομικών και Κοινωνικών Επιστημών* 2: 95–182.

Cigarette-machine, US 238640 A, Patented March 8, 1881. https://patentimages.storage.googleapis.com/c8/ea/24/463c1e13d10bd7/US238640.pdf. Accessed on 15 July 2022.

Constantinides, C.L. 1912. *Turkish Tobacco: A Manual for Planters, Dealers and Manufacturers*. London: W. & J. Rounce Ltd.

Εφημερίς των Συζητήσεω της Βουλής. 1911. *Ε. τ.* 1911. Β' Αναθεωρητική Βουλή (Vol. 1A) meeting 52, 17 March, 1126.

Εφημερίς της Κυβερνήσεως του Βασιλείου της Ελλάδος. 1918. Vol A, no. 6, 4 January.

Εφημερίς της Κυβερνήσεως του Βασιλείου της Ελλάδος. 1919. Vol A, no. 42, 27 February.

Εφημερίς της Κυβερνήσεως του Βασιλείου της Ελλάδος. 1920. Vol A, no. 279, 4 December.

Ηλιάδης, Γ. 1919. Το καπνεμπορείον Κ. Βάρκα & Σας. In *Η εργαζόμενη Ελλάς*, Vol 1: Αι Νέαι βιομηχανίαι της Ελλάδος, ed. Β. Γαβριηλίδης, 126–131. Athens: Εκδοτικά καταστήματα Ακροπόλεως.

Μικέλης, Ν. 1923. Ο καπνός και η βιομηχανία αυτού εν Ελλάδι. *Αρχείον Οικονομικών Και Κοινωνικών Επιστημών* 4: 340–356.

Ζολώτας, Ξ. 1940. Προβλήματα εργασίας και κεφαλαίου εις περίοδον πολεμικών ανωμαλιών. *Επιθεώρησις Κοινωνικής και Δημόσιας Οικονομικής* 9: 3–30.

Secondary Sources

Αβδελά, Έ. 1993. Ο Σοσιαλισμός των 'άλλων': ταξικοί αγώνες, εθνοτικές συγκρούσεις και ταυτότητες φύλου στη μετα-οθωμανική Θεσσαλονίκη.*Τα Ιστορικά*, τ. 10, τχ. 18–19: 171–204.

Αλέξης, Ν. 2021. Από τη "φυσική εισαγωγή" της προόδου στην πολιτική των αποζημιώσεων: για μια εξέταση των κοινωνικών αντιδράσεων στην τεχνολογία, από τις αρχές του 20 αιώνα μέχρι τον Μεσοπόλεμο".*Τα Ιστορικά* 72: 77–100.

Μηλιός, Γ. 2000. *Ο Ελληνικός κοινωνικός σχηματισμός: Από τον επεκτατισμό στην καπιταλιστική ανάπτυξη*. Athens: Κριτική.

Μόλχο, Ρ. 1988. Τα Ισπανοεβραϊκά: Μία Μεσογειακή γλώσσα στην καθημερινή ζωή της Θεσσαλονίκης του 20 αιώνα. *Τα Ιστορικά* 28–29: 123–146.

Μόλχο, Ρ. 2006. *Οι Εβραίοι της Θεσσαλονίκης, 1856–1919: Μια ιδιαίτερη κοινότητα*. Athens: Θεμέλιο.

Παλούκης, Κ. 2021. Ηθική οικονομία και ηθικός συνδικαλισμός. Συνδικαλιστικές πρακτικές στους μισθωτούς εργάτες τεχνίτες (απαρχές 20 αιώνα – Μεσοπόλεμος). In *Εκδοχές της ηθικής οικονομίας: ιστορικές και θεωρητικές μελέτες*. ed. Ν. Ποταμιάνος. 127–166, Ρέθυμνο: Ινστιτούτο Μεσογειακών Σπουδών - ΙΤΕ.

Ποταμιάνος, Ν. 2011. 'Ντόπιο πράμα!' Το αίτημα εθνικής προτίμησης και οι στρατηγικές ελέγχου της αγοράς εργασίας από τις εργατικές συλλογικότητες: Αθήνα και Πειραιάς, 1890–1922. *ΤαΙστορικά* 55: 283–322.

Φουντανόπουλος, Κ. 2005. *Εργασία και εργατικό κίνημα στη Θεσσαλονίκη, 1908–1936: Ηθική οικονομία και συλλογική δράση στο Μεσοπόλεμο*. Athens: Νεφέλη.

Χαριτάτος, Μ., and Γιακουμάκη, Π. 1998. *Η ιστορία του ελληνικού τσιγάρου*. Athens: ΕΛΙΑ.

Alford, B.W.E. 1973. *W. D. & H. O. Wills and the Development of the UK Tobacco Industry, 1786–1965*. London: Routledge.

Avdela, E. 1998. Class, Ethnicity and Gender in Post-Ottoman Thessaloniki: The Great Tobacco Strike of 1914. In *Borderlines: Genders and Identities in War and Peace 1870–1930*, ed. B. Melman, 533–551. New York: Routledge.

Balsoy, G. 2009. Gendering Ottoman Labor History: The Cibali Régie Factory in the Early Twentieth Century. *International Review of Social History* 54: 45–68.

Beckert, S. 2014. *Empire of Cotton: A Global History*. New York: Alfred A. Knopf.
Beinin, J., and Z. Lockman. 1988. *Workers on the Nile: Nationalism, Communism, Islam, and the Egyptian Working Class, 1882–1954*. London: I. B. Tauris & Co.
Betas, T. 2020. Cairo, Athens, Salonica: Strike Breaking and the Anti-labour Practices of Employers and the State in the Early Twentieth-Century Cigarette Industry. In *Corporate Policing, Yellow Unionism and Strikebreaking 1890–1930*, eds. M. Millan and A. Saluppo, 153–167. London and New York: Routledge.
Braverman, H. 1998. *Labor and Monopoly Capital: The Degradation of Work in the Twentieth Century*. New York: Monthly Review Press.
Carmona-Zabala, J. 2022. German Economic Power in Southeastern Europe: The Case of Reemtsma and the Greek Tobacco Merchants (1923–1939). *Business History* 64: 537–557.
Chandler, A. 1999. *The Visible Hand: The Managerial Revolution in American Business*. Cambridge, MA: Belknap Press.
Cooper, P. 1988. What This Country Needs Is a Good Five-Cent Cigar. *Technology and Culture* 29: 779–807.
Douglas, D. 2012. *Η Ενοποίηση της Ελλάδας, 1770–1923*. Athens: MIET.
Hadar, G. 2007. Jewish Tobacco Workers in Salonica: Gender and Family in the Context of Social and Ethnic Strife. In *Women in the Ottoman Balkans*, eds. A. Buturović and I.C. Schick, 127–152. London: I. B. Tauris.
Hannah, L. 2006. The Whig Fable of American Tobacco, 1895–1913. *The Journal of Economic History* 66: 42–73.
Hughes, T. 1993. The Evolution of Large Technological Systems. In *The Social Construction of Technological Systems*, eds. W. Bijker, T. Hughes, and T. Pinch, 51–82. Cambridge: MIT Press.
Khuri-Makdisi, I. 2010. *The Eastern Mediterranean and the Making of Global Radicalism, 1860–1914*. Berkeley and Los Angeles: University of California Press.
Καραμπάτσος, Χ. 2019. Ο Κωνσταντίνος Βάρκας και το "περίφημον μηχάνημα": Δυσλειτουργικές μηχανές και "τεχνικώς μορφωμένοι" εργάτες στην Ελλάδα μέσα από το παράδειγμα των σιγαροποιών, 1880–1920. *Τα Ιστορικά* 69: 59–96.
Labrianidis, T. 1982. *Industrial Location in Capitalist Societies: The Tobacco Industry in Greece, 1880–1980*. Ph.D Dissertation, London.
Ilicak, H.S. 2002. Jewish Socialism in Ottoman Salonica. *Southeast European and Black Sea Studies* 2: 115–146.
Montgomery, D. 1979. *Worker's Control in America: Studies in the History of Work, Technology and Labor Struggles*. Cambridge: Cambridge University Press.

Nacar, C. 2014. Labor Activism and the State in the Ottoman Tobacco Industry. *International Journal of Middle East Studies* 46: 533–551.

Nacar, C. 2019. *Labor and Power in the Late Ottoman Empire: Tobacco Workers, Managers, and the State, 1872–1912.* Basingstoke: Palgrave Macmillan.

Papastefanaki, L., and M. Erdem Kabadayi. 2020. Introduction and Historiographical Essay: Greek and Turkish Economic and Social History, and Labour History. In *Working in Greece and Turkey: A Comparative Labour History from Empires to Nation-States, 1840–1940*, eds. L. Papastefanaki and M.E. Kabadayi, 1–57. New York and Oxford: Bergham.

Porter, P. 1969. Origins of the American Tobacco Company. *Business History Review* 43: 68–69.

Radcliff, P. 1993. Elite Women Workers and Collective Action: The Cigarette Makers of Gijon, 1890–1930. *Journal of Social History* 27: 85–108.

Rifkin, J. 1996. *The End of Work: The Decline of the Global Labor Force and the Dawn of the Post-Market Era.* New York: Tarcher.

Roberts, B.W.W., and R. Knapp. 1992. Paving the Way for the Tobacco Trust: From Hand Rolling to Mechanized Cigarette Production by W. Duke, Sons and Company. *The North Carolina Historical Review* 69: 257–281.

Rogoff, L. 2001. *Homelands: Southern Jewish Identity in Durham and Chapel Hill, North Carolina.* Alabama: The University of Alabama Press.

Shechter, R. 2006. *Smoking, Culture and Economy in the Middle East: The Egyptian Tobacco Market.* New York: I. B. Tauris.

Smith, M.R. 1991. Industry, Technology and the "Labor Question" in 19th-Century America: Seeking Synthesis. *Technology and Culture* 32: 555–570.

Thompson, E.P. 1967. Time, Work-Discipline and Industrial Capitalism. *Past & Present* 38: 56–97.

PART III

Labour

CHAPTER 10

Tobacco Contestations: State, Planters, and Peasants in Besoeki Residency, East Java, Mid-Nineteenth to Early Twentieth Centuries

Ratna Saptari

In Southeast Asia, the globalisation of tobacco was marked by a striking transformation of regions formerly little involved in tobacco cultivation into export-oriented tobacco-growing regions. The Cultivation System (*Cultuurstelsel*), which the Dutch colonial government imposed between 1830 and about 1870, initially concentrated on indigo, coffee, and sugar. However, since the mid-nineteenth century, European planters had already started to get involved with finding other crops that could make their way on European markets, and tobacco gradually became a major commodity.[1] The decline in indigo production, and the large demand

[1] Broersma (1913, p. 17).

R. Saptari (✉)
Leiden University, Leiden, The Netherlands
e-mail: rsaptari2009@gmail.com

A. van Wickeren et al. (eds.), *Tobacco in Global Perspective, 1780–1960*, Cambridge Imperial and Post-Colonial Studies,
https://doi.org/10.1007/978-3-031-64411-5_10

for tobacco after the Franco-Prussian war in 1870, causing prices to increase significantly, resulted in a swarm of new tobacco entrepreneurs. They came not only to East Sumatra and the Vorstenlanden of Central Java, but also to the Besoeki residency in East Java.[2] European planters, concentrating on obtaining profits through tobacco production and trade, expanded their control over land and labour.

The rush into tobacco had a forceful impact on peasant economies, as Sugiyanto Padmo has thoroughly examined in his research on the tobacco economy in Central and East Java.[3] Padmo elaborately examines the development of the plantation system in the Principalities in Central Java and the Besoeki Residency since the early nineteenth century. Initially, the Dutch colonial government stimulated the development of small-scale enterprises run by individual Dutch or other European planters. This was followed by companies with large capital investing in tobacco and taking control of larger expanses of land. From the 1920s to the Japanese occupation in 1942, the tobacco economy experienced periods of boom and bust.

Padmo argues that tobacco plantations in the Vorstenlanden (Principalities of Central Java) were similar to those of the Deli plantations of East Sumatra, where Dutch companies held a monopoly over the tobacco industry, and local smallholders were never allowed to grow cigar tobacco independently. Padmo further shows how processes of change combined structural and local dynamics. However, Padmo, as he also acknowledged, is more limited in elaborating the spatially specific processes of negotiation and resistance that shaped the tobacco industry in the Besoeki residency, where tobacco cultivation took place within a social context that was entirely different. This is the subject of this chapter, in which I use the colonial term 'Besoeki' (Besuki) and the local term 'Djember' (Jember).

Many scholars have shown that multi-level dynamics are significant in shaping the production, consumption, and trade of commodities.[4] As in the case of other commodities, the spread of tobacco cultivation within and across imperial and national boundaries has always been rife with tensions, conflicts, and concessions between different colonial and local

[2] Padmo (1994).

[3] Padmo (1994, p. 80).

[4] Stubbs (2010, 2013).

powers. This transformed the landscapes of trade and production, and repositioned the different powers and actors involved at various levels. The late nineteenth and early twentieth centuries represented a peak in such tension.[5]

Access to land was a fundamental point of contestation. There were different opinions among government officials, plantation owners, and local leaders regarding what fell under the categories of 'native' land and 'waste' land. The boundaries between these types of land, and understandings about the rights of 'natives' and 'non-natives', became contentious. The parallel categories of ***bevolkingstabak*** (smallholders' tobacco) and ***ondernemingstabak*** (plantation tobacco) reflected these problems. In particular, access to land by plantation owners often came from hiring land, whether through short-term land renting of 'native' land, or through long-term leases (***erfpacht***) of 'waste' land. Furthermore, the successes and failures of experiments with cultivating different sub-species of tobacco affected not only the power play between plantation owners, traders, peasants, landless workers, and the colonial government, but also tensions within these groups.

Colonial authorities monitored the incidence of violations of regulations, and the most overt forms of attacks on property, which took the form of burning tobacco sheds. Such incidents of arson often occurred in East Java. These shed burnings, I would argue, provide insights into the nature of conflict, negotiation, and resistance in the period between the mid-nineteenth century and the 1920s.

Tensions in East Java's newly developed export-oriented tobacco industry were also an expression of the liberalisation processes that began in the 1870s. From that time onwards, tobacco companies expanded their control over land. However, local groups exploited newly introduced colonial regulations in a struggle to protect their interests. The chapter discusses how legal and political circumstances of liberalisation exacerbated conflicts. While European companies demanded access to land, labour and tobacco leaf, local landowners sought to retain (or obtain) access to land and rights to cultivate tobacco, in combination with other crops. All actors in the tobacco economy were interested in legislation by the Dutch colonial administration that represented their interests.

[5] Goodman (1993).

However, there was a de facto imbalance of power between European entrepreneurs and local landowners and farmers, which was particularly evident in the arbitrary price reductions imposed by European companies on leaf tobacco. Apart from negotiation and compromise-seeking, the asymmetry of power produced symbolic acts of resistance, which testify not least to the relative powerlessness of local actors. Negotiation and resistance in the East Java tobacco economy were thus intertwined processes. The actual actions of the European companies undermined negotiated rules, and thus brought about resistance.

The Development of Indonesia's Tobacco Economy

Tobacco has a long history in Indonesian consumption cultures and Indonesian tobacco cultivation was initially aimed mostly at the domestic market. As Anthony Reid noted, accounts of when tobacco was first introduced to the Indonesian archipelago usually refer to the Javanese courts, where the local royalty employed a long reed pipe, similar to royal consumption in Europe.[6] Around the mid-seventeenth century however, a cheaper, more popular way of smoking appeared, namely the *bungkus* (which means package or bundle), which was especially suited to ordinary people.[7] *Bungkus*, or *klobot*, was a type of cigarette that consisted of shredded 'Java tobacco' wrapped in dried leaf of maize or banana. *Bungkus* preceded and influenced the Indian and Burmese cheroot, of which the earliest recorded citations are in the eighteenth century.

In Sumatra, as in Malaya, homemade cigarettes were *nipah* or palm leaf-wrapped tobacco, referred to as *rokok*. This was assumed to have been spread by Dutch seamen, as the name is probably associated with the Dutch term for smoking, *roken*. The growing popularity of smoking intensified the need for the supply of tobacco. In the eighteenth century, Old Kedoe (Kedu, presently called Temanggung and Magelang), in Central Java, was already a thriving centre of tobacco cultivation, where Chinese merchants played a role in establishing a lease system in 1746, and where profits accrued to the East India Company.[8]

[6] Reid (1985, p. 536).

[7] Ibid., p. 537.

[8] Hall and Koppel (1949, p. 417).

During the nineteenth century, economic and social differentiation in lifestyles was retained, in part, by the way one smoked, or what one smoked. The elite of Batavia and the Javanese aristocracy used the pipe, the middle and upper classes smoked imported cigars or cigarettes, while the *bungkus* remained the preference of the lower classes.

These different patterns of consumption were closely related to the types of tobacco leaves cultivated, sold, or controlled by traders and tobacco companies. *Gekorven tabak* (*rajangan* in Indonesian), for instance, was notably aimed at domestic markets, whereas *krosok* was grown mainly for export. *Krosok* was dried by farmers and sold to traders, or to tobacco estates, which were responsible for fermentation, sorting and packing the product. The lower leaves of the *krosok* plant had a thinner structure and were lighter in weight, and they thus became an important product for the European tobacco industry from the mid-nineteenth century.[9] Quite often the farmer cultivated tobacco without yet having an idea whether it should be for *gekorven tabak* or for *krosok*.

In addition to the different types of tobacco leaves, there were two types of harvests, namely the *voor oogst* (early harvest) and the *na oogst* (late harvest). The *voor oogst* occurred in the dry season (April–June) and fell exclusively into the category of *bevolkingstabak* (native tobacco), whereas the *na oogst* took place in the rainy season (October–December) and was under the control of plantations.

During the Cultivation System, between 1830 and about 1870, indigo, sugar, and coffee were the major products exported to European markets, and tobacco was not yet a primary cash crop. The Cultivation System has often been conceived as a period in history where state regulation dominated the appropriation of land and labour for the production of export crops. This regulation compelled Javanese villages to set aside a portion of their land, normally one-fifth, to grow crops (in this case indigo, coffee, and sugar) designated by the government. The produce of this portion of the village's land was delivered to the government at a fixed price.[10]

The period of the Cultivation System witnessed the beginnings of intensive commercialisation of local economies, which intensified after the system was slowly ended. A flow of foreign capital entered the economy, resulting in the growth of the European community, who took charge

[9] Van den Broek (1949, pp. 523–525).

[10] Van Niel (1972, pp. 89–109).

of much of the expansion of plantation and trade networks. As Ulbe Bosma has argued, it was through the Cultivation System that there was an initial rise in the number of Europeans, whether technicians, military veterans, representatives of trading houses, or employees of estate owners and other private entrepreneurs.[11] State intervention, which had been highly uneven during the Cultivation System, gave way to a larger role for private enterprise after about 1870. More Dutch entrepreneurs flowed into the colony in search of profit, although locally settled Chinese and Arabs also remained very significant intermediaries.

In the attempt to obtain better results in the tobacco areas in the colonies, colonial companies had to deal with local powers or communities, either to conduct negotiations or treaties with local rulers for access to irrigated land, or to open areas which were considered to be 'waste land' or 'frontiers'. Ever since the land rent system had been introduced in the early nineteenth century, debates among colonial authorities regarding the land rights and obligations of natives and non-natives became a contentious issue. The idea of either obtaining tax or labour, especially from the cultivation of *sawah* (irrigated) land, or of protecting the rights of natives to maintain their own subsistence needs, was constantly debated among colonial officials and plantation owners. The basic question was, should communal land be maintained, or should private ownership be stimulated?[12] The Government Act of 1853 allowed the leasing of 'wild lands' or 'waste land'. This gave an entrepreneur the opportunity to obtain land by two means, either renting from the government for a period of not more than twenty years, or entering into arrangements with natives to have them grow products on their land. Both options were a problem for the entrepreneurs. In the first case, the duration of the lease was considered too short, and, in the second case, the entrepreneur had too little control over the production process. In the first ten to fifteen years of colonisation, land lease contracts varied. Some concessions were for 70 years, some for 75 years, and some up to 99 years. These contracts quite often took into account customary law. In the early years the main contention was how much land planters were allowed to have under their control, either through *erfpacht* (long lease) or shorter-term rents.

[11] Bosma (2007).

[12] See Kano (1977).

East Sumatra was already producing tobacco, pepper, rattan, gold, and rice for export, before it became the world-famous producer of Deli tobacco, a fine wrapper leaf for the manufacture of cigars. Nienhuys, who tried his luck on the East Coast of Sumatra in 1863, was the first to investigate the possibility of cultivating a commercial crop in Deli.[13] He was given a concession by the Sultan of Siak to clear and bring under cultivation empty land for 99 years without having to pay land rent. The Sultan would get a percentage of the proceeds when the tobacco had been exported.[14]

As for the Principalities of Central Java, they were already important producers of sugar, coffee, and indigo, and they had an elaborate land appropriation system grounded in the feudal apanage system and became famous for their filler leaf. The companies had to deal with the Sultan of Surakarta, who was customarily considered to own all agricultural land. The royal family members and royal officials had the privilege to use the apanage land. In the apanage system, peasants were allotted plots of land and had the right to use a portion of the land to grow food crops, in exchange for unpaid labour. This labour was not restricted to agricultural work, but could include other types of work. The Dutch planters were able to take over this system. With concessions from the sultan, they could have access to apanage land, together with the labour attached to it.[15]

The increased demand for local tobacco accelerated colonial attempts to develop tobacco as a profit-bearing commodity. The popularity of Havana cigars in the West stimulated the search for other areas that could produce good quality leaf tobacco.[16] In 1834, the Dutch government sent a Dutch official, N. G. de Voogt to Cuba to learn the technique of tobacco cultivation there. Four years later, he was sent to Java to assist in the cultivation of tobacco in the Rembang residency of Central Java. However, the initial experiments did not produce the desired results. In 1854, the Dutch government thus sent O. W. Swaving and H. J. van Swieten to Cuba again, to investigate more intensively the production of

[13] Pelzer (1982, pp. 32–35).

[14] Breman (1992) and Pelzer (1978).

[15] Padmo and Djatmiko (1991, pp. 29–36).

[16] Stubbs (2010).

tobacco there. Upon their return, they were appointed to assist in the tobacco industry in Rembang, Central Java.[17]

In Besoeki, unlike in Central Java, the first Dutch planters did not have to deal with an established aristocratic elite. Land that was considered unused was directly under the control of the colonial government, and therefore, planters had to obtain permission to rent it from the government. Land that was already cultivated by local peasants could only be rented under agreement with individuals. Thus, different kinds of arrangements were made, mainly with the local peasantry in the northern part, and mainly with the government in the southern areas, where there was more uncultivated land.

Since the 1850s Dutch planters had attempted to grow tobacco in the northern regions of East Java, particularly in Bondowoso. In 1860 C. H. Doup and J. G. Berkholst used a combination of methods to obtain the right to land. Apart from purchasing *na-oogst* tobacco from the peasants, they also rented peasant land on a 5-year basis. Since this was considered insufficient, they requested government permission to cultivate government land. In the end they managed to acquire 30 *bouw* (21 hectares) of land spread over six villages, even before they obtained a contract with the Dutch colonial government. Similarly, Fransen van de Putte (who later on became Minister of the Colonies) initially started a rice mill in the Djember district in 1856. When this did not succeed, he went on to tobacco, and set up with A. H. Lorenty a tobacco company in Soekowono, Besoeki residency. In 1857 he obtained 60 *bouw* (42 hectares) of land from the Dutch government. And D. J. Uhlenbeck obtained 106 *bouw* (74.2 hectares) of land rented from the peasants in Bondowoso. In 1853, Uhlenbeck grew *na-oogst* tobacco on the land rented from the peasants and recruited them in its production. In 1863 he obtained 106 *bouw* of land in Wonosari district, with government consent.[18] Depending on the ecology of the area, the land grown with *na-oogst* tobacco was widely spread and interspersed with land grown with other crops, even though they could be all leased or rented by a tobacco company. The cultivation of tobacco was undertaken alternately

[17] Padmo and Djatmiko (1991, p. 29).

[18] Ibid. (1991, p. 40).

with other crops, although the sequences of cultivation varied from area to area.[19]

George Birnie headed the largest tobacco company in the region. Initially, Birnie had been a Dutch civil servant (*controleur*) in charge of the supervision of crop cultivation, initially in the area of Kediri and Blitar, and then in Djember, all of which were located in East Java. During his period as *controleur* he studied and observed the environmental condition in the Djember area and made notes regarding the rainfall and tobacco cultivation, after which he decided to leave government service.[20] Because of limited capital, he initially rented only 15 *bouw* (10.5 hectares) of land from the local peasants. In order to obtain more capital to develop a plantation, Birnie joined with C. Sandenberg-Mathiessen and A. D. van Gennep to found the plantation company, NV Landbouw Maatschappij Oud Djember (LMOD) on 21 October 1859.[21] In an attempt to capture the European market, the tobacco planters experimented with crossing Havana, Kedoe, and Banjoemas varieties, which were all tobacco types that sold well on European markets.

Contesting Land Appropriation

Fransen van de Putte was of the opinion that "communal land possession or ownership is a cancer, which gnaws at native society in Java, hinders all further development and is a powerful impediment to the prosperity and progress of land and people".[22] Already during the period of the Cultivation System, there were indications of encouraging private entrepreneurs to obtain communal land. The Government Act of 1853 gave the entrepreneur the opportunity of renting government land or entering agreements with the peasants to grow the crops on their own and communal land.

The Agrarian Law of 1870 was a milestone in the development of the market economy, as well as the transformation of the agrarian structures in the colony. Now, all land not in private ownership was declared to

[19] Broersma (1913, p. 19).

[20] De Birnies (1992, p. 38).

[21] Padmo and Djatmiko (1991, p. 71). See also Jaeggi (1949, p. 491) and Padmo (1994).

[22] Elson (1997, p. 416).

belong to the state, and a distinction was drawn between two types of land. 'Free' land was not subject to native rights, as it was deemed to be waste and unoccupied, whereas 'unfree' land was subject to native rights. The government was empowered to lease 'free' land to Dutch subjects residing in the colonies and to companies registered in the Indies, for a term of not more than 75 years. Such *erfpacht* leases were attractive to Western planters, for the period was long enough to justify the planting of slow-maturing perennials and the investment in processing factories and other buildings. Consequently, there was a sharp increase in the area held in *erfpacht* after 1870.

In the 1860s and 1870s, the NV Landbouw Maatschappij Oud Djember (LMOD) faced various problems. In 1861, two years after its establishment, one of its founders, Van Gennep, died, and his shares went to the other two shareholders. But Matthiesen also sold his shares in 1875, and George Birnie's cousin Gerhard David took Matthiesen's place. Gerhard David had already worked for Oud Djember since 1860. During and after the Franco-Prussian War in 1870, the price of tobacco increased significantly from *f* 1,20 to *f* 1,60 per pound. This development induced a large number of tobacco planters to establish themselves in the region resulting in various arrangements being made with regard to land control. In 1875, in order to safeguard his rights to land, George Birnie requested the right to obtain 500 *bouw* of land in Soekoredjo by *erfpacht* leasehold, which became officially registered in 1879. However in 1875 George Birnie left the company and went with his wife, Rabina, to Europe.[23]

By 1893, LMOD had become the largest tobacco plantation in Besoeki, occupying 2,600 *bouw* of irrigated land, 15,000 *bouw* of non-irrigated land or *tegalan*, 16,000 *bouw* of *erfpacht* land, 150 *bouw* of land with *opstal* rights (the right to erect buildings), and 60 *bouw* of irrigated land with *eigendom* (ownership) rights.[24] Even when in the late nineteenth century the Oud Djember tobacco company had already become an important player in the tobacco business and gradually brought other estates under its control, the cousin and successor of George Birnie, Gerhard David Birnie, still made regular visits to Solo and also to Klaten,

[23] Birnie (1992, p. 126).

[24] Landbouw Maatschappij Oud-Djember (1909).

in Central Java, to study the intricacies of tobacco cultivation and to improve the techniques in his own estate.[25]

Reports regarding the land coverage and the annual tobacco production of these estates hardly mention the status of the land rights of the local peasants. Although it has been said that Birnie opened up forest lands to start his tobacco enterprise, Jos Hafid, an Indonesian scholar, states that there were cases of appropriation of inhabited land. Thus, in 1845, in the area of Rambipoedji, south of the town of Djember, both Javanese and Madurese groups had opened up the forest land before the arrival of the Dutch planters, totalling an area of approximately 2,465 *bouws*. Although it is not clear where Hafid obtained his data from, the figures seemed to be a good indicator for Javanese and Madurese activities at the time.[26]

The increasing power of private planters in controlling the allocation of capital, land, and labour became a concern of the colonial government, although perceptions were mixed regarding this situation. On the one hand, some favoured free market principles, with peasants paid on the basis of the quality of tobacco sold in the free market. On the other hand, others wanted a tighter control of tobacco cultivation and sale, to ensure that good quality tobacco could be linked to particular brands, or particular plantations. Those who advocated free market principles were traders, who wanted to be able to buy tobacco in the open market, and not be restricted by various government regulations that limited the sale of the Besoeki *na-oogst* tobacco crop to a few. These traders or 'buyers-up' did not need to make investments involving much capital, and therefore could offer higher prices.[27]

Those who favoured regulation were the descendants of the planters who had 'opened up' Djember, but there were significant tensions among them. Within the Birnie family, disagreements regarding the running of the LMOD became part of the management dynamics, as seen in family correspondence.[28] For instance, in Elisabeth Birnie's book it was stated that George had mentioned to his cousin, Gerhard David, that the harvesting wage should be changed. Gerhard David did not agree,

[25] Birnie (1992, p. 34).

[26] Hafid (2001).

[27] Jaeggi (1949, p. 489).

[28] Birnie (1992).

because he said the wage should be consistent with the verbal and written contract. It is not clear, in these letters, whether George was suggesting an increase or decrease of wages. However, the disagreement apparently resulted in Gerhard David's response that the company should be split in two, and George's decision to leave the company in 1874.[29] Negotiations among planters had to be made not only on how to control the quality of the crop, but also on its marketing. And this was reflected in the number of agreements they had to make among themselves, and the negotiations they had to make with the peasants. Local land-owning peasants also tried to benefit from their relationship with plantation owners and traders, sometimes renting out the same land twice.

The constant grouping and regrouping of interests between tobacco capitalists led to political lobbying regarding regulations, and to private agreements between planters. *De Rotterdam-Overeenkomst* (the 'Rotterdam Agreement') of 4 September 1907 involved six tobacco companies: Landbouw Maatschappij Oud-Djember, Besoeki Tabak Maatschappij, Cultuur Maatschappij Djelboek, L. M. Soekokerto Adjong, L. M. Soekowono and L. M. Soekasari. The agreement, which was initially valid for five years but was then extended to 1927, stated that these companies should respect the rights of each company to the land that they had rented from local landowners; introduce as much as possible the same requirements regarding tobacco cultivation; and refrain from buying tobacco cultivated on the land rented by others.[30] The 1908 *Tabaksverordening* (Tobacco Ordinance) was then meant to protect the rights of the *aanplant-ondernemer* (cultivator-planter), who cultivated tobacco on rented land. It was intended to put an end to 'free cultivation', where buyers-up would buy tobacco from the peasants, quite often at a better price than what the plantation owners offered. The consequence of these regulations and agreements was that plantations had almost unlimited power concerning the production of tobacco, and no space was given for free cultivation. However, with these arrangements, the planter also had to shoulder most of the risks. Even though on paper they were supposed to be protected in cases of harvest failure, in practice they usually got very little.[31]

[29] Birnie (1992, p. 42).

[30] Van Hoboken et al. (1932, p. 8).

[31] Anonymous (1919).

Moreover, regulations and agreements were often violated. In a report from 1913, R. Bosman, the resident of Besoeki, stated that the Tobacco Ordinance and the Rotterdam Agreement should be strictly implemented. If this did not happen, there would be 'unloyal competition' which would demoralise the population, various abuses of rights, uncertainty among the companies, etc. As examples, he mentioned two planters who took control of land already under the ownership of existing companies, and another planter, a member of a Trust Company, who threatened to violate the Rotterdam Agreement.

The rhetoric employed in these debates contrasted 'the common good' (*algemeen belang*), which the planters often referred to, with the interests of the *Inlandsche bevolking* (indigenous population), which those who were for free market tended to stress, as observed by the retiring resident of Bondowoso, Broekveldt.[32] In any case, the factors seen as impeding production and business stability were clashes between tobacco companies, that is planters and merchants, or the frustrations of local peasants, whose payments did not concur with their expectations.

Labour Types and Social Unrest

Examining the categories of labour needed for the cultivation of tobacco is highly complicated. The relationship of the producer to the land, the type of tobacco cultivated, and the different phases of tobacco processing need to be kept in mind. In the Besoeki residency, there were three types of relationships between landowners and the tobacco companies or buyers. There were those whose land was leased in *erfpacht* to European plantations for an extended period of time, which mainly applied to the Landbouw Maatschappij Oud Djember. Others rented out their land for five years, but retained the right to cultivate their own crops outside the tobacco season. Yet others were 'free' planters, who could sell their tobacco to any buyer. The first and second types of relationships are often difficult to distinguish, since in the *erfpacht* areas peasants were also allowed to use half the allocated land for tobacco, while the other half remains 'uncultivated'. In the case where all land is used for tobacco, peasants were also allowed to cultivate other crops between January and the end of May. However, because the cultivation and processing of tobacco

[32] See Saptari (2016, p. 97).

are a highly intensive affair, many peasants were often unable to prepare themselves sufficiently for the planting of secondary crops.

Under these conditions different types of agreements with the local peasantry were made to induce the cultivation of tobacco. If in the reports we see reference mostly to 'land-owning peasants' it should be underlined that the peasantry was not as homogeneous as formally stated. Peasants in the area could already be divided into those who were landowners, those who were landless, and those who had some degree of control of the means of production and sold their tobacco to tobacco traders or on the free market. Carpentier Alting's 1902 report stated that among all peasants involved in tobacco cultivation, around 26,619 were landowners, and 15,694 were landless, of whom 11,704 were local peasants, and 3,990 were migrants from elsewhere.[33]

Compared to central Java and Madura, the residency of Besoeki, especially its southern part, was sparsely populated, which made the appropriation of land in practice more negotiable. The situation became more complicated when the flow of migrants into the area increased, and new claims to land emerged. Migration from Madura, Central Java, and other parts of East Java had already occurred since the early nineteenth century.[34] Views regarding the characters of the migrants became much discussed in the reports of the residents at the end of their term. For instance, Bosman, in 1913, stated in a rather stereotypical way that there was no need to worry about the Madurese, who constituted a significant number of the population, because even though they were religious and noisy they did not tend to initiate protest actions.[35]

Regarding the production process and the gender division of labour, although it is not mentioned where these workers come from, a report of the NV Landbouw Maatschappij Oud Djember (LMOD) presented on the occasion of its 50th anniversary, stated that planting was usually done by men, and that women and girls watered the recently planted tobacco. For the first few days (usually five days) the young plant was watered every day. The field *mandor* (foreman) made sure that there was enough irrigation water in the vicinity. During the harvest, leaves were picked according to the degree of maturity. The tobacco was picked

[33] Anonymous (1902, p. 2).

[34] Bleeker (1847, p. 143). See also Tennekes (1963).

[35] Mailrapport no 2143/13.

by women wage workers, placed in harvest baskets, and brought to the drying shed.[36] What was remunerated by the wages paid was not only the work in the field, but also all the preparatory work before that; the tools needed for the work; the wages of the helpers in the field who the workers had to find themselves; worm searching by women and children; and the tying of leaves in a row and hanging up of sheaves in drying sheds. Even though in theory peasants were allowed to grow food crops, quite often no time was available to do so, as in practice the wives and children of peasants in the tobacco villages were usually recruited by the tobacco companies, either as permanent or daily labourers, to work in the smokehouses or sorting sheds.

The location of the drying sheds differed from place to place, depending on the layout of tobacco estates. In Besoeki, drying sheds were clustered together. Usually, the various phases of tobacco processing were conducted in one shed. It was in these drying sheds that most female and child labour was used. Because the sheds were clustered together, whereas rented lands were mostly located far from each other, women workers (who came from the peasant families) had to walk relatively long distances to get to the sheds. Sorting was done by Javanese or Madurese women. After the tobacco was dried, it was brought to the fermentation shed, which was the most important building in the estate. Fermentation took about two to four months, and sometimes even longer. If this period was too short, the quality of the tobacco declined. The leaves sometimes went through an additional pre-fermentation period.

The *mandor* was meant to control the sorting of leaf tobacco in the drying shed, but this was difficult to implement with limited personnel and means of control. Some foremen had their land rented out to the estate. As they were responsible for recruiting labour for the production and processing of tobacco, their position was crucial. Broersma mentions that the LMOD, which in 1884 had five tobacco estates, had only 60 European personnel, surrounded by around 500 foremen and an indefinite number of workers.[37] In Deli, in comparison, for one plantation with 280 hectares of land, work in the field would be supervised by 1 administrator, 4 assistants, 1 head foreman, and 12 sub foremen, with at

[36] Landbouw Maatschappij Oud-Djember (1909).

[37] Broersma (1913, p. 23).

least 200 coolies per foreman.[38] In Besoeki, limited personnel could at best regulate the harvesting times, when the bottom, the middle, and the top leaves had to be picked.[39] Yet, controlling even this process was difficult, and ultimately the only way to accord the proper value to the tobacco plant, according to company officials, was to pay peasants according to the tobacco's quality. Debates regarding the quality of the tobacco and the profits obtained through market sales often became a reason for non-payment or low payment.

Many calculations were made regarding the economic benefits that could accrue to peasants from tobacco cultivation. However, these calculations did not take into account various factors involved in the production of tobacco.[40] Even if the seeds distributed to the peasants were of high quality, the complex process of production, planting and watering the seedbeds, the transplanting of the young plants, the maintenance, and the harvesting were highly labour-intensive, which made it difficult for peasants to find time to produce staple crops that would help to increase their income.

The Tobacco Ordinance of 1908 ended free cultivation according to Broekveldt, who referred to an article published in numbers 75 and 76 of the *Javasche Courant* 18 and 22 September 1908. This led to peasant complaints recorded in the government reports, as peasants often preferred to sell to traders rather than to plantation owners. In Besoeki, Resident Broekveldt, in his report at the end of his term of office, referred to written complaints addressed by the Sarekat Islam organisation, a social movement concerned with land and labour issues, regarding the condition of 'native tobacco'.[41] This reflected a study on tobacco cultivation conducted by Liefrinck, a member of the Raad van Indie, between 29 November and 21 December 1917, regarding the situation of the *bevolkingstabak*.[42] In a provocatively formulated report, he disagreed with the view that companies rented land from the indigenous population. He stressed that most tobacco estates were not companies (*ondernemingen*)

[38] Breman (1992, p. 130).

[39] Anonymous (1902, p. 19).

[40] Vleming (1925, p. 69).

[41] See Saptari (2016, p. 97).

[42] The results regarding the situation of the bevolkingstabak were reported in Mailrapport no. 1324, 1918.

at all but just buyers. According to him, the peasants did all the work, then they brought the tobacco to the sheds, and were paid according to quality. If the tobacco was not up to the standards required, they were not paid at all.[43] This situation was a source of disenchantment for the peasants, as the tobacco company with which they had a contract would pay high prices for tobacco of good quality, and lower prices for bad quality leaves, rather than pay a standard price for all the delivered tobacco.[44]

Initially, complaints had been expressed by more liberal-minded civil servants or bureaucrats, who were worried by various forms of unrest that occurred from time to time. This was because payment would only be made when the tobacco had been sold, or because families could not grow other crops in the land that they used for cultivating tobacco, since their labour was needed in tobacco processing. However, the expansion of tobacco plantations or native tobacco production for the estates continued unabated. In some cases, if the tobacco was not according to the standards required, then producers would not be paid at all.

As competition between tobacco companies and merchants allowed peasants to sell on the free market for prices that were more advantageous than what companies offered, this stimulated heated controversy among the companies. Since 'free' peasants were not tied to the companies, they could plant tobacco of their own choosing and sell to any trader who offered good prices.[45] Additionally, it was often reported that these land-owning peasants could get quality seeds from their contacts among the *mandor*. With the *mandor*'s help, they might even have their own tobacco dried in the drying sheds of the companies.[46] Deviations from contracts could not be used by companies to bring legal action against land-owning peasants, for lack of evidence.

In order to deal with this situation, it was felt that security measures had to be improved, and a new category of personnel, the 'tobacco police', was introduced. These tobacco police were recruited for the period of planting and harvesting. The members of the police team consisted of native police officials and European *controleurs*, who, in

[43] Koloniën/Memorie van Overgave, National Archief, The Hague, hereafter NL-HaNA, Inv. Nr 2.10.39, Nr 1270/9, p. 9.

[44] Anonymous (1902).

[45] Vleming (1925, p. 61).

[46] Broersma (1913, p. 28).

collaboration with the plantations, were appointed by the local government. The costs were entirely in the hands of the estates. Control checks were to be made at the most important train stations and at various cross-roads with control posts along the road. A company such as the LMOD, for instance, would transport the tobacco from the fermentation sheds with ox carts to the various train stations, where the State Railways transported them to the storage houses of the Maatschappij Panarukan. From these sheds, the bales were brought by *prauw* (boats) to the waiting ship of the Stoomvaartmaatschappij Nederland, which brought them to Rotterdam and to the Firma Hoboken. This implied that, at every checkpoint, intensive security control needed to be done.[47]

Controllers checked whether the amounts transported corresponded to the *pipil*, papers detailing the tobacco, which every tobacco cultivator had to have. Every 'free cultivator' received a *pipil* on which were written name, address, number of tobacco plants, and amount of dry tobacco leaves. To ensure the accuracy of the information, the tobacco company also made its own check on the leaves coming from their territory, and then compared this with the list made by the tobacco police. At the control posts, the amounts of tobacco were checked with the *pipil* that had earlier been distributed, to find out whether they were from the same planter. If the inspectors discovered that either the quality or the quantity of the leaves was not in accordance with what was written on the *pipil*, then the tobacco would be confiscated, and the origins of the tobacco investigated.[48]

This form of strict control, however, could not entirely guarantee honest delivery of the product by those who were working on the land controlled by the companies. Peasants were able to take advantage of the situation by not delivering the amount of tobacco stipulated in the earlier agreement. Land-owning peasants could rent the land to two parties at the same time, which was confirmed in the reports written by the government officials. These security measures also did not guarantee the actual tobacco cultivation process prescribed by the company.

The anger of local peasants, who felt cheated in the payments that they received, impeded production and business stability. These frustrations were manifested in frequent burnings of the sheds where dried

[47] Landbouw Maatschappij Oud-Djember (1909).

[48] Jaeggi (1949, pp. 492–493).

tobacco was kept. In his 1902 report Bergh van Heinenoord stated that quite often the direct reasons for the fires were difficult to uncover, despite public and secret investigations by European and native officials, even with the help of spies. However, a number of interpretations were noted: the dismissals of some *mandor* and their malevolence, planters not paying the agreed price for tobacco, and dishonest management. Van Heinenoord also mentioned issues within local politics, such as non-sanctioning of village elections, or a grudge against a district head.[49] Conflicts also arose over land rents. Thus, it was mentioned that in the Soekowono plantation a number of peasants complained that in 1902 only half the rental price of the land had been paid. A complaint was also addressed to the Boender plantation, because the delivered tobacco was not paid according to the initial agreement.[50]

The role of political organisations in carrying out acts of discontent was further mentioned. In his report from 1913, R. Bosman stated quite strongly the need to monitor the role of Sarekat Islam in other parts of East Java, close to Besoeki, such as Panaroekan and Banyoewangi, as this might affect the situation in Besoeki. However, there is no clear evidence that Sarekat Islam was actually stirring up peasant discontent.

In the late nineteenth and early twentieth centuries, workers' conditions were little discussed. It was only in the 1920s, when the Labour Office started investigating workers in certain sectors of the economy, that debates emerged regarding how to deal with the rights of workers, and which standards to use. It was in this period that much attention was given to workers in the cigarette and tobacco sectors, since these absorbed a large proportion of the working population.[51]

Conclusion

The emergence of tobacco cultivation for export and the establishment of large tobacco companies in Djember was a contentious process. This chapter has attempted to examine the contestations between the different political actors in the regulation, production, and marketing of

[49] Van Heinenoord and van den Bergh (1902). Mailrapport no 1121, NL-HaNA, Ministry of Colonies. Box 2.10.36.02.

[50] Mailrapport no 1121, NL-HaNA, Ministry of Colonies, Box 2.10.36.02.

[51] See de Kat Angelino (1929). And also van der Reijden (1934–1936).

tobacco. State regulations attempted to mediate the conflicts between planters, or between planters and peasants. State officials held different views regarding priority issues. As for the crop itself, whether produced by individual peasants or plantation companies, value was determined by differences in taste and brand. Competition among planters, and between planters and merchants, affected the race to control land, and the quality of crop and labour. Peasant strategies in dealing with existing, and changing, power structures shaped their access to land and tobacco profits.

Boundaries between planters, traders, peasants, and wage workers could not easily be sharply defined, especially as there were many kinds of peasants. Some were contracted to companies on the basis of leasing. Others rented out land directly to companies, and then provided the labour, and some of the capital, to produce tobacco. Yet others were on short-term rents, and they often had the flexibility and agility to sell their tobacco either to the company or to 'buyers-up', depending on the price offered. And there were 'free peasants' who planted their own tobacco to sell to whatever buyer, and at whatever price was profitable. Moreover, peasants could sell tobacco already under contract with companies to independent brokers, and company employees could become brokers. The types of tobacco leaves that were cultivated further shaped the spread of the crop, and the tussles over it.

Tobacco-shed burnings were a manifestation of diverse forms of discontent or conflict, not only between peasants and plantation companies, but also among peasants themselves, who were positioned at different levels of the production hierarchy. Arson could also reflect tensions between village authorities and the local community. The colonial government attempted to reduce contestation, and to broker compromises and collaboration between various actors, by encouraging agreements and meetings. In this way, the authorities sought to increase stability in tobacco production and marketing. State regulations were attempts to control existing conflicts, and the possibility of future ones, and they also shaped the strategies of tobacco companies and traders. These endeavours depended on existing power structures, which were at times fluid and at other times more consistently maintained.

Acknowledgments I would like to thank the editors of this volume: Alexander van Wickeren, Jean Stubbs, William Clarence-Smith, and also Ben White, for intensively reading and commenting on this chapter.

References

Primary Sources

Unpublished

Van den Bergh, and E.M. van Heinenoord. 1907. *Memorie van overgave van de residentie besoeki*. Ministry of Colonies, National Archives, The Hague.
Van Heinenoord E.M., and van den Bergh. 1902. *Mailrapport no 1121. box 2.10.36.02*. Ministry of Colonies, National Archives, The Hague.

Published

Anonymous. 1902. *Voordracht in eene onder Voorzitterschap van den Resident van Bezoeki gehouden Bijeenkomst van Tabaksondernemers en Geemployeerden Bij de Tabakscultuur te Bondowoso 16 Februari 1902*. No place: No publisher.
Anonymous. 1919. *De Tabaksverordening, benevens eenige andere gewestelijke verordeningen van de Residentie Besoeki, ten dienste van de Tabaksondernemers. 1919*. No place: No publisher.
Bleeker, P. 1847. Bijdragen tot de Statistiek der Bevolking van Java. *Tijdschrijft voor Nederlandsch Indië* 9: 143.
Broersma, R. 1913. *Besoeki, Een Gewest in Opkomst*. Amsterdam: Groesbeek & Nijhoff.
de Kat Angelino, P. 1929. *Verslag Betreffende Eene Door den Inspecteur bij het Kantoor van Arbeid op de Vorstenslandsche Tabaksondernemingen Gehouden Enquete. Publicatie no 5 van het Kantoor van Arbeid*. Weltevreden: Landdrukkerij.
Jaeggi, A.C. 1949. De Tabakscultuur van de Residentie Besoeki. In *De Landbouw in de Indische Archipel. Part 2*, eds. C.J.J. van Hall and C. van de Koppel. 's-Gravenhage: N.V. Uitgeverij W. Van Hoeve.
Landbouw Maatschappij Oud-Djember. 1909. *Kort Overzicht van Oprichting, Bestaan en Bedrijf der Onderneming 'Oud Djember'*. Ter Gelegenheid van haar 50-jarig Jubileum samengesteld, 1859–1909. No place: No publisher.
van der Reijden. 1934–1936. *Rapport Betreffende Eene Gehouden Enquete Naar de Arbeidstoestanden in de Industrie van Strootjes en Inheemsche Sigaretten op Java. Publicatie van het Kantoor van Arbeid*. No place: No publisher.
Van Hoboken, A., et al. 1932. *Belanghebbenden Bij de Tabakscultuur in de Residentie Besoeki Thans in het Regentschap Djember*. No place: No publisher.
Vleming, J.L. Tabak. 1925. *Tabakscultuur en Tabaksproducten van Nederlandsch-Indië*. Weltevreden: Landsdrukkerij.

Secondary Sources

Birnie, E. 1992. *De Birnies*. Twello: No Publisher.

Bosma, U. 2007. The Cultivation System (1830–1870) and its Private Entrepreneurs on Colonial Java. *Journal of Southeast Asian Studies* 38: 275–291.

Breman, J. 1992. *Koelies, Planters en Koloniale Politiek*. Leiden: KITLV.

Elson, R. 1997. *The End of the Peasantry in Southeast Asia: A Social and Economic History of Peasant Livelihood*. London: Macmillan Press.

Goodman, J. 1993. *Tobacco in History: The Cultures of Dependence*. London: Routledge.

Hafid, J.O.S. 2001. *Perlawanan Petani. Kasus Tanah Jenggawah*. (Peasant Resistance. The Case of the Jenggawah Lands) Jakarta: Latin, LSPP.

Hall, C.J.J., and C. van de Koppel. 1949. *De Landbouw in de Indische Archipel. Part IIb*. 's-Gravenhage: W. Van Hoeve.

Kano, H. 1977. *Land Tenure System and the Desa Community in Nineteenth Century Java*. Tokyo, Institute of Developing Economies. Special Paper no. 5.

Padmo, S. 1994. *The Cultivation of Vorstenlands Tobacco in Surakarta Residency and Besuki Tobacco in Besuki Residency and Its Impact on the Peasant Economy and Society: 1860–1960*. Yogyakarta: Aditya Media.

Padmo, S., and E. Djatmiko. 1991. *Tembakau, Kajian Sosial Ekonomi*. Yogyakarta: Aditya Mediap.

Pelzer, K.J. 1978. *Colonial Policy and the Agrarian Struggle in East Sumatra*. The Hague: Martinus Nijhoff.

Pelzer, K.J. 1982. *Planters Against Peasants: The Agrarian Struggle in East Sumatra, 1947–1958*. The Hague: Martinus Nijhoff.

Reid, A. 1985. From Betel-Chewing to Tobacco-Smoking in Indonesia. *Journal of Asian Studies* 44: 529–547.

Saptari, R. 2016. Keeping Land and Labour Under Control? Reporting on Tobacco Shed Burnings in Besoeki (Java). In *Embedding Agricultural Commodities: Using Historical Evidence, 1840s–1940s*, ed. W. van Schendel, 78–98. London: Routledge.

Stubbs, J. 2010. El Habano and the World It Has Shaped: Cuba, Connecticut and Indonesia. *Cuban Studies* 41: 39–67.

Stubbs, J. 2013. El Habano: The Global Luxury Smoke. In *Global Histories, Imperial Commodities, Local Interactions*, ed. J. Curry-Machado, 248–276. Palgrave Macmillan.

Tennekes, J. 1963. *Bevolkingsspreiding der Residentie Besoeki in 1930*. Amsterdam: TKNAG.

Van den Broek, P.J. 1949. Bevolkingstabak. In *De Landbouw in de Indische Archipel, 1875–1947*. ed. C.J.J. van Hall and C. van de Koppel, 523–525. Gravenhage: W van Hoeve.

Van Niel, R. 1972. Measurement of Change Under the Cultivation System in Java, 1837–1851. *Indonesia* 14: 89–109.

CHAPTER 11

State Labour Control and Women's Resistance in Austro-Hungarian Transylvania Tobacco Manufacturing (1897–1918)

Alexandra Ghiţ

In late March 1897, after a week-long strike, the more than 1,000 women workers in the state-owned, and until 1911 fully non-mechanised, tobacco factory in the Transylvanian, eastern Austro-Hungarian city of Kolozsvár/Cluj Napoca/Klausenburg (Kolozsvár for short) succeeded in having an unpopular manager dismissed.[1] In the aftermath of the strike, in order to secure the women's loyalty and prevent another publicly visible labour conflict, the factory management introduced a range of site-specific paternalistic practices and institutions, including a library, cafeteria and crèche. Over a decade later, between late April and late

A. Ghiţ (✉)
Department of History, Department of Gender Studies, Central European University, Vienna, Austria
e-mail: ghita@ceu.edu

[1] Anonymous (1897b).

A. van Wickeren et al. (eds.), *Tobacco in Global Perspective, 1780–1960*, Cambridge Imperial and Post-Colonial Studies,
https://doi.org/10.1007/978-3-031-64411-5_11

May 1911, the women tobacco workers from Kolozsvár made the pages of the Budapest press, when a strike over wages and increased social insurance contributions met with a management-ordered factory lockout. According to a June 1911 issue of the social-democratic daily *Népszava*, the representatives of the Tobacco Directorate in the Ministry of Finance of the Hungarian Kingdom were unwilling to negotiate with the several hundred protesting workers for fear their demands would spread to other tobacco factories.[2]

Homing in on the Austro-Hungarian, Kingdom of Hungary, region of Transylvania between the 1890s and the end of World War I, this chapter examines how the increasing use of women workers in tobacco product manufacturing during the second globalisation of tobacco was accompanied by gendered labour policies and control measures on the part of the Hungarian state tobacco administration. The measures challenged and undercut an increasingly organised female workforce affiliated with broader social and political movements, through strikes and other practices. State-building and industrialisation in the Kingdom of Hungary after the Austro-Hungarian Dualist Compromise of 1867 was shaped by responses to workers' activism including that of an increasingly female tobacco-processing labour force across Hungary, including in peripheral Transylvania. The 1867 Dualist Compromise transformed the Habsburg Monarchy into an alliance of two states—Austria and Hungary—which had very similar institutions but a high degree of policy autonomy in most areas, including in most fiscal matters. By the 1890s, the rapid integration of a low-paid female workforce enabled the Hungarian state tobacco monopoly, which had been created in 1867 and legally strengthened in 1887, to retain its profitability in an increasingly liberalised tobacco world.

My case study of women tobacco workers' history of labour activism in Kolozsvár takes into account a very old historiography of labour in Transylvania and builds on a new wave of gender-sensitive scholarship on activism and imperial rule in Austria-Hungary and beyond. Eszter Varsa's reconstruction of late nineteenth-century peasant women's labour activism in Eastern Hungary's "stormy corner" (Viharsarok) reveals that 1897 was a peak year for women's organising in rural areas, within the Independent Socialist movement, led by István Várkonyi and benefitted

[2] Anonymous (1911f).

from the organising and editorial skills of his daughter Mariska Várkonyi.[3] My findings here strengthen Varsa's argument that the year represented a high-point of women's labour activism in Hungary—especially in light of 1950s research documenting harvest strikes in Transylvania at the same time as in Viharsarok, with a peak in 1897.[4] Rachel Trode focuses on bureaucratic conflicts surrounding a 1906 strike wave that began in a tobacco factory in Habsburg-ruled Sarajevo and considers the events as enabling interactions between local people and Austrian administrators in Bosnia and Herzegovina.[5] She argues that tobacco factories were sites where imperial rule on the Austrian side of the Austro-Hungarian Monarchy was negotiated. I pay similar attention to gendered workers' networks, legal frameworks and economic priorities linked to constructing and maintaining imperial rule. However, I investigate more closely the limits to workers negotiating imperial and state power, especially in highly profitable industrial sectors, such as tobacco manufacturing.

In explaining the changes that took place in the Hungarian tobacco industry, I accord more power to women's labour activism than is found in the labour history of Transylvania in the 1950s and 1960s in Romania.[6] I provide new perspectives on the lifeworld of women workers, evidencing their complaints, discourses and organising practices. Extrapolating from contemporary attention to factory-specific benefits and welfare institutions present in several studies on Austrian and Hungarian tobacco factories, I also aim for a more critical understanding of how social conflict was managed by means of factory-specific welfare infrastructure and practices as well as of discipline and control linked to state-building.[7]

I argue that women tobacco workers in Kolozsvár were more willing to become engaged in labour conflicts and had stronger links with the regional and national labour movement than presumed in the historiography of Transylvanian workers' movements, links which strengthened their position vis-à-vis management. I show how their demands—rooted in their specific experiences as women and as workers—could also be countered and neutralised through site-specific techniques of control

[3] Varsa (2024, pp. 119–126) .

[4] Egyed (1959, p. 227).

[5] Trode (2022).

[6] Fodor and Vajda (1957). Egyed (1957, pp. 33–56) and Deac (1962).

[7] Csóka (1958). Bauer (2015) and Wernitznig (2022).

by Hungarian tobacco monopoly civil servants. This closer look at the state's control measures, which were increasingly refined in retaliation for worker resistance, contributes to a better understanding of women's labour organising practices and of how their capacity to organise and resist was eventually undermined. It also contributes to developing our understanding of labour unrest in Austria-Hungary.

The first part of the chapter documents the backdrop of how tobacco factories became key pillars of a state-driven Hungarian industrialisation policy, whose profitability partly stemmed from gender inequality. The second part traces the formation of a female tobacco workforce in Hungary, analysing the agendas and forms of action during a March 1897 strike initiated and led by women in the Kolozsvár factory. Workers' demands for lower social contributions, an end to harsh treatment by the director and workshop foremen, and access to medical care were appeased through an array of factory-based welfare institutions, such that a certain level of peace was secured in the factory for the better part of the 1910s. The focus of the third part is on the 1911 strike that met with a lockdown, and on strengthening ties with the Social Democratic Party and local trade unions. I conclude by suggesting points of continuity in post-1918 developments, when Kolozsvár became part of the Kingdom of Romania and the factory the property of the Romanian state. I also offer more general reflections as to how the specific case of Austria-Hungary provides insights into the late nineteenth- and early twentieth-century interplay of a majority-women workforce, organisation of tobacco workers and state tobacco monopolies still found today in many parts of the world.

For my analysis I draw on a broad range of print sources, including a selection of recently digitised newspaper collections available in a comprehensive database of Hungarian language publications.[8] While series of newspaper articles on strikes may help construct a fairly clear timeline of key events, or may capture unusual details of events, they may misconstrue or misrepresent the complex motivations and even the actions of participants, especially when many of the decisive occurrences do not happen in front of the eyes of the journalists reporting them. To mitigate for biases and omissions inherent in press reporting, I sought to integrate sources produced across the diverse political spectrum of the

[8] The main database for digitalised Hungarian language press and government publication used in this chapter is Arcanum Digiteca (https://adt.arcanum.com/en/).

Hungarian press,[9] assembling and comparing the different angles in reports from distinct ideological standpoints. Information from the post-1918 Romanian-language archives of the tobacco factory was invaluable, especially a detailed, unpublished factory monograph covering the period 1851–1930.[10]

State Industrialisation of the Tobacco Sector

The Kolozsvár tobacco factory was founded in 1851, a year after the state tobacco monopoly was established in the Habsburg Empire. A state monopoly framework was adopted by Vienna to combat smuggling, to collect revenues via indirect taxation and to favour the development of industry.[11] The monopoly framework was maintained in Hungary after the Compromise. According to György Képes, considered a remnant of the Austrian neo-absolutist period and meant to be abolished by the late 1860s, the tobacco monopoly was consecrated as a "*necessarium malum*" by the mid-1870s, on account of the indispensable revenues that the full monopoly on tobacco cultivation, production and sale brought to the coffers of the Kingdom of Hungary.[12] A dedicated, "praiseworthy (nagytekintetű)", Royal Hungarian Tobacco Excise Central Directorate (Magyar Királyi Dohányjövedéki Központi Igazgatóság, the Tobacco Directorate hereafter), subordinate to the Hungarian Ministry of Finance, was created in 1882. The head of the Directorate had a function equal to that of state secretary. In 1887, the tobacco monopoly framework was reformed, to further increase tobacco revenues.[13] The Kolozsvár tobacco factory was one of the four earliest tobacco factories in what would be the Hungarian part of the Austro-Hungarian Monarchy after 1867. In the 1860s, the factory produced fine and lesser-quality tobacco, for pipes and chewing, as well as cigars (*szivar* in Hungarian, *ţigări de foi* in Romanian sources), before specialising in the former and, after 1883, also

[9] Ternay (1957) and Horváth (1999).

[10] Monografia fabricii 1851–1930 [Factory monograph 1851–1930], 1930, DJAN Covasna, Sfântu Gheorghe, Romania, File 40/1966, Fond 179 - Întreprinderea de Ţigarete Cluj.

[11] Wickett (1897, p. 210).

[12] Képes (2019).

[13] Képes (2019, pp. 71–74).

producing cigarettes (*szivarka*). By 1906, it was one of twenty-one factories of the state tobacco monopoly in the Kingdom of Hungary,[14] and by the outbreak of World War I had an annual output of 2,000,000 kg cut (pipe) tobacco, 175,000,000 cigarettes and 30,000,000 cigars.[15] It was one of the five largest in Hungary, and from the 1890s to the 1910s employed between 1,000 and 1,200 workers. As in all the tobacco factories, most of the workers were women: in 1911, for example, there were 1,112 women and 132 men, with most of the women working in cigars (526), followed by cigarettes (309).[16] Although there was an attempt at mechanisation in 1883, and machinery was successfully introduced in 1911, production remained primarily manual until the 1920s.[17]

By the late nineteenth century, tobacco was an increasingly important source of revenue for a Hungarian state that pursued, with some success, a costly policy of jumpstarting internal capital accumulation via tax breaks and investment in infrastructure. Scholarship on (semi)peripheralisation in the nineteenth century, especially Berend and Ránki's research from the late 1970s, argued—drawing on Myrdal—that in the late nineteenth century, the Kingdom of Hungary could avoid becoming strictly a supplier of raw materials for "core" industrialised countries in Europe. Hungarian government policy favoured internal capital accumulation.[18] Yet the development of modern infrastructure in the kingdom turned out to be more costly than expected. From the 1867 Dualist Compromise until the late 1890s, the state budget ran a deficit,[19] a situation of course complicated by the 1873 financial crisis generated by the crash of the Viennese Credit-Anstalt. The end of the nineteenth century represented a turning point. Tobacco was meant to become increasingly profitable for the Tobacco Directorate and its ownership of tobacco factories became a priority. By 1898, revenues from the sale of tobacco products (cut tobacco, cigars, cigarettes) had increased by 167% compared to 1870. In the Statistical Yearbook for 1898, the government reported that "[t]he excise sale of manufactured tobacco yielded over 100 million crowns; after

[14] Bányász (1906b, p. 808).

[15] Monografia fabricii 1851–1930 [Factory monograph 1851–1930]: 4.

[16] A M. Kir. Kormány (1906, p. 193).

[17] Monografia fabricii 1851–1930 [Factory monograph 1851–1930]: 5–8.

[18] Berend and Ránki (1980, p. 25). Myrdal (1957) and Szávai (2012, p. 43).

[19] Szávai (2012, p. 43).

deducting 40,906,000 crowns for the cost of manufacture and handling, the treasury surplus in money was 59,134,000 crowns."[20] The numbers indicate a profit margin (not taxed, of course) of more than 60%.[21]

The factories were profitable because the Tobacco Directorate kept production costs low by employing primarily women. After 1891, the number of women employed in tobacco manufacturing in the Kingdom of Hungary increased by about 1,000 women a year, from 12,201 in 1891 to 16,082 in 1895 and 17,876 in 1898.[22] In 1911, 18,497 women were working in tobacco factories,[23] with the number decreasing only slightly by 1914. The overall increase of women workers was not specific to the tobacco industry—in 1897, of the 170,267 workers employed in Hungarian factories (defined as enterprises with more than 10 workers) 41,868 (25.5%) were women—but 17,000 (40%) of female workers did work in tobacco manufacturing[24]; and the Tobacco Directorate was the leading employer for women employed in industry.

Recent economic history emphasises that Hungarian industrialisation vis-à-vis the Austrian side of the Austro-Hungarian Monarchy had limited redistributive effect and may have contributed to inequalities between various regions in Austria-Hungary. Living standards for wageworkers improved in the northern and western Cisleithanian, Austrian, part of the monarchy, between 1850 and 1915. However, the growth in Gross Domestic Product did not lead to improvements in workers' wages and living standards in Transleithania, the Monarchy's Hungarian part.[25] Other similarly predominantly agricultural regions, such as Austrian-ruled Bukovina and Galicia, registered a clear improvement from the 1890s until the 1910s.[26] In the 1890s, however, peasants in various parts of Transylvania, as in other parts of Hungary, experienced an accelerated process of immiseration, as smallholding rural households lost land and many were forced to seek agricultural work as wage labourers on estates.[27]

[20] A M. Kir. Kormány (1914, p. 254).

[21] Compare with Allen (2009).

[22] A M. Kir. Kormány (1914, p. 432).

[23] A M. Kir. Kormány (1914, p. 278).

[24] A M. Kir. Kormány (1914, p. 254).

[25] Cvrcek (2013, pp. 25–26).

[26] Ibid., p. 29.

[27] Deac (1962, p. 51) and Varsa (2024, 105–107).

The Hungarian government (and implicitly, the Tobacco Directorate) also saw tobacco factories such as the one in Kolozsvár as the core of a development strategy for the economically troubled areas in their peripheries where labour was cheap and plentiful. Politicians and the administration presented tobacco factories as pioneering industrial and charitable institutions that could develop "backward" regions and rescue their inhabitants from dire poverty.[28] This mirrored a process documented by Ingrid Bauer for the Austrian parts of the Monarchy.[29] Contemporary observers noted that the tobacco factories were supported by agricultural pressure groups, and press articles suggested that cities were particularly keen to have factories built in certain areas where major landowners had a vested interest in supplying the tobacco grown on their own estates.[30]

In the early decades of the nineteenth century, according to some sources, Hungary was the fourth-largest leaf tobacco producer in the world, ahead of Cuba and Brazil and surpassed only by production in the US, British India and Russia.[31] At the time, the central Hungarian Tolna and Heves counties produced "distinctive, superior varieties of tobacco" while less subtle tobacco varieties were grown in over two-thirds of the other Hungarian counties.[32] By the end of the nineteenth century, Hungary was still a leading producer of tobacco in Europe (second after Russia), but had long been surpassed by other countries globally, especially the US.[33] Tobacco was increasingly cultivated in different areas of the country, where less fine sorts grew better. For some Hungarian observers, including Vilmos Daróczi, the publisher of the *Magyar Dohány Ujság (Hungarian Tobacco News)*, this shift of cultivation areas meant a decline in quality. Daróczi used familiar stereotypes about the "innovation-incompetent" farmer by arguing that although the soil in Eastern Hungarian counties was fully suited for more flavourful tobacco, underdeveloped methods meant that growers (many of them

[28] Járó (1883).

[29] Bauer (2015, p. 74).

[30] Anonymous (1897c).

[31] Nemes (2016, p. 180).

[32] Ibid., p. 193.

[33] Magyar Tudományos Akadémia (1896, p. 213).

still poor land holders) preferred sturdy, long-leaved, high-yield varieties.[34] Hungary's already modest tobacco product exports declined. As Austria, the traditional client for Hungarian tobacco leaf, began expanding production in Galicia, and countries in the Americas increased their production, the Hungarian tobacco industry focused on selling its tobacco products to consumers in Hungary even more than before. Varieties of cigars, and from the mid-1900s, as elsewhere, cigarettes became increasingly important.

With the construction of new factories, the Hungarian government tried to keep at bay the unrest that was sweeping the Hungarian countryside, especially in the first half of the 1890s, when an agrarian socialist movement rapidly gained support, intensifying and coordinating the riots and harvest strikes of peasants. A central reason for agrarian socialist activism was the concentration of land in the hands of landowners, increasing the number of landless peasants.[35] The Hungarian Social Democratic Party was founded in 1890 and organised May Day celebrations in various Transylvanian cities, including Kolozsvár.[36]

Fear of disorder and attempts to curb the growing power of the labour movement led to an overhaul of welfare policies in the Kingdom of Hungary. In 1891, Act XIV introduced compulsory social insurance for all industrial workers, after half a decade of more comprehensive but unsuccessful drafts. Hungary became the third country in Europe, after the German Empire and the Austrian side of the Austro-Hungarian Monarchy, to introduce such insurance. In regard to the amounts available for sick pay or cover for family members, the system was more generous than in Austria and Germany.[37] Yet the new insurance system, as in Austria and Germany, was set up with the clear intention of weakening workers' mutualist associations. The influential General Workers' Insurance Office, a workers' mutual aid association that insured workers and provided healthcare, also "financed strikes and printed workers' leaflets and papers."[38] In this context, the government was intent on preventing

[34] Nemes (2016, p. 193).

[35] Drosick (1976). Csóka (1958) and Varsa (2022).

[36] Deac (1962, pp. 79–96).

[37] Szikra (2004, p. 263).

[38] Szikra (2004, p. 261). see Zimmermann (2011, pp. 97–106).

some of the large Budapest-based mutualist associations from expanding to other cities, preventing them from opening new local offices.

In Hungarian tobacco factories, workers had already had insurance through factory-based schemes but with the 1891 Act XIV tobacco workers could be admitted to a broader "Tobacco Sickness Insurance Fund." Tobacco workers had access to sickness benefits and a funeral allowance. After at least ten years of employment, workers were entitled to a small monthly retirement pension.[39] Employment in the tobacco factories also appears to have been a coveted position particularly because of the small pension available to workers in old age.[40] Under the 1891 social insurance act, the contribution rate of workers was 2% of the daily pay. Two-thirds of that contribution was deducted from a worker's salary, while the employer paid the remaining third, and workers were to have a two-third majority in administering the new insurance offices.[41] The Tobacco Sickness Insurance Fund was maintained even after the 1907 reform of health (and introduction of accident) insurance, which aimed to centralise and unify the previously large variety of funds.[42] Significantly, benefits provided to workers in tobacco manufactories were higher for men than for women, and amounts varied depending on the location of the factory.

From the late 1890s, practices to foster worker loyalty were enhanced in many Hungarian tobacco factories. Besides health insurance and retirement benefits, tobacco factories were to offer workers access to facilities such as on-site libraries, cafeterias and crèches. Remarkably, however, by 1906 the Kolozsvár factory was the only one in Hungary which had set up the entire gamut of on-site welfare facilities that the Tobacco Directorate considered desirable. The Kolozsvár library—one of only two such tobacco factory libraries in Hungary—was opened to "ennoble the morals and thinking of the workers."[43] "*Bildung*" through reading seemed to be a means of taming the workers, who were perceived as out of control, familiarising them with the behaviour of bourgeois society, without in turn erasing the actual class distinction. At the same time, a factory library

[39] Bányász (1906a, p. 580).

[40] Mérey (1997, p. 241).

[41] Szikra (2004, p. 263).

[42] Bányász (1906b, p. 807).

[43] Bányász (1906b, p. 823).

was a way to counter socialist publications and the libraries socialist organisations set up. The Kolozsvár factory cafeteria was among only five that were left by 1906, and a free crèche existed only in one other Hungarian factory, its cost being shared with the rail company.

By the end of the nineteenth century, tobacco factories had become highly profitable establishments and important tools in the Hungarian state's fiscal and industrial policies for the peripheries. As the next section reveals, press articles discussing these policies show how the factories were closely linked to public reflection on the peripheral regions and increasing internal inequalities within Hungary, and how the peripheries became increasingly sites of policy innovation in Hungary, in response to workers' demands, aimed at fostering loyalty and discipline among a female workforce that kept production costs low.

Women's Labour Activism and Paternalistic State Control

The Romanian-language labour historiography of Transylvania has portrayed tobacco workers as reluctant to engage in labour conflict. Historians have argued that workers feared losing their employment in workplaces better regulated and more stable than in other industries, and that their reluctance was further due to the 'barracks-like' discipline state manufacturing imposed on and demanded of workers.[44] The regulations for tobacco factory workers in the Kingdom of Hungary were particularly explicit about the expectation of discipline in such factories.[45]

There was, however, already conflict in the tobacco factories dating back to before state investment intensified in the sector, deepening social tensions in the 1890s. In August 1882, women tobacco workers in Budapest clashed with the local management and urban police next to the Soroksár street factory after the director had read a decree by the Ministry of Finance according to which all women were to learn how to make cigars according to a new, faster, rolling method, without their pay being increased.[46] In 1886, female workers in the Transylvanian Temesvár/

[44] Fodor and Vajda (1957, p. 75).

[45] Bányász (1906a, p. 583).

[46] Anonymous (1882).

Temeswar/Timişoara tobacco factory went on strike over pay,[47] and in 1887 women workers in Pozsony/Pressburg/Prešporok/Bratislava went on strike and rioted, demanding the dismissal of a manager, better work materials and better pay.[48] Rather than displaying disciplined attachment to the factory-specific benefits, workers also frequently highlighted changes and malfunctions in the dedicated insurance system. This was the case in Temesvár where women not only demanded higher pay but also a part of the money they paid weekly towards their health insurance.[49] It was also the case that same year, when 800 women workers from one of the three Budapest tobacco factories attended a gathering in an inn close to the factory. There, one of the women speakers argued that if the Minister would not rescind a new, five-forint, tax on wages, she herself would be the first to declare a strike. She also proposed to found a trade union and inform the "socialist party" in Budapest of its founding.[50]

An increase in taxes that was not accompanied by an increase in wages was at the core of the 1897 strike in the Kolozsvár tobacco factory and was well reported in the national and local press. The strike came on the heels of an uptick in social-democratic organising and trade unionisation in Transylvania in the 1890s, and also of increased surveillance of the labour movement, especially during the 1895–1899 premiership of Dezső Bánffy.[51] The statutes for new trade unions and worker associations were approved by the Ministry of the Interior with great difficulty, and on the condition that any organisation refrain from aiding striking workers.[52] Because of the significance of the General Workers' Insurance Office for the labour movement, issues related to social insurance played a frequent part in labour conflict, at least in Transylvania.[53]

Although press reporting on the 1897 strike of the women tobacco workers did not reveal any direct ties with the Social Democratic Party or workers' associations in Kolozsvár, the demands made, the organised ways in which workers proceeded and surveillance by the local police suggest

[47] Anonymous (1886).

[48] Anonymous (1887).

[49] Dohánygyári munkásnők strájkja [Tobacco factory workers' strike].

[50] Anonymous (1896).

[51] Fodor and Vajda (1957, pp. 36–46).

[52] Ibid., pp. 30–45.

[53] Ibid., p. 29.

that their protest was part of a broader trend of labour organising in the city. Thus, in March 1897, the Kolozsvár factory management announced that women workers would pay 4.7–7.98 forint, while the men were to be taxed 7.98–9.98 forint.[54] The higher taxes covered an increase in workers' insurance contributions, as well as municipal and road taxes specific to Kolozsvár. As of 1896, tobacco workers were already paying an increased yearly tax—of 4.74 forint for women, whose salaries were lower than men's, as against 7.98 forint for men—an increase that likely triggered the women workers' meeting in Budapest.

After the announced increase, as allowed under the 1895 regulations on tobacco factories,[55] women workers' representatives (a delegation of no more than six persons) had an unsuccessful meeting with the Kolozsvár factory director, Sándor Hadházy, to present their complaints, which triggered dramatic events on Saturday 20 March 1897.[56] Hadházy ordered the women workers be locked in their workshops for the rest of the day, presumably so as not to be able to stage a walk out. The press reported that after the locked-in women workers began screaming male colleagues broke down the door, and 1,000 women left the factory building, assembled on the adjacent street and declared a strike.[57] One of the women workers assembled outside the factory's gates, Mrs. György Zachariás, was reported as "shouting over the heads of others" that work in the Kolozsvár factory would be resumed on Monday only if the level of taxation from three years before, of 3.24 forint per person, was reinstated. When police arrived, protestors quickly dispersed so that no one would be taken to the police section.

The day after, some 50 male workers in the factory also joined the women to protest calmly outside the factory gates. Small groups of strikers were seen in the streets that day, all reported to have been behaving calmly. Speaking to the correspondent of one of the newspapers, the argument of the workers was that although they paid 0.08 forint a week for sickness insurance, the designated factory doctor also worked for the railway company and as a private practitioner and was unable to

[54] Anonymous (1897d).

[55] Bányász (1906a, p. 587).

[56] Anonymous (1897d).

[57] Ibid.

genuinely attend the needs of 1,040 factory workers.[58] Hadházy emerged as a deeply unpopular figure in the factory and the strikers wanted him dismissed. He was considered a disciplinarian who was unwilling to demand that his foremen stop their verbal abuse of women workers.[59] A newspaper sympathetic to the management reported that in the initial meeting with women workers Hadházy claimed to not have any power to influence taxation but that he promised he would seek to remedy the problems. While male workers could be convinced to stand in solidarity with female workers during certain strikes and conflicts, in the tobacco industry in general these solidarities could be complicated by the sometimes distinct interest of workers considered skilled (men) and by the social advantages men as a group enjoyed in and outside the factory.[60]

As had happened during the Pozsony labour conflict a decade before,[61] the Kolozsvár strike soon involved the local city authorities, and a conciliation committee was organised. A senior official of the Tobacco Directorate arrived in Kolozsvár from Budapest and held meetings with the factory manager and other local representatives in one of the city's main hotels. The workers—who had not appointed a ten-person delegation, as proposed by the Budapest envoy—gathered in front of the building. Rózsa Dézsi, a woman appointed by her co-workers, "read the agreement and conditions of the strikers to the crowd."[62] Eventually, Dézsi and several other workers were taken by the police for interrogation but were soon released.

The strike ended on March 26, with a victory for the strikers. A newly dispatched representative of the Tobacco Directorate promised that all would be done to lower workers' taxes, while Hadházy was put "on leave" and temporarily replaced by his deputy, György Hirth.[63] Rezső Kazay, seemingly an official who was well liked among workers, was soon appointed director,[64] and under Kazay carefully choreographed fatherly benevolence towards women tobacco workers was devised and displayed

[58] Anonymous (1897a).

[59] Anonymous (1897d).

[60] Ghiţ (2023) on constructions of skill in the same factory, after World War I.

[61] Anonymous (1896).

[62] Anonymous (1897a).

[63] Anonymous (1897b).

[64] Anonymous (1898).

to the public. The following year, Kazay organised a lavish "May Festival" (*majális*) in the local, beautifully decorated park, where more than 2,000 people connected to the factory gathered to listen to the playing of a brass band. When Kazay, Hirth and their families arrived in the park, a delegation of women workers presented each of them with a bouquet of flowers. Oranges were distributed to the women workers' children, and Kazay personally invited the children to accompany him to enjoy cakes in a nearby confectionery.

When in 1901 the factory celebrated 50 years of existence, the symbolic markers and rhetoric of paternalism were further evidenced. The celebrations took place in the presence of representatives of the Hungarian Tobacco Directorate and other government officials from Budapest. Newspaper articles mentioned the "spirit of peaceful agreement," love, respect and trust for the factory managers.[65] Repeatedly, speakers at the event presented the factory as not only an industrial enterprise but also as a charitable and humane institution in which "the poor, the widow and the orphan" had always found refuge. Various speeches referenced the "paternal kindness" of representatives of the Tobacco Directorate and especially Kazay, who, in turn, praised the charitable hearts of the women workers, noticeable—he declared—in the donations workers had made to the local school for blind children. An enthusiastic speech delivered by a young woman worker encouraged colleagues to cheer for the factory's "benevolent bosses."[66]

The 1901 celebration also proved to be an occasion to review the activities of several factory-based welfare institutions created since Hadházy had been ousted. As part of the classical repertoire of paternalist institutions, such facilities helped justify the levying of high taxes on wages, increased the authority of the managers and were designed to enhance workers' loyalty to the company.[67] The most important among these institutions was a credit cooperative. Started in September 1900 it had helped workers with small loans,[68] to help build homes and pay for food.[69] In September 1900, Kazay had asked the city of Kolozsvár to

[65] Anonymous (1901).

[66] Ibid.

[67] Reid (1985).

[68] Anonymous (1900a).

[69] Anonymous (1901).

assist with the expenses of setting up the crèche for the children of the factory workers,[70] and the factory cafeteria was established for workers to have a cheap daily meal with meat. Workers could also join a choir.

At the same time, the support of the local labour movement for tobacco factory workers, likely veiled for strategic reasons in previous years, became clearer. This was most evident in public contestations by social-democrats of the industrial paternalism practices pursued in the tobacco factory. In 1903, an article by Mór Rappaport in *Erdélyi Munkás*, a short-lived social-democratic newspaper that had begun publishing in Kolozsvár that year, claimed the tobacco factory management "robbed" the workers and sought to control their every move. He argued that "our mothers, our sisters" became sick working in the factory, while the management underpaid them, and complained that the workers were expected to work very fast and pay could vary because management set women's wages at its discretion. Moreover, he declared: "it is not enough for them to exploit the workers who toil under their management, they also want to control the workers outside the factory, by ordering them where to go, what to read and what to wear."[71]

The article in *Erdélyi Munkás* is significant not only for the passion of its language but also its mention of tobacco women workers' contact with social-democratic organisers and socialist literature. In Rappaport's view, it was in vain for the manager to ban women workers from attending social-democratic meetings, or from reading social-democratic pamphlets, since the cause of social democracy ended up triumphing wherever there was oppression. He ended his article demanding that factory women be treated decently, as the patience of the women's family members was already running thin. Interestingly, the following day, a women's delegation from the factory contested Rappaport's account in a statement of their own, which suggested that loyalty-producing practices in the factory were not entirely unsuccessful.[72]

In the period 1904–1907, Transylvania was swept by a wave of strikes, as was the rest of the Kingdom of Hungary. State socialist historians in Romania have suggested that these occurred despite a strong legalistic approach to labour struggle favoured by the Budapest-based Trade

[70] Anonymous (1900b).

[71] Anonymous (1903b).

[72] Anonymous (1903a).

Union Council, and as expressed in a 1904 Strike Regulation created by the Council.[73] The women tobacco factory workers in Kolozsvár did not declare another strike until 1909, during an attempted city-wide general strike, one that failed due to quick repression by the authorities.[74] Their labour activism subsequently developed in tandem with the broader social-democratic trade union movement in the region; shared some demands with the broader (male-dominated) union movement; and strategised how to organise within the specific framework of the new rules, regulations and paternalistic institutions which governed the tobacco industry.

Cost Cutting and Labour Activism

In 1911, a late April week-long protest followed by a bitter May lockout once again drew the attention of the Hungarian press to the Kolozsvár factory, revealing key changes in managerial tactics and labour politics in the decade since Hadházy was replaced by Kazay, and Kazay himself replaced in 1909 by his long-time deputy Hirth. In terms of managerial strategies, 1911 represented a shift towards cost cutting, with faster work expected for the same pay, less willingness to appease via paternalist institutions and greater willingness to take hard-line stances.

In terms of labour politics, the years 1908–1910 were a period of reflux after the uptick in organising in the period 1905–1907. In 1911, the pace of unionisation in Transylvania picked up again, with the Trade Union Council recognising that too little attention had been granted up to that point to workers in larger factories, especially state-owned ones, as energies had concentrated on unionising skilled workers in small and medium-sized enterprises.[75] Protests and strikes across the region highlighted the intensification of the pace of work and the increase in the cost of living.[76] The Trade Union Council (a Szakszervezeti Tanács) was created in 1892, with its first congress held in 1899. It was associated with the Social Democratic Party.[77]

[73] Fodor and Vajda (1957, pp. 60–61).

[74] Anonymous (1909).

[75] Fodor and Vajda (1957, pp. 101, 103).

[76] Ibid. (1957, p. 95).

[77] Fodor and Vajda (1957, p. 38).

Despite criticism by an early state socialist historiography highly critical of the social-democratic trade unions' approach towards unskilled workers in large industrial establishments during this period, the development of the 1911 labour conflict in the Kolozsvár factory shows that local trade unionists supported the demands of women piece-rate workers. The tactics of "slowdown" and "passive resistance" and the careful attempts at compliance with factory regulations and those governing local assemblies, point to how workers involved in labour conflict elaborated their own strategy to protect workers at risk of dismissal. Importantly, press reports made it clear that workers marshalled a history of failed management promises by, for example, comparing the situation in Hungary with the higher pensions in the tobacco industry in the Austrian side of the Monarchy. In addition, a mid-May appeal of the locked-out women to local public opinion revealed that the workers sought to turn to their advantage the paternalistic practices and the community's attachment to the smooth functioning of the factory, the very practices and attachments cultivated by factory management over the previous decade.

As revealed by a factory monograph drawn up in 1930, eight Semenoff tube-making machines were introduced in the Kolozsvár factory in 1911, to respond to growing domestic demand for various kinds of cigarettes.[78] That year the Tobacco Directorate had set out to increase tobacco revenues by increasing tobacco prices and efficiency in the factories.[79] The combination of mechanisation and drive for increased profits affected the piece rates of some 500 women workers employed in the factory's "most difficult piecework."[80] At the end of April, the Tobacco Directorate announced that wages might be increased in May for workers in certain factory departments, but not for the workers doing piecework and hired on a daily or weekly basis.[81] A delegation representing the 500 women pieceworkers in the factory sought unsuccessfully to meet with Hirth to discuss a wage increase that would also include them.

Seeing this, the signal was given for the 500 women pieceworkers to "slowdown" for the rest of the day, engaging in what was known

[78] Monografia fabricii 1851–1930 [Factory monograph 1851–1930 and Ghiţ (2023, pp. 14–16) for production processes after World War I].

[79] A M. Kir. Kormány (1914, p. 34).

[80] Anonymous (1911i).

[81] Anonymous (1911j).

as *amerikázni* (Americanising)—a term that began to circulate in the Hungarian labour press around 1906, meaning to "work less than before during the allotted time."[82] Whereas "go slows" or "slowdowns" were a part of labour activism repertoires elsewhere, the association with the US may have been due to the relatively strong ties between the Hungarian and the American labour movements at the turn of the century.[83] The workers knew that under factory regulations, absence from factory premises during work hours for more than three days constituted grounds for dismissal and could lead to the loss of accumulated benefits. After the failed meeting with Hirth, the women remained in the workshops, not leaving even for lunch for fear of being locked out of the factory. But otherwise "busy hands stood still," so that at the end of the workday "less than a quarter of the usual quantity of cigarettes had been delivered."[84]

Slowdown, in American trade union practice sometimes described as "goldbricking," had as its objective to reduce the anticipated volume of production to obtain concessions from management. Researchers investigating the practice during the 1950s argued that slowdowns were used as a tactic especially by workers doing piecework, often with the aim of lowering production quotas that were considered too high. Generally, the method required a high degree of solidarity on shop floors since a slowdown is of consequence only if a cumulative effect is achieved. The tactic could be quite discreet, in that in most factories it was still difficult to pinpoint who had started the slowdown, who was intentionally participating in it and who was simply suffering the consequences of others' slowness.[85] This meant that workers at risk could protect themselves more from dismissal, the tactic was less disruptive than a full-blown strike and it could be used especially when the workers involved had little job security.

One day after the beginning of the slowdown, most of the workers in the factory joined this "passive resistance" initiated by women pieceworkers. Circumventing the regulation that they could be dismissed after three days of being absent, the women arrived at work on time but did not start work at their tables, milling about in their locker area instead.

[82] Anonymous (1906a).

[83] Jemnitz (1963).

[84] Anonymous (1911j).

[85] Hammett, Seidman and London (1957, p. 126).

Other workers who depended on the work done by the women could also not do much, and increasingly would not.[86]

Workers demanded a general increase in wages and an increase in the level of their pensions, pointing out that the pensions of the tobacco workers from the Austrian side of the monarchy had already been increased. They claimed that for years management had been making promises about an increase in wages.[87] Three days after the slowdown began, Minister Counsellor Haracsek travelled from Budapest to Kolozsvár to appease the workers. In meetings with workers from each workshop, he promised that a wage increase might be possible the following month.[88] As the workers felt they had been deluded with promises for several years, they continued their slowdown.

Haracsek ordered the workers on slowdown out of the factory and barred their return to the premises. The move meant the Directorate was willing to risk a strike, and thus a stoppage in production, in the hope that the threat of having everyone dismissed would make workers drop their demands. The now locked-out workers formed a strike committee and asked the authorities for permission to picket in front of the factory.

When strikers arrived in the afternoon for their picket, the police violently disbanded their protest. At the end of that day, the Tobacco Directorate issued an ultimatum: workers could either return to work by 4 May or be dismissed. Once the slowdown had become a strike and an ultimatum issued, the involvement of local social-democrats in helping to organise the workers became visible. On 3 May, Izsák Berkovics and Gyula Tatay, representing the Social Democratic Party leadership and both editors of the party's *Erdélyi Munkás*, encouraged workers to hold out on strike, offering financial support for the strikers while encouraging them to organise in a trade union.[89]

The city authorities' investment in social peace at the local tobacco factory was also rendered more visible, as had been the case in 1897. The mayor of Kolozsvár asked the strikers to return to work for two weeks while waiting for a final decision of the Directorate on the matter of planned wage increases. At this point, most of the women workers

[86] Anonymous (1911g).

[87] Anonymous (1911h).

[88] Anonymous (1911g).

[89] Anonymous (1911d).

decided to continue with their strike, while knowing they were taking a great risk with their stable, albeit underpaid and deeply unhealthy work.[90] On 5 May, with only 133 workers reporting for work, a notice that the factory would be closed indefinitely was posted on the factory gate. The women on strike subsequently launched an appeal, distributing a leaflet on 18 May among the citizens of Kolozsvár, asking for support for themselves and their children and urging any member of the public who wanted to help to contact them via the Trade Union Council secretariat ("*Szakszervezeti Tanács titkársága*"), located in "Kolozsvár, Mátyás király street 4."[91]

Hirth, they stated, had been interrogating various workers in his office in an attempt to learn who were the leaders of the protest. Asking "who is an agitator (...) Mr. Hirth?," they urged he "just reach up to the shelves... where the payrolls are" to identify the actual source of the discontent. They denounced him for behaving not like the father figure he often claimed to be but with the arrogance of a medieval lord of the castle. By contrast, the women claimed to have been good paternalist subjects. Rather than making their demands in a spirit of human dignity, as they could have, they had appeared humbly at the door of his office, having believed management promises and waited patiently for their raise. They also referred to women workers' participation in the (gendered) rituals of citizenship in Hungary, mentioning how on Children's Day that year they had donated for the benefit of poor children. The women signatories argued that despite their donations to charity, they were now seeing their own children threatened by hunger. They concluded: "In the wretched hovels of our homes, our children weep with hunger, their anguished sobs blessing the fatherly kindness of the tobacco factory director."[92]

As the standoff between management and workers continued after mid-May 1911, several representatives of the city of Kolozsvár sought to have the ear of the Tobacco Directorate. Local members of a city council that was not known for being either too progressive or worker friendly travelled to Budapest to speak to the heads of the Directorate on behalf of the women who had been locked out. Repeatedly, Tobacco

[90] Anonymous (1911c).

[91] Anonymous (1911e).

[92] Ibid.

Directorate representatives argued that they had no intention of negotiating with either the workers, who had sent also their own representative, or their intermediaries. According to *Népszava*, Tobacco Directorate officials made it explicit that they were adopting a hard line because if wages were increased for the women workers of the Kolozsvár tobacco factory, women workers in Budapest factories would immediately make similar demands.[93]

When the factory reopened, at the end of May, strikers faced retaliation. After holding out for several weeks, 800 women who reapplied for work were asked to line up in the factory yard. The women who were identified as agitators were rudely chased away. Then every third woman lined up in the yard was told she was dismissed and would no longer have access to the pension into which some of them had been paying via the Tobacco Insurance Fund for decades. "Now you can strike forever," they were told.[94] New workers were recruited to make up for most of the dismissals.

It is unclear if up to the eve of World War I labour organising in the Kolozsvár tobacco factory further intensified or whether labour conditions and pay improved. Between 1914 and 1918 the Kolozsvár factory functioned at reduced capacity, producing only lower-quality cigarettes to supply the front.[95] After 1918, women workers' labour activism in the factory was periodically noticeable, as for instance in the late 1920s. However, such moments of contestation took place in quite different circumstances, as the city became part of the Kingdom of Romania and the factory was incorporated into the Romanian Régie of State Monopolies. In this new Romanian context, the key factory-based workers' welfare facilities were kept but became part of a broader attempt to transform the city through rapid nationalisation.[96]

The tobacco factory became a preoccupation for an emerging network of Romanian-speaking social reform actors, who, in the early 1920s, were encouraged by the Régie to become involved in factory-based welfare institutions and practices.[97] Thus, in 1920, the "Prince Mircea" women's

[93] Anonymous (1911f).

[94] Ibid.

[95] Monografia fabricii 1851–1930 [Factory monograph 1851–1930]: 5.

[96] Livezeanu (2000). Ghiț (2023, p. 15).

[97] Stanca (1927, pp. 18, 30).

society, focused on children's welfare, was appointed to manage the on-site crèche that had been functioning in the factory since the 1890s.[98] The "Prince Mircea" Society for the Protection of Children was one of a plethora of women's societies founded after World War I. It focused on healthcare for children, was generously subsidised by the Direction of Social Assistance in the Ministry of Labour and enjoyed the patronage of Queen Marie of Romania.[99] The social reformers included middle-class women's organisations and physicians; the latter were interested in social medicine, industrial hygiene and the "social hygiene" strand of eugenics which focused on welfare policies to improve the health of ethnic Romanians in Transylvania.[100] The social reformers sought to de-link the factory from some of the Austria-Hungary-specific networks that had shaped its existence in the previous 60 years, and instead link it to networks that were beginning to define a post-imperial world, including those forged between European scientists and American institutions such as the Rockefeller Foundation.[101] In this context, the factory was left with a heavily constrained labour movement, which built on the history of trade unionism as it had developed in the factory since the 1890s, with only limited success.[102]

Conclusion

As I document here, the increase of women workers in the successful consolidation of the Hungarian state tobacco monopoly, aimed at keeping production costs down, was accompanied by a back-and-forth between state policies of labour restriction and appeasement and the protests of an increasingly organised female labour force. The history of the Transylvanian Kolozsvár factory in the late Austro-Hungarian Empire evidences how women developed a new dynamic of labour organisation, adapted to their own ends. Their protests, strikes and slowdowns helped ensure social improvements for those working in the factories and a strengthening and expansion of the workers' movement.

[98] Stanca (1927, p. 18).

[99] Asociaţia Ştiinţifică pentru Enciclopedia României (1938, p. 529).

[100] Bucur (2002, p. 48).

[101] Weindling (1993).

[102] Ghiţ (2020). Ghiţ (2023, p. 16).

The 1897 strike reveals how the women tobacco workers' demands ushered in a period of factory-based, partly locally funded, welfare institutions and paternalistic practices. The limited success of the labour movement in the later period, however, can be seen as the flip side of this, leading to a consolidation of the state tobacco monopoly and a strengthening of its labour policies. The strikes and the alliance of the tobacco workers with socialist and social-democratic initiatives after the 1890s heralded a change in state labour policy from a paternalistic and benevolent approach to one of cost cutting. After 1911, the intensification of the pace of work accelerated and was accompanied by lower piece rate pay, so that workers opted for a failed slowdown that resulted in mass dismissal and an undercutting of women's labour organising.

After World War I, the newly expanded Romanian state was able to draw on structures and experience in the control of female factory workers that state officials had successfully assembled and applied to consolidate and expand the administrations of the state tobacco organisation in Transylvania within the Hungarian Kingdom. This is suggestive of how state monopoly longevity in tobacco, during a time of increasing global liberalisation of the tobacco economy, at least in regard to a trend of dissolution of state monopoly organisations, was to a significant extent grounded on the monopoly's ability to manage protest. The emergence of a better organised female labour force had represented a challenge, one which the monopoly was able to contain to its advantage.

Women's work in tobacco manufacturing was clearly instrumental to capital accumulation, with the state in the Hungarian case becoming the main employer of women workers in industry and engaging in the development of social policies specific to this sector. This was not unique to Transylvania, a region on the supposed periphery of Europe, but was also to be observed in the apparent centres, such as the state-owned factories of the French tobacco monopoly in Paris or the privately operated factories in the Southern German states. The extent to which the successes and failures of the Hungarian tobacco monopoly's back-and-forth between control measures and worker protest and the containment of the women's organisation were replicated in other states, however, remains to be seen.

Acknowledgements This work has received funding from the European Research Council (ERC) under the European Union's Horizon 2020 research and innovation programme (Grant agreement No. 833691). Susan Zimmermann provided highly relevant Hungarian language scholarly and newspaper articles and pointed me towards the statistical yearbooks available online. Farkas Sipos Erika Márta and Simongáti-Farquhar András kindly checked the accuracy of Hungarian to English automatic translations Varsa Eszter kindly helped me double-check the Hungarian in the proofs stage. Early versions of this chapter benefited from the comments and feedback of colleagues in the ZARAH project.

References

Primary Sources

Unpublished

Arhivele Naţionale ale României, Direcţia Judeţeană a Arhivelor Naţionale Covasna, Sfântu Gheorghe, Romania.

- Fond 179 - Întreprinderea de Ţigarete Cluj, File 40/1966.

Published

A M. Kir. Kormány 1906. *Évi működéséről és az ország közállapotairól szóló jelentés és statisztikai évkönyv 1905* [The Royal Hungarian Government Annual Report and Statistical Yearbook for 1905]. Budapest: Nyomdai Részvénytársulat Könyvnyomdája.

A M. Kir. Kormány 1914. *Évi működéséről és az ország közállapotairól szóló jelentés és statisztikai évkönyv 1912* [The Royal Hungarian Government Annual Report and Statistical Yearbook for 1912]. Budapest: Az Athenaeum Irodalmi és Nyomdai Részvénytársulat Könyvnyomdája.

Anonymous. 1882. Munkásnők harcza [The Fight of the Female Workers]. *Ellenzék*. 16 August.

Anonymous. 1886. Dohánygyári munkásnők strájkja [Tobacco Factory Female Workers' Strike]. *Pesti Hírlap*. 14 January.

Anonymous. 1887. Nők strike-ja [Women's Strike]. *Fővárosi Lapok*. 9 September.

Anonymous. 1896. Sztrájk az adó miatt [Strike over Tax]. *Kis Ujság*. 23 October.

Anonymous. 1897a. A kolozsvári sztrájk [The Kolozsvár Strike]. *Magyarország*. 25 March.

Anonymous. 1897b. A kolozsvári sztrájk [The Kolozsvár Strike]. *Budapesti Hírlap*. 25 March.

Anonymous. 1897c. Miskolcz nem liczitál. [Miskolcz Does Not Bid]. *Szabadság*. 16 January.

Anonymous. 1897d. Munkássztrájk Kolozsvártt [Workers' Strike in Kolozsvár]. *Magyarország - Reggeli Magyarország*. 24 March.

Anonymous. 1897e. Sztrájk a dohánygyárban [Strike in the Tobacco Factory]. *Magyar Polgár - Kolozsvár*. 23 March.

Anonymous. 1898. A dohánygyár majálisa [Tobacco Factory May Festival]. *Magyar Polgár - Kolozsvár*. 23 May.

Anonymous. 1900a. Iparosok szövetkezetei [Industrialists' Cooperatives]. *Hazánk*. 15 September.
Anonymous. 1900b. Városi közgyűlés [Municipal Assembly]. *Magyar Polgár - Kolozsvár*. 27 September.
Anonymous. 1901. A dohánygyár ünnepe [The Anniversary of the Tobacco Factory]. *Magyar Polgár – Kolozsvár*. 31 August.
Anonymous. 1903a. A dohánygyári munkások tiltakozása [The Tobacco Factory Workers' Protest]. *Magyar Polgár - Kolozsvár*. 4 August.
Anonymous. 1903b. Rablógazdálkodás a kolozsvári dohánygyárban [Robber Management in the Tobacco Factory in Kolozsvár]. *Erdélyi Munkás*. 1 August.
Anonymous. 1906a. Az öngyilkos építőmester [The Suicidal Builder]. *Pesti Napló*. 9 November.
Anonymous. 1909. A kolozsvári szakszervezetek [The Trade Unions in Kolozsvár]. *Pesti Hírlap*. 20 January.
Anonymous. 1911a. A kolozsvári sztrájk [The Strike in Kolozsvár]. *Az Ujság*. 15 January 1909.
Anonymous. 1911b. 2,600 munkást kizártak—A Kolozsvári állami dohánygyárból [2,600 Workers Locked Out—From the Kolozsvár State Tobacco Factory]. 26 April.
Anonymous. 1911c. A kolozsvári dohánygyári sztrájk [The Strike at the Tobacco Factory in Kolozsvár]. *Budapesti Hírlap*. 4 May.
Anonymous. 1911d. A kolozsvári dohánygyári sztrájk [The Strike at the Tobacco Factory in Kolozsvár]. *Világ*. 4 May.
Anonymous. 1911e. A kolozsvári nagy kizárás [The Great Kolozsvár Lockout]. *Népszava*. 18 May.
Anonymous. 1911f. "Csak éhezzenek a disznók, ha sztrájkolni tudtak!" A Kolozsvári dohánygyári harc [Let the Pigs Starve If They Can Go on Strike! The Conflict at the Tobacco Factory in Kolozsvár]. *Népszava*. 2 June.
Anonymous. 1911g. Dohánygyári munkások sztrájkja [Strike by Tobacco Factory Workers]. *Pesti Hírlap*. 26 April.
Anonymous. 1911h. Sztrájk a kolozsvári dohánygyárban [Strike at the Tobacco Factory in Kolozsvár]. *Népszava*. 22 April.
Anonymous. 1911i. Sztrájk a kolozsvári dohánygyárban [Strike at the Tobacco Factory in Kolozsvár]. *Pesti Hírlap*. 21 April.
Anonymous. 1911j. Sztrájk a kolozsvári dohánygyárban [Strike at the Tobacco Factory in Kolozsvár]. *Világ*. 23 April.
Asociaţia Ştiinţifică pentru Enciclopedia României. 1938. *Enciclopedia României* [Encyclopedia of Romania]. vol. 1. Bucharest, Romania: Imprimeriile Naţionale.
Bányász, L. 1906a. *munkásviszonyok és munkásjóléti intézmények a m. kir. dohánygyárakban* [Working Conditions and Workers' Conditions and Workers'

Welfare Institutions in the Royal Tobacco Factories]. Közgazdasági Szemle 36(3): 577–590.

Bányász, L. 1906b. *Munkásjóléti intézmények a m. kir. dohánygyárakban* [Workers' Welfare Institutions in the Royal Tobacco Factories]. *Közgazdasági Szemle* 36(6): 805–829.

Járó, K. 1883. A legjobb minőségű ... [The Best Quality...]. *Ellenzék*. 15 November.

Magyar Tudományos Akadémia. 1896. *Közgazdasági és statisztikai évkönyv 1894–1895* [Economic and Statistical Yearbook 1894–1895]. Budapest: Athenaeum Részvénytársulat.

Stanca, D. 1927. *Organizarea igienico-socială a muncii. O anchetă sanitară la Fabrica de Tutun din Cluj* [The Hygenic-Social Organisation of Labour. A Sanitary Inquiry in the Cluj Tobacco Factory]. Cluj Napoca: Imprimeria Dr. Sebastian Bornemisa.

Wickett, S.M. 1897. Studien über das Österreichische Tabakmonopol. *FinanzArchiv/Public Finance Analysis* 14: 198–284.

Secondary Sources

Allen, R.C. 2009. Engels' Pause: Technical Change, Capital Accumulation, and Inequality in the British Industrial Revolution. *Explorations in Economic History* 46: 418–435.

Bauer, I. 2015. *"Tschikweiber haums uns g'nennt..." Die Zigarrenfabriksarbeiterinnen von Hallein: Frauen, Arbeit, Geschichte*. Berlin: Die Buchmacherei.

Berend, I.T., and G. Ránki. 1980. *Underdevelopment in Europe in the Context of East-West Relations in the Nineteenth Century*. Budapest: Akadémiai Kiadó.

Bucur, M. 2002. *Eugenics and Modernization in Interwar Romania*. Pittsburgh: University of Pittsburgh Press.

Csóka, J. 1958. Az egri dohánygyár 60 éve, 1895–1955 [The Eger Tobacco Factory at 60]. *Az Egri Pedagógiai Főiskola Évkönyve - Acta Academiae Paedagogicae Agriensis* 4: 375–397.

Cvrcek, T. 2013. Wages, Prices, and Living Standards in the Habsburg Empire, 1827–1910. *The Journal of Economic History* 73: 1–37.

Deac, A. 1962. *Mişcarea muncitorească din Transilvania, 1890–1895* [The Labour Movement in Transylvania, 1890–1895]. Bucharest: Editura Ştiinţifică.

Drosick, S.D. 1976. *The Agrarian Socialist Movement in Hungary 1890–1899*. Ph.D. Dissertation: Columbia University.

Egyed, A. 1957. *Despre miscarea muncitoreasca din Transilvania intre anii 1880-1890* [On the Labour Movement in Transylvania Between 1880–1890]. *Studii - Revista de Istorie* 10: 33–56.

Egyed, A. 1959. Grevele de seceriş din Transilvania de la sfârşitul sec. XIX şi începutul sec. XX [Harvest strikes in Transylvania from the end of the XIXth and the beginning of the XXth centuries]. *Anuarul Institutului de Istorie din Cluj* I–II: 219–40.

Fodor, I., and L. Vajda. 1957. *Contribuţii la istoria mişcării sindicale din Transilvania: 1848–1917* [Contributions to the History of the Trade Union Movement in Transylvania 1848–1917]. Bucharest: Editura Consiliului Central al Sindicatelor.

Ghiţ, A. 2020. Re-Reading Local Sources: Finding Gendered Trade Unionism in a Transylvanian Factory Newspaper. *ZARAH Blog*. https://zarah-ceu.org/re-reading-local-sources-finding-gendered-trade-unionism-in-a-transylvanian-factory-newspaper/. Accessed 3. January 2024.

Ghiţ, A. 2023. Gendered Work, Skill, and Women's Labor Activism in Romanian Tobacco Factories from the 1920s to the 1960s. *International Labor and Working-Class History* 104:11–31.

Hammett, R.S., J. Seidman, and J. London. 1957. The Slowdown as a Union Tactic. *Journal of Political Economy* 65: 126–134.

Horváth, Z. 1999. The Metropolitan Press. *East Central Europe* 26: 73–86.

Jemnitz, J. 1963. The Relations of the American and the Americo-Hungarian Labour Movements as Revealed in the Correspondence of Ervin Szabó. *Acta Historica Academiæ Scientiarum Hungaricæ* 9: 179–214.

Képes, G. 2019. A magyar dohánypiaci szabályozás története az osztrák-magyar kiegyezés fényében [The history of Hungarian tobacco market regulation in the light of the Austro-Hungarian Compromise]. *Acta Universitatis Szegediensis: Forum: Acta Juridica et Politica* 9(1): 57–83.

Livezeanu, I. 2000. *Cultural Politics in Greater Romania: Regionalism, Nation Building, and Ethnic Struggle, 1918–1930*. Ithaca: Cornell University Press.

Mérey, K.T. 1997. A pécsi dohánygyár dolgozói, 1912-1948 [The Workers of the Tobacco Factory in Pecs, 1912–1948]. *Történelmi Szemle* 39: 237–256.

Myrdal, G. 1957. *Economic Theory and Under-Developed Regions*. London: G. Duckworth.

Nemes, R. 2016. *Another Hungary: The Nineteenth-Century Provinces in Eight Lives*. Stanford: Stanford University Press.

Reid, D. 1985. Industrial Paternalism: Discourse and Practice in Nineteenth-Century French Mining and Metallurgy. *Comparative Studies in Society and History* 27: 579–607.

Szávai, F. 2012. The Late Industrial Revolution in Hungary (1867–1918). In *Hungary and the Hungarians*, ed. S.J. Magyarody. Budapest: Matthias Corvinus Publishers.

Szikra, D. 2004. The Thorny Path to Implementation: Bismarckian Social Insurance in Hungary in the Late 19th Century. *European Journal of Social Security* 6: 255–272.

Ternay, K. 1957. Hungarian Journalism 1900–1943. *Gazette* 3: 131–137.
Trode, R. 2022. The Sarajevo Tobacco Factory Strike of 1906: Empire and the Nature of Late Habsburg Rule in Bosnia and Herzegovina. *Central European History* 55: 493–509.
Varsa, E. 2022. 'Let Us All Stand Under the Banner of Freedom and Sisterly Love': Gender, Anarchist Thought and Women in the Agrarian Socialist Movement in Hungary and Internationally. *ZARAH Blog*. https://zarah-ceu.org/let-us-all-stand-under-the-banner-of-freedom-and-sisterly-love-gender-anarchist-thought-and-women-in-the-agrarian-socialist-movement-in-hungary-and-internationally/. Accessed 3 January 2024.
Varsa, E. 2024. "The Women of Viharsarok: Peasant Women's Labour Activism in 1890s Hungary." *International Review of Social History* 69, 1: 99–126. https://doi.org/10.1017/S0020859024000130.
Weindling, P. 1993. Public Health and Political Stabilisation: The Rockefeller Foundation in Central and Eastern Europe Between the Two World Wars. *Minerva* 31: 253–267.
Wernitznig, D. 2022. Rauchzeichen: Tabakproduktion und Gender im globalen und historiographischen Kontext. *Österreichische Zeitschrift für Geschichtswissenschaften* 33: 58–78.
Zimmermann, S. 2011. *Divide, Provide and Rule: An Integrative, History of Poverty Policy, Social Policy, and Social Reform in Hungary Under the Habsburg Monarchy*. Budapest: Central European University Press.

CHAPTER 12

Global Labour and Management Migrations: BAT-China, 1910s–1930s

Nan Enstad

On a typical 1920s weekday in Pudong, China, thousands of workers and hundreds of supervisors and managers poured through the British American Tobacco Company (BAT) factory gates for the start of the workday. Virtually everyone had migrated to be there, whether from Britain, the US, India, or multiple regions in China. Workers checked in by their assigned number rather than by name because of the many languages and dialects spoken there. Once through the gates, workers streamed to their workshops and managers to their offices and, as they did so, they sorted into job classifications determined by gender and native place origin.

Fully two-thirds of the workers and floor supervisors were young Chinese women; their jobs were considered less skilled and paid less than jobs held by male workers. Women workers were further sorted into the job hierarchy by regional origin, with women from rural provinces working in the less desirable, dirtier, and lowest paid positions. Male

N. Enstad (✉)
University of Wisconsin, Madison, WI, USA
e-mail: nenstad@wisc.edu

A. van Wickeren et al. (eds.), *Tobacco in Global Perspective, 1780–1960*, Cambridge Imperial and Post-Colonial Studies,
https://doi.org/10.1007/978-3-031-64411-5_12

workers, likewise, worked with, and under the supervision of, men from their native place and were further sorted into job hierarchies by age, with young men and boys earning less. White managers from the US South and Britain occupied the main offices with Chinese office staff. This complex and teaming production force gathered each day with one directive: to produce thousands upon thousands of cigarettes for the vast and still barely tapped Chinese and East Asian markets.

This chapter explores how BAT-China generated new labour flows and labour management systems, considering especially the question of the production of difference. At the turn of the twentieth century, the global tobacco and cigarette industry occupied the cutting edge of capitalism's increasing capacity to initiate labour flows and manage large and diverse workforces. By looking at the case of BAT-China, this chapter argues first that tobacco companies, along with textiles and garments, innovated by drawing on young female labour, making "girls" as labourers central to their business model, a phenomenon that is widely known but chronically undertheorised. Second, expansionist tobacco companies also relied on a global migration of managers well-versed in running factories based on machine production. In BAT-China, many such managers hailed from the US South and implemented management techniques learned under Jim Crow segregation, making revisions in concert with Chinese supervisors. While race did not pertain in the same way in China, managers utilised Jim Crow segregation as a model for the "production of difference"[1] through categories of age, gender, and native place.

For decades, many scholars privileged class division as an inherent force in capitalism and saw managers' deployment of race, native place, gender, and age difference in job recruitment, assignment, and supervision as a manipulation of identities that fragmented the working class or, at worst, slowed class consciousness. Drawing on Marx's notion of abstract labour, these scholars saw capitalism's effect primarily as homogenising: it standardised workers' movements, deskilled the work process, and thereby eliminated the significance of differences between workers. The dynamic development of a working class, by this view, is the relevant focus for understanding capitalism; differences of gender and race are fixed, pre-capitalist and secondary.

[1] Lowe (2009) and Roediger and Esch (2012).

This view has faced a host of challenges over decades, from feminist historians who documented the significance of women to the capitalist workplace rather than only to family and reproduction, to historians of race who argued that global capitalism's origins lie in plantation slavery, not solely in the industrial workshop. This chapter takes on one portion of this vast topic, drawing on recent scholarship that analyses how managers not only utilised categories of gender, race, and native place to divide or segment the workforce but actively produced such categories. It does so by exploring the production of difference at two levels: the inducement of labour flows and strategies of factory-floor management.

Successful capitalist expansion across most of the globe in the early twentieth century relied centrally on the establishment of factory infrastructures and labour forces. Today, finance capital likely would be the primary point of inquiry for understanding a similar degree of expansion because companies may produce in few places and ship product cheaply across long distances. At the turn of the twentieth century, though the steamship had greatly reduced time and cost of transport, perishability and transport costs remained significant concerns, including for cigarettes. In addition, national tariffs and battles over exclusive, nation-based patents for machinery—again, including new cigarette machines—accentuated the importance of factory production in key national markets. Companies with ambitions for global expansion prioritised purchasing or building factories and retaining or constituting a workforce.[2] When BAT set its sights on a truly global market, then, it focused on factories and workers as much as on finance and technology.

BAT-China offers an especially interesting case for the investigation of labour migration and the production of managerial hierarchies because the transnational corporation built a massive factory system in China from scratch. When BAT's precursor, the American Tobacco Company (ATC), began its 1890s merger spree, taking over companies across the US as well as in Mexico, Europe, and Japan, its method was to force the purchase of an existing cigarette factory. Once the purchase was secured, the corporation sent a small number of executives and managers to slowly revamp the functioning of the existing factory while keeping most local supervisors and workers in place. Indeed, former company owners often became factory managers. In 1902, ATC merged with Britain's Imperial

[2] Enstad (2018) and Beckert (2014).

Tobacco Company (ITC) to form BAT, one of the world's first multinational corporations, and BAT continued the ATC strategy. However, BAT's 1905 expansion into China relied on a purchased factory that was no longer functioning. Unlike most other BAT acquisitions, the Chinese factory had no workforce, no trained managers, no branded products, and no established markets. But the factory did have the exclusive rights in China to the Bonsack cigarette machine and the shared, extravagant rights for foreign-owned companies in Chinese treaty ports. To expand in China, BAT had no choice but to constitute the entire corporate and factory hierarchy on site, from executives to managers to factory-floor supervisors to workers of many classifications.[3]

The chapter begins with a discussion of scholarship on abstract labour and the production of difference. It moves from there to the topic of how the tobacco industry, including BAT-China, accessed labour flows via the production of difference, especially its participation in the production of girls as a significant global capitalist labour flow of the late nineteenth and early twentieth centuries. This section also examines the migration of white male managers from the US and Britain in the constitution of BAT-China's corporate structure and factory workforce. While the question of labour flows and migration takes a bird's-eye view of the industry, the production of difference also occurs at the granular level of everyday life at the factory. This chapter therefore also investigates how the struggle between management and labour shaped the meaning of categories of difference within the everyday management of workers' movements in the factories.

Abstract Labour and the Production of Difference

Scholars have recently revised understandings of how capitalism produces homogeneity and difference. Certainly, the foundational role of slavery, racism, and white supremacy in capitalism is now widely accepted, overturning an earlier interpretation that tied capitalist development exclusively to the industrial factory and cast slavery as pre-industrial. Historians have definitively demonstrated that financialisation, plantation economies of scale, global commodity markets, and the dispossession and

[3] Enstad (2018). Cox (2000). Cochran (1980) and Perry (1993).

subjugation of labour made the institution of slavery a central location for capitalism's development.[4] Historians have also demonstrated that capitalism relied on racialised workforces across the globe in the nineteenth and twentieth centuries and have tracked their histories, which has required an implicit or explicit shift in understandings of class and the function of abstract labour. In addition, social scientists have created a body of literature on the global 'feminisation of labour' in industry since 1980 and its impact on models of national citizenship.[5] I engage here with a subset of these scholars who focus explicitly on how capitalism not only utilises but produces differences, including race, gender, age, and native place, and who make their theoretical interventions explicit.[6]

Understandings of capital that sidelined difference had been based partly on Karl Marx's notion of abstract labour. Marx argued that capitalism's development relied on the abstraction of labour, that is, the removal of idiosyncrasies of workers' personality, culture, and identity in order to standardise the function of labour. The abstraction of labour is epitomised by the machine's imposition of isolated, repetitive movements on the worker—any worker—at a particular point of the factory assembly line. The abstraction of labour includes deskilling work tasks, limiting advancement, and lowering wages.[7] The abstraction of labour did not only serve capitalist profit but made possible the ideas of global labour and an international working class that were critical to the rise of a global labour movement. As Lisa Lowe argued, an immigrant woman of colour making a garment in a Los Angeles sweatshop may be seen as fundamentally part of the same workforce as a migrant woman making a similar garment in Taiwan, Thailand, or China, even when she worked for a different contractor, who supplied to a different corporation.[8] Such workers make many of the same movements, draw a similarly low wage, and face a similar kind of workplace precarity and discipline. Michael Denning points out that even our idea of 'labour' as a global category, separate from this task, that place, these workers, is indebted to the process of abstract

[4] Robinson (1983). Johnson (2013). Baptist (2014). Beckert (2014) and Jenkins and Leroy (2021).

[5] Lowe (2009) and Ong (1999).

[6] Lowe (1996). Lowe (2009) and Roediger and Esch (2012).

[7] Chakrabarty (2000).

[8] Lowe (2009).

labour.[9] The homogenising force of capitalism is an undeniable factor in BAT-China, as managers from Britain and the US sought to train a new workforce to use Bonsack cigarette machines, much as workers did in New York City, Liverpool, Dresden, Mexico City, and many other places.

Though the abstraction of labour is a function of capitalist industrial workplaces, capitalism both has a homogenising impact and produces categories of difference like race, native-place origin, gender, and age.[10] Critics of labour systems have long argued that managers *exploited* lines of difference to divide workers and set them against each other. The use of workers of colour or women as strikebreakers for a white male workforce is an example of this, as is the segmentation of the positions by race, native place, gender, or age. Lowe, however, went further, arguing that the *production* of difference is as important to capitalist profits as abstraction. As Lowe wrote, "In the history of the United States, capital has maximized it profits not through rendering labor 'abstract' but precisely through the social production of 'difference',... marked by race, nation, geographic origins, and gender."[11] Lowe was part of a wave of scholarship in literary studies, sociology and anthropology confronting capitalist globalisation, the feminisation of the low-wage labour force globally, and its implications for racialised gender, citizenship, and precarity.[12] Lowe argued that Marx's theory of abstract labour was not able to account for the "racialized relations of production" historically nor the post-1980 turn to "racialized immigrant female labor." Weakening national boundaries and "eroding national political institutions like citizenship" created new precarities for migrants; companies responded by creating profitable labour flows based in differences of race, gender, age, and native origin.[13]

Historians David Roediger and Elizabeth Esch applied Lowe's theoretical foundation to the history of labour management practices in the US, finding that the production of difference as a capitalist technique has its roots in the management of enslaved people. By drawing on professional management literature produced decades before scientific management, when many historians see management literature originating, they clearly

[9] Denning (2007).

[10] Lowe (2009). Roediger and Esch (2012) and Esch (2018).

[11] Lowe (1996, p. 25).

[12] Ong (1999). Sassen and Hong (2006).

[13] Lowe (2009, pp. 182, 183).

demonstrated the intentional development of management techniques that constructed new racialised structures, meanings, and values. They also developed an idea of "whiteness-as-management," by which they meant that white manhood in the nineteenth-century US came to mean that one was civilised, rational, and a manager of both household (women and children) and workers. By conflating management with whiteness and maleness,[14] whiteness-as-management became an embodied racialised and gendered practice, not just a set of techniques. While "whiteness-as-management" first developed in the context of slavery, Roediger and Esch argued, it became fundamental to the expansion of the US West, imperialist ventures, and the mobilisation of numerous other labour flows, including the global migration of Chinese male workers. Managers as well as workers are produced historically via regimes of racial difference.

Considering "Girls" as a Global Labour Flow

Despite drawing on Lowe, Roediger and Esch paid minimal attention to women or girls as workers. Whatever the reason for this omission, it a serious one for work that purports to analyse capitalism and difference in the late nineteenth and early twentieth centuries. The migration and employment of girls of many nations and races was integral to the expansion of at least three global industries, each so large that it has been taken as paradigmatic of capitalism itself: cotton textiles, garments, and tobacco, especially cigars and cigarettes. Because both regional and international migrations are central to this deployment, "girls" should be seen as a major global labour flow in this period, nearly one hundred years before the so-called feminisation of industrial labour post-1980. Historians of gender have worked for decades to demonstrate the centrality of women's labour globally in the capitalist transformation from 1870 to 1930, but the significance of this global labour flow to broader histories and theories of capitalism is still muted in scholarship.[15]

Girls may seem not to fit the definition of a large labour flow because they do not originate from a single region, like the flow from Africa's west coast in the slave trade or the migration from the Guangdong region of China in the so-called coolie trade. Likewise, they vary by race and ethnic

[14] Roediger and Esch (2012, p. 14).

[15] Maynes and Waltner (2018).

origin and do not share a culture. Their migration cannot, therefore, be likened to a diaspora. Nevertheless, there was a global pattern of labour migration of girls from rural to urban areas, both within nations and internationally, for industrial work in factories. This labour flow grew out of the disruption of rural family-based economic systems that included women's home production. Sometimes, young women migrated alone, and at other times they were part of a family migration. Even when part of a family migration, women sorted into a particular job classification for girls at their destination.

Gender historians indicate that the factory labour category of girls emerged globally (but not everywhere identically) first within the textile industry as their proto-industrial market activity in textiles moved outside the home to the factory setting. Spinning in Europe, the US and China were firmly established as women's work; weaving also fell to women in China. It is important to recognise, then, that the shift was not from reproductive to productive/market labour but from home to factory of an essentially similar labour. In addition, such home labour had widely worked in concert with agriculture to support families. Understanding how the category of girls emerged as a wage-labour category in different countries' textile industries requires careful parsing of the interrelationship between changing agricultural economies and opportunities for wage work, the increasing need for cash, and shifting household economic strategic decisions, including age of marriage and use of child labour.[16] Maynes and Waltner point out that rural families in Europe shifted to a later age of marriage for women by the seventeenth century largely to promote land ownership before childbearing began. With marriage ages of 20 or even higher for women, Europe was an outlier. Some historians believe that this landowner strategy, generating a supply of single women who could do wage work, was a critical factor that allowed Europe to advance rapidly in industrialised textiles in the decades around 1800.

Some historians treat gender, age, and marital status as self-evident demographic categories but others point out that a new category of girls was being socially constructed. Gender and childhood historians have argued that this transformation was a critical moment in the development of notions of adolescence and girlhood as a stage of life.[17] The emerging

[16] Maynes and Waltner (2018). Boydston (1996) and Honig (1986).

[17] O'Dowd and Purvis (2018).

labour category of girls, then, must be seen in more than demographic terms. By the 1870–1930 period, when girls became known as a labour force across the globe, the meaning of that category the meaning of that category varied greatly. Girls could be anywhere from 9 to 30 years old—their status being defined as much by holding the job as by their birthdate. They also were widely seen as single, but the reality varied greatly, with married and widowed women also working. One cigarette worker I interviewed in North Carolina began working in the 1920s at age 13, the same year that she married.[18] In China, enough young female cigarette workers were married and mothers that the company had to develop a maternity policy. How the category of girls travelled between different places and industries deserves much more attention. What is clear is that the industry definition of them as single and young justified paying them poorly in relationship to married male workers, even though many were heads of households.

The international ready-made garment industry also relied primarily on girls during the period 1870–1930, spurring intra- and international labour migrations.[19] New York City became the centre of global industrial production of inexpensive clothing, but it was by no means alone: factory manufacturing sprang up in cities around the world. The industry drew on a combination of women's home work and factory work. As with textiles, though girls were central to the business model, companies defined them as inherently auxiliary—and therefore worthy of less pay—because of their subservient place in the patriarchal family ideal, regardless of their actual circumstances.

The international tobacco industry turned to girls first in the emerging cheap cigar sector in the 1870s in order to deskill what had been a male artisanal system.[20] Cigar company owners created a deskilled component of the industry in the late nineteenth century in pursuit of the cheap five-cent cigar. Cigars were de rigueur for business deals in the US and Europe and, once the cheap cigars hit the market, the cigar became a massively successful tobacco product. Though there would be no machines that could manage the tight rolling of a cigar for several decades, cigar employers introduced moulds to create a uniform shape

[18] Enstad (2018).

[19] Guglielmo (2010). Gabaccia (2000). Hewitt (2001) and Tilburg (2019).

[20] Cooper (1987) and Hewitt (2001).

and segmented and standardised the labour process so that rolling a perfect shape became a guarantee rather than a skilled accomplishment. With skill less important, cigar employers increased the size of operations to take advantage of economies of scale. The result was a two-tier cigar industry divided by quality, price, and type of worker.

Nowhere is it clearer than in the US cigar industry that employers considered girls a labour option comparable to Chinese men. In California, cigar production owners hired Chinese immigrant men; in New York and Florida, they hired European immigrant girls. Artisanal cigar workers fought back against this change on both coasts and, in California, adopted virulent anti-Chinese tactics that directly influenced the development of the US Chinese Exclusion laws as well as the strategy and structure of the American Federation of Labor (AFL). Samuel Gompers, British immigrant and head of the AFL, got his start as a cigar roller. He penned a famed Sinophobic document, "Meat versus Rice: American Manhood Against Asiatic Coolieism, Which Shall Survive" that committed skilled white workers to a racist campaign for exclusion as a union strategy. Presented in 1902 to the US Senate as a plea to renew the Chinese Exclusion Act, the document asserted that Chinese men were rice-eating, opium-smoking, emasculated, unfree, diseased, and lived in 'colonies' rather than families. Nevertheless, the document continued, they could outcompete whites in social evolution because they work for half the pay, threatening the survival of "Christian society and Christian civilization." "None can withstand their silent and irresistible flow," the document warned, evoking the image of a sinister horde.[21]

In New York, artisan cigar makers also opposed the hiring of girls in defence of a white man's living wage, but recast all girls not as workers but as the mythic daughters and wives of skilled workers.[22] This representation was as fictional as the rendition of Chinese men as criminals, but far less violent and inflammatory in its implications. Most young women in cigar work had migrated from Southern and Eastern Europe, areas deemed less "civilised." Indeed, the AFL in "Meat vs. Rice" also decried the high numbers of migrant workers coming to the US from Europe. Nevertheless, in the struggle over cigar labour on the US East Coast, AFL rhetoric attempted to contain the threat of European female migrants

[21] Anonymous (1902). Young (2015). Saxton (1995).

[22] Cooper (1987) and Glickman (1993).

with family-based rhetoric: daughters should not be in the workforce but should be supported by well-paid fathers. This obscured young women's foreign origins, while the violent rhetoric of anti-Chinese labour activism rendered the Chinese as permanently alien.[23]

Assembling a Factory Labour Force in Shanghai

By 1905, when BAT-China began recruiting workers for its Shanghai cigarette factory, both textile and cigarette companies globally typically turned to girls for a significant portion of their labour. BAT-China tapped labour migrations already underway to Shanghai because of the textile industry. The first textile factory opened in Shanghai in 1889 and foreign production greatly expanded after the 1895 Sino-Japanese war forced the Chinese government to lift the prohibition against foreigners owning factories. British and German companies built textile factories in Shanghai in the 1890s and Japan built its first textile factories by 1904. All hired girls.[24]

The cigarette industry in China grew at an astonishing rate and the large labour demand greatly increased the flow of girls from rural regions of China to the cosmopolitan city of Shanghai. In 1906, BAT-China opened a new factory in Pudong, the industrial suburb of Shanghai. This factory would grow to massive proportions by the 1920s with thousands of workers. BAT-China also added a second factory in the city of Shanghai in 1917. As BAT-China's factories grew, large competitors like the Nanyang Brothers Tobacco Company also located in the Shanghai area. By 1916, just over a decade after the first executives arrived, half to two-thirds of the 12 billion cigarettes that BAT sold in China were supplied by its China factories rather than imports. By the end of World War I, considerably before the heyday of BAT-China, 25,000 Chinese people worked in BAT's cigarette factories, the majority female, and in the 1920s, BAT-China became the city's largest employer.[25] In addition to its Shanghai area factories, BAT-China built new factories in Hankow in 1907, Mukden in 1909, Harbin in 1914, Tianjin in 1921, Tsingtao in 1925 and Hong Kong in 1929.

[23] Ngai (2004) and Lee (2019).

[24] Honig (1986). Perry (1993). Cochran (1980) and Enstad (2018).

[25] Cochran (1980) and Perry (1993).

As BAT-China's factories grew, the need for managers and supervisors from the US, Britain, and China also increased. As one of the world's first multinational corporations, BAT balanced the demands of its executives in Britain and the US. The corporation emerged from a price war between ATC and ITC; the two companies agreed to stay out of the other's domestic markets and to pursue foreign markets together through the new corporation of BAT. James B. Duke of ATC was the first director of BAT and stayed in that position until 1923; the board of directors generally was evenly split between American and British executives. Duke was adamant that the director of BAT-China be appointed from the American contingent; James A. Thomas of North Carolina took the helm in 1905 and held the position through the end of World War I, when he was replaced by another American, Thomas Cobb. Foreign representatives in China came from both countries but the US contingent strongly dominated until a shift in power in BAT in the 1920s.[26]

Thomas hired foreign representatives primarily from a network of white men connected to the bright leaf tobacco industry in North Carolina and Virginia—managers who shared his own race, gender, and native place. He justified tapping this network because of a knowledge of bright leaf tobacco farming: "Most of the Far Eastern representatives of the company in the early days were recruited from North Carolina and Virginia. There was no rule about this, but as most of the company's men at home came from these two states, they knew where to find assistants who from infancy had cultivated, cured and manufactured tobacco, so that it was second nature to them."[27] However, men from the US dominated positions throughout BAT-China's organisation, including at headquarters and in factory and sales management, not just in the agricultural programme. Nevertheless, the argument about bright leaf tobacco justified the migration of hundreds of young, white men from the US South to China from 1905 until the Japanese war of the late 1930s. Ivy G. Riddick of Raleigh, North Carolina, demonstrates the importance of this network to factory management styles. Riddick went to China in 1914 and in 1919, became the manager of the stemmery at BAT-China's factory in Hankow, and later served as factory manager there. In 1931,

[26] Cox (2000) and Cochran (1980).

[27] Thomas (1928, pp. 85–86).

he became a special labour consultant at BAT's massive factory complex at Pudong, a job he held until 1939.[28]

Despite the dominance of the bright leaf network, both British and US representatives worked for BAT-China and the company culture mixed elements from the US South and the British imperial elite. Foreign representatives' contracts with BAT, for example, were drawn up according to policies for British agents in the Empire, namely that employees must be unmarried, no more than 25 years old, and willing to sign a four-year commitment after which they would have a four-month home leave[29] British representatives, in general, came from a higher class background and had more formal education than their US counterparts, and Shanghai's treaty port culture as a whole was dominated by British colonial practices. British representatives could be found at headquarters, in factories and in sales (though not in the agricultural programme). British representative H. A. Keily was BAT's first factory manager in Shanghai[30] and some mechanics at the Pudong factory in the 1920s were decommissioned soldiers who had served the British empire.

Chinese businessmen, managers, and staff were also critical to BAT-China's success, though their impact was chronically underplayed by British and American executives. From the outset, Thomas relied on two very important Chinese businessmen, Zheng Bozhao and Wu Tingsheng, who provided advice, cultural competency, and served as agents for the purchase of property as well as managing cigarette sales. By 1912, Thomas partnered with each of these executives on sales and corporate subsidiaries and Zheng became the second-most powerful person in BAT-China (and arguably its most indispensable) by the end of World War I. BAT-China's executive offices and the factory's main office was staffed largely by Chinese male clerks.[31]

BAT-China factory management also recruited both male and female floor supervisors from various regions of China who in turn recruited workers from their native place for their shops. BAT-China drew on Chinese practices when making native place a foundation for labour

[28] 9 March 1934, Ivy G. Riddick Papers, hereafter RIDDICK, Southern Collection, University of North Carolina, Chapel Hill, NC.

[29] Hutchison (1936).

[30] Cox (2000, p. 126).

[31] Cox (2000) and Thomas (1928).

recruitment. In China, native place functioned as a significant identity category referring to the rural origins of one's family and ancestors. Chinese people had long created guilds and business networks through native place and tapped those associations when hiring as well. In addition, Chinese regions carried very different levels of status, with poorer and more rural regions at the lower end of the spectrum. BAT hired supervisors from different native places for different workshops, scaling the prestige of the native place to the status that they wished to give to the work.[32] As was typical in China, supervisors then hired workers of their own gender and from their own native place, segmenting the factory workforce in the process. If BAT wished for the packing department to be staffed by women of a high-ranking province like Zeijiang, then, management hired a female supervisor from Zeijiang, who would hire female workers from there. In this way, BAT created a functional hybrid, joining its desire to segment the workplace with normative Chinese business practice.[33]

Despite foreign managers' power to set factory-wide policy, Chinese supervisors held enormous power to hire, fire, and discipline workers. Supervisors' labour recruitment consisted of hiring only workers of one's native place and gender who offered gifts, cash, or a banquet. Zhang Yongsheng began working at BAT's Pudong factory at age nine after his father paid 17 yuan (a very high fee) to the supervisor. Another worker paid cash and hosted a dinner at Da Hong restaurant. Even after obtaining a position, workers continued to offer periodic gifts, especially at holidays, to supervisors in order to remain in good standing. "Those who gave generous gifts," recalled one worker, "would be sent to perform work at a higher piece rate or be given more and better raw material." Supervisors "found fault in everything," when workers did not offer gifts. One supervisor gained the nickname "Invitation Party Queen" because she required that so many events be thrown for her.[34] Qian Meifeng reported that one cigarette department supervisor would only hire male rollers who were part of his gang. He also ran a gambling business on

[32] Li interview and Riddick Factory Report 1932, both Shanghai Academy of Social Sciences, hereafter SASS, British American Tobacco Company Records, Economic Division. Perry (1993).

[33] US Bureau of Foreign and Domestic Commerce (1922) and Perry (1993).

[34] Zhang interview 1958. Zikun interview 1958. Chen interview 1963 Hao interview 1958, all SASS, British American Tobacco Company Records, Economic Division.

the side that he expected workers to pay into.[35] Factory manager I. G. Riddick, from North Carolina, noted that "shroffs" occupied the "'No Man's Land' of Pootung, between the foreigner and the labour. Practically all of our shroffs are worthless as interpreters, and otherwise, in matters of discipline."[36]

BAT-China's Shanghai cigarette factories, then, assembled a diverse population speaking many dialects and languages through labour and management recruitment that produced new and salient significance for gender, age, race, and native place. Likewise, BAT-China's business and factory culture emerged from the interaction of British, American, and Chinese practices, with foreign managers by no means imposing entirely foreign models or controlling all aspects of the workplace. At all levels, the industrial process did not erase differences but rather reconfigured and produced new material significance for them.

The Production of Difference in the Factory

In addition to initiating labour migrations, daily workplace discipline at the factory proved another location for the production of difference. Managers utilised social categories of gender, age, and race or native place origin to order the division of labour and create differential status and wages on the job. Managers did not simply replicate already existing categories, however, but infused these markers of difference with new purpose. Managers created disciplinary regimes that directed workers' movements through the factories, marked different jobs with uniforms, and augmented the status of certain workers through gratis cigarettes.

Managers created status and stigma at the factories first by creating a functional and spatial division between the leaf and cigarette departments and endowing that division with markers of gender and native place. In the leaf department, workers prepared tobacco leaves for manufacturing by removing the stems, checking for impurities, treating the leaves to achieve an appropriate moisture content, and sometimes adding flavourings. They also chopped, shredded, and sorted the leaves. On the cigarette side, workers ran the cigarette machines, caught cigarettes as they came

[35] Qian interview 1963, SASS, British American Tobacco Company Records, Economic Division.

[36] Riddick Factory Report 1932, SASS, British American Tobacco Company Records, Economic Division.

out of the machines, weighed, counted, packed, and labelled cigarettes, packs, cartons, and cases. All of the jobs in both the leaf and cigarette departments could be learned quickly and none took exceptional strength, with the exception of moving tobacco around the factory. Though they often came to seem natural, status and pay differentials did not track to skill but were almost entirely arbitrarily assigned in the interest of labour control.

By the 1910s, US managers created loose parallels between the labour systems in the US and China. In the US, white women packed; in BAT-China, women from higher status, urban areas packed. In both countries, men worked in the leaf department, though not usually as stemmers. In the US, black men performed leaf department work; in BAT-China, men from lower status regions performed it. The main difference came in the cigarette-making department. In the US, white women performed all of the tasks through World War I, after which both white men and women worked in this high-status department, with white men working the machines and white women catching the cigarettes. In China, only men worked in the cigarette-making room, with adult men running the machines and boys serving as catchers. Considered apprentices, these boys were in line for the privileged positions of running the cigarette-making machines. Unlike the boys in China, women in the cigarette-making room in the US had no expectation of advancement.[37]

The arbitrary nature of workplace values becomes especially clear when considering the job of stemming tobacco. In factories managed by white southerners in both the US and China, leaf department jobs carried the lowest status and lowest pay. In the US, such work had been associated with African Americans since slavery. In the US, African American women stemmed tobacco leaves; in China, BAT assigned women from a low-status Northern province to stem tobacco leaves. However, BAT-China's most significant competitor, the Nanyang Brothers Tobacco Company *only* hired workers from the company owners' native-place origin, making native place the determining factor in hiring but not relevant to further workplace segmentation. Nanyang hired women as stemmers, as did BAT-China but Nanyang paid stemmers *more* than women in the cigarette department because they determined the work to be more difficult

[37] Janiewski (1991) and Perry (1993).

and otherwise less desirable.[38] Nanyang's difference signals that BAT's constructed work values may not have seemed reasonable to Chinese workers who did not associate tobacco leaf preparation with slave labour.

BAT-China workers found themselves sorted by gender and race or native-place origin upon arriving at the factory. Workers entered the factory compound by one of two gates, the men's entrance or the women's entrance.[39] Gender, this practice declared, was not just important for family life but was of utmost significance in modern factory life as well. Chinese workers next travelled within the compound to their department, typically segregated by native-place origin. Through these movements, workers' investments in these categories deepened, especially because their job and pay were also scaled to differentials of gender and native place.

At the factory gate, each worker presented an identity card with their employee number. Assigning workers a number depersonalised them and also allowed for record keeping in English in the factory office, accommodating foreign managers' varying levels of skills in Chinese.[40] However, workers used their anonymity in the eyes of foreign company executives to manage their family economies. Mothers, especially, would 'loan' their identity card to daughters so that they could stay home with new babies, giving evidence to why girls seemed a reasonable labour category for employees as well as for industry. Chinese supervisors could be offered a gift in exchange for turning a blind eye.[41]

By the 1930s, managers accentuated job classifications with uniforms for women only. Women in the packing department wore blue jackets with white aprons, and women in the lower-paid stemmery wore all blue jackets and aprons. Uniforms made job classifications visible on the body: they simultaneously abstracted workers and attached them even more tightly to gender and race or native-place origin categories. In large factory compounds, the uniform was the first thing that any coworker or supervisor saw. If someone were out of place, the uniform would announce it. The colour differences between uniforms would not likely

[38] Perry (1993).

[39] Ibid.

[40] Wage Record, SASS, British American Tobacco Company Records, Economic Division. Anonymous (1929a).

[41] Perry (1993).

mean the same things to Chinese workers and supervisors as they would to foreign managers. Blue was widely associated with labour in China's twentieth-century treaty ports, a fact likely related to the strong presence of British and US industries. The uniforms in BAT's cigarette and leaf departments both featured blue jackets and more privileged cigarette packers' uniforms included a white apron. In China, however, white did not signal purity and race privilege as it did in the US and England, in fact, Chinese cultures associated white with funerals and death. There is fragmentary evidence that uniform policies may have originated to control sexual expression and prevent women from dressing up at the factories. Despite their low wages, some female workers participated in consumer culture and creatively engaged with popular styles. Cigarette workers from Jiangsu Province were known for their stylish clothes and boots.[42] If muting individual sexual expression at the workplace was one motivation for the uniform policies, it had a paradoxical effect of making gender and sexuality especially visible.

BAT-China gave free cigarettes to higher status workers, underscoring gender hierarchy. The company gave male workers 50–100 cigarettes a week regardless of their native-place origin, while women received only 50 cigarettes per year.[43] This practice likely grew out of the need to manage workers' ability to pocket cigarettes on the job. Cigarettes were small, easy to lift from the line and conceal on the body. Managers regularly dismissed workers caught "pilfering" cigarettes. Managers allotted free cigarettes to the category of worker who had the most access to manufactured cigarettes in the cigarette-making room, which meant men. Gratis cigarettes decreased the number of people who would lift cigarettes from the line, making it possible for supervisors to define the practice as aberrant and punishable when discovered.

Free cigarettes served as a management strategy beyond simply staunching the flow of pilfered cigarettes, however, because managers gave them out not by department but by identity category. Women in the packing department had daily and easy access to cigarettes, but their 50 cigarettes per year were certainly not enough to deter them from helping themselves. The differential distribution of free cigarettes, then, acted as

[42] Perry (1993) and Anonymous (1925).

[43] Perry (1993).

another disciplinary device that constructed status at the workplace and built investments in gender identities.

Free cigarettes had significant value whether or not workers intended to smoke them. Urban China still operated partly as a barter economy. In Shanghai, the inflation rate was so volatile that the company paid workers in a combination of cash and rice so that people could eat even if the cash lost value.[44] By paying some people cigarettes, furthermore, management used the commodity to create workplace identities. When workers smoked, sold, bartered, or gave away the cigarettes, they performed workplace privilege.

For workers who did not receive free cigarettes, it was easy to see cigarettes as compensation for inadequate wages. Management continued to struggle to curtail losses of cigarettes. Riddick, head manager of the Pudong plant, noted in 1932 that their losses from cigarette pilfering were considerable, and attributed it to the fact that the factory failed to pay a living wage to a large number of its workers.[45] Supervisors regularly fired workers caught with even a single cigarette in their possession.[46] Women in the packing department proved particularly difficult to control. In one skirmish, a "foreign overseer" caught a woman in Pudong taking cigarettes out of the packing department, and management fired her on the spot. When word reached the packing department, the women immediately struck. Management somehow convinced the workers to cease their strike, probably by threatening their jobs. However, at the end of the workday the women of the packing department made their point. They concealed and carried out hundreds of cigarettes and destroyed them on the street in front of the factory in protest.[47]

These women demonstrated the limits of managers' ability to discipline the bodies of the workers through these cultural techniques. Just as managers' techniques—uniforms, differential doors, perks—were personal and performed via the body, so did workers assert their bodily autonomy in their protest. Cigarettes were easy to conceal underneath clothing, and

[44] Conversation at Mr. TV Soong's House 1928, SASS, British American Tobacco Company Records, Economic Division.

[45] Riddick Factory Report 1932, SASS, British American Tobacco Company Records, Economic Division.

[46] Qiao Jinding interview 1963, SASS, British American Tobacco Company Records, Economic Division. Anonymous (1929b, c).

[47] Anonymous (1929c).

allowed women to assert their bodily will and their ability to pursue a need or desire beyond the reach of factory control. By destroying the commodity in front of the factory, rather than smoking or selling it, they asserted their ultimate power to define its meaning. In this situation, they made the company's cigarettes into a symbol of women workers' power and defiance.

As this example shows, though the labour category of girls was designed to garner less pay and power at the factory and despite the outsized power of supervisors, in daily life women did not simply accept a disempowered position. This was true, too, for young mothers. Workers would lose their jobs if they missed too many days in a row, which led to pregnant women coming to work until the day they gave birth and returning immediately afterwards. Zhang Yongsheng recalled, "Some gave birth in the lavatory. Some on the road. Some on the little sampan. A female worker had a son who was born on the sampan and his nick-name was 'little sampan.'"[48] Mu Guilan recalled that family members would bring babies to the factory gate at lunch break to meet mothers. "I chewed dry bing and ran to breast feed."[49] In response to major strikes, BAT did implement some maternity policies in January 1928, including a six-week leave without pay for childbirth and a flat payment of $30.[50]

It is important to recognise that, because two-thirds of its workers were women, any factory-wide strike at BAT was a strike of women. Over its tenure, BAT was subject to more strikes than any other company in China: 56 strikes between 1918 and 1940.[51] Strikers were up against enormous odds, including a private, armed factory police force, but they made significant gains nonetheless. In 1928, the company agreed in writing to workers' right to form a union and bargain collectively, seven years before Southern cigarette workers gained this right in the US. In addition, workers argued with some success for the right, at least on paper, for no dismissal without cause, compensation for injury on the job, and the six-week unpaid maternity leave already mentioned. They also won

[48] Zhang interview 1958, SASS, British American Tobacco Company Records, Economic Division.

[49] Mu interview 1958, SASS, British American Tobacco Company Records, Economic Division.

[50] Terms for Mutual Assistance 1928, SASS, British American Tobacco Company Records, Economic Division.

[51] Perry (1993).

some paternalist programmes, including health benefits and a company-funded school for the children of workers at the Pudong plant.[52] These gains did not extend across all of BAT's factories and could remain subject to some supervisors' discretion, but they did shift daily life in the factories.

Conclusion

The global tobacco industry was one of a handful of 'light' industries at the forefront of the mobilisation and migration of girls as an industrial labour force between 1870 and 1920. The significance of the word "girls" here is paramount: companies across the globe seized on an idealised configuration of gender, age, and marital status, most likely following the success of the European textile boom in utilising single women under 30 as workers, and applied it in widely varied places and conditions. This category is best seen not simply as reflective of demographic information but as a category that shaped and defined—and sometimes distorted—experience. The category of "girls" defined all women workers as young, single, and supplemental to a family income supported by other wage earners, rendering them auxiliary and not in need of a living wage. Of course, this was very often untrue. Furthermore, the category was flexible and vague and did not always mean the same thing. In the US South and China, where the age of marriage was much younger than in Western Europe, girls at the factory might indeed be teenagers but also married and mothers. The term "girls," then, likely served ideological purposes in obscuring labour practices in public discourse; certainly it has done so in historical discourse.

The success of the tobacco industry and other industries in mobilising this category in vastly different sex and gender systems across the globe is a remarkable testimony to the homogenising power of abstract labour and capitalist development. Historians working across the globe have remarked on the vast changes that follow the entrance of women into public wage work, a change that sometimes is taken to define global modernity and capitalist standardisation. At the same time, the success of mobilising girls is testimony to the ways that capitalism also produces difference in its pursuit of profit. BAT-China produced difference when recruiting a labour force using gender and native place as well as at the

[52] Terms for Mutual Assistance 1928, SASS, British American Tobacco Company Records, Economic Division.

factory itself through job segmentation and daily workplace discipline, including directing movements through the factory, the uniform requirement, and the differential use of free cigarettes. Men and women and people of different native places would take different pathways through the compound and work in different workshops and jobs under supervisors who shared their identities. Women workers would wear distinctive uniforms while men in the cigarette department received the valuable "gift" of free cigarettes.

Management's tactics were impersonal and bureaucratic but affected each worker on a personal level: by amplifying the differences of gender and native-place origin, managers rendered other differences between workers less visible and less relevant. In other words, managers used highly personal and bodily tactics to render workers as anonymous and interchangeable as possible while still constructing gender and native-place difference as a central workplace disciplinary mechanism. The abstraction of labour did not mean complete homogenisation and it did not mean that class was the only ascendant capitalist identity category.

This change in perspective on abstract labour matters greatly because many scholars had long seen class as the primary category of capitalism and class consciousness as the goal of workers' organising; gender and race or native-place self-consciousness in this view becomes 'identity politics,' merely cultural investments in personal identities that obstruct the kind of critical class consciousness required for organisation. This tired formulation not only leaves the white male worker as the unmarked or iconic worker in much European and North American scholarship—and tends to miss female-centred labour activism—but it misunderstands the formation of *structures* in global capitalism. That is, the intervention in this chapter is at once structural and cultural. In its fundamental workings, twentieth- and twenty-first-century capitalism does not only assert a homogenising force but a force that produces gender and race and/or native-place differences. Historians of capitalism need to read deeply in the histories of gender and race not simply to be 'inclusive' but to understand the fundamental workings of capital.

References

Primary Sources

Unpublished Sources

Shanghai Academy of Social Sciences
- British American Tobacco Company Records.
University of North Carolina, Chapel Hill, NC
- Ivy G. Riddick Papers.
Eastern Carolina University, Greenville, NC
- James N. Joyner Papers.

Published Sources

Anonymous. 1902. *Some Reasons for Chinese Exclusion: Meat vs. Rice, American Manhood Against Asiatic Coolieism, Which Shall Survive?* 57th Cong., 1st sess., S. Doc. No. 137 (statement of Samuel Gompers). Washington, DC: Government Printing Office.

Anonymous. 1925. *North China Herald* Newspaper, 15 November.

Anonymous. 1929a. *Eastern Times* Newspaper, 5 June.

Anonymous. 1929b. *North China Herald* Newspaper, 8 June.

Anonymous. 1929c. *North China Herald* Newspaper, 2 February.

Hutchison, J.L. 1936. *China Hand*. New York: Lathrop, Lee and Shepherd.

Thomas, J. 1928. *A Pioneer Tobacco Merchant in the Orient*. Durham: Duke University Press.

US Bureau of Foreign and Domestic Commerce. 1922. *Supplement to Commerce Reports Trade Information Bulletin No. 61 "Industrial Conditions in China,"* 18 September, published by the Bureau of Foreign and Domestic Commerce, US Department of Commerce.

Secondary Sources

Baptist, E.E. 2014. *The Half Has Never Been Told: Slavery and the Making of American Capitalism*. New York: Basic Books.

Beckert, S. 2014. *Empire of Cotton: A Global History*. New York: Alfred A. Knopf.

Boydston, J. 1996. The Woman Who Wasn't There: Women's Market Labor and the Transition to Capitalism in the United States. *Journal of the Early Republic* 16: 183–206.

Chakrabarty, D. 2000. *Provincializing Europe: Postcolonial Thought and Historical Difference*. Princeton: Princeton University Press.

Cochran, S. 1980. *Big Business in China: Sino-Foreign Rivalry in the Cigarette Industry, 1890–1930*. Cambridge, MA: Harvard University Press.
Cooper, P.A. 1987. *Once a Cigar Maker: Men, Women, and Work Culture in American Cigar Factories, 1900–1919*. Urbana: University of Illinois Press.
Cox, H. 2000. *The Global Cigarette: Origins and Evolution of British American Tobacco, 1880–1945*. London: Oxford University Press.
Denning, M. 2007. Representing Global Labor. *Social Text* 25: 125–145.
Enstad, N. 2018. *Cigarettes Inc.: An Intimate History of Corporate Imperialism*. Chicago: University of Chicago Press.
Esch, E. 2018. *The Color Line and the Assembly Line: Managing Race in the Ford Empire*. Berkeley, CA: University of California Press.
Gabaccia, D.R. 2000. *Italy's Many Diasporas*. New York: Routledge.
Glickman, L. 1993. Inventing the 'American Standard of Living': Gender, Race, and Working-Class Identity, 1880–1925. *Labor History* 34: 221–235.
Guglielmo, J. 2010. *Living the Revolution: Italian Women's Resistance and Radicalism in New York City, 1880–1945*. Chapel Hill: University of North Carolina Press.
Hewitt, N. 2001. *Southern Discomfort: Women's Activism in Tampa, Florida, 1880–1920*. Urbana: University of Illinois.
Hong, G.K. 2006. *Ruptures of American Capital*. Minneapolis: University of Minnesota Press.
Honig, E. 1986. *Sisters and Strangers: Women in the Shanghai Cotton Mills, 1919–1949*. Stanford: Stanford University Press.
Janiewski, D. 1991. Southern Honor, Southern Dishonor: Managerial Ideology and the Construction of Gender, Race and Class Relations in Southern Industry. In *Work Engendered: Toward a New History of American Labor*, ed. A. Baron, 70–91. Ithaca: Cornell University Press.
Jenkins, J., and J. Leroy, eds. 2021. *Histories of Racial Capitalism*. New York: Columbia University Press.
Johnson, W. 2013. *River of Dark Dreams: Slavery and Empire in the Cotton Kingdom*. Cambridge: Harvard University Press.
Jung, M.-H. 2006. *Coolies and Cane: Race, Labor, and Sugar in the Age of Emancipation*. Baltimore: Johns Hopkins University Press.
Lee, E. 2019. *America for Americans: A History of Xenophobia in the United States*. New York: Basic Books.
Lowe, L. 2009. Work, Immigration, Gender: New Subjects of Cultural Politics. In *American Studies: An Anthology*, eds. J.A. Radway et al., 31–49. Malden, MA: Wiley-Blackwell.
Maynes, M.J., and A. Waltner. 2018. Young Women, Textile Labor, and Marriage in Europe and China Around 1800. In *A History of the Girl: Formation, Education, and Identity*, eds. M. O'Dowd and J. Purvis, 75–102. Basingstoke: Palgrave Macmillan.

Ngai, M. 2004. *Impossible Subjects: Illegal Aliens and the Making of Modern America*. Chicago: University of Chicago Press.
O'Dowd, M., and J. Purvis, eds. 2018. *A History of the Girl: Formation, Education, and Identity*. Basingstoke: Palgrave Macmillan.
Ong, A. 1999. *Flexible Citizenship: The Cultural Logics of Transnationality*. Durham: Duke University Press.
Perry, E.J. 1993. *Shanghai on Strike: The Politics of Chinese Labor*. Stanford: Stanford University Press.
Robinson, C. 1983. *Black Marxism: The Making of the Black Radical Tradition*. London: Zed Books.
Roediger, D.R. and E.D. Esch. 2012. *The Production of Difference: Race and the Management of Labor in US History*. New York: Oxford University Press.
Sassen, S. 2003. Strategic Instantiations of Gendering in the Global Economy. In *Gender and U.S. Immigration: Contemporary Trends*, ed. Pierrette Hondagneu-Sotelo, 43–60. Berkeley: University of California Press.
Saxton, A. 1995. *The Indispensable Enemy: Labor and the Anti-Chinese Movement in California*. Berkeley: University of California Press.
Tilburg, P. 2019. *Working Girls: Sex, Taste and Reform in the Parisian Garment Trades, 1880–1919*. London: Oxford University Press.
Young, E. 2015. Chinese Coolies, Universal Rights, and the Limits of Liberalism in an Age of Empire. *Past and Present* 227: 121–149.

CHAPTER 13

Palestinian *Fellahin* Tobacco 'Smuggling' Under Late Ottoman, British, and Israeli Rule

Basma Fahoum

Introduction

The spread of commercial tobacco cultivation in twentieth-century Palestine brought with it a proliferation of what state and tobacco companies viewed as 'smuggling' on the part of tobacco-growing peasants (*fellahin*, sing. *fellah*), whose family households depended on part-subsistence and part-surplus agriculture. During the period of the late Ottoman Empire, the colonial British Mandate of 1923–1948 and then the Israeli state, repressive legal and police measures were constantly taken against the smuggling. In response, *fellahin* developed their own justification strategies to differentiate themselves from those who were professional smugglers in the region. With Israeli restrictions on movement, access to land, access to water, and the de-development of Arab agriculture,

B. Fahoum (✉)
Ben Gurion University of the Negev, Beersheba, Israel
e-mail: fahoumb@bgu.ac.il

A. van Wickeren et al. (eds.), *Tobacco in Global Perspective, 1780–1960*, Cambridge Imperial and Post-Colonial Studies,
https://doi.org/10.1007/978-3-031-64411-5_13

however, the Palestinian *fellahin* were gradually forced to give up their own farming and take on wage labour.[1] By the 1980s, when the region was thrown into deep conflict, tobacco cultivation had declined and the conflicts over *fellahin* tobacco smuggling were consigned to history.

Smuggling has been a constant in tobacco history, and the global tobacco industry, despite its own centuries-long involvement in smuggling, in the main tried to ban small tobacco growers from taking any part in it.[2] Growers were promised that the cash crop would lift them out of poverty and into the modern world, to operate freely, unattached to previously restrictive customs and obligations. While theoretically they could sell their crop to whomsoever they wanted, in practice the market was often monopolised and highly regulated, and the state, recognising the revenue potential of tobacco, levied excise and other taxes. Over time, as imperial state monopolies gave way to other colonial state, parastatal and corporate monopolies, taxes increased. The growers, mostly peasant family households, involving the work of men, women, and children, did not enjoy a liberalised free market: they were to sell their tobacco to the companies, and any sold informally or independently was banned and considered smuggling.

As this chapter documents, up until the 1980s, Palestinian *fellahin* smuggled tobacco across the Palestine/Israeli northern border and traded illegally, seeing this as a social and cultural norm, a just practice and a right. Their long-standing struggle over the right to sell untaxed tobacco, which they consumed in the form of hand-rolled cigarettes, under colonial rule took on additional meaning and created a discourse tied to nationalist aspirations and beliefs about economic justice, notably who has the right to grow, sell, smoke, and profit from tobacco. Like alcohol, tobacco was a special commodity requiring a different form of taxation. Since it has been viewed both as a luxury and later as a harmful

[1] Rosenfeld (1968, pp. 732–752).

[2] Gilmore and Rowell (2018). OCCRP (2022). OCCRP. 2022. Smoke and Mirrors: How the 'Father' of Iraq's Cigarette Smugglers Built an Empire. OCCRP. https://www.occrp.org/en/investigations/smoke-and-mirrors-how-the-father-of-iraqs-cigarette-smugglers-built-an-empire. Accessed 14 August 2022.

substance, it was often very highly controlled and taxed, as it was seen as unworthy of the ideals of free trade. *Fellahin* fundamentally rejected this characterisation.

Fellahin conceptualised their right to sell the tobacco they grew based on two main sets of justifications. First and foremost, they recognised the tobacco they grew as inalienably theirs. They did not allow the law to define them, but rather denied any attempt to define the informal trade in tobacco as smuggling (*tahrīb*) or themselves as smugglers (*muharribin*). The term in Arabic does not carry specific connotations apart from the illegality of spatial movement and transfer of goods, and there are no additional meanings that would make *fellahin* particularly resistant to using the word, besides the legal violation. They also condemned colonial economic policy and its claim to support free trade while in fact nurturing an environment conducive to monopsonies and mercantilism.

They gave their own justifications and rationales to settle the discrepancy between whom they believed they were and their illegal actions. This was especially true for the period of the 1948 War and the Palestinian *Nakba* [Ar. Catastrophe], and the subsequent criminalisation of Palestinian refugees who attempted to return to their villages, called 'infiltration' by Israeli officials and the press. *Nakba* describes the destruction of Palestinian life and society, and the displacement of the vast majority of the country's Palestinian inhabitants during the 1948 War. After the war, the State of Israel was established on 78% of Mandatory Palestine, and 160,000 Palestinians who remained within this area became citizens of Israel. In this new situation, *fellahin* were worried about how they were publicly and privately perceived. They believed that what they did could not be called smuggling, insisting it was their natural right, especially because it was a necessary means to make a decent living. They used subterfuge and negotiated with officials to bridge the gap between the colonial legal framework and the survival needs of their families. They also saw themselves as the 'cooks of the poison'—whose essential, inalienable right it was to smoke the tobacco they grew and to sell it independently. Whether this 'poison' or 'drug' was harmful or of bad quality, *fellahin* could not see how the different legal systems governing them could prevent them from engaging freely with the product of their labour. Peasants and their households continued to adapt and take advantage of loopholes in the letter of Ottoman, British, and Israeli law, contending with the legal ramifications of their actions.[3] They wanted to enjoy the fruit, or rather leaf, of their hard work and trade freely.

Tobacco cultivation began in Palestine when the state monopoly on tobacco was granted to the Ottoman Public Debt Administration (OPDA),[4] through a company it formed, called the *Societé de Régie co-interessée des tabacs ottomans*, in 1883. The *Régie* introduced many new norms for the tobacco trade, as a single-buyer, or monopsony, under the banderole system of stamps which the department of excise sold to producers, signifying that excise had been paid.[5] These included, among others, annual licences; the establishment of supervised warehouses; the ban on personal consumption and the transportation of tobacco; the encouragement of tobacco cultivation in certain areas and discouragement in others through extending or withholding cheap credit; and the introduction of guards to monitor planting areas. Some of these norms, like the banderoles, warehouses and ban on personal consumption, were introduced to battle what had become an unintended but prominent feature of the trade: the creation of a widespread market for contraband tobacco.

Although the British Mandate abolished the monopoly of the *Régie* in 1921,[6] and even claimed to have established a free market for tobacco, most of these features were replicated in the Tobacco Ordinance of 1925. Palestinian growers still had to sell only to licensed manufacturers; could only grow, transport, and store tobacco with a licence; and could be prevented from cultivating tobacco if their leaf was deemed of 'bad quality.' The conditions were ripe for one of the world's largest tobacco companies, the British American Tobacco Company (BAT), to re-monopsonise the local tobacco market and set prices.

After establishing its first factory, Maspero Frères Ltd. in Jaffa in 1921, BAT started acquiring and merging or entering partnerships with local factories. By the late 1920s, it had all but monopolised the cigarette market, by controlling the largest Arab and Jewish factories and dictating prices. BAT remained active in Israel after 1948 through Maspero Frères,

[3] See ISA-MandatoryOrganizations-SecretaryCommerce-000o4ex, ISA-MandatoryOrganizations-SecretaryCommerce-000o0zu.

[4] Chaker (2012).

[5] Ibid., p. 33.

[6] El-Eini (2006, p. 121).

but finally left the country in 1956 as the Suez Crisis and the Arab League's boycott of Israel intensified.[7] BAT marketed its cigarettes as either 'Jewish' (manufactured by Maspero) or 'Arab' (manufactured by its 'Arab' factories, most importantly Karaman, Dick, and Salti, or KDS in Haifa), thus using the colonial struggle in Palestine as a sales tactic.[8]

The Israeli regime, at its inception in 1948, then adopted the British ordinance, and in 1953 only made several amendments to its main articles, including provisions to produce duty-free cigarettes for the use of Israel Defense Forces (IDF) soldiers, police, prison guards, and their families, and the conversion of fines from Palestine Pounds to Israeli Pounds.[9] The Egyptian Pound (LE) had been the legal tender in British Mandate Palestine until the Palestinian Pound (LP) replaced it in 1927, with both currencies pegged to the British Pound Sterling. The Palestine Pound was replaced by the Israeli Pound (IP) in 1952. With the departure of BAT from the country four years later, conditions were ripe for one company, Dubek, an Israeli producer, to slowly acquire and merge with the other producers, finally becoming the single official buyer of tobacco leaf in 1971.

Legal Obstacles to Informal Trade Under Ottoman and British Rule

Tobacco was only one of several taxed, banned, or scarce commodities in which Palestinian peasant households, embedded as they were in capitalist markets from the onset of tobacco cultivation, traded in both the formal and informal markets. The formal market proved unfree for most, extracting the most value at the expense of those who provided it with raw material and labour by creating a captive market, preventing competition, and over time reducing the price paid for the leaf. Growers often turned to the informal market as the only 'free market' available to them, and perceived legality and justice as two distinct concepts across changing political and economic scenarios. Smuggling, however, remained a constant in the local tobacco trade, as in many other products of peasant households.

[7] Fahoum (2020).

[8] Fahoum (2023, chap. 2).

[9] ISA-mof-mof-000lyir, 28–32, 90, 108–113.

Under Ottoman rule, transporting tobacco illicitly was widespread, accounting for an estimated half of tobacco consumption in the 1880s,[10] and 9% of all tobacco grown in the empire in the 1910s.[11] It is hard to determine how much was smuggled in Palestine alone, but smuggling by tobacco traders and growers existed in all parts of the empire, including the most high-yielding regions. The Ottoman Empire had its own legal, political, and financial reasons not to completely curb the informal trade in tobacco, not only before 1883 but also after. It understood the importance of this trade for smallholders and the rural economy more broadly.[12] The *Régie's* attempts to control smuggling were stricter than those of the Ottoman government, which did not restrict growing areas, ban personal use or uproot plots with mature plants,[13] and considered anyone growing without a licence, or anyone cutting, transporting, or trading in tobacco independently, a smuggler.

To enforce its rules without the help of the Ottoman government, the *Régie* created a force numbering up to 7,000 guards (*kolcu/coldji*), who toured the countryside looking for unlicensed tobacco plots, especially smaller ones for personal consumption and small-scale trade.[14] When they found plots of unlicensed tobacco, they fined the grower, confiscated the crop, and kept records of the infraction to deny any future permit. In practice, this only served to encourage those caught to grow without a licence and sell independently to others trading in smuggled tobacco.

When the British Mandatory Government abolished the *Régie*, many more peasant households from villages across Palestine started growing tobacco. From 1917 until the Mandatory Government issued the Tobacco Ordinance of 1925—when the government started to monitor tobacco cultivation and manufactured tobacco products—virtually anyone, anywhere, could freely grow tobacco. Replicating the

[10] Chaker (2012, p. 39).

[11] Zlocisti (1925, p. 16).

[12] Chaker (2012, chap. V).

[13] Ibid., pp. 73–74.

[14] Vardağli. E. T. (2014, pp. 606–621, 611).

Ottoman monopoly rules, the Tobacco Ordinance of 1925 then prohibited growers from selling or transporting their excisable product—manufactured or unmanufactured, and in any quantity—to anyone but licensed manufacturers.

Unlike the Ottoman Government, which often negated the rules of the *Régie*, the British Mandatory Government considered anyone who broke the law—even by keeping some for personal consumption or by selling tobacco to their neighbours—as a smuggler, subject to heavy fines of up to three pounds per kilogram of tobacco. This was often converted to time in jail, and, in the case of a recurrent violation, in addition to being fined, the violator could face incarceration for up to six months. While the Mandatory Government attempted without success to export Palestinian tobacco, growers sold tobacco domestically and to neighbouring countries informally and illegally.

The British administration also brought a much tighter enforcement of customs laws and agreements, while making provisions for border villages in Upper Galilee, the mountainous area straddling what today is northern Israel and southern Lebanon, which were now expected to recognise the new frontier between British-administered Mandatory Palestine and French-administered Mandatory Lebanon. These changes were gradual and never went into full effect until much later in the twentieth century. According to the *bon voisinage* (good neighbour) customs agreement between the British and French Mandates in Syria and Lebanon and the supplementary International Conventions Ordinance of 1925, if goods were to be transported outside the prescribed trade routes, they were to be deemed contraband—unless the people carrying them were "[p]ersons living near the frontier whose business obliges them to cross the frontier daily" for "the carriage of small quantities of goods; and the products of the soil in small quantities."[15] The French and British Mandates also established a common customs house in Ras al-Naqura.[16] The agreements with Syria and Lebanon came to an end in May 1948, when both countries declared war on Israel. This first phase of the First Arab–Israeli War disrupted the northern border with Lebanon and Syria and many of the connections between people living on the two sides.

[15] ISA-MandatoryOrganizations-MandateAtrnGen-00077im, 11.

[16] Ibid., p. 4.

Duties on tobacco made up a substantial part of the British Mandatory Government's income. For example, in 1937, excise taxes on tobacco alone constituted 5% of all government revenue on tobacco produced in Palestine from local and foreign leaf for cigarette production.[17] Foreign leaf was a small fraction of all tobacco used during the Mandate; was mostly Greek, Turkish, and Bulgarian; and was mostly to blend cigarettes. Rewards to informers were directly linked to the revenue potential of tobacco, and the Department of Customs and Excise handed out rewards to anyone willing to provide information about smuggling operations and growers selling tobacco independently. The department paid very large amounts in rewards to informants, sometimes up to LP 1,000 a month.[18]

A major factor affecting the Palestinian tobacco market in the years 1921–1956 was the presence of BAT. Throughout the 1920s, BAT bought many cigarette factories in Palestine, both Arab- and Jewish-owned, practically monopolising the market. It had very close connections to the government and was very interested in curbing the informal trade. It successfully effected the drafting of the Tobacco Ordinance, thus tying its interests with those of the government.

While officials knew that smuggling was widespread throughout the country, very few reports clearly indicated the amounts of smuggled tobacco. A 1924 government report noted that peasants produced their own tobacco, which they then cut in the villages, and recommended that this tobacco be exempt from taxation.[19] It estimated that 1,235 tons of Turkish tobacco and 450 tons of *Baladi* (the local variety of tobacco, sometimes called *'Arabi'* or 'Arabic') tobacco would be grown in Palestine in 1924. Given that the estimated consumption of processed tobacco in Palestine was 300 tons of Turkish leaf, and an additional 300 tons of Baladi mixed with Turkish which "might be consumed unmanufactured, that is to say, cut by the peasants for personal consumption," it followed that the difference (935 tons of Turkish and 150 tons of Baladi) "would probably be smuggled into Syria and Trans-Jordan."[20]

In 1933, the northern district's agricultural officer noted that the number of tobacco-related contraventions was stable over the previous

[17] Himadeh (1939, p. 512).

[18] See ISA-MandatoryOrganizations-SecretaryCommerce-000o0zu.

[19] ISA-MandatoryOrganizations-MandateFishery-000nduz, 224.

[20] ISA-MandatoryOrganizations-MandateFishery-000nduz, 203.

five years, with almost 5,000 excise tax offences each year.[21] These were recorded instances, therefore we must assume that the actual number of informal sales was much higher. Tobacco manufacturers also warned the government about smuggling, stating that excess quantities of lower-grade tobacco were sold illegally, and that tobacco produced in the areas around Nazareth, Jenin, and Tiberias was specifically grown for illicit trade.[22]

Fellahin growers, especially from the areas that produced tobacco desirable for the cigarette industry, boldly used the issue of smuggling to further their participation in decision-making. A letter to the department of agriculture from growers in the villages around Tarshiha asked that areas of land under cultivation be restricted because the inferior tobacco produced there would end up being smuggled.[23] In another letter, representatives of 24 tobacco-growing villages repeated the same claim, saying that producing excess tobacco, which the local industry could not absorb, "could depress [the value of] this crop, dissuade growers from producing saleable crops, and encourage smuggling, making the farmer subject to prosecution and loss of business, which is not only harmful to the grower, but also to the government, because smuggling diminishes [legal] consumption greatly, and reduces revenues of the treasury from banderole and other taxes."[24]

The *fellahin* understood the importance of custom and tax revenues, and they might have preferred the government ensure that the legal price for tobacco remained high and able to sustain them and their families, instead of having to sell their tobacco informally and risk getting caught. They would have also preferred if the law was more lenient towards personal use of tobacco, which was also illegal according to the 1925 ordinance. They openly challenged the restrictions on personal consumption, as stated in the 1930 Hope-Simpson report, commissioned following the violent events of the Buraq Uprising in August 1929:

[21] ISA-MandatoryOrganizations-MandateFishery-000nduz, 158. Hope-Simpson (1930, Chapter VIII, Section G).

[22] ISA-MandatoryOrganizations-MandateFishery-000nduz, 96.

[23] ISA-MandatoryOrganizations-MandateFishery-000ndv0, 82.

[24] ISA-MandatoryOrganizations-MandateFishery-000ndv0, 45.

> On the part of the cigarette merchants it is alleged that smuggling is rife, especially after the disturbances of August last [1929], and it was urged that much more severe measures are required on the part of the authorities in order to combat that evil. On the other side there were frequent complaints on the part of the *fellahin* that the Tobacco Ordinance is not only harsh in its terms, but is, in addition, administered in a cruel manner.[25]

In 1934, the attorney general recommended that the clause relating to punishment for smuggling be amended "with the object of making it possible to deal with poor persons convicted of being in possession of small quantities of contraband tobacco without undue severity."[26] This amendment, passed on October 2, 1934,[27] made it possible for peasants to keep small quantities up to one kilogram for personal use, but also probably made it possible for them to evade punishment when caught red-handed in possession of untaxed tobacco they continued to sell informally.

The *Nakba* and Israeli Rule

The 1925 Tobacco Ordinance, along with the Customs Ordinance, of the British mandate continued to be the legal foundation for tobacco regulation in what became Israel, and Palestinian *fellahin* continued to be the main growers of tobacco selling their crops to local manufacturers, including BAT's one remaining factory Maspero. After the 1948 War, however, which saw the expulsion of 750,000 Palestinians and depopulation of hundreds of villages, the *fellahin* who remained in Israel were only a small minority of those who had lived in Palestine and cultivated its land.[28] The economy of what became Israel faltered in the absence of the expelled Palestinians, who used to provide the labour, raw material, trade connections, and know-how; but for many of those who did remain in what was a country suffering from inflation, monetary instability, scarcity, and austerity, cultivating tobacco became their lifeline.

[25] Hope-Simpson (1930).

[26] ISA-MandatoryOrganizations-MandateFishery-000ndv0, 71.

[27] Anonymous (1934).

[28] Zureik (1976, p. 48).

Israeli cigarette manufacturers were eager to secure tobacco leaf, and *fellahin*, in turn, needed money. However, this was not a simple supply-and-demand scenario, as Israeli officials often portrayed it. Palestinians in Israel became citizens, but their rights in the Zionist state were structurally limited. In the first 18 years of Israeli statehood, Palestinians in most areas were placed under military government, which controlled their movement, employment, education, and property. Under the emergency regulations (still in force in Israel today), the government gave itself the power to expropriate land, limit, or extend labour in certain industries, and direct the economy as it saw fit. Research conducted by Gadi Algazi, for example, demonstrates how the command economy of Israel in the first two decades was fertile ground for profit-making.[29]

In the tobacco sector, military and civilian officials and business connected to them profited in the name of the Jewish-Zionist hegemonic group and national home at the expense of the remaining Palestinian economic institutions. Palestinian cigarette manufacturers in Israel, The Arab Cigarette & Tombac Co., and Ibten Tobacco Co., for example, were excluded from the Joint Pool Committee for Tobacco Leaf in which the four largest Jewish manufacturers Dubek, Bejarano Bros., the Israel Cigarette Company, and Maspero participated. Many smaller factories were established during or right after the Mandate, but Maspero was the only one BAT controlled after 1948.

The Ministry of Finance, Zionist development agencies, and Jewish manufacturers never supported the Palestinians financially. Smuggling was therefore crucial for peasant households during and in the immediate aftermath of the War. Concomitantly, for the Israeli authorities, an issue primarily of *what* was being smuggled became an issue of *who* was doing the smuggling. Palestinians crossing the border became the main threat, and anything they carried across the border was seen as contraband. Questions of taxation, which until then were the main motivation for curbing smuggling, became irrelevant. The military and political institutions in Israel acted against it in the name of the security and demographic composition of the new state.

In August 1949, Amos Elon, in an article in *Bamahane* [ba-Mahane], the Hagana and later the IDF's weekly magazine,[30] described beginning

[29] Algazi (forthcoming).

[30] Bamahane, 4 August 1949, 9–13.

his reporting at the customs station in the depopulated border village of Tarbikha, one of the seven Shi'a villages of Mandatory Palestine. The main crop grown in Tarbikha before the expulsion was tobacco. The village had a customs station and one of the Tegart Forts built during the British Mandate as a measure against the 1936–1939 Arab Revolt due to its proximity to the border and its involvement in the tobacco market.[31] In his report, tobacco features as a sort of currency. Traffickers returned to Lebanon with their sacks full of shillings and ***kuruşlar***, equal to one hundredth of the Ottoman Lira or post-Ottoman currencies like the Syrian or Lebanese Pound or Lira, and also tobacco. "Tobacco grows everywhere in the Upper Galilee. Its price in [Israel] is much lower than in Lebanon or Syria. It is smuggled into Lebanon in exchange for sunglasses. Hundreds of kilograms—without banderoles." Elon also makes the point that tobacco smuggling represented a loss of hundreds of thousands of Israeli Pounds in state revenue.

The issue of infiltration became a key feature in political and public discourse in early Israel, fomenting a sense of constant threat to the very existence of the state. Historian Benny Morris calls infiltration "the core phenomena of the Arab–Israeli conflict in the years 1949–1956,"[32] and *fellahin* growing tobacco were some of these 'infiltrators.' Elias Shoufani, a scholar and native of Mi'ilya, writes in his account of the fall of the village about the pre-war significance of smuggling tobacco and the post-war tobacco-harvesting operation. Smuggling in the 1947 season was a necessity, he argued, since the violence had already begun and selling it to licensed manufacturers was impossible. Established growers, who used to sell their crop, the best in the country, for a good profit now needed to hire others to traffic their leaf across the border. He remembers how "the farmers harvested their tobacco, packed it in packages of one kilo each, and smuggled it across the border and sold it in other villages where tobacco was not grown."[33]

During the war, as floods of refugees moved north, many villagers in Lebanon hosted refugees in their homes, and continued to trade with refugees and peasants who remained in their villages, like the ones in Mi'ilya. During the first truce, and after the village's occupation in May

[31] ISA-moch-mmi-000g1wc.

[32] Morris (1997, p. v).

[33] Shoufani (1972, p. 116).

1948, they had to harvest the crop by late June in a clandestine operation. To do so, villagers set up nightly scouting missions to see whether soldiers patrolled the fields or the footpaths.[34] When they established that it was safe, they sneaked out to harvest. Women and children participated, and women learned how to fire rifles to protect themselves.

After the ceasefire agreement was signed, cigarettes were not included in the price-controlled, rationed commodities during the decade of the 1949–1959 command economy, the austerity regime or *tsenaʿ* in Hebrew.[35] News reports from the 1950s show just how prevalent smuggling operations were for the *fellahin* in Galilee. The devaluation of the Israel Pound made cash payment in exchange for Lebanese goods impossible. This, coupled with an import deficit and limited production in Israel, drove many, including many Palestinian villagers who did not receive rations, to seek out goods on the black market. A 1952 report notes that instead of cash payments people buying Lebanese smuggled goods started to barter.[36] Essential goods, like shoes, clothes, foodstuffs, coffee, and sugar brought from the Lebanese side of the border, were exchanged for medicine, tobacco, and food preserved in olive oil.

These smuggling operations were some of the first instances of Arab–Jewish cooperation after 1948, and many intercepted trafficking rings were 'Jewish–Arab.' 'Arabs', more likely Palestinians on both sides of the border, often undertook the more dangerous role of moving contraband across the border, and then Jewish distributers and intermediaries (men and women) mediated between the smugglers and the traders. One customs report draft stated that smugglers were assisted by Palestinians in border villages and Jews resident in frontier settlements and the *maʿabarot* immigrant camps.[37] But the report omitted to mention Jewish collaboration with smugglers, laying the blame solely at the feet of the Palestinians.[38] By the late 1950s, most of the Israeli demand for manufactured goods like shoes and clothes were met through legal imports and improved manufacturing. Preventative customs operations, in cooperation with the Israel Border Police, had brought much of the earlier

[34] Ibid., p. 117.

[35] ha-Tsofeh, 22 May 1949, 3.

[36] 'Al Hamishmar, 8 February 1952, 8.

[37] ISA-mof-mof-000lecz, 47.

[38] Ibid., 39.

trafficking under control by then. A report from 1958, however, listed the commodities still trafficked widely, including tobacco.[39]

Tobacco smuggling had by then taken the familiar form of internal smuggling or informal sale. As an excisable commodity, the state considered any failure to report the accurate quantity of tobacco a *fellah* household grew as smuggling. This points to the final remaining survival strategy of tobacco-growing *fellahin* at the time: "In the last few years a pattern is consolidating, whereby the residents of Arab villages in Israel only declare part of the tobacco they grow and use the remaining tobacco for 'internal' trafficking."[40] The report noted the high price of Israeli-manufactured cigarettes as key for the proliferation of this trade, which was made possible by the trafficking of thin rolling papers for domestic cigarettes. Rolling papers, cigarette cutters, and other paraphernalia for domestic cigarette production were banned under the stipulations of the Tobacco Ordinance. Data published in the press shows a leap in siezures of contraband tobacco and its paraphernalia for the years 1953–1957, with leaf being internally smuggled and rolling papers and lighters moved across the border to make the untaxed informal trade in tobacco leaf possible.[41]

This internal smuggling was harder to monitor or prevent and posed a serious challenge to the Department of Customs and Excise. The director of customs stated that tobacco growers cannot be accused of tobacco smuggling just because they sold crops that manufacturers deemed to be "too small."[42] Without tangible evidence, the authorities had no grounds on which to accuse the growers of smuggling or other violations of the tobacco ordinance, like not reporting the destruction of crops or the true extent of cultivation.

Small quantities of untaxed tobacco and rolling papers were apprehended at different times,[43] but selling tobacco informally rested on a network of people united by the same goal—to trade freely in tobacco. This meant that in groups with a high level of social and political cohesion, like the Palestinians in Israel and, as detailed below, the *fellahin*

[39] Ha-Aretz, 7 February 1958, p. 3.

[40] Ibid.

[41] ha-Aretz, 7 February 1958, p. 3.

[42] ISA-mof-mof-000lyir, p. 12.

[43] ha-Boker, 10 August 1958, 6. Herut, 12 January 1955, p. 4.

tobacco growers, as long as everyone kept quiet the informal trade went on uninterrupted.

Fellah Narratives

Under Ottoman, British, and Israeli rule tobacco-growing *fellahin* used methods that were delegitimised and punishable by law to make a living from the tobacco they grew, which they colloquially called *'Arabi*. These included smuggling tobacco to and from neighbouring countries, such as South Lebanon, also a tobacco-growing area known for smuggling[44]; selling tobacco to neighbours and other villagers who did not grow it themselves; smoking it without paying taxes; and manufacturing and smuggling banned tobacco cutters, rolling papers, and related equipment. Most did not partake in the bigger cross-border smuggling operations, and, as we shall see in this section, from interviews I conducted, did not identify as organised criminals breaking the law for a substantial profit. The illegal trade in tobacco by *fellahin*, rather than professional smugglers, is rarely reported in the press. By comparison, newspapers and archival documents provide many examples of smuggling by professional traffickers. Unlike peasants, professional smugglers, especially during the mandate, were less afraid of the authorities, and openly challenged law enforcement, for example by pretending to be informants and collecting rewards,[45] or by suing customs officers for compensation in case of bodily harm.[46] *Fellahin*, on the other hand, were more wary and less proud of their participation in the informal trade, especially since at the time of our conversations they still lived under Israeli rule and were governed by its legal system.

They had reason to be cautious. When newspapers covered seizures of tobacco in peasant households, they reported crimes for which punishments were astonishingly grave. In 1940, the Central Court of Acre heard six cases and sentences were, on average, a fine of LP 384, enough to reduce the household to financial ruin. Ahmad 'Assaf was fined PL 414, Mahmoud Diyab LP 608, Hasan Yasin LP 539, Muhammad Sa'id Sun'-allah LP 204, Fayyad 'Omar Muhammad LP 212, and Ragheb Rashid

[44] Abisaab (2009, pp. 483–501). Chaker (2016, pp. 27–51).

[45] Anonymous (1932, p. 7).

[46] PRO CO 733/270/9.

'Abd al-Halim LP 324.[47] The fine could be converted to three months' imprisonment, a choice some of the accused likely made since the average peasant household only made LP 25–30 annually.[48] Most active in the informal trade were men, but since tobacco cultivation depended on the labour of the entire household, all members of the family participated in the cultivation, manipulation, transportation, and sale of the leaf.

When I first started interviewing, I was not aware of the hesitation to talk about the informal trade and began directly asking about smuggling. I soon learned that *fellahin* seldom called tobacco that would otherwise be classified as 'smuggled' but used the euphemism "tobacco for smoking" (*Dukhan li-shurub*). They often chose some of the best of their tobacco 'for smoking', thus failing to report the accurate amount of excisable tobacco they produced and failing to sell it to a tobacco company as the law required.

When asked, Hanna Abu 'Oqsa (b. 1926) from the village of Mi'ilya answered:

B: And smuggling?
H: Where to? Smuggling what?
B: Wherever you want.
H: We did not deal with smuggling.
B: No, but did you hear that some people smuggled?
H: There was some smuggling. We heard rumours… We can't tell you anything about it, I mean, we cannot know the truth of it, whether it's true or not. Smuggling… Whoever smuggles does so quietly. Will they show off what they smuggle?
B: And you, you did not smuggle, right?
H: No, I did not work in smuggling.[49]

For him, keeping tobacco for personal use had nothing to do with smuggling. Smuggling was something a career criminal would do, and he was nothing of the sort. If he had smuggled, he had done so quietly. Later in the conversation, I tried a different tactic. I asked him about tobacco for personal use:

[47] Anonymous (1940, p. 3).

[48] El-Eini (2006, p. 119).

[49] Hanna Abu 'Oqsa, interview with author, 29 June 2014, min. 6:56.

B: What about tobacco for smoking?
H: They used to take some, keep some and smoke it, whoever smoked kept some...
B: Where did they hide it?
H: They didn't hide it, they just put it in a place where it can't be [found].
B: And they didn't come searching for it?
H: No, they would look and not find it. They used to put it aside.[50]

Hanna's admission, that people who used to smoke tobacco kept some for personal use, did not contradict his insistence on not having smuggled himself. To stress the point, he insisted that people did not 'hide' it, just 'put it aside' where it could not be found. Moreover, in a peasant economy where many goods and objects change hands without having been bought or sold, 'personal use' could plausibly be interpreted not only as serving the needs of the immediate family but possibly a much larger group through gift-giving.

Hanna's knowledge of trafficking operations at the border perfectly matches press reports and scholarly literature about organised trafficking operations and especially that of hashish, which was smuggled by professional smugglers from Lebanon through Palestine (which was not a consumer of hashish) to Egypt.[51] Together with his denial of keeping tobacco for personal use or selling it independently, he knew intimately how the traffickers operated:

H: There were two or three smugglers in the village. Some of them were caught and some were not. Smugglers would charge their "tax" [...] People from Lebanon would come here. The borders were easy [to cross], not like today.
B: Would they come often?
H: Yes, often.
B: What would they bring apart from hashish?
H: Hashish, that's it.

Hanna further specified the networks used for smuggling purposes:

[50] Hanna Abu 'Oqsa, interview with author, 29 June 2014, min. 3:38.
[51] Ram (2020).

B: Did people here [in Palestine] buy hashish?
H: No.
B: [in disbelief] No? So where would they move it?
H: To Gaza, to Egypt.
B: From Lebanon to Egypt.
H: They would bring it here, through here, and take it to Gaza.
B: And on its way there, would anybody…
H: They would, it is smuggling after all…
B: Yes, but would anybody buy from them?
H: [Decisively] No. No. Nobody here, or very few. Besides, how much [hashish] would one require? A small piece? We're talking kilograms here.
B: How did they come? On foot?
H: On foot, how else?!
B: I don't know…
H: Walking, it was all on foot. This was trafficking at night. People would bring it to the border, other people would bring it here [to the village] and from here they would take it to their people in Nazareth, Kafr Qar', etc. [..] They would take it from one [town] to the next until it gets to Gaza and then Egypt.

Similarly, when I asked Hanna's sister, Agnes (b. 1920), related questions, this time without saying the word 'smuggling,' she evaded the issue:

B: Did you leave some tobacco on the side?
A: Leave tobacco on the side? Why?
B: For the neighbours, for your father, I don't know, for your family, for you…
A: I don't know…
B: Did you not smoke it?
A: Why? Was it considered poison?
B: No, I ask because it was forbidden.
A: No, it was not forbidden, they could not have banned it. Whoever was smart used to hide it and they could not do anything about it. The police conducted searches, and when they caught something they penalised us. This whole thing just required some humouring and it would all be resolved.

B: They would humour the officials?
A: They would humour the Arabs and the Arabs would humour [the officials] ...[52]

"Why? Was it considered a poison?" is a question she fired after she thought I had implied the tobacco her family grew was of poor quality. *Samm*, the word she used, also means drug in Arabic, so it could be understood both in terms of legality as well as social acceptability. When she realised I was asking about informal tobacco's legality, she summarily denied any illegality. Her answer reflected a very basic rejection of the law, and small, everyday ways to circumvent what she saw as its arbitrariness and injustice. 'Humouring,' or bribing, the officers was also illegal, but she had no problem talking about that.

This must be seen as closely related to national and social cohesion among the growers, who had to rely on each other not to inform the authorities and collect rewards, which would be easy money for the indebted. In her book *Palestinian Village Histories: Geographies of the Displaced*, anthropologist Rochelle Davis tells the story of the now-depopulated village of al-Shajara. Palestinian customs officers employed by the British Mandate came to a guesthouse (*madafeh*). While there, they went through the cigarettes offered to the guests and found some containing untaxed, locally grown tobacco. The officers fined the host for having untaxed cigarettes, whereupon they were not served lunch in a breach of local social norms.[53] The officers left annoyed and went to the neighbouring village of Tamra, where they complained to their hosts that the people of al-Shajara did not serve them lunch. The *mukhtar* [Ar. village chief] of Tamra said that was impossible because the people of al-Shajara were known for their generosity. When the officers told him why this had happened, the *mukhtar* became angry and told them to leave, also without feeding them.

Davis argues that this portrays the values of the villagers and demonstrates the defence of Palestinian values in the face of British colonial authority. It also demonstrates how the officers, some of whom were Palestinians, were caught in a non-market economy of gift-giving and hospitality. This point arose in the interview with Hanna Shoufani (b.

[52] Agnes Abu 'Oqsa Ma'louf, interview with author, 29 June 2014, min. 13:42.
[53] Davis (2011, p. 74).

1930) from Mi'ilya, the brother of Elias Shoufani. He labelled customs officers "traitors" who treated them with incriminating suspicion and disrespect:

H: The government of Israel used to [employ] one man from customs who was called Abu Nadeem, from, from, from Jdaideh, here, when he used to come weigh the tobacco, he would go around our house as if I'm hiding a bunch or two of tobacco that I want to cut and steal cigarettes. I mean, they're the lowest of the low.
B: And did they use to do the same in the times of *El-Ingleez* [the British Mandate]?
H: In the times of *El-Ingleez* they also used to do so.
B: They used to search and see if you kept some for yourself?
H: Yes, they would look whether you'd left a bunch or two of tobacco. The cook of the poison tastes it.[54]

Hanna spoke of his own agency and rejected notions of colonial lawfulness. Echoing Agnes, he insisted that he was "the cook of the poison" and had every right to taste it. He denied the alienation between him, the producer, and the product of his labour, even if that product were poison. For him, it was preposterous that a grower, who together with his household toiled all year round to cultivate tobacco, should be prevented from disposing of his crop however he desired. The tone he used conveyed his contempt towards the British Mandate and its laws and policies.

Nationally construed social cohesion was not only important to safeguard peasants against colonial officers but also to market tobacco informally across the countryside. Hanna Shoufani demonstrated the contradiction between hiding tobacco and spreading the word about its quality as a commodity:

H: I mean, [my tobacco] had a good reputation, the tobacco I made for myself to smoke was recommended, and people would come take from it, they knew about my tobacco.
B: Did you hide the tobacco you produced somewhere?

[54] Hanna Shoufani, interview with author, 7 April 2014, min. 21:01.

H: I used to cut it, I'm telling you, I used to cut it, no, when it was cut I didn't... I put it next to my bed. <laughing> I hid it of course...

Wife: He used to shove it under the bed.[55]

On the one hand, Shoufani hid the tobacco leaf under his bed, but it had a good reputation, people knew about it and recommended it for its quality. He chose to say that they would "take from it," maybe to dissimulate the economic exchange. His pride in his tobacco leaf was not hampered by the illegality of the practice or the fact that he had to hide it. He was a third-generation grower, following in the footsteps of his grandfather. His son, Fai'z, also went back to growing tobacco with his children, making five generations of tobacco growers in their family.

'Orsan Tarabe (b. 1913), from Sakhnin, described a different sales practice—that of the travelling salesman:

B: Did they smoke this tobacco here?

O: Yes, yes, we would smoke it and carry it with us, whoever did not have would buy from me, and people started cutting tobacco, the blade on one side and a mortar [on the other], [the blade] would shave [the tobacco] like a razor into the basin, it would condense the tobacco and with the blade the person cutting would go ahead...

B: And cut it. And did you sell all the tobacco to Qaraman, or would you smoke...?

O: No, to Qaraman, some was for Qaraman, and some, that was good to smoke, we would cut it [and] divide it into *Ūqiyahs* [*Okas* or ounces] and an *Ūqiyah* is one half of a *Ratl*. We would wander around the villages. Yes we would sell it, in Loubieh, in Saffurieh, in Reineh, in Mashhad, in Iksal, in Kufr Masr and those villages, [we sold it for a price that was] enough to provide for ourselves.[56]

Orsan is one of the oldest peasants I interviewed, and his language, as well as rationale, was the farthest from the present. His family usually sold its tobacco to Karaman, Dick, and Salti, the largest manufacturer

[55] Hanna Shoufani, interview with author, 7 April 2014, min. 41:25.

[56] Orsan Tarabe, interview with author, 21 July 2013, min. 27:48.

of cigarettes in Palestine during the Mandate, which was the flagship 'Arab' BAT-associated factory. His justification for going village-to-village to sell tobacco was simple: his family needed to provide for itself. Peasants further to the south grew very little tobacco, and the quality was not good enough to smoke on its own. He had a market available, and he was willing to take his chances with customs patrols, which could get him fined, imprisoned, or lose the donkey he used to go around on selling his merchandise.

Despite their belief that it was their right, and even though it had turned into something of a national tradition, this practice put the *fellahin* in situations where they had to hide their involvement in the informal trade in tobacco. Hanna Shoufani told a famous story in Mi'ilya, mixing humour with a recipe to elude punishment. The man in the story had gone to the judge to plead that his donkey, used to transport contraband, not be confiscated:

> H: There was this man from our village who got caught [illegally transporting tobacco], he was a simple man but a clever one. They caught him and his donkey here, at the entrance [to the village] and fined him. He went to the courthouse, where the judge asked him: "how old is this donkey?" The man held his hand out, [...] and answered: "I swear to your honour, I forgot the donkey's birth certificate at home!" The judge yelled at him <loudly>: "leave!!" <laughing>[57]

Without being able to identify the specific donkey, it could not be taken away from the *fellah*. So, by denying knowing his age, the *fellah* successfully avoided losing his main means of transportation. 'Humouring' colonial officers, or rather using humour, were effective methods not only to evade punishment but also narrative methods through which the *fellahin* could insist on their subjectivity in the face of draconian law and law enforcement. Humour took the brunt of injustice, and made it socially deliberated, and even laughed at.

[57] Hanna Shoufani, interview with author, 7 April 2014, min. 25:26.

Conclusion

The commercial cultivation of tobacco was the main source of livelihood for many Palestinian peasant households. While it presented them with many challenges under three different regimes and with changing borders, they managed to withstand imperial and colonial monopolistic practices and make a livelihood cultivating tobacco commercially and often selling it independently. This informal market had been active and even widespread since the introduction of the Ottoman *Régie*, in the late nineteenth century. With their occupation of Palestine in World War I, the British promised to liberalise the market, but in fact replicated the *Régie's* monopolistic rules, and codified them into the Tobacco Ordinance of 1925, which allowed BAT to effectively monopolise the market. Israeli authorities would later adopt the British Ordinance and recreate the same conditions that would make it easy for one company, Dubek, to become a single-buyer of tobacco leaf in 1971.

Particularly in times of need, as during and after the 1948 War, when most Palestinians became refugees, the informal sale of tobacco provided *fellahin* who grew tobacco with a way to make some income. The ones who were refugees crossed back to harvest their tobacco crops. The minority who remained in Palestine had to cross into Lebanon to sell the tobacco leaf, which became important as a form of currency. Both groups did so at great risk, as they could get caught or worse.

Despite these ostensibly illegal actions, most *fellahin* would never identify themselves as smugglers. They rejected this completely, seeing themselves as law-abiding people who have done nothing that warrants such a negative, criminal identification. They found justifications for their actions and ways to make sense of the gap between what they knew was formally illegal but believed was their inalienable right, and they argued that the law was unjust in its attempt to ban their independent sale of tobacco. They were proud of what they grew and did their best not to lose their sense of humour and innate sense of justice.

Without being overtly nationalist and anticolonial, they managed to express their own sense of justice as colonised indigenous peasants. They called the untaxed tobacco 'Arab,' expressed disdain for colonial laws and policies, and did not shy away from talking about their work and their tobacco with others within the community. In fact, the entire market was constructed through long-standing social ties between Palestinians sharing the same understanding of the peasants' right sell the tobacco they grow as they please.

References

Primary Sources

Unpublished

Agnes Abu 'Oqsa Ma' louf, interview with author, 29 June 2014.
Hanna Shoufani, interview with author, 7 April 2014.
ISA-mof-mof-000lyir
ISA-mof-mof-000lecz
ISA-moch-mmi-000g1wc
ISA-MandatoryOrganizations-MandateFishery-000ndv0
ISA-MandatoryOrganizations-MandateFishery-000nduz
ISA-MandatoryOrganizations-SecretaryCommerce-000o0zu
ISA-MandatoryOrganizations-SecretaryCommerce-000o4ex
ISA-MandatoryOrganizations-MandateAtrnGen-00077im
Orsan Tarabe, interview with author, 21 July 2013.
PRO CO 733/270/9

Published

Anonymous. 1932. *Filastin*, 08 October, 7.
Anonymous. 1940. a*l-Difa*, 09 July, 3.
Anonymous. 1949. *ha-Tsofeh*, 22 May, 3.
Anonymous. 1955. *Herut*, 12 January, 4.
Anonymous. 1958(a). *ha-Boker*, 10 August, 6.
Anonymous. 1958(b). h*a-Aretz*, 7 February, 3.
Himadeh, S.B. 1939. *Economic Organization of Palestine*. Beirut: American Press.
Hope-Simpson. J. 1930. *Report on Immigration, Land Settlement and Development*. Presented by the Secretary of State for the Colonies to Parliament by Command of His Majesty. London: H.M. Stationery Office.
Shmueli, Yermiyahu. 1952. *'Al Hamishmar'*, 08 February, 8.
The Government of Palestine. 1934. Supplement no. 1 to the *Palestine Gazette*, no. 470, 4 October, 4.
Zlocisti, T. 1925. *The Cultivation and Manufacture of Tobacco in Palestine*. Tel-Aviv: Palestine Economic Society.

Secondary Sources

Abisaab, M. 2009. Shiite Peasants and a New Nation in Colonial Lebanon: The Intifada of Bint Jubayl, 1936. *Comparative Studies of South Asia, Africa and the Middle East* 29: 483–501.

Chaker, J. 2012. Eastern Tobacco and the Ottoman Régie: A History of Financiers in the Age of Empire. MA Thesis, American University of Beirut.

Chaker, J. 2016. Mule Drivers in Nineteenth-Century Lebanon: From Local Social History Towards Global History. *Almanack* 14: 27–51.

Davis, R. 2011. *Palestinian Village Histories: Geographies of the Displaced*. Stanford, CA: Stanford University Press.

El-Eini, R.I.M. 2006. *Mandated Landscape: British Imperial Rule in Palestine, 1929–1948*. London and New York: Routledge.

Fahoum, B. 2020. Weaponizing Global Consumers: Big Tobacco's Arab Boycott and the 'Jewish Problem'. *Journal of Levantine Studies* 10. https://levantine-journal.org/product/weaponizing-global-consumers-big-tobaccos-arab-boycott-jewish-problem/. Accessed by 2 January 2024.

Fahoum, B. 2023. Tobacco Cultivation and Production in Twentieth-Century Palestine/Israel. Ph.D. Dissertation, Stanford University.

Gilmore, A.B., and A. Rowell. 2018. The Tobacco Industry's Latest Scam: How Big Tobacco Is Still Facilitating Tobacco Smuggling, While Also Attempting to Control a Global System Designed to Prevent It. Blog—Tobacco Control, 19 June. https://blogs.bmj.com/tc/2018/06/19/the-tobacco-industrys-latest-scam-how-big-tobacco-is-still-facilitating-tobacco-smuggling-while-also-attempting-to-control-a-global-system-designed-to-prevent-it/. Accessed by 2 January 2024.

Morris, B. 1997. *Israel's Border Wars, 1949–1956: Arab Infiltration, Israeli Retaliation, and the Countdown to the Suez War*. Oxford: Oxford University Press.

OCCRP. 2022. Smoke and Mirrors: How the 'Father' of Iraq's Cigarette Smugglers Built an Empire. OCCRP. https://www.occrp.org/en/investigations/smoke-and-mirrors-how-the-father-of-iraqs-cigarette-smugglers-built-an-empire. Accessed 14 August 2022.

Ram, H. 2020. *Intoxicating Zion: A Social History of Hashish in Mandatory Palestine and Israel*. Stanford, CA: Stanford University Press.

Rosenfeld, H. 1968. Change, Barriers to Change, and Contradictions in the Arab Village Family. *American Anthropologist* 70: 732–752.

Shoufani, E. 1972. The Fall of a Village. *Journal of Palestine Studies* 1: 108–121.

Vardağli, E. T. 2014. International Tobacco Politics and the Question of Social Movements in the Middle East: A Comparative Analysis of Ottoman and Iranian Cases. *Middle Eastern Studies* 50: 606–621.

Zureik, E. 1976. Transformation of Class Structure Among the Arabs in Israel: From Peasantry to Proletariat. *Journal of Palestine Studies* 6: 39–66.

CHAPTER 14

Afterword: Tobacco's Glocal Worlds

Kathinka Sinha-Kerkhoff

> In the final analysis, any global history of tobacco is a broad outline of events that should more cautiously or glocally be told worldwide.[1]

My research in colonial Bengal, on tobacco, indigo, and sugar,[2] over almost the same time frame as this volume, made me acutely aware of the distinctions among various crops and locales, and the need to broaden my story.[3] It made me see the need for a comparative perspective within the overarching history of capitalism, whereby empirical case studies can act as building blocks for garnering a much-needed local and global historical perspective. For many years, attempts on the part of several of us to hold an international tobacco conference that could advance such a

[1] Quote taken from Relli Shechter's Chapter 3.
[2] Sinha-Kerkhoff (2014, 2016, 2017).
[3] Sinha-Kerkhoff (2020).

K. Sinha-Kerkhoff (✉)
International Institute of Social History (IISH), Amsterdam, The Netherlands
e-mail: kathinkasinhakerkhoff64@gmail.com

A. van Wickeren et al. (eds.), *Tobacco in Global Perspective, 1780–1960*, Cambridge Imperial and Post-Colonial Studies,
https://doi.org/10.1007/978-3-031-64411-5_14

glocal tobacco narrative failed to materialise. Funding for this proved difficult to obtain in a world that increasingly viewed tobacco as a public health concern and advocated for its global eradication. In December 2021, however, a group of scholars physically dispersed across the globe convened online to share their passion for researching the profound implications of tobacco's global dissemination across diverse settings. At the end of three days of intense discussion of tobacco histories in a range of countries, I had the honour of delivering the concluding remarks which form the basis for what I now elaborate on here.

Commodity history all too often draws predominantly from English-language sources, and the conference organisers particularly sought out new and established scholars whose research was based on linguistically diverse sources, from various disciplines and employing different methodologies, relying not only on textual evidence but also delving into statistical data, visual materials, archaeological findings, and oral histories. With the exception of two chapters, this edited volume comprises a selection of papers originally discussed during the conference that have been worked on since. It stands as testimony to the effort on the part of authors and editors, given the linguistic diversity of the source materials, the variety of languages in which conference papers were originally written, and the subsequent substantial work of translation and revision. The authors provided fresh perspectives on the global history of tobacco, crafting new narratives from previously untapped historical sources that provided ample documentation of the widespread dissemination of tobacco.

While following diverging historical paths, tobacco gained prominence as a lucrative cash crop in colonial and postcolonial landscapes, under shifting political regimes and often tobacco monopolies. In colonial and metropolitan environments, documents yielded valuable information on how different tobacco varieties were grown, dried, cured, harvested, and processed, as well as on the diseases associated with them. Scientific texts examined various aspects of different tobacco plants—American, Turkish/Oriental, Cuban, and the many domestic varieties, graded according to quality (superior/inferior), colour (dark/bright), and forms of consumption. Treatises offered instruction on soils, irrigation, and how to prepare the tobaccos, often by blending with locally available varieties, whether for chewing or smoking, or snuff. Statistics, business and economic reports, and other source material provided information on markets, investment, import and export, expenditure and income, retail, pricing, and revenue.

Knowledge was shared about agriculture, commerce, industry and technology; innovations in tobacco growing, processing, and manufacturing; and the tools and machinery used, as in hand-rolled or machine-made cigars and cigarettes. Consumption added another layer to the multifaceted tobacco narratives. Detailed descriptions of tobacco use and artefacts circulated. Some contemporary treatises were explicitly intended for smokers, extolling the plant's sublime qualities, while others warned of its detrimental health effects. Ethnographic monographs contributed valuable insights into the cultural and social significance of tobacco among various populations around the world. Tobacco featured prominently in prose, poetry, anecdotes, and myths, spanning ever more diverse languages and regions, in addition to travelogues, artwork, images, architectural elements, and advertisements. All attested to tobacco's pervasive global presence in a range of consumption practices and material cultures.[4]

Tobacco is far from monolithic. It encompasses different plant varieties, irrigation and land issues. Its processing results in loose or dried, flue- or sun-cured leaf, shredded or powdered tobacco, and plug or shag. Tobacco might refer to filler or wrapper leaf, tobacco transformed into "carottes," or tobacco mixed with other kinds of leaf. Tobacco can be either a luxury or a necessity, and has different meanings, often symbolic. It was used as currency in financial transactions and barter, and gifted, a sign of hospitality or sociability.

Tobacco was embodied in non-human objects such as warehouses, factories, machines, financial institutions and retail structures; in laws, regulations, advertisements, branding and design; in a variety of finished products, such as pipes, cigars, and cigarettes; and in a whole paraphernalia for consumption, such as pouches, stoppers, match- and snuff-boxes, containers, cutters, filters, graters, and raspers. There was "foreign" and "indigenous" tobacco, including, in the British context, "Empire" vs "non-Empire" tobacco, and tobacco for the domestic and export markets.

Most of all, this tobacco universe was inhabited by people—seafarers, slaves, labourers, missionaries, scientists, and soldiers, who diffused it all over the globe to leave its imprint on the lives of consumers, producers, traders, the rich and the poor, the powerful and the marginalised, and everyone in between. In this universe, tobacco played a role in shaping

[4] As documented, for example, in Brennan (1915).

identities, based on class, gender, ethnicity, age, and native place, giving rise to intricate power dynamics.

The chapters in this volume collectively reveal to us such a tobacco universe, encompassing plants, objects, and people, interconnected across geographical locations, located spatially and temporally to document not only how tobacco was diffused globally but also how it became embedded or rejected locally. A promising new history has been written, exploring the three components of tobacco, as a plant, an object, and a living being, in worlds where human and non-human elements are entangled. Plants, and objects associated with them, are seen in interaction with humans, in a sense possessing their own agency.[5]

Authors were asked to pay special attention to agency, and, while not always engaging with some of the more innovative approaches, they all show agency in one or more of its multiple forms roaming the world. There was the agency of factory owners and managers, politicians, policy-makers, businessmen, and scientists, some with more and others with less power, some representing the interests of conglomerates and monopolies. Foregrounding colonial, national, ethnic, racial, class, gender, age, and birthplace divides, there were those who challenged the conditions under which they laboured and claimed what they perceived as their rights and rightful identities, through their involvement in illicit trade, picketing, strikes, slowdowns, and acts of vandalism and other so-called felonies. The whole gamut of agency, as a product of social relations, is thus well evidenced.

There are historians over the centuries who have called for the inclusion of tobacco's place in world history on a par with war and revolution. As quoted by Thomas Höllman, the German historian August Ludwig von Schlözer, in his *Briefwechsel* (Göttingen 1775–1781), came to the following conclusion: "A history of tobacco drawn from the sources (…) is (…) for the history of the world at least as attractive a subject as the history of the great Tamerlane, or that of the old Assyrian empire."[6] By then already advanced in age, he had come to understand that the story of tobacco "elsewhere in the world" was of as much importance in a true commodity history of the world as was the introduction of tobacco in Europe.

[5] Russell (2019).

[6] Höllmann (2015, p. 127).

The Austrian historian Count Egon Caesar Corti similarly reiterated in his 1931 history of smoking that tobacco was of universal interest and had to be seen in its religious, therapeutic, medicinal, and sociological entirety. Corti referred to other historians who had followed the path outlined by von Schlözer and had produced exhaustive works on tobacco. Yet most, he judged, had been "handling the subject under various specific aspects" and had not surveyed "the matter as a whole." In spite of their "excellent qualities," Corti still felt the need to pen a global history of tobacco "something which plays an important part in the daily life of the great majority of people."[7]

A decade before Corti's work, the Tobacco Leaf Publishing Company in New York released Carl Avery Werner's *Tobaccoland*,[8] which was a book about tobacco that provided a geographical and chronological account of the wild tobacco plant, its transformation into several species of cultivated plants, and their manufacturing into consumption commodities that could be chewed, smoked, puffed, drunk, or sniffed. Werner depicted this land of tobacco extending its frontiers all over the world, a world created by commerce for profit pursued by individuals, communities, corporations, nation-states, and empires, the dynamic of which transformed the prevailing geopolitical and economic structures of capitalism. He detailed how tobacco's introduction in different regions in the world generated socio-cultural change as well as changing cultivation systems, industrial processes, commercial development, and government regulations. However, like so many others before and since, he provided the reader with few social, economic, legal, artistic, scientific, or technological references beyond those that were generated in North America and Europe. The scope of a truly global tobacco history remained an ongoing challenge.

This volume goes well beyond a solely Anglocentric or Eurocentric approach. It incorporates regions that have previously received little to no attention, and skilfully interweaves major aspects of global tobacco trade, production, and consumption into the narratives. It highlights how a particular region can evolve from being a central player in global tobacco production to a peripheral one over time, as well as the reverse, and

[7] Corti (1931, pp. 7–9).

[8] Russell (2019).

how a territory primarily catering to its domestic market is not necessarily missing out on a vibrant and constantly evolving consumer culture.

Connections are made between various global processes, from the spread of capitalism and the global ebb and flow of commodities to industrialisation, mechanisation, and migration. Authors show how these processes were intertwined in the local tobacco worlds explored, in the context of world-changing wars—from the Seven Years' War, the American War of Independence, and the War of the Spanish Succession to World War I and World War II, the Franco-Russian War, the Russo-Ottoman War, the Balkan Wars, and the Arab–Israeli War—and landmark moments such as the Austro-Hungarian Dualist Compromise, the establishment of the Armenian Patriarchate in Turkey, the Treaties of Carlowitz and Passarowitz, and the Palestinian Nakba. Longue-durée processes span the transformation of states, monarchies, and empires; state alliances; the formation and abolition of tobacco monopolies, liberalisation, and nationalisation; colonisation, decolonisation, and corporate imperialism; the feminisation of labour, racism, and genocide; and natural disasters, impacting on, and influenced by, the various tobacco worlds featured in the volume.

A common thread that runs throughout is the role of individuals in positions of power in states, empires, monopolies, and multinational corporations, alongside others in small local companies playing important roles in agro-industrial and market complexes, and a long list of government officials, customs officers, controllers, influential business figures and their family members, experts, technicians, scientists, sellers and buyers, managers, planters, settlers, landowners, policymakers, and politicians. And yet, their efforts to introduce new practices, change existing ones, or even maintain the status quo in tobacco production, commerce, and consumption often met with reactions from those with less power, from traders, producers, and workers to consumers, and the outcomes of their interactions were complex, contentious, diverse, and often unpredictable.

In conclusion, this volume skilfully intertwines histories of tobacco on a global scale, delving into complex interplays across a variety of contexts, and what stands out is how vividly tobacco's trajectories were never unilateral or unidirectional. The twelve narratives make a compelling case for how tobacco played a pivotal role in shaping the modern world we inhabit today.

Fig. 14.1 Title: 1944: Calcutta Street Scene "Smoking Passing Show and Enjoy Good Health" (*Source* Photograph by Frank Bond held by the University of Chicago Library, Southern Asia Department.Courtesy James Nye and Laura A. Ring)

The contemporary landscape of tobacco has undergone significant transformations. Many of the worlds depicted here have faded into history, as fleeting representations of a bygone era. The brand "Passing Show" was once associated with the most affordable machine-made cigarettes of its time made with Virginia-type tobacco. Manufactured in London and also exported to British India, it faced competition there from a locally produced brand called "Charminar." In colonial India, the "foreignness" of the Passing Show was clear to see, symbolised by the image of a top-hatted, monocled British gentleman displayed prominently on a 1940s billboard in the heart of Calcutta, the former colonial capital, yet it was popular due to its affordability (Fig. 14.1).

"Passing Show" also served as the title of a Bengali stage play that revolves around Atin, a character whose existence straddles the boundary between the present and the past. In the play, Atin's imaginative worlds seamlessly traversed different spaces, times, and people. The core message of the play emphasises that the past holds significance not merely as nostalgia, but also as a vital lens for comprehending the contemporary world that Atin inhabits.[9]

The glocal tobacco worlds in this volume evolved over time and space, and many of their traditions and artefacts now reside in museums. Yet, despite the global transformations in tobacco consumption and production, practices, tastes, advertising, and the meanings and identities associated with tobacco, the in-depth histories recounted here remain crucial. Much like the Bengali play illustrates, these histories are essential for our present-day comprehension of not only the who, where, and what of tobacco consumption, but also the broader complexities of tobacco's reach. They shed light on past "smoking geographies"[10] shaping current identities and interests intertwined with tobacco and underscore the formidable challenges faced today in pursuit of tobacco's eradication.

References

Barnett, R., G. Moon, J. Pearce, L. Thompson, and L. Twigg. 2017. *Smoking Geographies. Space, Place and Tobacco*. Chichester: Willey Blackwell.

Brennan, W.A. 1915. *Tobacco Leaves. Being a Book of Facts for Smokers*. Menasha, WI: George Banta Publishing Company.

Chatterji, S.A. 2016. Passing Show: A Search into One's Past? The Citizen (TC) I S Queer +, 17 April. http://dev.thecitizen.in/en/NewsDetail/index/9. Accessed by 5 October 2023.

Corti, C.E.C. 1931. *A History of Smoking*. London: George G. Harrap.

Höllmann, T.O. 2015. Review. Golden-Silk Smoke: A History of Tobacco in China, 1550–2010. *East Asian Science, Technology, and Medicine* 41: 127–129.

Russell, A. 2019. *Anthropology of Tobacco. Ethnographic Adventures in Non-Human Worlds*. London and New York: Routledge.

Sinha-Kerkhoff, K. 2014. *Colonising Plants in Bihar: Tobacco Betwixt Indigo and Sugarcane (1760–1950)*. Gurgaon: Penguin Random House.

Sinha-Kerkhoff, K. 2016. Yellow Tobacco. Black Tobacco: Indigenous (desi) Tobacco as an Anti-commodity. In *Local Subversions of Colonial Cultures*.

[9] Chatterji (2016).

[10] To borrow the term from Barnett et al. (2017).

Commodities and Anti-commodities in Global History, ed. S. Hazareesingh and H. Maat, 29–49. Hampshire: Palgrave Macmillan.

Sinha-Kerkhoff, K. 2017. Embedding Cigarette Tobacco in Colonial Bihar (India): A Multi-dimensional Task. In *Embedding Agricultural Commodities. Using Historical Evidence, 1840–1940s*, ed. W. van Schendel, 99–119. London: Routledge.

Sinha-Kerkhoff, K. 2020. Wooing Indians with New Smokes: Cigarette and Bidi Advertising in British India. In *Globalising Everyday Consumption in India. History and Ethnography*, ed. B. Bhattacharya and H. Donner, 98–121. London and New York: Routledge.

Werner, C.A. 1922. *Tobaccoland*. New York: The Tobacco Leaf Publishing Company.

Index

A. van Wickeren et al. (eds.), *Tobacco in Global Perspective, 1780–1960*, Cambridge Imperial and Post-Colonial Studies,
https://doi.org/10.1007/978-3-031-64411-5

SPRINGER NATURE

GPSR Compliance

The European Union's (EU) General Product Safety Regulation (GPSR) is a set of rules that requires consumer products to be safe and our obligations to ensure this.

If you have any concerns about our products, you can contact us on ProductSafety@springernature.com

In case Publisher is established outside the EU, the EU authorized representative is:

Springer Nature Customer Service Center GmbH
Europaplatz 3
69115 Heidelberg, Germany

The manufacturer's authorised representative in the EU is Springer Nature Customer Service Centre GmbH, Europaplatz 3, 69115 Heidelberg, Germany. If you have any concerns regarding our products, please contact ProductSafety@springernature.com

Printed and bound by CPI Group (UK) Ltd, Croydon, CR0 4YY
01/10/2026
02225913-0005